Rock and Roll
Baby Names

ROCK AND ROLL

Over 2,000 Music-Inspired Names

from Alison to Ziggy

Margaret Eby

GOTHAM BOOKS

BABY NAMES

GOTHAM BOOKS
Published by Penguin Group (USA) Inc.
375 Hudson Street, New York, New York 10014, U.S.A.
Penguin Group (Canada), 90 Eglinton Avenue East, Suite 700, Toronto, Ontario M4P
2Y3, Canada (a division of Pearson Penguin Canada Inc.); Penguin Books Ltd, 80
Strand, London WC2R 0RL, England; Penguin Ireland, 25 St Stephen's Green, Dublin
2, Ireland (a division of Penguin Books Ltd); Penguin Group (Australia), 250 Camber-
well Road, Camberwell, Victoria 3124, Australia (a division of Pearson Australia Group
Pty Ltd); Penguin Books India Pvt Ltd, 11 Community Centre, Panchsheel Park, New
Delhi—110 017, India; Penguin Group (NZ), 67 Apollo Drive, Rosedale, North Shore
0632, New Zealand (a division of Pearson New Zealand Ltd); Penguin Books (South
Africa) (Pty) Ltd, 24 Sturdee Avenue, Rosebank, Johannesburg 2196, South Africa

Penguin Books Ltd, Registered Offices: 80 Strand, London WC2R 0RL, England

Published by Gotham Books, a member of Penguin Group (USA) Inc.

First printing, April 2012

1   3   5   7   9   10   8   6   4   2

Copyright © 2012 by Margaret Eby

LIBRARY OF CONGRESS CATALOGING-IN-PUBLICATION DATA

Eby, Margaret.
Rock and roll baby names : over 2,000 music-inspired names, from Alison to Ziggy /
Margaret Eby.
p. cm.
ISBN 978-1-59240695-1
1. Names, Personal—Dictionaries. 2. Rock music—Miscellanea. 3. Rock musicians—
Miscellanea. I. Title.
CS2377.E29 2012
781.66092—dc23   2011035393

Printed in the United States of America

Set in Cosmiqua Com

Designed by Sabrina Bowers

*For my parents, Tom and Mary,
who always suspected their names would show up
in a book of mine.*

Contents

Introduction

What's the first thing you think of when you hear the name Layla? Probably not its Greek definition. If you're a music fan, your answer is likely the finger-snapping sweetness and searing riffs of Eric Clapton's song "Layla," and maybe the tortured love triangle between Clapton, George Harrison, and Pattie Boyd that inspired it. Names are more than a collection of Latin root words and their attributes, they're affected by the people who wear them and particularly by the way they're used in movies, television, books, and, most importantly, in music.

Today's babies are as likely to be named for a favorite rock song as a great-uncle. And why not? Rock music has long been the arbiter of cool, and it's brimming with naming ideas. My high school class had both an Aja, for Steely Dan's epic jazz-rock album, and a Rhiannon, for the bewitching character in a Fleetwood Mac song. For the musically inclined parent, there's no better place to look for inspiration than the vast collection of leather-clad guitar gods, wispy folk strummers, rowdy riot grrrls, and sugar-sweet pop singers and the names that inspired them.

Rock and Roll Baby Names collects them all, from R&B singer Aaliyah to David Bowie's "Ziggy Stardust" and everything in between. The definitions in this book aren't from forgotten ancient languages (though, yes, it has those too), they're derived from memorable lyrics and musicians—the girl next door in "Caroline, No" and "Sweet Caroline" or the twitchy hammer-wielding protagonist of "Maxwell's Silver Hammer." Everyone wants his or her own theme song. Rock and roll–named babies have them from birth.

Because rock is a nebulous genre that grabs influences from all over the place—South African jazz, harp music, a guy on the street playing the spoons—this book also has chapters for genres outside of rock that rub up against it, like hip-hop and country. If the name is common (like Jane), I've included a sampling of the most significant bearers and songs instead of listing them all. Ditto for names that are places or common words, like Geneva or Joy. If you want to submit a song or artist you think should have been included, you can do so on *rockandrollbabynames.com*, which is full of other goodies.

For the adventurous, the sky is pretty much the limit—you could name your tiny tyke Velouria for the Pixies song or take a page from David Bowie and name your son Zowie. But if your taste veers more toward the traditional, keep in mind that names like John, Alex, and Kim have just as much music snob cred. Contrarily, some of the people who make the most earth-shatteringly great music aren't necessarily the best namesakes. Yes, U2 is great. No, you probably shouldn't name your child The Edge. (Though his daughter's name, Blue, is pretty darn cute.) But you knew that. No matter what name you choose, your baby's going to rock.

1950s:
Rock and Roll Pioneers

The 1950s are where it all really started: rockabilly cats, beach parties, teddy boys, and gum-snapping poodle skirt girls. This is the era of doo-wop groups and "Long Tall Sally," a bonanza for a parent looking for a name that's gone the cycle from cool to stuffy to cool again—like Addie or Elias.

GIRLS

Addie, Addy

ENGLISH: Variation of Adelaide, Addison, or Adeline; noble
ROCK AND ROLL: Bubbly, bright, friendly
RELATED ARTISTS/SONGS: Addie McPherson (The Shirelles), "Addie Bowie" by The Glove, "For Addie Rose" by Jason Ringenberg, "Addie" by Greg Maroney, "Dear Addy" by King Creole and the Coconuts
LINER NOTES: Addie McPherson met the other Shirelles in high school; the group was called The Poquellos, and then Shirley & the Shirelles, before The Shirelles.

Arlene, Arleen

IRISH: Variation of Arlyn, blessed
ROCK AND ROLL: Takes pleasure from simple things, loves traveling
RELATED ARTISTS/SONGS: Arlene Smith (The Chantels), Arleen Lanzotti (The Delicates), "Arlene" by The Handsome Family, "Arlene" by Crystal Bowersox, "Arlene" by Marty Stuart, "Arleen (aka Arlene)" by Widespread Panic
LINER NOTES: Crystal Bowersox wrote the song "Arlene" for her tour bus driver.

Babette

FRENCH: Form of Barbara, foreigner
ROCK AND ROLL: Sultry, sophisticated, stylish
RELATED ARTISTS/SONGS: Babette Chinery (The Beverley Sisters), Babette Ory, "Babette" by Mantovani, "Babette" by Bob Gordon, "Babette!" by Pepper Rabbit, "Babette" by Vector Lovers

LINER NOTES: The Beverley Sisters were older sister Joy, Babette, and her twin sister Teddie; the Girls were the highest paid entertainers in Europe for twenty years.

Bonnie, Bonny

SCOTTISH: Pretty
ROCK AND ROLL: Gorgeous, glamorous, and totally gangster
RELATED ARTISTS/SONGS: Bermuda Bonnie, Bonnie Raitt, Delaney & Bonnie, "Bonnie" by Supertramp, "Bonnie" by Big Dipper, "Bonnie B," by Jerry Lee Lewis, "Bonnie Taylor Shakedown 2K4" by Hellogoodbye, "Bonny" by AC/DC

"Bonnie B, she's like a little queen bee."
—JERRY LEE LEWIS

Brenda

CELTIC: Blade
ROCK AND ROLL: A spunky sweetheart
RELATED ARTISTS/SONGS: Brenda Fassie, Brenda Kahn, Brenda Lee, "Brenda" by The Four Tops, "Brenda" by Memphis Slim, "Brenda" by The Jon Spencer Blues Explosion, "Brenda's Got a Baby" by 2Pac, "Brenda" by the Cupids
LINER NOTES: Brenda Lee's nickname was "Little Miss Dynamite," thanks to her hit song "Dynamite" and her small stature.

Caledonia

LATIN: Scotland
ROCK AND ROLL: Exotic, dreamy, an artist
RELATED ARTISTS/SONGS: "Caledonia" by Dougie MacLean, "Caledonia Mission" by The Band, "Caledonia" by The Gourds, "Caledonia" by Cromagnon, "Caldonia" by Louis Jordan
LINER NOTES: Folk songstress Shawn Colvin named her daughter Caledonia.

Carol, Carole

FRENCH: Joyful song
ROCK AND ROLL: Lyrical, talented, good at dancing
RELATED ARTISTS/SONGS: Carole King, Carol Sloane, "Carol" by Chuck Berry, "Carol" by Slint, "My Carol" by Mark Olson, "Hello Carol" by The Gladiators, "Carol" by Al Stewart
LINER NOTES: Chuck Berry's song "Carol" has been covered by The Beatles, The Rolling Stones, The Doors, Charlie Daniels, and The Flamin' Groovies, among others.

Chloe

GREEK: Young green shoot

ELTON JOHN:
"I will always be your friend, Chloe."

LOUIS ARMSTRONG:
"I'll roam through the dismal swamplands, searching for you."

BLOOD OR WHISKEY:
"She was my soapbox derby queen."

MOTHER LOVE BONE:
"Chloe's just like me, only beautiful."

Clarabella, Clarabelle

LATIN: Combination of Clara and Bella, bright and beautiful
ROCK AND ROLL: Eager, literary, sweet
RELATED ARTISTS/SONGS: "Clarabella" by The Jodimars, "Clarabella" by Francisco Repilado, "Clarabelle" by Todd Howarth
LINER NOTES: "Clarabella" was first recorded by The Jodimars, but it's best known from The Beatles' recording of the song on the radio show *Pop Go the Beatles*.

Claudette

FRENCH: Form of Claude, deliberate
ROCK AND ROLL: Pretty, lucky, loving
RELATED ARTISTS/SONGS: Claudette Robinson (The Miracles), Claudette Soares, Claudette Ortiz, "Claudette" by Roy Orbison, "Claudette" by Status Quo
LINER NOTES: Berry Gordy called Claudette Robinson the "First Lady of Motown" because she was the first woman signed to his label; she had taken her brother's place in The Miracles after he was drafted into the army.

Connie

LATIN: Short for Constance, unwavering
ROCK AND ROLL: Sweet-talkin' girl, loves poodle skirts and bouffants
RELATED ARTISTS/SONGS: Connie Dover, Connie Francis, Connie Smith, "Connie" by Duane Eddy, "Connie" by Neil Sedaka, "Connie" by Commander Cody and His Lost Planet Airmen, "Connie" by The Dubs, "Connie O" by The Four Seasons
LINER NOTES: Before he married Sandra Dee, Bobby Darin dated Connie Francis, offering to elope with her. Francis's father ran Darin out of the house at gunpoint when he heard of their plans, effectively ending their relationship.

3

Darla

ENGLISH: Dear girl
ROCK AND ROLL: Cute, sweet, trusting
RELATED ARTISTS/SONGS: Darla Farmer, "Darla" by Buck Evans, "Darla" by Lali Puna, "Darla" by Robert J. Kral, "Chasin' Darla" by Cows, "Darla" by Why?
LINER NOTES: Darla Records, an independent label based in San Diego, was named in the tradition of 1950s labels with women's names.

Edna

HEBREW: Pleasure
ROCK AND ROLL: Dark and glamorous, a renegade
RELATED ARTISTS/SONGS: Edna's Goldfish, Edna Lewis, Edna May, "Evil Edna" by Bob Seger, "Edna" by The Medallions, "Songs for Edna" by Caroline Weeks, "Edna Frau" by Jeff Buckley
LINER NOTES: Doo-wop group The Medallions coined the phrase "pompatus of love," which Steve Miller used in the song "Joker."

Faye, Fay

ENGLISH: Fairy
ROCK AND ROLL: Mystical, beautiful, swift, believes strongly in tradition.
RELATED ARTISTS/SONGS: Faye Adams, Faye Wong, "Faye Dunaway" by Edie Sedgwick, "Run Fay Run" by Isaac Hayes, "Miss Fay Regrets" by The Pretty Things, "Faye Tucker" by Indigo Girls, "Faye" by Jandek
LINER NOTES: R&B pioneer Faye Adams became known on the 1950s nightclub circuit as "Atomic Adams" in tribute to her powerful voice.

Gertie

ENGLISH: Form of Gertrude, strength of spear
ROCK AND ROLL: Sunny, blond, doesn't take any guff
RELATED ARTISTS/SONGS: Noel and Gertie, Gertie Gitana, "Flirty Gertie" by The Jiv-A-Tones, "My Gal Gertie" by Dub Dickerson, "(Heartless) Hertie Gertie" by Crazy Elephant, "Ah Gertie" by The Caresser, "Grandma Gertie" by Shelley Hirsch
LINER NOTES: Texas rockabilly singer Dub Dickerson's biggest songs besides "My Gal Gertie" were "Owl Hoot Blues" and "Sweet Bunch of Bittersweets."

Ginger

ENGLISH: Red-haired
ROCK AND ROLL: Freckle-faced and adorable, has a wild side
RELATED ARTISTS/SONGS: Ginger Hildebrand, Ginger Smock, Ginger Rogers, "Jack & Ginger" by We Are Scientists, "Ginger Snaps" by Dean & Britta, "Ginger Ale" by The Clean, "Ginger (Bein' Free)" by Oneida, "Ginger" by Lilys

LINER NOTES: Ginger Rogers had an ice cream soda fountain installed in her house to entertain guests.

Ginny, Jinny

ENGLISH: Form of Ginger, Virginia, or Jennifer; fair

ROCK AND ROLL: Adorable, courageous

RELATED ARTISTS/SONGS: Jinny Osborn (The Chordettes), Ginny Owens, Ginny Arnell, "Ginny" by The Duprees, "Ginny" by The Smart Tones

LINER NOTES: The Chordettes' Jinny Osborn was born Virginia Cole; her father was then the president of the Barbershop Harmony Society.

Glenda

SCOTTISH: Feminine version of Glen, valley

ROCK AND ROLL: An old-fashioned girl, doe-eyed, warm, innocent

RELATED ARTISTS/SONGS: Glenda Collins, Glenda Millar (Juluka), Glenda Lynn, "Glenda and the Test" by Toy Dolls, "Glen or Glenda" by Howard Shore

LINER NOTES: Though Glenda Collins's musical career was short-lived, her association with famed Merseybeat producer Joe Meek has made her albums valuable collector's items, fetching around $100 each.

Irene

GREEK: Peace

ROCK AND ROLL: Funny and pretty but flighty

RELATED ARTISTS/SONGS: Irene Cara, Irene Kral, Irène Schweizer, "Goodnight, Irene" by Leadbelly, "Irene" by Caribou, "Irene" by The Fugs, "Irene" by John Carroll

LINER NOTES: Though "Goodnight, Irene" was first recorded by blues musician Leadbelly, The Weavers, Frank Sinatra, and Moon Mullican all recorded hit cover versions of the song; it also inspired Hank Thompson's 1954 answer song, "Wake Up, Irene."

Jacqueline

FRENCH: Variation of Jacques, supplanter

ROCK AND ROLL: Sentimental, loves the summer, classy, spunky

RELATED ARTISTS/SONGS: Jacqueline Boyer, Jacqueline Schwab, Jacqueline Steiner, "Jacqueline" by Big Bill Broonzy, "Jacqueline" by Hugh Mandell, "Jacqueline" by Franz Ferdinand, "Jacqueline" by The Durutti Column, "Jacqueline" by The Coral

*"Spicy as a magazine and
twice as sassy."*
—BOBBY HELMS

Jaime, Jamie

SPANISH: Variation of James, replacement
ROCK AND ROLL: Divine, long-haired, fresh, loves The Beach Boys
RELATED ARTISTS/SONGS: Jamie Kyle, "Jamie" by Weezer, "Jamie" by Eddie Holland, "Jamie" by Ray Parker Jr., "Jamie's Cryin'" by Van Halen
LINER NOTES: Before recording "Jamie's Cryin'," David Lee Roth quit smoking and drinking to get a cleaner sound. The recording turned out so poorly on the first take that Ted Templeman ordered him to go outside and smoke before recording another version.

Joy

ENGLISH: Happiness
ROCK AND ROLL: Exuberant, peppy, cute
RELATED ARTISTS/SONGS: Joy Layne, Joy DeCastro (The DeCastro Sisters), Joy Division, "Road to Joy" by Bright Eyes, "Joy" by Isaac Hayes, "Joy" by The Minutemen, "Joy" by Marvin Gaye
LINER NOTES: Joy Layne recorded her biggest hit, a cover of The Poni-Tails' "Your Wild Heart," when she was just fifteen.

Julie

LATIN: Youthful

DAVID BOWIE:
"I'm yours 'til the end."

JENS LEKMAN:
"Oh, Julie . . . you could have me for a cigarette lighter."

WAYLON JENNINGS:
"Pretty as the answer to any man's dream."

THE BOBBY FULLER FOUR:
"Julie, I need your love so bad."

THE KINKS:
"She had a timeless glow, she was the image of youth."

Kay

ENGLISH: Variation of Katherine, pure
ROCK AND ROLL: Elegant, sweet, kindhearted
RELATED ARTISTS/SONGS: Kay Starr, Kay Strother (The Bell Sisters), "Kay" by Eric Sloss, "Kay" by Nino Rota, "Kay" by Alain Marion, "If You See Kay" by The Script
LINER NOTES: Pop and jazz singer Kay Starr, best known for "The Wheel of Fortune" and "The Rock-and-Roll Waltz," grew up on a farm, where she serenaded the chickens.

Lizzie, Lizzy

HEBREW: Form of Elizabeth, God's promise
ROCK AND ROLL: Hypnotizing, a fun dance partner, the lifeguard of the year
RELATED ARTISTS/SONGS: Thin Lizzy, Lizzy Mercier Descloux, "Dizzy Miss Lizzy" by Larry Williams, "Lizzy" by the Melvins, "Lizzy" by Ben Kweller
LINER NOTES: "Dizzy Miss Lizzy" is modeled on Little Richard's "Good Golly, Miss Molly." The Beatles covered the song at the suggestion of Ringo Starr.

Lois

GREEK: Friendly
ROCK AND ROLL: Laid-back, adventurous, wonderful
RELATED ARTISTS/SONGS: Lois Reeves (The Vandellas), Lois Maffeo, "Lois" by Mystic Shake, "Dennis and Lois" by The Happy Mondays, "Lois Ann" by Wes Montgomery, "Lois" by Dirge
LINER NOTES: At five-foot-one, The Vandellas' Lois Reeves went by the nickname "Pee-Wee."

Lucille

FRENCH: Light
ROCK AND ROLL: Beautiful, independent, impetuous
RELATED ARTISTS/SONGS: "Lucille" by Little Richard, "Lucille" by The Drifters, "Lucille" by Kenny Rogers, "Lucille Talks Back" by B.B. King
LINER NOTES: B.B. King once ran into a burning building to rescue his guitar. The next day, King found out that two men died in the blaze, fighting over a woman named Lucille. King named his guitar Lucille as a reminder to never run into a fire again.

Lulu

ARABIC: Form of Luella, pearl
ROCK AND ROLL: Sensible during the day, a club queen at night, stylish
RELATED ARTISTS/SONGS: Lulu, "Lawless and Lulu" by Buckcherry, "Lulu" by James Taylor, "A Happening for Lulu" by The Jimi Hendrix Experience, "Bang Bang Lulu" by The North Mississippi Allstars, "Lulu Walls" by John Prine

"Crazy and a nighttime angel, she had a colorful career."
—BUCKCHERRY

Maybellene

ENGLISH: Form of Mabel, friendly
ROCK AND ROLL: A teenage dream, flighty
RELATED ARTISTS/SONGS: "Maybellene" by Chuck Berry, "Maybellene" by Elvis Presley
LINER NOTES: Chuck Berry adapted the song "Maybellene" from Roy Acuff's "Ida May"; he named the protagonist after glancing at a mascara box on the floor of the studio.

Nadia

ARABIC: Delicate
ROCK AND ROLL: Feisty, worldly, intelligent
RELATED ARTISTS/SONGS: Nadia Ali, Nadia Boulanger, Nadia Oh, "Nadia" by Jeff Beck, "Nadia" by Sonny Red, "Nadia" by David Monte Cristo
LINER NOTES: Nadia Boulanger, known as the "tender tyrant," taught composition to both Quincy Jones and Philip Glass.

Nadine

FRENCH: Hope
ROCK AND ROLL: Sophisticated, pretty, breezy
RELATED ARTISTS/SONGS: Nadine Coyle (Girls Aloud), Nadine Shamir, "Nadine" by Chuck Berry, "Nadine" by Frank Black and the Catholics, "Nadine" by Mos Def, "Nadine" by Led Zeppelin, "Nadine" by Levitation
LINER NOTES: Chuck Berry's "Nadine" was his foray into go-go; it rocketed up the charts thanks to the frug dance craze, in which dancers would shake their hips from right to left without moving their feet.

Nan

ENGLISH: Form of Nancy or Nanette, generous
ROCK AND ROLL: Sweet, old-fashioned, wise
RELATED ARTISTS/SONGS: Nan Castle, "Nan You're a Window Shopper" by Lily Allen, "Nan Ding" by Slint, "Nan" by Ween, "Nan's Song" by Robbie Williams
LINER NOTES: Rockabilly singer Nan Castle, known for her song "Star Light, Star Bright," was born Nancy Castleberry; she was one of Chet Atkins's early recruits for the Grand Ole Opry.

Patience

ENGLISH: Virtuous
ROCK AND ROLL: Calm, generous, sweet
RELATED ARTISTS/SONGS: Patience McIntyre (Patience & Prudence), "Patience" by Guns N' Roses, "Is Patience Still Waiting?" by The Juliana Theory, "Patience" by Rites of Spring
LINER NOTES: Sister singing act Patience & Prudence McIntyre were the daughters of Mark McIntyre, an orchestra leader in Frank Sinatra's entourage.

Peggy, Peg

GREEK: Variation of Margaret, pearl
ROCK AND ROLL: Enchanting, blond, sassy
RELATED ARTISTS/SONGS: Peggy Lee, Peggy March, Peggy Seeger, "Peggy Sue" by Buddy Holly, "Peggy Day" by Bob Dylan, "Pretty Peggy-O" by Simon & Garfunkel, "Peggy Gordon" by The Corrs, "Peggy" by Phish
LINER NOTES: Buddy Holly's song "Peggy Sue" was originally titled "Cindy Lou," after his niece; he changed the title for Crickets' drummer Jerry Allison's girlfriend.

Priscilla

LATIN: Old
ROCK AND ROLL: Rambunctious, strong, a wild child
RELATED ARTISTS/SONGS: Priscilla Presley, Priscilla Ahn, Priscilla Price, "Priscilla" by Meat Loaf, "Priscilla" by Soft Machine, "Priscilla" by Suzanne Vega, "Priscilla" by Graham Central Station
LINER NOTES: Elvis first met Priscilla Presley in Germany when he was in the army; she was only fourteen at the time. They kept in touch via phone and letters for four years, and then she moved to Graceland and married him.

Queenie

ENGLISH: Ruler
ROCK AND ROLL: Statuesque, charming, a temptress
RELATED ARTISTS/SONGS: Queenie Smith, Little Queenie, "Too Cool Queenie" by Stone Temple Pilots, "Little Queenie" by Chuck Berry, "50 Ft. Queenie" by PJ Harvey, "Queenie's Suite" by Nick Cave, "Teenage Queenie" by Pussycat

"Lookin' like a model on the cover of a magazine."
—CHUCK BERRY

Ruth

HEBREW: Companion
ROCK AND ROLL: Sassy, bold, confident
RELATED ARTISTS/SONGS: Ruth Brown, Ruth Price, Ruth Etting, "A Rose and Baby Ruth" by Marilyn Manson, "Ruth" by Herbie Mann, "Ruth" by Hot Chocolate, "Red Bowling Ball Ruth" by The White Stripes, "Ruth Is Sleeping" by Frank Zappa
LINER NOTES: 1950s R&B sensation Ruth Brown only came out of retirement in the 1970s at the urging of comedian Redd Foxx; she went on to play DJ Motormouth Maybelle in John Waters's *Hairspray*.

Sally

ENGLISH: Form of Sarah, princess
ROCK AND ROLL: Slender, fun-loving, a dreamer
RELATED ARTISTS/SONGS: "Sally Gal" by Bob Dylan, "Long Tall Sally" by Little Richard, "Mustang Sally" by Wilson Pickett, "Sally Simpson" by The Who, "Sally Can't Dance" by Lou Reed
LINER NOTES: A little girl named Enotris Johnson passed songwriter Robert Blackwell a scrap of paper with the lyrics "Saw Uncle John with Long Tall Sally," and Blackwell wrote the rest.

Sparkle

ENGLISH: Shimmer
ROCK AND ROLL: Luminous, peppy, beautiful
RELATED ARTISTS/SONGS: Sparkle Moore, Sparklehorse, "Sparkle City" by Shuggie Otis, "Sparkle" by Cameo, "Sparkle" by Phish, "Jewel to Sparkle" by The Juliana Theory, "Sparkle" by Everclear
LINER NOTES: Rockabilly pioneer Sparkle Moore, born Barbara, got her nickname from a character in the comic *Dick Tracy*; she was known for wearing men's clothing and an Elvis-style pompadour on stage.

Theresa, Teresa

GREEK: Harvester
ROCK AND ROLL: Kind, funny, sparkling
RELATED ARTISTS/SONGS: Teresa Brewer, Teresa De Sio, Theresa Nervosa (Butthole Surfers), "Theresa's Sound World" by Sonic Youth, "Theresa" by Citien Cope, "St. Teresa" by Joan Osborne, "Teresa" by Eddie Cochran, "Teresa" by Charles Brown
LINER NOTES: Teresa Brewer wrote "I Love Mickey" about her crush on baseball player Mickey Mantle; her other novelty hits included "Choo'n Gum" and "Molasses, Molasses."

Wanda

SLAVIC: Shepherdess
ROCK AND ROLL: Powerful, the life of the party, self-sufficient
RELATED ARTISTS/SONGS: Wanda Jackson, Wanda Hutchinson (The Emotions), Wanda Young (The Marvelettes), "For Wanda" by A Silver Mt. Zion, "Wicked Wanda" by Stephen Malkmus and the Jicks, "Wanda" by The Forester Sisters
LINER NOTES: Self-proclaimed First Lady of Rockabilly Wanda Jackson briefly dated Elvis when she was still a teenager; she later recorded a tribute album to Presley, *I Remember Elvis*.

Zola

FRENCH: From the earth
ROCK AND ROLL: Quirky, witty, brave
RELATED ARTISTS/SONGS: Zola Jesus, Zola Taylor (The Platters),

"Zola Budd" by Chumbawamba, "Zola" by Fred Simon, "Zola" by Joseph Robichaux & His New Orleans Rhythm Boys

LINER NOTES: The Platters' Zola Taylor was one of three women who claimed to be Frankie Lymon's wife; Halle Berry played Taylor in *Why Do Fools Fall in Love*.

BOYS

Billy

ENGLISH: Diminutive of William, staunch defender

ROCK AND ROLL: Childhood friend, intellectual, adventurous, drawn to guns

RELATED ARTISTS/SONGS: Billy Corgan (Smashing Pumpkins), Billy Idol, Billy Joel, "Billy Breathes" by Phish, "C'mon Billy" by PJ Harvey, "Billy's Bones" by the Pogues, "Billy" by Lou Reed, "Billy's Third" by the Undertones

"Billy was a friend of mine/I grew up with him ever since we were nine."
—LOU REED

Bo

NORDIC: Full of life

ROCK AND ROLL: An original, bouncy, funny

RELATED ARTISTS/SONGS: Bo Bice, Bo Carter, Bo Diddley, "Story of Bo Diddley" by The Animals, "Bo Demmick" by The Fall, "Bo Bo" by Boogie Down Productions

LINER NOTES: Bo Diddley pioneered the "Bo Diddley beat," created by slapping parts of the body and used in songs from George Michael's "Faith" to The Stranglers' "I Want Candy," while he was trying to play Gene Autry's "(I Got Spurs That) Jingle, Jangle, Jingle."

Boyd

SCOTTISH: Blond

ROCK AND ROLL: Southern, sweet, well mannered

RELATED ARTISTS/SONGS: Boyd Bennett, Boyd Rice, Joe Boyd, "Mr. Boyd" by Argosy, "Mr. Boyd" by My Life Story

LINER NOTES: Boyd Bennett, best known for the rockabilly hit "Seventeen," later formed a music variety show called *Boyd Bennett and His Space Buddies* about a crew of singing astronauts.

Bud, Buddy

ENGLISH: Friend
ROCK AND ROLL: Pioneer, original, pal, sometimes used as slang for weed or weed dealer
RELATED ARTISTS/SONGS: Bud Freeman, Buddy Guy, Buddy Holly, "My Name Is Buddy" by Ry Cooder, "Buddy" by De La Soul, "Buddy Holly" by Weezer, "Buddy" by Willie Nelson, "Billy Bud" by Morrissey
LINER NOTES: Buddy Holly had a dog named Alonzo and a cat named Booker T.

Byron

ENGLISH: Cottage for cows
ROCK AND ROLL: Eccentric but educated, a poet
RELATED ARTISTS/SONGS: Byron Case, Byron Lee, Byron Roberts (Bal-Sagoth), "Byron" by The Mekons, "Byron" by Liam Gallagher, "Lord Byron's Luggage" by Warren Zevon
LINER NOTES: Ska bandleader Byron Lee named his group the Dragonaires after his college soccer team.

Carl, Karl

SWEDISH: King
ROCK AND ROLL: Supportive, often overshadowed
RELATED ARTISTS/SONGS: Carl Palmer (Emerson Lake & Palmer), Carl Perkins, Karl Kaiser, "Carl's Big Chance" by The Beach Boys, "Carl" by J Mascis, "Carl Perkins' Cadillac" by Drive-By Truckers
LINER NOTES: Though Elvis made it famous, Carl Perkins was the musician who wrote "Blue Suede Shoes." He was inspired after seeing a man get angry at his date for scuffing his shoes.

Chuck

GERMAN: Diminutive of Charles, manly
ROCK AND ROLL: Cool, innovative, guitar genius, demanding
RELATED ARTISTS/SONGS: Chuck Berry, Chuck D, Chuck Dukowski (Black Flag), "Chuck" by Maximillian Colby, "Chuck Baby" by Chuck Brown, "Chuck's Beat" by Chuck Berry and Bo Diddley, "Chuck" by Sum 41, "Good Luck Chuck" by The Dandy Warhols
LINER NOTES: Chuck Berry owns a warehouse full of Cadillacs, one of almost every model back to the 1950s; he has four children, Ingrid, Chuck Jr., Aloha Isa, and Melody Exes.

Clarence

LATIN: Bright
ROCK AND ROLL: Creative, a daydreamer, a problem solver
RELATED ARTISTS/SONGS: Clarence "Gatemouth" Brown, Clarence Clemons (The E Street Band), Clarence Greenwood (aka Citizen Cope), "Clarence" by Shel Silverstein, "Clarence in Wonderland" by Soft Machine, "Clarence in Wonderland" by Gong
LINER NOTES: Guitarist Clarence "Gatemouth" Brown fused blues

music with zydeco, jazz, and R&B; he was Frank Zappa's favorite musician.

Cully, Culley

IRISH: Variation of Culver, dove

ROCK AND ROLL: Mellow, a good friend

RELATED ARTISTS/SONGS: Culley Holt (The Jordanaires), Frank Culley, "Culley on Bleecker Street" by Nice Beaver, "Cully" by Sarah-Jane Himmelsbach

LINER NOTES: The founding members of The Jordanaires were all ordained ministers; they went on to play with Elvis until he moved to Las Vegas.

Dick

GERMAN: Form of Richard, leader

ROCK AND ROLL: A friend, goofy, loves to play practical jokes

RELATED ARTISTS/SONGS: Dick Clark, Dick Dale, "Handsome Dick" Manitoba (The Dictators), "Dick" by The Dandy Warhols, "Dick's Slow Song" by The Tindersticks, "Dick" by Penthouse, "Dick" by Guano Apes

LINER NOTES: King of Surf Guitar Dick Dale played in several beach party movies in the 1950s and 1960s, including *Muscle Beach Party* and *A Swingin' Affair*.

Elias

GREEK: Variation of Elijah, the Lord is my God

ROCK AND ROLL: Daring, proud

RELATED ARTISTS/SONGS: Elias Bates (aka Bo Diddley), "Elias" by Dispatch, "Elias" by Wolfsheim

LINER NOTES: Whenever he was credited as a songwriter, Bo Diddley used the name Elias McDaniel.

Fabian

LATIN: Bean seller

ROCK AND ROLL: A smooth talker, handsome

RELATED ARTISTS/SONGS: Fabian Forte, Lara Fabian, "Fabian" by Tripod, "Fabian" by Nordafjells, "Fabian's World" by Mustasch

LINER NOTES: The 1980 film *The Idolmaker* was a thinly veiled account of teen pop icon Fabian Forte's rise and fall from fame, the rise mostly due to electronic manipulation of his voice; Fabian has three children, Christian, Julie, and Ava.

Grady

IRISH: Hardworking

ROCK AND ROLL: Adventurous, loves a good time, a gentleman

RELATED ARTISTS/SONGS: Grady Martin, Grady Tate, Grady Nichols, "Grady and Dubose" by Nana Grizol, "Grady" by Ronny Cox, "Grady" by Rhonda Robinson

LINER NOTES: Nashville A-Team session musician Grady Martin headed Willie Nelson's band and played on Roy Orbison's "Pretty Woman"; he's credited with inventing the fuzzy, distorted guitar sound by playing a session with a malfunctioning mixing board.

Harris

ENGLISH: Harry's son
ROCK AND ROLL: Mischievous, fun, sprightly, and cool
RELATED ARTISTS/SONGS: Calvin Harris, Eddie Harris, Emmylou Harris, Hal Harris, "Harris" by Sam Dickens, "Harris" by Mansun
LINER NOTES: Texas rockabilly singer Hal Harris was nicknamed "Fuzzy" for his murky, bluesy guitar solos.

Herman

GERMAN: Soldier
ROCK AND ROLL: Creative, introverted, whimsical, has a rich fantasy life.
RELATED ARTISTS/SONGS: Herman's Hermits, Herman Rarebell (Scorpions), Herman Santiago (The Teenagers), "Herman the Human Mole" by The Residents, "Herman" by The Jerky Boys, "Herman" by Uncle Mingo
LINER NOTES: Songwriter Herman Santiago penned the song "Why Do Fools Fall in Love"; his group was originally called The Ermines, then The Coupe de Villes, and then The Premiers before finally settling on The Teenagers.

Hugh

GERMAN: Intellectual
ROCK AND ROLL: Brave, resourceful, nobly born
RELATED ARTISTS/SONGS: Hugh Cornwell (The Stranglers), Hugh Hopper (Soft Machine), Hugh Masekela, "Hugh" by Nightnoise, "Courage (for Hugh MacLennan)" by The Tragically Hip, "Sir Hugh" by Andrew King
LINER NOTES: South African flugelhornist Hugh Masekela, best known for his work with Miriam "Mama Africa" Makeba, has a son, Salema, who hosts extreme sports shows on ESPN.

Ike

HEBREW: Variation of Isaac, laughter
ROCK AND ROLL: Quirky, cool, rowdy, has a few bad habits
RELATED ARTISTS/SONGS: Ike Quebec, Ike Turner, "Ike's Mood" by Isaac Hayes
LINER NOTES: Ike Turner began working at Clarksdale, Mississippi's radio station WROX when he was eight years old. He ran the elevator and changed records for the DJ.

Jay

SANSKRIT: Victory
ROCK AND ROLL: Brainy, devastatingly witty, flighty
RELATED ARTISTS/SONGS: Jay Bennett (Wilco), Jay Reatard, Screamin' Jay Hawkins, "Jay" by Andy Williams, "Jay" by Grace Slick, "Jay" by Eek-A-Mouse, "Blue Jay Way" by The Beatles
LINER NOTES: Screamin' Jay Hawkins once emerged from a coffin on stage to win a $300 bet with a local DJ.

Jerome

GREEK: Sacred name
ROCK AND ROLL: Rugged, a pioneer, a lady killer
RELATED ARTISTS/SONGS: Jerome Arnold (The Paul Butterfield Blues Band), Jerome Green, Jerome Kern, "Jerome" by Galaxie 500, "Jerome" by Barenaked Ladies, "Jerome" by Lykke Li, "Jerome" by Jim Sullivan, "Bring It to Jerome" by Bo Diddley
LINER NOTES: Jerome Green played the maracas with Bo Diddley's band; he was originally recruited to pass the hat around while Diddley busked on the street.

Jerry

GREEK: Variation of Gerald or Jerome, sacred name

SMASHING PUMPKINS:
"You are forever my star."

QUIMBY:
"Jerry can dance, finally."

JOHN MELLENCAMP:
"He sees the world through a ten-year-old boy's eyes."

BURNING SPEAR:
"Play, Jerry, play, play your guitar."

Link

ENGLISH: Form of Lincoln, town by the pool
ROCK AND ROLL: Experimental, adventurous, dramatic, rowdy
RELATED ARTISTS/SONGS: Link Wray, "Link" by Robyn Miller, "Link" by Bananarama, "Link" by Mike Stern
LINER NOTES: Link Wray was part Shawnee Indian; he was posthumously inducted into the Native American Music Awards Hall of Fame.

Louie

GERMAN: Variation of Louis, brave warrior
ROCK AND ROLL: Pale, fun-loving, a romantic
RELATED ARTISTS/SONGS: Louis Bellson, "Louie Louie" by The Kingsmen, "Louie" by Allen Touissant, "Brother Louie" by Stories
LINER NOTES: Though the FBI conducted a two-year obscenity investigation on the song "Louie Louie," the song remained uncensored because researchers found that the lyrics are "unintelligible at any speed."

Mitch

ENGLISH: Form of Michael, Who is like God?
ROCK AND ROLL: Funny, mellow, well organized
RELATED ARTISTS/SONGS: Mitch Miller, Mitch Mitchell, Mitch Ryder, "Mitch" by Paul Heaton, "Mitch" by Tom Garvin, "Mitch" by Phil Woods
LINER NOTES: Winona Ryder took the pseudonym "Ryder" when she saw a Mitch Ryder LP in her dad's record collection.

Morris

ENGLISH: Form of Maurice, dark-skinned
ROCK AND ROLL: Smart, loves the open road
RELATED ARTISTS/SONGS: Morris Stoloff, Morris On, "Morris Brown" by OutKast, "Morris Day" by Felt, "Morris" by The Middle Men
LINER NOTES: Morris Stoloff's biggest pop hit was "Moonglow," the love theme from the movie *Picnic*; he later became Frank Sinatra's musical director.

Nolan

IRISH: Renowned
ROCK AND ROLL: Suave, wordly, likes to hang with the boys
RELATED ARTISTS/SONGS: The Nolan Sisters, John Nolan, Nolan Strong, "Nolan" by Wally, "Nolan" by Jeff Stanley, "Nolan" by Scott Foster, "Nolan Ryan" by The Winks
LINER NOTES: Doo-wop crooner Nolan Strong was so influential on a young Lou Reed that in one *Rolling Stone* interview the Velvet Underground singer said, "If I could really sing, I'd be Nolan Strong."

Obie, Obi

ENGLISH: Form of Obadiah, servant of God
ROCK AND ROLL: Politically aware, soulful, kind
RELATED ARTISTS/SONGS: Obie Benson (The Four Tops), Obie Trice, Obi Best, "Obi" by Toots Thielemans, "Obi" by Lori Bell
LINER NOTES: The Four Tops' bass singer Obi Benson cowrote Marvin Gaye's "What's Going On?"; he had two daughters, Ebony and Toby.

Presley

ENGLISH: Holy meadow
ROCK AND ROLL: Royalty, revered, fresh-faced
RELATED ARTISTS/SONGS: Elvis Presley, "Presley" by Le Bambine
LINER NOTES: When Elvis visited Richard Nixon in the White House in 1970, Nixon greeted him with "You dress kind of strange, don't you?" to which Elvis replied, "Mr. President, you got your show, and I got mine."

Raymond

ENGLISH: Protector
ROCK AND ROLL: Beloved son, unconventional, handsome
RELATED ARTISTS/SONGS: Raymond Scott, Raymond Burrell (Bad Company), Raymond McGinley (Teenage Fanclub), "Raymond" by Bellini, "Raymond" by Space, "Raymond" by Brett Eldredge
LINER NOTES: Composer Raymond Scott invented several instruments, including the Clavivox, a synthesizer that translated levels of light into musical notes.

Richard

ENGLISH: Powerful leader
ROCK AND ROLL: Practical, dependable, steadfast
RELATED ARTISTS/SONGS: Little Richard, Richard Hell, Richard Berry, "Richard III" by Supergrass, "Richard" by Slowdive, "The Last Time I Saw Richard" by Joni Mitchell, "Richard Cory" by Simon & Garfunkel, "Postcards from Richard" by Elton John
LINER NOTES: Little Richard presided over Demi Moore and Bruce Willis's wedding in 1987; actress Ally Sheedy was a bridesmaid.

Rochester

ENGLISH: Fortress on a rock
ROCK AND ROLL: Sly, witty, a Northerner
RELATED ARTISTS/SONGS: Rochester Neal (The Dixie Nightingales), Rochester Fosgate, Anthony Rochester, "Rockin' Rochester" by the 5.6.7.8's, "Rochester" by Craig Armstrong, "Rochester's Farewell" by Michael Nyman, "Rochester" by Tackhead
LINER NOTES: Southern gospel group The Dixie Nightingales' David Ruffin was later the lead singer of The Temptations.

Roosevelt

DUTCH: From the rose field
ROCK AND ROLL: A showman, bold, cheerful
RELATED ARTISTS/SONGS: Roosevelt Mays (The Danleers), Roosevelt Sykes, "Hotel Roosevelt" by Augustana, "Roosevelt Room" by Conor Oberst, "Roosevelt" by Missing Joe
LINER NOTES: Boogie-woogie pianist Roosevelt Sykes, nicknamed "The Honeydripper" for his way with the ladies, was known for continually smoking a cigar as he played.

Ronnie

NORSE: Variation of Ronald, royal advisor
ROCK AND ROLL: A small-town boy, brave, good-hearted
RELATED ARTISTS/SONGS: Ronnie Earl, Ronnie Hawkins, Ronnie James Dio, "Ronnie" by Metallica, "Ronnie" by Tracker
LINER NOTES: Also known as Rompin' Ronnie, Ronnie Hawkins was known for his talent-scouting; the members of his backup band, The Hawks, went on to form The Band and Janis Joplin's Full Tilt Boogie Band.

Roy

SCOTTISH: Roy
ROCK AND ROLL: An improviser, sensitive, a stand-up guy
RELATED ARTISTS/SONGS: Roy Acuff, Roy Orbison, Roy Milton, Roy Wood (ELO), "Roy" by C.W. McCall, "Roy" by Slim Dusty, "Roy" by Richard Harris, "Roy" by RB Morris, "Roy Walker" by Belle & Sebastian, "Hats Off to (Roy) Harper" by Led Zeppelin
LINER NOTES: Roy Orbison was Johnny Cash's lifelong friend and next-door neighbor. When Orbison's house burned down in 1968, Cash bought the property and planted an orchard on it in tribute to the Orbisons.

Rudolph, Rudolf

GERMAN: Famous wolf
ROCK AND ROLL: Speedy, an underdog, forever associated with the red-nosed reindeer
RELATED ARTISTS/SONGS: Adam Rudolph, Rudolph West, Kevin Rudolf, "Run Rudolph Run" by Chuck Berry, "Rudolf" by White Trash Debutantes, "Rudolf" by Bobo Stenson
LINER NOTES: Johnny Marks, the songwriter who wrote the original version of "Rudolph the Red-Nosed Reindeer" also wrote the rock version "Run, Rudolph, Run" for Chuck Berry.

Scotty

ENGLISH: Variation of Scott, Scottish
ROCK AND ROLL: Loyal, intellectual, a fan favorite
RELATED ARTISTS/SONGS: Scotty, Scotty Moore, "Scotty Doesn't Know" by Lustra, "Beam Me Up Scotty" by Nicki Minaj, "Watching Scott Die" by The Dead Milkmen, "Watching Scotty Grow" by Bobby Goldsboro, "Scotty Doesn't Know" by Sum 41
LINER NOTES: Elvis's backing guitarist Scotty Moore was a major influence on Keith Richards; in his memoir, Richards commented, "Everyone else wanted to be Elvis—I wanted to be Scotty."

Seymour

ENGLISH: Marshland
ROCK AND ROLL: Brainy, conservative, shy
RELATED ARTISTS/SONGS: Seymour Spiegelman (The Hilltoppers),

Seymour Stein, "Seymour Stein" by Belle & Sebastian, "Seymour" by Vapnet, "Seymour" by The Ominous Seapods, "Seymour" by The Spoils

LINER NOTES: Sire Records cofounder Seymour Stein was a pivotal figure in new wave music, signing The Ramones, The Talking Heads, and Madonna for the first time.

Stewart, Stuart

ENGLISH: Guardian of the house

ROCK AND ROLL: Forthright, courageous, has a terrible sense of direction

RELATED ARTISTS/SONGS: Stuart Sutcliffe, Stuart Zender (Jamiroquai), Stuart Murdoch (Belle & Sebastian), "Stuart" by The Dead Milkmen, "Stuart" by Ruby Blue, "Stuart and the Ave." by Green Day, "Stuart Gets Lost Dans Le Metro" by Someone Still Loves You Boris Yeltsin

LINER NOTES: Stuart Sutcliffe, the original bass player of The Beatles, is pictured on the covers of both *Sgt. Pepper's Lonely Heart's Club Band* and *Anthology 1*.

Tab

AMERICAN INVENTED, CIRCA 1952

ROCK AND ROLL: Handsome, a dreamboat

RELATED ARTISTS/SONGS: Tab Hunter, Tab Smith, "Tab" by Monster Magnet, "Tab" by The Hellacopters, "Tab" by Komet

LINER NOTES: Teen Idol Tab Hunter was known as "the Sigh Guy" for his dreamy good looks.

Vito

ITALIAN: Life

ROCK AND ROLL: Wealthy, spiritual, a flashy dresser

RELATED ARTISTS/SONGS: Vito Picone (The Elegants), Big Vito, "Vito's Ordination Song" by Sufjan Stevens, "Remember Vito Andolini" by Nino Rota

LINER NOTES: The Elegants founder Vito Picone played bit parts in *Goodfellas*, *The Sopranos*, and *Analyze This*.

Wydell

ENGLISH: Form of Wade, river ford

ROCK AND ROLL: Spiritual, clever

RELATED ARTISTS/SONGS: Wydell Jones (The Edsels), Wydell Croom, "Tiny Snaps Wydell" by Tyler Bates, "The Last Triumphant Ride of Sheriff Wydell" by A House Cursed

LINER NOTES: Wydell Jones's group The Edsels are known for their big hit "Rama Lama Ding Dong."

Rock Pioneers' Children

Rock stars in the 1950s were pioneering more than the music genre; they were kicking off a tradition of children with superstar names. Chuck Berry's daughters Aloha Isa and Melody Exes have names that seem just as fresh and original now as they did in the 1950s and 1960s. Take some inspiration from the rock parents of yesteryear for names with some spunk and flash to them.

BABY NAME	ROCK PIONEER PARENT
Aloha Isa	Chuck Berry
Doreen	Bill Haley
Jay Perry	The Big Bopper
Jolie	Brenda Lee
Knox	Sam Phillips
Link Elvis	Link Wray
Lisa Marie	Elvis Presley
Martha Maria	Bill Haley
Melody Exes	Chuck Berry
Mona Kay	Link Wray
Roy DeWayne	Roy Orbison
Sherri Ann	Gene Kelton
Terri Lynn	Bo Diddley

Famous Guitars'
Nicknames

S ome rock stars are known for smashing their instruments, but others treat their guitars almost like children. They get pampered, cleaned, and a few of them even get names. Below are rock musicians and the names they gave their musical instrument babies.

Eric Clapton	Blackie, Brownie
Bo Diddley	Big B, The Twang Machine
Rory Gallagher	Ex-Sunburst
Jerry Garcia	Alligator
Billy Gibbons	Pearly Gates
George Harrison	Rocky
Jimi Hendrix	Betty Jean
Albert King	Lucy
B.B. King	Lucille
Bob Marley	Old Faithful
Brian May	Red Special
Tom Morello	Soul Power, Arm the Homeless
Willie Nelson	Trigger
Les Paul	The Log
Randy Rhoads	Harpoon
Eddie Van Halen	Frankenstrat
Stevie Ray Vaughan	Number One or First Wife
Neil Young	Old Black

Elvis
Baby Names

Maybe no figure in rock and roll history has been as influential on the world of baby names as Elvis Presley. In fact, it took until 2011—thirty-four years after the King took his final bow—for Elvis to leave the top 1000 names in the United States. While naming your tot Elvis might put a lot of expectations on his wee shoulders, there are plenty of sources of inspiration in Presley's lyrics.

GIRLS	BOYS
Annie	Aaron
Aubrey	Abraham
Blue	Adam
Cindy	Antonio
Creole	Danny
Frankie	Jericho
Gladys	Jesse
Guadalajara	John
Hawaii	Johnny
Hula	Joshua
Judy	Mojo
Kentucky	Penn
Leilani	Presley
Lucia	Sam
Mamie	Teddy
Marie	Tennessee
Maybellene	Tupelo
Memphis	
Mona	
Petunia	
Queenie	
Sally	
Violet	
Viva	

Just Names:
Legends

From Axl to Elvis to Ozzy, if you want a name that's instantly recognizable as a music fan's choice, you couldn't do much better than to select from the icons below.

GIRLS

Beyoncé

AMERICAN: Derived from Beyince, blessed

LINER NOTES: Beyoncé Knowles got her unusual name from her mother's maiden name, Biyince; her family nicknames are Bee and Juju.

Dolly

AMERICAN: Dainty

LINER NOTES: Dolly Parton's advocacy efforts to save the bald eagle earned her the Partnership Award from the U.S. Fish and Wildlife Service.

Fiona

GAELIC: Fair

LINER NOTES: Fiona Apple has a tattoo of the letters "FHW" on her back, a reference to a dream about flying, in which the people below her cried "Fiona Has Wings!"

Janis

HEBREW: Variation of Jane, God is merciful

LINER NOTES: Though Janis Joplin's best-known nickname is Pearl, her close friends and family called her "Tex," an homage to her home state of Texas.

Liza

HEBREW: Variation of Elizabeth, God's promise

LINER NOTES: Liza Minnelli's first film appearance was as a baby, in the last shot of mother Judy Garland's 1949 film *In the Good Old Summertime*.

Madonna

LATIN: My lady
LINER NOTES: Madonna has a tattoo of Marilyn Monroe's face on her butt.

Stevie

ENGLISH: Variation of Stephanie, laureled
LINER NOTES: Stevie Nicks was runner-up for prom queen in high school.

BOYS

Axl

GERMAN: Peaceful
LINER NOTES: In his youth, William "Axl" Rose taught Sunday school at his church. He adopted the stage name Axl after a band he once played in.

Bono

LATIN: Good
LINER NOTES: Before Bono's band named itself U2, it went by The Hype and, briefly, by the name Feedback.

Bruce

ENGLISH: From the willows
LINER NOTES: An ice cream stand in Belmar, New Jersey, is named "10th Avenue Freeze Out" in honor of the Bruce Springsteen song.

Duke

ENGLISH: Royalty
LINER NOTES: Duke Ellington's first job was hawking peanuts at baseball games in Washington, D.C.

Elton

ENGLISH PLACE NAME: Eel town
LINER NOTES: Elton John's son, Zachary Jackson Levon, got his second middle name from John's song "Levon."

Elvis

NORSE: All wise
LINER NOTES: Elvis Presley had a pet turkey named "Bowtie."

Jimmy, Jimmie, Jimi

HEBREW: Variation of James, he who supplants

LINER NOTES: Left-handed Jimi Hendrix played with his right hand in front of his father, who believed left-handedness was a sign of the devil.

Keith

SCOTTISH: Forest

LINER NOTES: Keith Richards estimates that he only slept two nights out of every week for many years, and therefore he has "been conscious for at least three lifetimes."

Les

ENGLISH: Form of Leslie, fortified

LINER NOTES: Before settling on his stage name (his birth name was Lester Polsfuss), Les Paul used the names Rhubarb Red and Red Hot Red.

Mick

ENGLISH: Form of Michael, Who is like God?

LINER NOTES: Mick Jagger has seven children by four women: daughters Karis, Jade, Elizabeth, and Georgia May, and sons James Leroy, Gabriel Luke, and Lucas Maurice.

Miles

LATIN: Soldier

LINER NOTES: At Miles Davis's wedding to Cicely Tyson, Bill Cosby was his best man.

Ozzy

HEBREW: Variation of Oz, courageous

LINER NOTES: Ozzy Osbourne's "O-Z-Z-Y" tattoo across the knuckles of his left hand was one he did himself with a sewing needle and pencil lead.

Ringo

ENGLISH: Form of Richard, leader

LINER NOTES: Ringo Starr's son, Zakk, went on to play drums with The Who.

Sting

AMERICAN INVENTED

LINER NOTES: Sting got his nickname from the yellow and black striped sweater he wore when playing with The Phoenix Jazzmen.

Pop Icons: Divas, Crooners, and Bubblegum

From Elton to Whitney, Bette to Wayne, pop rock is rich in possibility for names with star potential. If you want your li'l bit to have his or her name in flashing lights, there's no one better to look to than divas, crooners, and boy bands, those that have brought inspiration to their bubblegum and found something one-of-a-kind and simply sweet.

GIRLS

Alexandra

GREEK: Defender
ROCK AND ROLL: A nightclub queen, joyful, boisterous, and brassy
RELATED ARTISTS/SONGS: Alexandra Burke, "Alexandra Leaving" by Leonard Cohen, "Back to Alexandra" by Dave Matthews Band, "Alexandra" by Aventura
LINER NOTES: Leonard Cohen's song "Alexandra Leaving" is an adaptation of the poem "God Abandons Antony" by Constantine P. Cavafy.

Aretha

GREEK: Virtue
ROCK AND ROLL: Exuberant, warm, the undisputed queen, loves unusual hats
RELATED ARTISTS/SONGS: Aretha Franklin, "Aretha, Sing One for Me" by George Jackson
LINER NOTES: Aretha Franklin's youngest son, Kecalf, is a Christian rap artist. His name is a combination of the initials of his parents' names: Kenneth E. Cunningham Aretha Louise Franklin.

Barbara, Barbra

LATIN: Foreigner, stranger
ROCK AND ROLL: Loves to dance, the hometown girl who makes it big

"There's no one like her, like Barbara."
—FRANK SINATRA

Bette

HEBREW: Variation of Elizabeth, God is abundance
ROCK AND ROLL: Brassy, confident, bright, and blond
RELATED ARTISTS/SONGS: Bette Midler, "Bette" by the Jesse Green Trio
LINER NOTES: Bette Midler starred in the first professional production of *Tommy*, The Who's rock opera.

Brandi, Brandy

DUTCH: Brandy wine
ROCK AND ROLL: A good girl with a mischievous streak, intoxicating
RELATED ARTISTS/SONGS: Brandy (Norwood), Brandi Shearer, "Blackberry Brandy" by T Bird and the Breaks, "Brandy (You're a Fine Girl)" by Looking Glass, "Too Much Brandy" by The Streets, "Brandy" by Kenny Chesney, "Brandy" by the O'Jays
LINER NOTES: R&B singer Brandy is Snoop Dogg's first cousin.

Brittany, Britney

CELTIC: A Breton
ROCK AND ROLL: Sultry, resilient, sensitive
RELATED ARTISTS/SONGS: Brittani Senser, Britney Spears, Brittany Wells, "Brittany" by Lil' Louis & the World, "Brittany's Back" by The Love Language
LINER NOTES: Britney Spears was the point guard on her high school's basketball team; her childhood nickname was "Pinky."

Carly, Carli

GERMAN: Free
ROCK AND ROLL: Romantic, sensitive, mysterious
RELATED ARTISTS/SONGS: Carly Simon, "Carly" by The Capes, "Age of Loneliness (Carly's Song)" by Enigma, "Carly" by Jack Nietzsche, "Carly" by The Higher
LINER NOTES: Though it's been more than thirty years since the song was written, Carly Simon refuses to divulge who "You're So Vain" is about; contenders include Warren Beatty, James Taylor, and David Geffen.

Cassandra, Cassie

GREEK: Prophet

ROCK AND ROLL: Intuitive, wise, knowing, has a hard time getting people to listen

RELATED ARTISTS/SONGS: Cassie Ramone (Vivian Girls), Cassandra Ventura (aka Cassie), Cassandra Wilson, "Cassie" by Dolly Parton, "Cassandra" by ABBA, "Cassandra Gemini" by The Mars Volta, "Cassandra" by Dave Brubeck, "Cassandra" by Dennis Brown

LINER NOTES: Dolly Parton's song "Cassie" is about her sister; Parton has three other sisters, Willadeene, Freida, and Stella.

Celia

LATIN: Musical

NECARE:
"She is God's own art."

PHIL OCHS:
"The vision of my Celia make dreams to dream upon."

KICKS:
"There was something about that girl."

THE CARDIGANS:
"You won't say you're not moved by her beauty."

ANNAH MAC:
"Girl I'll always be here waiting for you."

Cilla

LATIN: Variation of Priscilla, old

ROCK AND ROLL: Carefree, breezy, sweet, and cheerful; probably British

RELATED ARTISTS/SONGS: Cilla Black, "Lilla Cilla" by Orsa Spelman, "Cilla & Marg" by Paul Rose

LINER NOTES: Cilla Black, born Priscilla White, became friends with John Lennon and Paul McCartney while working as a coat-check girl at the Liverpool club they played weekly gigs at.

Chaka

HEBREW: Life

ROCK AND ROLL: Dancing queen, a party girl

RELATED ARTISTS/SONGS: Chaka Khan, "Chaka" by the Manhattan Brothers

LINER NOTES: Chaka Khan's sister, Yvonne Stevens, gained success as a funk singer under the name Taka Boom.

Cher

FRENCH: Dear
ROCK AND ROLL: Formidable, fashion forward
RELATED ARTISTS/SONGS: Cher (née Cherilyn Sarkisian), "Cher" by Brigitte Fontaine, "Cher" by The Celebrities
LINER NOTES: The first Sonny and Cher album was released under the pseudonyms Caesar and Cleo.

Christina, Cristina, Kristina

GREEK: Form of Christian, bearer of Christ
ROCK AND ROLL: Daredevil, a great dancer, chic
RELATED ARTISTS/SONGS: Christina Aguilera, Christina Blust, Christina Milian, "Kristina" by Rick Springfield, "Christina" by Memphis Slim, "Christina" by Waylon Jennings, "Christina" by Super Furry Animals, "Christina" by The Oblivians
LINER NOTES: Christina Aguilera named her son Max Liron because the name combination in Hebrew translates to "My greatest song."

Deanna, Deana, Deanne

LATIN: Divine
ROCK AND ROLL: Partner in crime
RELATED ARTISTS/SONGS: Deanna Bogart, Deana Carter, Deanna Durbin, "Deanna" by Nick Cave & the Bad Seeds, "Deanna" by Johnny & the Moon
LINER NOTES: Actress and singer Deanna Durbin was the top-salaried woman in the United States in 1945 and 1947.

Delores, Dolores

SPANISH: Sorrowful
ROCK AND ROLL: One of a kind, gorgeous, edgy
RELATED ARTISTS/SONGS: Dolores Keane, Dolores Fuller, Dolores O'Riordan, "Dinner with Delores" by Prince, "Dolores" by The Mavericks, "Todo Los Dolores" by Devendra Banhart, "Dolores" by Frank Sinatra, "Dolores" by Miles Davis

 "A voice like music, lips like wine/what a break if I could make Dolores mine."
—FRANK SINATRA

Diana

LATIN: Divine
ROCK AND ROLL: Charming, effervescent, and seductive
RELATED ARTISTS/SONGS: Diana King, Diana Krall, Diana Ross,

"Diana" by Herbie Hancock, "Diana" by Bryan Adams, "Diana" by The Misfits, "Dirty Diana" by Michael Jackson, "Diana" by Paul Anka
LINER NOTES: Diana Ross has five children: Rhonda, Tracee, Chudney, Ross, and Evan.

Doris

GREEK: Sea nymph
ROCK AND ROLL: Has a beautiful voice, sentimental, girlish
RELATED ARTISTS/SONGS: Doris Day, "Doris" by Shellac, "Doris" by Dirty Three, "Shoot Doris Day" by Super Furry Animals, "Doris Dub" by Tosca
LINER NOTES: Doris Day's real last name is Kappelhoff; Day was a suggestion from the bandleader Barney Rapp after she sang the song "Day After Day."

Edith

ENGLISH: Rich in war
ROCK AND ROLL: Stylish, sophisticated, upper crust
RELATED ARTISTS/SONGS: Edith Piaf, "Edith and the Kingpin" by Joni Mitchell, "She Thinks She's Edith Head" by They Might Be Giants, "Edith" by Big Dipper, "Calloused Fingers Won't Make You Strong, Edith Wrong" by Casiotone for the Painfully Alone, "Edith" by The Hot Melts
LINER NOTES: Chanteuse Edith Piaf was great friends with German singer Marlene Dietrich, who was Piaf's maid of honor at her wedding to Jacques Pills.

Florence

LATIN: Blossom
ROCK AND ROLL: Intrepid, a brassy, adventurous lady
RELATED ARTISTS/SONGS: Florence Ballard (The Supremes), Florence Welch (Florence and the Machine), "Florence" by the Paragons, "Florence" by Fats Waller, "Florence" by Gargoyles, "Florence" by Crooked Still
LINER NOTES: When Florence Ballard helped found The Supremes, their group name was The Primettes. The ladies were supposed to be the all-woman supporting act for doo-wop group The Primes, who later became The Temptations.

Frieda, Frida

GERMAN: Peaceful
ROCK AND ROLL: Artistic, a revolutionary; linked to the Mexican painter Frida Kahlo
RELATED ARTISTS/SONGS: Frida (Anni-Frid Lyngstad, ABBA), Frida Hyvönen, "Frida" by The Minders, "Frida" by Yann Tiersen, "Frida" by Bongusto, "Freida" by Porter Wagoner
LINER NOTES: ABBA's Frida Lyngstad is now a member of German royalty, owing to her third marriage, to Prince Heinrich Ruzzo Reuss of Plauen.

Gabriella, Gabrielle

HEBREW: Feminization of Gabriel, God's messenger

ROCK AND ROLL: A trustworthy confidante, effortlessly beautiful

RELATED ARTISTS/SONGS: Gabriella Cilmi, Troy & Gabriella, "Gabriella" by The Avett Brothers, "Gabriella" by The Ladybirds, "Gabrielle" by Ween, "Gabrielle" by Johnny Hallyday

LINER NOTES: Australian-Italian songstress Gabriella Cilmi was discovered when she sang the Rolling Stones song "Jumpin' Jack Flash" at a street festival in Melbourne.

Gladys

WELSH: Royalty

ROCK AND ROLL: Sentimental, romantic, a Southern belle

RELATED ARTISTS/SONGS: Gladys Knight, "Gladys" by Stan Getz, "Gladys" by The Scallions, "Goddess Gladys" by Puggy

LINER NOTES: Gladys Knight's son Shanga owns an Atlanta-based restaurant chain called Gladys Knight & Ron Winans' Chicken & Waffles.

Janet

ENGLISH: God's gift

ROCK AND ROLL: Flirty, fun, energetic; a crossover hit

RELATED ARTISTS/SONGS: Janet Jackson, Janet Lennon (The Lennon Sisters), Janet Weiss (Sleater-Kinney), "Janet" by The Commodores, "Janet" by Duke Ellington, "Janet" by Ralph Towner

LINER NOTES: Michael Jackson nicknamed his sister Janet "Dunk" because he thought her petite stature made her look like a donkey.

Kylie

ABORIGINAL: Boomerang

ROCK AND ROLL: Bubbly, effervescent, friendly, loves a good party

RELATED ARTISTS/SONGS: Kylie Minogue, "Kylie" by Pinback, "Kylie" by Bear vs. Shark

LINER NOTES: Kylie Minogue's singing career took off after she performed "I Got You Babe" with John Waters at a Football Club benefit concert.

Lesley, Leslie

SCOTTISH: Gray fort

ROCK AND ROLL: Cute, carefree, fun-loving

RELATED ARTISTS/SONGS: Lesley Gore, "Lesley" by Joe Tex, "Lesley" by Muck and the Mires, "Lesley's Song" by Fred Hand, "Leslie Anne Levine" by The Decemberists

LINER NOTES: Lesley Gore was a junior in high school when her song "It's My Party" topped the *Billboard* charts in 1963.

Linda

GERMAN: Tender
ROCK AND ROLL: Charming, aloof
RELATED ARTISTS/SONGS: Linda Jansen (The Angels), Linda McCartney, Linda Ronstadt, "Linda" by Jan & Dean, "Linda" by Clinic, "Linda" by Fleetwood Mac, "Linda on My Mind" by Conway Twitty, "Linda" by Wyclef Jean
LINER NOTES: In the 1980s, Linda Ronstadt was engaged to director George Lucas.

Mandy

LATIN: Diminutive of Amanda, much loved
ROCK AND ROLL: Happy, nurturing, smarty, a good girlfriend
RELATED ARTISTS/SONGS: Mandy Moore, Mandy Patinkin, "Mandy" by Barry Manilow, "Mandy" by Irving Berlin, "Mandy" by The Jonas Brothers, "Mandy" by Fats Waller, "Mandy" by Citizen Cope
LINER NOTES: Barry Manilow's song "Mandy" was originally titled "Brandy," but he changed it in order to avoid confusion with the Looking Glass song "Brandy (You're a Fine Girl)."

Mariah

HEBREW: Variation of Moriah, the Lord is my teacher
ROCK AND ROLL: Glossy, put-together, playful
RELATED ARTISTS/SONGS: Mariah Carey, "Mariah" by The Kingston Trio
LINER NOTES: Mariah Carey named her twins Monroe, in honor of Marilyn Monroe, and Moroccan, the style of room in which Nick Cannon proposed to her.

Monica

LATIN: Counselor
ROCK AND ROLL: Soulful, earnest, smooth, nocturnal
RELATED ARTISTS/SONGS: Monica, "Monica" by The Kinks, "Monica" by Tortoise
LINER NOTES: Monica is related to rapper Ludacris through her mother's second marriage.

Nancy

HEBREW: Variation of Anna, grace
ROCK AND ROLL: Friendly, stylish, healthy, has a certain glow, angelic
RELATED ARTISTS/SONGS: Nancy Sinatra, Nancy Spungen, Nancy Wilson, "For Nancy" by Pete Yorn, "Nancy (With the Laughing Face)" by Frank Sinatra, "Nancy" by Ray Charles, "Nancy Boy" by Placebo
LINER NOTES: Frank Sinatra wrote the song "Nancy (With the Laughing Face)" for his daughter Nancy's fourth birthday.

Nicolette

FRENCH: Variation of Nicholas, people of victory

ROCK AND ROLL: A city girl with a country twang, spontaneous, rosy-cheeked

RELATED ARTISTS/SONGS: Nicolette Aubourg, Nicolette Larson, Nicolette Palikat, "Nicolette" by The Cambridge Singers, "Nicolette" by Kenny Wheeler

LINER NOTES: Nicolette Larson and Linda Ronstadt were credited on Neil Young's album *American Stars 'n Bars* as "the Saddlebags."

Olivia

LATIN: Olive

ROCK AND ROLL: Mellow, soft, sultry, and elegant

RELATED ARTISTS/SONGS: Olivia Harrison, Olivia Newton-John, "Olivia" by Henry Rollins, "Olivia" by Trey Anastasio, "Olivia" by Rick Trevino, "Olivia" by Edie Brickwell

LINER NOTES: Due to a zipper breaking, Olivia Newton-John had to be sewn into the leather pants she wore as Sandy in the last sequence of *Grease*.

Pamela

ENGLISH: All sweetness

ROCK AND ROLL: Curious, saucy, adventurous

RELATED ARTISTS/SONGS: Pamela Green (Salt-N-Pepa), Pamela Rose, "Pamela" by Bobby Fuller, "Pamela" by Toto, "Pamela" by Art Blakey, "Pamela" by The Key, "O Pamela" by Nouvelle Vague

"Pamela, heaven in a box."
—NOUVELLE VAGUE

Petula

ENGLISH: Variation of Petunia, flower

ROCK AND ROLL: Tender, dramatic, and elegant

RELATED ARTISTS/SONGS: Petula Clark, "Petula" by Bert Kaempfert

LINER NOTES: Petula Clark's first public performance was at a department store. She was paid with a tin of toffees and a gold watch.

Rihanna, Rianna

WELSH: Variation of Rhiannon, divine queen

ROCK AND ROLL: Caribbean bombshell with a tough edge

RELATED ARTISTS/SONGS: Rihanna, "Rianna" by Paul Schwartz, "Rianna" by Fisher

LINER NOTES: Rihanna was a cadet in a sub-army program that trained with the Barbadian military.

Rosemary

ENGLISH PLANT NAME
ROCK AND ROLL: Colorful, a survivor, well dressed
RELATED ARTISTS/SONGS: Rosemary Clooney, "Rosemary" by The Grateful Dead, "Why Didn't Rosemary" by Deep Purple, "Dear Rosemary" by Foo Fighters, "Love Grows (Where My Rosemary Goes)" by Edison Lighthouse, "Rosemary" by Lenny Kravitz
LINER NOTES: Edison Lighthouse was a fake group formed so that the studio-created "Love Grows (Where My Rosemary Goes)" could be on the TV show *Top of the Pops*.

Shakira

ARABIC: Woman of grace
ROCK AND ROLL: Saucy, sultry, multilingual
RELATED ARTISTS/SONGS: Shakira, "Shakira" by Prestige, "Shakira" by Shanti Roots
LINER NOTES: Shakira, whose full name is Shakira Isabel Mebarak Ripoli, learned bellydancing from her Lebanese grandmother.

Tina, Teena

ENGLISH: River
ROCK AND ROLL: Clear-eyed, honest, irresistible
RELATED ARTISTS/SONGS: Tina Marie, Tina Turner, Tina Weymouth (Talking Heads), "Tina" by Camper van Beethoven, "Tina" by The Mekons, "Tina" by Frank Sinatra, "Tina Toledo's Street Walkin' Blues" by Ryan Adams, "Tina" by The Weavers
LINER NOTES: Tina Turner was born Anna Mae Bullock. Ike gave her the stage name "Tina" after *Sheena, Queen of the Jungle*.

Toni

LATIN: Variation of Antonia, praiseworthy
ROCK AND ROLL: Sultry, romantic, sophisticated, high-class
RELATED ARTISTS/SONGS: Toni Basil, Toni Braxton, Toni Childs, "Toni" by Herb Ellis, "Toni" by Michaux
LINER NOTES: Toni Braxton has two sons, Denim Cole and Diezel Ky.

Vanessa

ENGLISH: Star
ROCK AND ROLL: Bubbly, strong, elegant, has got it all together
RELATED ARTISTS/SONGS: Vanessa Carlton, Vanessa Williams, "Vanessa" by Gene Clark, "Vanessa" by Billy Swan, "Vanessa" by Chet Atkins, "Vanessa Paradis" by Chet Baker
LINER NOTES: Vanessa Williams was offered Halle Berry's Oscar-winning role in *Monster's Ball* but turned it down. She has four children, Melanie, Jillian, Devin, and Sasha.

Whitney

ENGLISH: White water
ROCK AND ROLL: Fierce, determined, spiritual, beautiful
RELATED ARTISTS/SONGS: Whitney Houston, "Don't Call Me Whitney, Bobby" by The Islands, "Whitney Walks" by Jawbox, "Early Whitney" by Why?
LINER NOTES: Dee Dee and Dionne Warwick are Whitney Houston's cousins, and Aretha Franklin is Houston's godmother.

Yvette

FRENCH: Variation of Yves, archer
ROCK AND ROLL: Spontaneous, magnetic, a heartbreaker
RELATED ARTISTS/SONGS: Yvette Giraud, Yvette Michele, Yvette Nelson, "Yvette" by Gerald Wilson, "Yvette" by Stan Getz, "Dear Yvette" by LL Cool J
LINER NOTES: Chaka Khan's birth name was Yvette Marie Stevens; an African shaman associated with the Black Panthers renamed her Chaka Adunne Aduffe Hodarhi Karifi.

Yvonne

FRENCH: A coniferous tree
ROCK AND ROLL: Dependable, summery, tempting
RELATED ARTISTS/SONGS: Yvonne Chaka Chaka, Yvonne Elliman, "Yvonne" by Marshall Crenshaw, "Yvonne" by James Moody, "Yvonne" by Paul McCartney, "Yvonne" by The Saw Doctors
LINER NOTES: The Bee Gees wrote the song "If I Can't Have You" for Yvonne Elliman.

BOYS

Al

ENGLISH: Variant of Albert, Alexander, or Alan; noble, great
ROCK AND ROLL: Curious, quirky, the class cutup
RELATED ARTISTS/SONGS: "Weird Al" Yankovic, Al Green, Al Casey, Al Hirt, "You Can Call Me Al" by Paul Simon
LINER NOTES: During his 1992 campaign for the vice presidency, Al Gore used Paul Simon's song as an unofficial theme for his entrance.

Andy

GREEK: Form of Andrew; masculine
ROCK AND ROLL: Rugged but sweet, loyal, hates winter
RELATED ARTISTS/SONGS: Andy Williams, Andy Gibb, Andy Rourke (The Smiths), "Andy" by Frank Zappa, "Me & Little Andy" by Dolly

Parton, "Andy" by Neko Case, "Andy" by Indigo Girls, "Desperate Andy" by The Cranberries

LINER NOTES: Frank Zappa's "Andy" is a tribute to Andy Devine, a character actor best known for his work in Westerns.

Bert, Burt

ENGLISH: Variant of Albert, Herbert, or Bertram; bright

ROCK AND ROLL: An awful nice guy, either rough-hewn or silky smooth

RELATED ARTISTS/SONGS: Bert Jansch, Bert Kaempfert, Burt Bacharach, "Bert" by R. Stevie Moore, "Lonesome Cowboy Burt" by Frank Zappa, "Closer, the Ballad of Burt and Linda" by Cheap Trick, "Yellow Burt" by Toy Dolls

LINER NOTES: Burt Bacharach had a cameo appearance in all three *Austin Powers* movies.

Bing

ENGLISH: Onomatopoeia of a bell sound

ROCK AND ROLL: Fun, laid-back, sharp, smooth

RELATED ARTISTS/SONGS: Bing Crosby, "Bada Bing" by Danger-doom, "Bing" by Mark Verbos, "Bing" by Andy Sheppard, "Bing" by Bonham

LINER NOTES: In his early films, Bing Crosby habitually wore hats or hairpieces to cover up his big ears. One studio executive complained that he looked "like a taxi with both doors open."

Bobby

ENGLISH: Diminutive of Robert, bright flame

ROCK AND ROLL: Dashing, a heartbreaker

RELATED ARTISTS/SONGS: Bobby "Blue" Bland, Bobby Brown, Bobby Darin, "Song to Bobby" by Cat Power, "Bobby Brown" by Frank Zappa, "Bobby" by Wooden Wand, "Me and Bobby McGee" by Janis Joplin, "B.O.B.B.Y." by the RZA

LINER NOTES: Bobby Brown has five children, Landon, La'princia, Bobby Jr., Bobbi Kristina, and Cassius; Brown is also a distant cousin of disco queen Donna Summer.

Cliff

ENGLISH: Ford by a cliff

ROCK AND ROLL: An uncrowned king, well loved

RELATED ARTISTS/SONGS: Cliff Burton (Metallica), Cliff Carlisle, Cliff Richard, Cliff William (AC/DC), "Cliff" by The Marshes, "Cliff" by Ovuca

LINER NOTES: Yodeler Cliff Carlisle pioneered the use of Hawaiian steel guitar in country music.

Cole

ENGLISH: Dark-haired
ROCK AND ROLL: Dapper, part of a legacy
RELATED ARTISTS/SONGS: Cole Porter, "Cole" by Fiendz, "Old King Cole" by Accelerator
LINER NOTES: Cole Porter was the head of the glee club and a football cheerleader at Yale.

Dean

ENGLISH: Leader
ROCK AND ROLL: The king of cool, dapper, the dude in charge
RELATED ARTISTS/SONGS: Dean Fertita (The Dead Weather), Dean Martin, Dean Ween (Ween), "James Dean" by The Eagles, "Dean" by Dizzee Rascal, "Dean" by Terry Reid, "The Dean and I" by 10cc
LINER NOTES: At the age of fifteen, Dean Martin boxed under the name "Kid Crochet."

Don

SCOTTISH: Short for Donald, world leader
ROCK AND ROLL: Top dog, untouchable, a serious gangster
RELATED ARTISTS/SONGS: Don Henley (The Eagles), Don McLean, Don Van Vliet (aka Captain Beefheart), "Don't Don" by Super Junior, "We Did It All for Don" by Against Me!, "Don" by Need New Body, "Don" by Albert Ayler, "Mr. Don" by Disco Biscuits
LINER NOTES: Songwriter Lori Lieberman wrote "Killing Me Softly" about Don McLean.

Errol

GERMAN: Noble
ROCK AND ROLL: Confident, quiet, intelligent
RELATED ARTISTS/SONGS: Errol Brown (Hot Chocolate), Errol Parker, Erroll Garner, "Errol" by Australian Crawl, "Errol" by James Reyne
LINER NOTES: Hot Chocolate's Errol Brown has two daughters, Leone and Collette.

Frank

LATIN: Free man
ROCK AND ROLL: Inventive, wild, a standard-bearer
RELATED ARTISTS/SONGS: Frank Black (Pixies), Frank Sinatra, Frank Zappa, "Frank" by Ween, "Frank" by Steve Vai, "Frank Sinatra" by Cake, "Frank's Theme" by Tom Waits, "Just Like Frank" by Less Than Jake, "Dirty Frank" by Pearl Jam
LINER NOTES: Frank Zappa was in a high school band called The Blackouts with Don Vliet, later known as Captain Beefheart.

Frankie

LATIN: Diminutive of Francis, free man

SISTER SLEDGE:
"I never loved anyone this much."

BETTY BLOWTORCH:
"Had a great smile and pretty green eyes."

CONNIE FRANCIS:
"Frankie, my darling, I'll never let you see me cry."

PHISH:
"Time is me and I should know."

Gilbert

GERMAN: Bright youth
ROCK AND ROLL: A free spirit, industrious, crafty
RELATED ARTISTS/SONGS: Gilberto Gil, Gilbert Mamery, Gilbert O'Sullivan, "Gilbert" by Calexico, "Gilbert Street" by Sweet Thursday
LINER NOTES: While in college, Gilbert O'Sullivan played drums in a band with a pre-Supertramp Rick Davies.

Guy

FRENCH: Leader
ROCK AND ROLL: Laid-back, hip, a chill dude
RELATED ARTISTS/SONGS: Guy Berryman (Coldplay), Guy Clark, Guy Picciotto (Fugazi), "Guy" by Jeff Merchant, "Song for Guy" by Elton John, "Jealous Guy" by John Lennon, "My Guy" by the Supremes
LINER NOTES: In the film *Sister Act*, motown hit song "My Guy" was adapted into the gospel track "My God."

Harry

ENGLISH: Variation of Henry, ruler
ROCK AND ROLL: A smooth-talking rebel, passionate and charming
RELATED ARTISTS/SONGS: Harry Belafonte, Harry Connick Jr., Harry Nilsson, "Harry's Song" by Ringo Starr, "Harry, You're a Beast" by Frank Zappa, "Harry" by Janis Joplin, "Harry Hood" by Phish, "Harry" by Macy Gray
LINER NOTES: Harry Nilsson's paternal grandparents were Swedish circus performers, inspiring Nilsson's album *Aerial Ballet*.

Herbert

GERMAN: Bright
ROCK AND ROLL: Artistic, intelligent, sophisticated
RELATED ARTISTS/SONGS: Herbert Joos, Herbert Feemster (Peaches & Herb), Herbert Grönemeyer, Herbert Rhoad (The Persuasions), "Herbert" by Le Hammond Inferno, "Herbert" by Gottlieb Wende-hals, "Herbert" by Ludwig Hirsch
LINER NOTES: The a cappella group The Persuasions has been active since the mid-1960s, recording tribute albums to The Grateful Dead, U2, and Frank Zappa.

Hoagy

AMERICAN INVENTED
ROCK AND ROLL: Sophisticate, suave, and sentimental
RELATED ARTISTS/SONGS: Hoagy Carmichael, Hoagy Lands, "I Remember Hoagy" by Ahmad Jamal, "Hoagy, Bix, & Johnny" by Bob Dylan
LINER NOTES: Hoagy Carmichael was named Hoagland after a circus troupe called The Hoaglands who lived in his mother's house while she was pregnant with him.

Irving

SCOTTISH: Green river
ROCK AND ROLL: Sophisticated, chic, aristocratic
RELATED ARTISTS/SONGS: Irving Azoff, Irving Berlin, "Irving" by Three Man Army, "Irving" by Austin Lounge Lizards
LINER NOTES: During the course of his career, Irving Berlin wrote more than fifteen hundred songs, including "There's No Business Like Show Business" and "God Bless America."

Jackson

ENGLISH: Son of Jack
ROCK AND ROLL: Polite, reserved, politically engaged, sensitive
RELATED ARTISTS/SONGS: Jackson Browne, Jackson Frank, "Jackson" by Jerry Lee Lewis, "Jackson" by Johnny Cash and June Carter, "Jackson" by the Kingston Trio
LINER NOTES: For a short time in the 1960s, Jackson Browne played in folk legend Tim Buckley's backup band.

Jordan

ARAMAIC: One who descends
ROCK AND ROLL: Capable, tall, good with his hands
RELATED ARTISTS/SONGS: Jordan Knight (New Kids on the Block), Jordan Officer, Jordan White, "Jordan" by Tara MacLean, "If You See Jordan" by Something Corporate
LINER NOTES: New Kid on the Block Jordan Knight has two sons, Dante Jordan and Eric Jacob.

Kenny

SCOTTISH: Variation of Kenneth, fiery
ROCK AND ROLL: Laid-back, down home, popular
RELATED ARTISTS/SONGS: Kenny Chesney, Kenny G, Kenny Rogers, "Kenny" by Sicko, "Kenny" by Medeski Martin & Wood, "Kenny" by Jodi Shaw
LINER NOTES: At seventeen, Kenny G's first professional gig was playing with Barry White and the Love Unlimited Orchestra.

Lawrence

LATIN: One with laurels
ROCK AND ROLL: Bubbly, effusive, friendly
RELATED ARTISTS/SONGS: Lawrence Donegan (The Bluebells), Lawrence Welk, "Lawrence" by Ani DiFranco, "Lawrence" by Jay & the Americans, "Lawrence" by 54-40
LINER NOTES: Lawrence Welk has a resort community named after him near Escondido, California.

Lee

ENGLISH: Clearing
ROCK AND ROLL: Kindhearted, a good friend, dependable
RELATED ARTISTS/SONGS: Lee DeWyze, Lee Ranaldo (Sonic Youth), Lee "Scratch" Perry, Lee Wiley, "Lee" by Henry Mancini, "Lee" by Stan Getz, "Lee" by Tenacious D
LINER NOTES: Some of the pseudonyms that Lee "Scratch" Perry went by include The Upsetter and Pipecock Jackson.

Leroy

FRENCH: The king
ROCK AND ROLL: Tough, a kingpin, a sharp dresser
RELATED ARTISTS/SONGS: Leroy Anderson, Leroy Carr, Leroy Jenkins, "Bring Back That LeRoy Brown" by Queen, "Mrs. Leroy Brown" by Loretta Lynn, "Leroy" by Anita Carter, "Bad, Bad Leroy Brown" by Jim Croce, "Leroy" by Wheatus
LINER NOTES: Jim Croce's song "Bad, Bad Leroy Brown" has inspired at least two pro wrestling names: Leroy Brown and Junkyard Dog.

Marvin

WELSH: Sea fortress
ROCK AND ROLL: Funky, smooth, powerful
RELATED ARTISTS/SONGS: Marvin Gaye, Marvin Hamlisch, "Marvin (Patches)" by Titas, "Marvin" by The Limeliters, "Marvin" by Norman Davis
LINER NOTES: Marvin Gaye's younger sister Zeola was his choreographer.

Maurice

FRENCH: Dark-skinned

ROCK AND ROLL: Savvy, artful, a charmer

RELATED ARTISTS/SONGS: Maurice Chevalier, Maurice Gibb, Maurice White (Earth, Wind & Fire), "Maurice" by Amy Stephen, "A Day in the Life of Maurice" by Caravan, "So Good (Maurice's Song)" by Destiny's Child, "Enter Maurice" by Steve Miller

LINER NOTES: Maurice Gibb's paintball team was called the Royal River Rats, a riff on his title as a Commander of the Order of the British Empire.

Michael

HEBREW: Who is like God?

ROCK AND ROLL: A great dancer, a child prodigy, stubborn, good-looking

RELATED ARTISTS/SONGS: Michael Bublé, Michael Jackson, Michael Stipe (R.E.M.), "Michael" by Franz Ferdinand, "The Ballad of Michael Valentine" by The Killers, "Michael" by The Highwaymen, "Michael" by Joan Baez, "Michael" by Suzi Quatro

LINER NOTES: Michael Jackson once had a boa constrictor named "Muscles" and a pet ram named "Mr. Tibbs."

Mickey

ENGLISH: Form of Michael, Who is like God?

ROCK AND ROLL: Popular, a teenage heartbreaker

RELATED ARTISTS/SONGS: Micky Dolenz (The Monkees), Mickey Hart (The Grateful Dead), Mickey Jones, "Mickey" by Toni Basil, "Mickey's Monkey" by The Miracles, "Mickey" by Jackie Gleason

LINER NOTES: "Mickey" was originally written as an ode to "Kitty," but Toni Basil adapted it to sing to a male character.

Nelson

ENGLISH: Son of Neil

ROCK AND ROLL: Virtuous, stalwart, chummy

RELATED ARTISTS/SONGS: Nelson Eddy, Nelson Riddle, Nelson Ned, "Nelson" by Laura Love, "Nelson" by Loraxx

LINER NOTES: Musical star Nelson Eddy taught himself how to sing by imitating opera recordings; he was distantly related to President Martin Van Buren.

Noel

FRENCH: Christmas

ROCK AND ROLL: Peaceful, joyful, always in a good mood

RELATED ARTISTS/SONGS: Noel Coward, Noel Gallagher (Oasis), Noel Paul Stookey (Peter, Paul, & Mary), "Noel" by Daniel Amos, "Stroke It Noel" by Big Star

LINER NOTES: *NME (New Musical Express)* dubbed a generation of

British pop bands "Noelrock" after the influence that Noel Galla-gher had on them.

Oscar

IRISH: Friend of deer
ROCK AND ROLL: Creative, affable, old-fashioned
RELATED ARTISTS/SONGS: Oscar Brand, Oscar Hammerstein, Oscar Moore, "Oscar the Angel" by Randy Travis, "Oscar See Through Red Eye" by Boards of Canada, "Oscar Wilde" by Company of Thieves
LINER NOTES: Musical theater legend Oscar Hammerstein studied law at Columbia University.

Pat

LATIN: Variation of Patrick, patrician
ROCK AND ROLL: Friendly, stalwart, sweet, a little nerdy
RELATED ARTISTS/SONGS: Pat Boone, Pat Martino, Pat Metheny, "Pat" by Duke Ellington, "Pat" by Serge Chaloff, "Pat" by Slint
LINER NOTES: Pat Boone was once Ozzy Osbourne's next-door neighbor.

Ricky

GERMAN: Variation of Richard, ruler
ROCK AND ROLL: Tricky, energetic, a heartthrob
RELATED ARTISTS/SONGS: Ricky Martin (Menudo), Ricky Nelson, Ricky Skaggs, "Ricky's Theme" by The Beastie Boys, "Ricky" by The Butthole Surfers, "Ricky" by Division Day
LINER NOTES: Boy band Menudo had a total of thirty members, including a young Ricky Martin; once a member turned sixteen or his voice changed, he was contractually required to leave the group.

Robbie, Robby

GERMAN: Form of Robert, famous
ROCK AND ROLL: The leader, brainy, quiet, the strong but silent type
RELATED ARTISTS/SONGS: Robbie Robertson (The Band), Robbie Williams, Robbie Shakespeare (Sly & Robbie), "Robbie" by Slices, "Robbie" by Yusef Lateef, "Hey Robby" by Tom Astor
LINER NOTES: Robbie Williams considers himself to be a nudist at heart, joking in interviews that he expects to be "one of those dads who embarrass their children."

Rod

ENGLISH: Variation of Rodney, island by the clearing
ROCK AND ROLL: An interpreter, virtuoso, dynamic
RELATED ARTISTS/SONGS: Rod Stewart, Rod Taylor, "Hot Rod" by Peaches

LINER NOTES: Before he became a professional musician, Rod Stewart was a newspaper boy, a screen printer, and an apprentice gravedigger.

Rudy

GERMAN: Diminutive of Rudolph, famous wolf
ROCK AND ROLL: A wild child, takes his time
RELATED ARTISTS/SONGS: Rudy Vallee, "Rudy" by Cher, "Rudy" by Supertramp, "A Message to You Rudy" by The Specials, "Rudy Wants to Buy Yez a Drink" by Frank Zappa, "Run Rudy Run" by the Toasters
LINER NOTES: One of crooner Rudy Vallee's radio shows was called *The Royal Gelatin Hour*.

Sammy

HEBREW: Diminutive of Samuel, told by God
ROCK AND ROLL: A happy child, prefers leather and gold
RELATED ARTISTS/SONGS: Sammy Cahn, Sammy Davis Jr., Sammy Hagar, "Sammy" by The Afghan Whigs, "Moon Sammy" by Soul Coughing, "Sammy" by GWAR, "Sammy" by The Roll-Ups
LINER NOTES: Sammy Davis Jr. was Tim Burton's first choice to star in *Beetlejuice*, but the studio refused.

Sigmund

GERMAN: Protection through victory
ROCK AND ROLL: Cerebral, cautious, friendly
RELATED ARTISTS/SONGS: Sigmund Romberg, Sigmund Groven, "Sigmund Freud's Impersonation of Albert Einstein in America" by Randy Newman, "Sigmund" by Chomsky, "Sigmund and the Sea Monsters" by Tripping Daisies
LINER NOTES: Before writing songs for Broadway musicals with the likes of George Gershwin, Sigmund Romberg worked in a pencil factory.

Sonny

ENGISH: Variation of Son, male child
ROCK AND ROLL: Mellow, friendly, beloved
RELATED ARTISTS/SONGS: Sonny Bono, Sonny Rollins, Sonny Boy Williamson, Sonny Sandoval (P.O.D.), "Sonny" by Christy Moore, "Sonny" by Rod Stewart, "Sonny" by Mary Black, "Sonny" by New Found Glory, "Sonny's Burning" by The Birthday Party
LINER NOTES: The *Simpsons* character Bleeding Gums Murphy is partly based on Sonny Rollins, who was also discovered while playing on a bridge at night.

Todd, Tod

ENGLISH: Fox
ROCK AND ROLL: Electric, a technical mastermind, cheerful, brainy
RELATED ARTISTS/SONGS: Big Head Todd and the Monsters, Todd Rundgren, Todd Terry, Todd Wilson, "Todd" by Jeff Allen, "Todd's Song" by The Bouncing Souls
LINER NOTES: Todd Rundgren is Liv Tyler's stepfather; he has three biological sons, Rex, Randy, and Rebop Rundgren.

Val

FRENCH: Variation of Valeria or Valentino, strong
ROCK AND ROLL: A charismatic rascal, handsome
RELATED ARTISTS/SONGS: Val Fuentes (New Riders of the Purple Sage), Val Doonican, Val Burke (Spooky Tooth), "Val" by The Czars, "Val" by Greg Serrato, "Val" by Carl Stone
LINER NOTES: Irish balladeer Val Doonican's trademarks were his cardigans and rocking chair, a gentle persona that earned him the nickname "Ireland's Bing Crosby."

Vincent

FRENCH: Conqueror
ROCK AND ROLL: Starry-eyed, an artist, often misunderstood
RELATED ARTISTS/SONGS: Vincent DeNunzio (The Feelies), "Vincent" by Don McLean, "Vincent" by Jane Olivor, "Vincent" by NOFX, "Vincent O'Brien" by M.Ward
LINER NOTES: Don McLean wrote "Vincent" as a tribute to Vincent Van Gogh.

Wayne

ENGLISH: Wagon-maker
ROCK AND ROLL: Mellow, smooth, loves spectacle
RELATED ARTISTS/SONGS: Lil Wayne, Wayne King, Wayne Newton, Wayne Shorter, "Wayne, Wayne (Go Away)" by R. Stevie Moore, "Wayne" by Jae Sinnett
LINER NOTES: Wayne Newton had a rockabilly band, The Rascals in Rhythm, with his older brother in the 1950s.

Xavier

BASQUE: New house
ROCK AND ROLL: Long-lived, passionate, popular, has a good ear
RELATED ARTISTS/SONGS: Xavier Cugat, Xavier Naidoo, Xavier Rudd, "Xavier" by Dead Can Dance
LINER NOTES: Bandleader Xavier Cugat helmed the Waldorf-Astoria Hotel's orchestra for sixteen years and was also a successful cartoonist.

Yves

FRENCH: Yew tree

ROCK AND ROLL: Fondly remembered, courageous, blessed

RELATED ARTISTS/SONGS: Yves Larock, Yves Montand, "Yves" by The Everly Brothers, "Yves" by The Spiders

LINER NOTES: Yves Montand had a long relationship with singer Edith Piaf.

Broadway
Baby Names

From fun-loving wise guys to spunky starlets, the matinee is a good place to look for names for your future star. There are beloved characters like *Wicked*'s Nessarose or *West Side Story*'s Tony, not to mention leading ladies like Idina Menzel or Julie Andrews. Ziegfield and Griselda didn't make the list—but here are some creative name suggestions from the world of musical theater:

GIRLS		BOYS	
Adelaide	Montego	Adolfo	Marcello
Aida	Musetta	Arvide	Nathan
Amneris	Nettie	Cipriano	Norbert
Anika	Orfeh	Clifford	Oliver
Carlotta	Patti	Conrad	Pippin
Cosette	Roxie	Cornelius	Raoul
Demeter	Sally	Enoch	Rodolfo
Dulcinea	Serena	Ernst	Sky
Eden	Texas	Fiorello	Tobias
Edna	Tovah	Gaston	Tulsa
Evita	Ursula	Herbie	Tyrone
Glinda	Uta	Hero	Victor
Goody	Velma	Hunter	Wilbur
Heather	Victoria	Jean-Michel	Yul
Helga	Vivian	Juan	Zero
Kristen	Zaza		

Frank Sinatra
Baby Names

If you can't get enough of Old Blue Eyes, you should look to his formidable repertoire for naming inspiration. From darling Charmaine to Mack the Knife, Sinatra songs offer a lot of choice. To wit:

GIRLS	BOYS
April	Abraham
Barbara	Andy
Bonita	Bob
Caroline	Dick
Charmaine	Jimmy
Dolly	Joe
Dolores	Johnny
Elizabeth	Leroy
Emily	Luigi
Felicia	Mack
Ginny	Michael
Jemima	Nelson
Judy	Noah
Laura	Peter
Lily	Tommy
Linda	Wenceslas
Lorraine	
Marie	
Marlene	
Misty	
Nancy	
Neiani	
Poinciana	
Sheila	
Stella	
Susie	
Tallulah	
Tina	

The Diva Name Generator

L et's face it: No matter how much you love the name, there's really only one Cher. To find a name for your very own little diva, look to your favorite pop songstress' lyrics.

SO YOU LIKE . . .	FOR A BOY	FOR A GIRL
Aretha Franklin	Jack ("The House That Jack Built")	Louise (Aretha's middle name)
Barbra Streisand	Nick (*Funny Girl*'s Nick Arnstein)	Jenny ("Jenny Rebecca")
Britney Spears	Jayden (Her son Jayden)	Lucky ("Lucky")
Cher	Jesse ("Just Like Jesse James")	Bonnie (Cher's original stage name)
Christina Aguilera	Cruz ("Cruz")	Genie ("Genie in a Bottle")
Diana Ross	Lee ("Mr. Lee")	Blue (Album *Blue*)
Janet Jackson	Jackson (Janet's last name)	Damita (Janet's middle name)
Lady Gaga	Alejandro ("Alejandro")	Stefani (Gaga's real name)
Madonna	Isaac ("Isaac")	Eva (Her character in *Evita*)
Mariah Carey	Alfred (Mariah's beloved dad)	Honey ("Honey")
Shakira	Carlos (Collaborator Carlos Santana)	Gitana ("Gitana")
Tina Turner	Craig ("Craig")	Zelma (Tina's mother)
Whitney Houston	Clive (Mentor Clive Davis)	Joy ("Joy")

Diva Babies & Crooner Babies

P op star babies are in the limelight from the moment they're born, and their diva mothers and crooner fathers often choose their names to stand out in the crowd. Check out the name choices that the reigning royalty of pop bestowed upon their little tykes:

BABY NAME	POP STAR PARENT(S)
Ava	Fred Astaire
Blue Angel	U2's The Edge
Bluebell Madonna	Geri Halliwell
Bobbi Christina	Whitney Houston and Bobby Brown
Brando	Frankie Valli
Bronx Mowgli	Ashlee Simpson
Carla	Frankie Avalon
Chastity Sun	Cher
D'Andrea	Tony Bennett
Daegel	Tony Bennett
Egypt	Alicia Keys
Elijah Blue	Cher
Emilio	Frankie Valli
Emma Maribel	Jennifer Lopez
Francesco	Frankie Valli
Kecalf	Aretha Franklin
Kenya	Gladys Knight
Kingston	Gwen Stefani
Lourdes	Madonna
Mary Frances	Bing Crosby
Melody	Gene Vincent
Mercy James	Madonna
Mirabella Bunny	Bryan Adams
Moroccan	Mariah Carey
Noelle	Andy Williams
Phoenix Chi	The Spice Girls' Melanie Brown
Ricci	Dean Martin
Shanga	Gladys Knight
Shari	Harry Belafonte
Zuma	Gwen Stefani

Roots of Rock: Jazz and Blues

The Rolling Stones named themselves after a Muddy Waters song and Pink Floyd took their name from bluesmen Pink Anderson and Floyd Council. You probably don't need a history lesson to know that not only did blues and jazz musicians provide the foundation of rock, they gave many budding young guitarists the inspiration for their band names. Browsing through the list of blues and jazz greats might provide you with a similar epiphany: from Southern charmers ripe for revival like Mahalia and Lottie to the untouchable cool of Bix and Coltrane, these are some standards worth breathing new life into.

GIRLS

Alberta

ENGLISH: Form of Albert, noble
ROCK AND ROLL: Bold, slender, outgoing
RELATED ARTISTS/SONGS: Alberta Hunter, Alberta Cross, "Alberta" by Leadbelly, "Alberta" by Bob Gibson, "Alberta" by Snooks Eaglin, "Alberta" by The Chad Mitchell Trio, "Alberta #1" by Bob Dylan
LINER NOTES: Memphis blueswoman Alberta Hunter inspired a musical called *Cookin' at the Cookery*; her trademark look was fringed shawls and enormous sparkly earrings.

Bess, Bessie, Bessy

HEBREW: Form of Elizabeth, God's promise
ROCK AND ROLL: Close friend, endearingly goofy, knows how to boogie
RELATED ARTISTS/SONGS: Bessie Smith, Dressy Bessy, "Jump Sister Bessie" by Otis Rush, "Bessie" by James Brown," "Bess, You Is My Woman Now" by Ella Fitzgerald, "You and Me, Bess" by Joanna Newsom, "Jog Along Bess" by Vashti Bunyan
LINER NOTES: Bessie Smith got voice lessons from blues legend Ma Rainey.

Betty

HEBREW: Variant of Elizabeth, God's promise
ROCK AND ROLL: A good girl gone bad, a little freaky
RELATED ARTISTS/SONGS: Betty Davis, Betty Boo, Betty Weiss (The Shangri-Las), "Iron Ore Betty" by John Prine, "Black Betty" by Leadbelly, "Mister Betty" by The Gourds, "Backyard Betty" by Spank Rock
LINER NOTES: Leadbelly's song "Black Betty" derives from a traditional marching song; a "black betty" was a musket and "bam-a-lam" the sound it made when it fired.

Beverley, Beverly

ENGLISH: Near the beaver stream
ROCK AND ROLL: Hardworking, dreamy
RELATED ARTISTS/SONGS: The Beverley Sisters, Beverley Knight, Beverly Lee (The Shirelles), "Beverly" by John Fahey, "Beverly" by Bobbie Gentry
LINER NOTES: Blues musician Beverly Watkins, who has collaborated with the likes of B.B. King and Ray Charles, is one of the few female blues guitarists of her era.

Billie

ENGLISH: Short for Wilma or Wilhelmina, defender
ROCK AND ROLL: Beautiful, sometimes clingy, regal on the stage
RELATED ARTISTS/SONGS: Billie Davis, Billie Holiday, Billie Piper, "Billie" by Pavement, "Billie Jean" by Michael Jackson, "Billie's Bounce" by Charlie Parker, "Billie Listens" by Joan Osborne, "Ballad of Billie Sol" by Phil Ochs
LINER NOTES: Billie Holiday was born Eleanora Fagan. She took her stage name from the actress Billie Dove and her father, musician Clarence Holiday.

Blanche

FRENCH: White
ROCK AND ROLL: Delicate, fair, pretty
RELATED ARTISTS/SONGS: Blanche Calloway, "Fleur Blanche" by Orsten, "Blanche" by Ken McIntyre, "Blanche" by Klaus Schulze
LINER NOTES: Blanche Calloway, Cab Calloway's sister, was the first woman to lead an all-male jazz orchestra; she also worked as a DJ for twenty years in Florida.

Clora

ENGLISH: Form of Clara, clear
ROCK AND ROLL: Sprightly, brave, talented
RELATED ARTISTS/SONGS: Clora Bryant, "Clora" by Mikkel Metal
LINER NOTES: Jazz trumpeter Clora Bryant was the only female musician to perform with Dizzy Gillespie.

Coco, Koko

SPANISH: Little coconut
ROCK AND ROLL: Chic, bouncy, bright
RELATED ARTISTS/SONGS: Koko Taylor, CocoRosie, CoCo Lee, "Coco" by Machito, "Coco" by Lee Baxter, "Coco" by Charlie Palmieri, "Koko" by Charlie Parker
LINER NOTES: Koko Taylor, the Queen of Chicago Blues, was born Cora; her nickname is from her love of chocolate.

Dinah, Dina

HEBREW: Vindicated
ROCK AND ROLL: A Southern belle, likes to play hard to get
RELATED ARTISTS/SONGS: Dinah Shore, Dinah Washington, "Dinah" by Chet Baker, "Dinah Moe Humm" by Frank Zappa, "Belly Dancin' Dina" by The Jungle Brothers, "Song for Dina" by Dan Deacon, "Dinah" by Fats Waller
LINER NOTES: Songstress Dinah Washington has an avenue in Alabama and a park in Chicago named in her honor.

Ella, Elle

FRENCH: Woman
ROCK AND ROLL: Tireless, sought after, colorful
RELATED ARTISTS/SONGS: Ella Jenkins, Ella Johnson, Ella Fitzgerald, "Ella" by M. Ward, "Elle" by The James Taylor Quartet, "Elle et Moi" by Lemongrass, "Elle" by Celine Dion, "Dear Ella" by Dee Dee Bridgewater
LINER NOTES: Ella Fitzgerald made her debut at Harlem's Apollo Theater, where she won $25 as the winner of one of its Amateur Nights.

Esperanza

LATIN: Hopeful
ROCK AND ROLL: Eclectic, clever, the dark horse
RELATED ARTISTS/SONGS: Esperanza Spalding, "Ultima Esperanza" by The Dresden Dolls
LINER NOTES: Esperanza Spalding was the first jazz musician to win the Grammy Award for Best New Artist.

Ethel

ENGLISH: Nobel
ROCK AND ROLL: Powerful, something special, tough, a brassy broad
RELATED ARTISTS/SONGS: Ethel Beatty, Ethel Merman, Ethel Waters, "Ethel" by Superblue, "Ethel" by Arcado, "Depth Charge Ethel" by Grinderman
LINER NOTES: Blues singer Ethel Waters was the second African-American to be nominated for an Oscar, for her 1949 film *Pinky*.

Etta

ENGLISH: Home ruler

ROCK AND ROLL: Gutsy, spontaneous, and bursting with life

RELATED ARTISTS/SONGS: Etta Baker, Etta James, "Etta" by Albert Nicholas, "Etta" by Andrea House

LINER NOTES: Etta James, born Jamesetta Hawkins, got the nickname "Miss Peaches" from her doo-wop group The Peaches. She has two sons, Donto and Sametto.

Felicia

LATIN: Happy

ROCK AND ROLL: Gutsy, laid-back, and boisterous; the gum-snapping cool girl in class

RELATED ARTISTS/SONGS: Felicia Day, Felicia Sanders, "Felicia" by Nat King Cole, "Felicia" by The Constellations, "Felicia" by Blues Traveler, "Felicia No Capecia" by Louis Prima, "Felicia" by Herb Alpert & the Tijuana Brass

"She's got a crocodile smile and a switchblade style."
—THE CONSTELLATIONS

Flora

LATIN: Flower

ROCK AND ROLL: The prettiest girl in town, mischievous

RELATED ARTISTS/SONGS: Flora Purim, Flora Reed, "Flora" by Gilberto Gil, "Flora" by Peter, Paul and Mary, "Flora's Secret" by Enya, "Alexander, Flora of Pom" by Elefant

LINER NOTES: Jazz singer Flora Purim has a voice that spans six octaves, a rare quality she shares with Mariah Carey and Bobby Brown.

Flossie, Flossy

LATIN: Variation of Florence, blossom

ROCK AND ROLL: Glamorous, lives life large, smokin' hot

RELATED ARTISTS/SONGS: Flossie and the Unicorns, "Flossie Lou" by Clifford Brown & Max Roach, "Flossie" by Carl Hodges, "Flossy" by Red Red Meat, "Flossie's Alarming Clock" by The Cuban Boys, "Flossie's Frolic" by Jeff Minter

LINER NOTES: Dizzy Gillespie was an early supporter of Clifford Brown, who wrote "Flossie Lou."

Francine

FRENCH: Feminine varation of François, French
ROCK AND ROLL: Fine and feisty, an angelic teenage queen
RELATED ARTISTS/SONGS: Francine Reed, "Francine" by ZZ Top, "Francine" by Tricia Greenwood, "Francine" by Azra
LINER NOTES: Blues singer Francine Reed has appeared in concerts with Miles Davis, Smokey Robinson, Etta James, and Willie Nelson.

Geneva

GERMAN: Juniper tree
ROCK AND ROLL: Intoxicating, petite, helpful, hypnotic
RELATED ARTISTS/SONGS: Geneva, "Geneva" by Henry Rollins, "Geneva Farewell" by Frank Zappa, "Little Geneva" by Muddy Waters, "Geneva's Lullaby" by The Amazing Rhythm Aces, "Geneva" by Alexis Korner

"I want to see Geneva so bad this morning, man, she heals my all in all."
—MUDDY WATERS

Gertrude, Trudy

GERMAN: Strength
ROCK AND ROLL: The pioneering matriarch, old-timey, had excellent taste
RELATED ARTISTS/SONGS: Gertrude "Ma" Rainey, Trudy Pitts, "Gertrude" by Jerry Jeff Walker, "Dear Gertrude" by Paula Cole, "Gertrude's Bounce" by Clifford Brown, "Trudy" by Band of Horses
LINER NOTES: Ma Rainey toured with her husband under the name "Rainey and Rainey, Assassinators of the Blues."

Gilda

ENGLISH: Golden
ROCK AND ROLL: A sultry bombshell, passionate, gorgeous
RELATED ARTISTS/SONGS: Gilda, Gilda Butta, "Gilda" by Momus, "Gilda" by Al Caiola
LINER NOTES: Michael Jackson used scenes from the 1940s film *Gilda* for one version of his music video for "Smooth Criminal."

Hattie

ENGLISH: Variation of Harriet, land ruler
ROCK AND ROLL: Fiercely independent, an eccentric matriarch, might have magical powers
RELATED ARTISTS/SONGS: Hattie Hart, "Batty Over Hattie" by

Dennis Wheeler, "Hurricane Hattie" by Jimmy Cliff, "Hattie" by Andrew Hill, "The Lonesome Death of Hattie Carroll" by Bob Dylan, "Hattie Blues" by Big Bill Broonzy

LINER NOTES: Country blues musician Hattie Hart, of The Memphis Jug Band, was famous for the wild, enormous parties she threw in Chicago during Prohibition.

Ida

GERMAN: Laborer

ROCK AND ROLL: Dusky, a beautiful bombshell, flirty but flighty

RELATED ARTISTS/SONGS: Ida Cox, Queen Ida, "Ida, Sweet as Apple Cider" by Frank Sinatra, "Ida" by The Annuals, "Don't Forget Me Ida" by The Bee Gees, "Ida" by Kid Ory

LINER NOTES: Blues singer Ida Cox managed her own vaudeville troupe, called Ida Cox and the Raisin' Cains.

Josephine

HEBREW: *Variation of Joseph, the Lord increases*

THE WALLFLOWERS:
"You must taste like sugar & tangerines."

BRANDI CARLILE:
"Take me back, Josephine."

CHRIS REA:
"Josephine, I'll send you all my love."

MANDO DIAO:
"She believes in magic and rhymes."

Lena

GREEK: Palm tree

ROCK AND ROLL: Tender, melodious, effortlessly glamorous

RELATED ARTISTS/SONGS: Lena Horne, Lena Katrina (t.A.T.u.), Lena Philipsson, "Lena" by Satellite, "Lena" by Joe Louis Walker, "Lena" by Cecil Taylor

LINER NOTES: Lena Horne was the mother-in-law of director Sidney Lumet, who married her daughter, Gail.

Lil

ENGLISH: Variation of Lillian, Lily

ROCK AND ROLL: Lighthearted, sassy, extroverted

RELATED ARTISTS/SONGS: Lil Hardin Armstrong, "Lil" by Excepter, "Lil" by Gordan Cheeks, "Lil" by Kamel Ziri

LINER NOTES: Lil Hardin Armstrong deemed Louis Armstrong's

clothes to be "too country" for Chicago; she used to make most of Armstrong's shirts.

Lindsay, Lindsey

ENGLISH: Linden tree by the sea
ROCK AND ROLL: Moon child, a dreamer, divine
RELATED ARTISTS/SONGS: Lindsay Cardinale, Lindsay Cooper, Lindsay Daenen, Lindsey Haun, "Lindsay" by Archie Fisher, "Lindsay" by Billy Klippert, "Lindsay" by Park, "Lindsey Quit Lollygagging" by Chiodos
LINER NOTES: Jazz oboist Lindsay Cooper toured with Captain Beefheart and became one of the main composers for John Peel's favorite avant-rock group, Henry Cow.

Lottie, Lotte

FRENCH: Variation of Charlotte, free woman
ROCK AND ROLL: Capricious, fun-loving, the life of the party
RELATED ARTISTS/SONGS: Lotte Lenya, Lottie Porter, Lottie Kimbrough, "Little Lottie" by Andrew Lloyd Webber, "Lottie Mo '68" by Lee Dorsey, "Lottie" by Jerry Reed, "Lottie Dottie" by Chuck Brown, "Lottie" by Ronny Elliott
LINER NOTES: Blueswoman Lottie Kimbrough was called "the Kansas City Butterball" for her large stature; record executives used pictures of her sister when billing her.

Mabel

LATIN: Lovable
ROCK AND ROLL: A great cook, loves to dance on the kitchen table
RELATED ARTISTS/SONGS: Mabel King, Mabel Mercer, "Mabel" by Procol Harem, "Mistress Mabel" by The Fratellis, "Mabel's Grievances" by Daniel Johnston, "Mabel" by Django Reinhardt
LINER NOTES: Cabaret singer Mabel Mercer's American fans included a young Frank Sinatra, who used to emulate her storytelling techniques.

Madeleine, Madalaine

GREEK: Variation of Magdalan, magnificent
ROCK AND ROLL: Cultured, curious, stylish
RELATED ARTISTS/SONGS: Madeleine Peyroux, "Madeleine" by Jacques Brel, "Madeleine-Mary" by Bonnie "Prince" Billy, "Madeleine" by Saint Etienne, "Madeleine" by Eugene McGuinness, "Madalaine" by Winger
LINER NOTES: Jazz songstress Madeleine Peyroux was inspired to begin singing by hanging out with the street musicians in the Latin Quarter of Paris.

Madison

ENGLISH: Son of Maud
ROCK AND ROLL: Well bred, polite, wealthy
RELATED ARTISTS/SONGS: "Madison" by The Attorneys, "Madison" by Talisman, "Madison Blues" by Fleetwood Mac, "Madison Blues" by Elmore James, "Madison" by Jude Cole
LINER NOTES: The Beatles' song "For You Blue" was inspired by Elmore James's "Madison Blues." In fact, midway through "For You Blue," George Harrison interjects, "Elmore James got nothing on this baby."

Mahalia

HEBREW: Tender affection
ROCK AND ROLL: Nurturing, soulful, earthy, strong
RELATED ARTISTS/SONGS: Mahalia Jackson, "Mahalia" by Ralph Alessi
LINER NOTES: Queen of Gospel Mahalia Jackson's childhood nickname was "Halie." She was named for her aunt Mahala.

Marlene, Marlena

GERMAN: Form of Maria, beloved
ROCK AND ROLL: Glamorous, alluring, magnetic
RELATED ARTISTS/SONGS: Marlene Dietrich, "Marlene on the Wall" by Suzanne Vega, "Marlene" by Todd Rundgren, "Marlene" by Lightspeed Champion
LINER NOTES: When Marlene Dietrich brought her cabaret act to Las Vegas, she hired a young Burt Bacharach as her music arranger.

Matana

ARABIC: Gift
ROCK AND ROLL: Worldly, elegant
RELATED ARTISTS/SONGS: Matana Roberts, "Matana" by Xangai, "Matana" by Steve Kroon
LINER NOTES: Free jazz saxophonist Matana Roberts published a zine, *Fat Ragged*, about her experiences busking in the New York subway.

Mildred

ENGLISH: Gentle strength
ROCK AND ROLL: Funny, loving, well read
RELATED ARTISTS/SONGS: Mildred Bailey, "Mildred Pierce" by Sonic Youth, "Mildred, Mildred" by Yoko Ono, "Mildred" by Edith Piaf, "Mississippi Mildred" by Jelly Roll Morton
LINER NOTES: Jazz singer Mildred Bailey and her husband Red Norvo earned the nickname "Mr. and Mrs. Swing" during the 1930s.

Monette

FRENCH: Variation of Mona, noble
ROCK AND ROLL: Lovely, bright, summery
RELATED ARTISTS/SONGS: Monette Moore, Monette Evans, "Monette's Ride" by Franck Valat, "Monette" by Gil Landry, "Monette" by Kenny Nolan
LINER NOTES: In the 1960s, blues singer Monette Moore briefly worked at Disneyland with The Young Men of New Orleans; she also recorded under the pseudonym Susan Smith.

Nanette

FRENCH: Form of Nancy, gracious
ROCK AND ROLL: Bouncy, not easily discouraged
RELATED ARTISTS/SONGS: Nanette Workman, Nanette Natal, "Nanette" by Someone Still Loves You Boris Yeltsin, "Nanette" by Thomas Cunningham, "The Story of Nanette" by Bette Midler, "No, No, Nanette" by Vincent Youmans
LINER NOTES: Blues singer Nanette Workman grew up in Mississippi but performs most of her songs in French; she sings backup on The Rolling Stones' "Honky Tonk Woman."

Nina

RUSSIAN: Form of Antonina, beautiful eyes
ROCK AND ROLL: Classy, bright, impetuous, lives for the weekend
RELATED ARTISTS/SONGS: Nina Hagen, Nina Simone, "Nina" by Lil Wayne, "Nina, Pretty Ballerina" by Abba, "Nina" by Holly Near, "Nina" by Gene Kelly

"She is the queen of the dancing floor."
—ABBA

Patricia

LATIN: Noble
ROCK AND ROLL: Strong, nurturing, a fighter
RELATED ARTISTS/SONGS: Patricia Bennett (The Chiffons), Patricia Kaas, Patricia Morrison (Gun Club), "Patricia's Moving Pictures" by The Go! Team, "Patricia" by Perry Como, "Patricia" by Art Pepper, "Patricia" by Perez Prado, "Patricia" by Genesis
LINER NOTES: The actor Gerard Depardieu produced French jazz singer Patricia Kaas's first single.

Phyllis

GREEK: Green leaf
ROCK AND ROLL: Warm, cheery, has a sunny smile

RELATED ARTISTS/SONGS: Phyllis Hyman, Phyllis Dillon, "Phyllis" by Major Lance, "Phyllis" by Apollo Sunshine, "Soul to Keep (For Phyllis)" by 7 Seconds, "Phyllis Ruth" by 16 Horsepower
LINER NOTES: Before gaining traction as a solo singer, Phyllis Hyman performed in clubs with Pharoah Sanders & the Fatback Band.

Rhoda

GREEK: Rose
ROCK AND ROLL: Youthful, a ray of sunshine, freckled
RELATED ARTISTS/SONGS: Rhoda Scott, Rhoda Dakar, Rhoda Hutchinson, "Rhoda" by Slint, "Rhoda" by Belle & Sebastian, "Rhoda Rhoda" by Robert Pollard, "Rhoda" by Nick Mason
LINER NOTES: Soul jazz organist Rhoda Scott would take her shoes off to work the pedals, earning her the nickname "The Barefoot Lady."

Rosetta

ENGLISH: Little rose
ROCK AND ROLL: Feisty, fearless, spiritual
RELATED ARTISTS/SONGS: Sister Rosetta Tharpe, "Rosetta" by Earl Hines, "Rosetta" by Joe Turner, "Rosetta" by Johnny Hodges, "Rosetta" by Ray Charles

 "In my heart dear there's nobody else but you."
—RAY CHARLES

Shemekia, Shemeika

AMERICAN: Derived from Melia, emulating
ROCK AND ROLL: Honest, brassy, confident
RELATED ARTISTS/SONGS: Shemekia Copeland, "Shemeika" by Ima-C
LINER NOTES: Shemekia Copeland is the daughter of blues guitarist Johnny Copeland; she first started singing when she accompanied him on his tours.

Stella

LATIN: Star
ROCK AND ROLL: Ethereal, artsy, expressive
RELATED ARTISTS/SONGS: "Stella Blue" by The Grateful Dead, "O Stella" by PJ Harvey, "Stella by Starlight" by Victor Young, "Stella" by Incubus, "Stella" by Al Jolson
LINER NOTES: Jazz standard "Stella by Starlight" was developed for

the 1944 film *The Uninvited*, but it also appears in *The Nutty Professor*, *Sabrina*, and *Casino*.

Valaida, Valeta

LATIN: Strong
ROCK AND ROLL: Good-natured, passionate
RELATED ARTISTS/SONGS: Valaida Snow, "Valeta" by Colette, "Valeta" by Lucero, "Valeta" by Henry Jimenez
LINER NOTES: Jazz trombonist Valaida Snow was nicknamed "Little Louis" after Louis Armstrong, who claimed that she was the second best trumpeter in the world, after him.

Viola

LATIN: Violet
ROCK AND ROLL: Musical, lighthearted, sweet
RELATED ARTISTS/SONGS: Viola McCoy, Viola Lee, "Viola" by Chuck Mangione, "Viola" by Butterfly Child, "Viola" by Anna Oxa, "Viola" by Michael Moore
LINER NOTES: Blues singer Viola McCoy, noted for her lively kazoo playing, recorded under various pseudonyms, including Amanda Brown, Gladys White, and Daisy Cliff.

BOYS

Alexis

GREEK: Guardian
ROCK AND ROLL: Southerner, free spirit
RELATED ARTISTS/SONGS: Alexis Korner, "Alexis" by Tommy Bolin, "Alexis" by Rory Gallagher
LINER NOTES: Father of British Blues Alexis Korner had a loose-knit electric blues group called Blues Incorporated, which included musicians Ginger Baker, Mick Jagger, Keith Richards, Rod Stewart, Brian Jones, and Jimmy Page.

Bix

AMERICAN INVENTED: Spunky
ROCK AND ROLL: Colorful, exuberant, a child prodigy
RELATED ARTISTS/SONGS: Bix, Bix Beiderbecke, "Bix" by Airplay
LINER NOTES: Jazz hero Bix Beiderbecke began playing the piano when he was only three years old, holding his hands way above his head to reach the keyboard; his cornet playing was described as "bullets shot from a bell."

Blake

ENGLISH: Dark-haired
ROCK AND ROLL: Mystic, wise
RELATED ARTISTS/SONGS: Blind Blake, Blake Mills, Blake Shelton, "One (Blake's Got a New Face)" by Vampire Weekend, "Blake's Jerusalem" by Billy Bragg
LINER NOTES: King of Ragtime Guitar Blind Blake honed a blues finger-picking style later used by Ry Cooder and Leon Redbone, among others.

Branford, Brantley

ENGLISH: Fiery torch
ROCK AND ROLL: Innovative, quirky, the black sheep
RELATED ARTISTS/SONGS: Branford Marsalis, Rick Brantley, "Branford" by Pete Rodriguez, "Branford Marsalis" by Marian McPartland
LINER NOTES: Saxophonist Branford Marsalis both acted in and played music for the soundtrack of Spike Lee's *School Daze*.

Cabell, Cab

FRENCH: Rope maker
ROCK AND ROLL: Energetic, cheerful, funny
RELATED ARTISTS/SONGS: Cab Calloway, "Cab" by Craig Harris, "Cab" by Shampoo, "Cab" by Train, "Cab" by Toy House
LINER NOTES: Cab Calloway's gliding backward dance moves, referenced in the Betty Boop short *Minnie the Moocher*, were the inspiration for Michael Jackson's moonwalk.

Cecil

LATIN: Stubborn
ROCK AND ROLL: Hardworking, long-suffering, has a good heart
RELATED ARTISTS/SONGS: Cecil Taylor, Cecil James McNeely (Big Jay McNeely), Cecil Womack (The Womack Brothers), "Cecil Brown" by Hank Williams III, "Cecil's Bells" by Sunset Rubdown, "Cecil" by Gary Chapman, "Star Cecil" by Coheed and Cambria
LINER NOTES: Free jazz pianist Cecil Taylor is also a ballet enthusiast; he composed a song for Mikhail Baryshnikov's ballet *Tetra Stomp: Eatin' Rain in Space*.

Charles

GERMAN: Manly
ROCK AND ROLL: A hard worker, the guy in charge
RELATED ARTISTS/SONGS:, Charles Brown, Charles Mingus, Charles Wright, "Charles" by The Skids, Charles in Charge" by Relient K, "Charles Atlas" by AFI, "Lake Charles" by Lucinda Williams, "The Charles C. Leary" by Devendra Banhart

Elmer

ENGLISH: Noble, famous
ROCK AND ROLL: Adventurous, a force of chaos
RELATED ARTISTS/SONGS: Elmer Bernstein, Elmer Food Beat, Elmer Snowden, "Elmer Karr" by Richard Buckden, "Elmer's Tune" by Glenn Miller, "Elmer's Song" by The Residents, "Elmer's" by 88 Fingers Louie
LINER NOTES: Composer Elmer Bernstein conducted the scores for *To Kill a Mockingbird* and *Ghostbusters*, among many other films.

Elmore

ENGLISH: Bright
ROCK AND ROLL: Gritty, electric, ferocious, influential
RELATED ARTISTS/SONGS: Elmore James, Elmore Judd, "Belle Elmore" by Mean Red Spiders, "Tribute to Elmore" by Eric Clapton
LINER NOTES: Early in his career, Jimi Hendrix sometimes played under the name "Maurice James," a pseudonym that he took in honor of bluesman Elmore James.

Erskine

SCOTTISH: High-minded
ROCK AND ROLL: Good-natured, old-fashioned, vivacious
RELATED ARTISTS/SONGS: Erskine Hawkins, Peter Erskine (Steely Dan), "The Erskine Bridge" by Errors, "Erskine Caldwell" by Bob Dylan
LINER NOTES: Jazz musician Erskine Hawkins, best known for his rendition of "Tuxedo Junction," was nicknamed the "20th Century Gabriel" for his trumpet skills.

Francisco

LATIN: From France
ROCK AND ROLL: Virtuosic, sunny, passionate
RELATED ARTISTS/SONGS: Francisco de Assis França (aka Chico Science), Francisco Mora, Francisco Pozo, "Francisco" by Brian Eno, "Francisco" by Jackie McLean
LINER NOTES: Chico Science, the Godfather of Merengue Beat, was sometimes known as "the Brazilian Jimi Hendrix."

Grover

ENGLISH: Gardener
ROCK AND ROLL: Smooth, sophisticated, and prolific
RELATED ARTISTS/SONGS: Grover Mitchell, Grover Washington Jr., "Grover" by Philadelphia Experiment, "Grover's Groove" by Rick Braun, "Groovin' for Grover" by Spyro Gyra
LINER NOTES: Grover Washington Jr. began sneaking into jazz clubs at the age of ten, hoping to catch a glimpse of his idols Harold Vick and Charles Lloyd.

Gus

LATIN: Variation of Augustus, revered
ROCK AND ROLL: Partner in crime, a political activist
RELATED ARTISTS/SONGS: Gus Backus (The Del-Vikings), Gus Cannon, Gus Gus, "Gus the Mynah Bird" by Stereolab, "Gus" by Lambchop & Hands Off Cuba
LINER NOTES: Bluesman Gus Cannon taught himself to play using a banjo he fashioned out of a frying pan and raccoon skin.

Herb, Herbie

GERMAN: Variation of Herbert, bright
ROCK AND ROLL: Smart, has rhythm, refined, stylish, innovative
RELATED ARTISTS/SONGS: Herb Alpert, Herb Fame (Peaches & Herb), Herbie Hancock, "Herbie" by Joseph Patrick Moore, "Herbie" by Madlib, "Herb" by Sly Dunbar
LINER NOTES: Jazz legend Herbie Hancock played a piano solo with the Chicago Symphony when he was just eleven years old.

Horace

LATIN: Timekeeper
ROCK AND ROLL: Shy, soulful, trustworthy, has a great sense of humor.
RELATED ARTISTS/SONGS: Horace Brown, Horace Painter (The Specials), Horace Silver, "Horace" by Ronnie Hawkins, "Horace" by J.J. Johnson, "Horace" by Madlib, "The Diary of Horace Wimp" by Electric Light Orchestra
LINER NOTES: Steely Dan based their hit song "Rikki, Don't Lose That Number" off of jazz saxophonist Horace Silver's "Song for My Father."

Humphrey

GERMAN: Peaceful warrior
ROCK AND ROLL: Old-fashioned, neat, good at improvising
RELATED ARTISTS/SONGS: Humphrey Lyttleton, Humphrey Searle, "Humphrey" by Benny Green, "Sir Humphrey" by Buck Clayton & His Swing Band
LINER NOTES: Jazz musician Humphrey Lyttleton, known for his work with Sidney Bechet, played trumpet on Radiohead's 2001 album *Amnesiac*.

Igor

NORSE: Protected
ROCK AND ROLL: Blue-blooded, serious, virtuosic
RELATED ARTISTS/SONGS: Igor Bril, Igor Yusov (Red Elvises), "Igor" by Woody Herman, "Igor" by Peter Jones, "Igor" by Patrick Doyle, "Prince Igor" by Warren G
LINER NOTES: Warren Zevon was inspired to take up music in high school when he met famed composer Igor Stravinsky.

Isaiah

HEBREW: God is salvation
ROCK AND ROLL: Humble, good-natured, knowledgeable
RELATED ARTISTS/SONGS: Isaiah Owens, Isaiah "Doc" Ross, "Isaiah" by Adult Rodeo, "Isaiah" by Dub Congress
LINER NOTES: Bluesman Isaiah Ross was nicknamed "the doctor" for his habit of carrying his harmonicas around in what looked like a black doctor's bag.

Ishmael

ARABIC: Outcast
ROCK AND ROLL: Adventurous, brave, but obsessive; avoid whales
RELATED ARTISTS/SONGS: Ishmael & the Peacemakers, "Ishmael" by Abdullah Ibrahim, "Ishamel & Maggie" by The Trews, "Ishamel" by Diamond Head, "Call Me Ishamel" by Get Cape Wear Cape Fly
LINER NOTES: Author Ishmael Reed has written ten novels and is also a jazz pianist, collaborating with the likes of Taj Mahal and Albert Ayler.

Jamal

ARABIC: Beauty
ROCK AND ROLL: Old school, thinks on his feet, clever
RELATED ARTISTS/SONGS: Ahmad Jamal, Jamal Phillips (Def Squad), "Jamal" by Dado Moroni, "Jamal" by Tony Forster
LINER NOTES: Pianist Ahmad Jamal is a favorite of actor Clint Eastwood, who used two of Jamal's recording in *The Bridges of Madison County*.

Kermit

IRISH: Without envy
ROCK AND ROLL: Old-fashioned, friendly, a little froggy
RELATED ARTISTS/SONGS: Kermit Driscoll, Kermit Ruffins, Kermit Whalin, "Kermit" by Hank Roberts, "Kermit" by Don Kohleone
LINER NOTES: Jazz musician Kermit Ruffins, founder of The New Orleans Rebirth Brass Band, has a recurring role on HBO's *Treme*.

Lewis, Louis

FRENCH: Famous warrior
ROCK AND ROLL: A film buff, clever, emotional
RELATED ARTISTS/SONGS: Louis Armstrong, Louis Clark, Louis Jordan, "Lewis" by Yo La Tengo, "Louis Collins" by The Grateful Dead, "Louis Riel" by Thee Headcoatees, "Louis" by Alexis Korner, "Louis" by The Roches
LINER NOTES: Louis Armstrong invented jazz scatting when he dropped the lyric sheet for "Heebie Jeebies" in the middle of recording, making up words to go along with the music.

Marcus

LATIN: Warrior
ROCK AND ROLL: A visionary, droll, has big ideas
RELATED ARTISTS/SONGS: Marcus Mumford (Mumford and Sons), Marcus Cooper (aka Pleasure P), Marcus Miller (The Crusaders), "Marcus Junior" by The Skatalites, "Marcus" by Tapper Zukie, "My Friend Marcus" by Manchester Orchestra
LINER NOTES: Jazz musician Marcus Miller composed the core for the sitcom *Everybody Hates Chris*.

Max

ENGLISH: Form of Maxwell or Maximillian, great stream
ROCK AND ROLL: High-strung, funky, clean and tidy
RELATED ARTISTS/SONGS: Max Richter, Max Roach, Max Priest, "Max" by The Future Sound of London, "Relax Max" by Dinah Washington, "The Max" by Prince, "Max" by Annie Gallup, "Max" by Paolo Conte
LINER NOTES: Bebop trailblazer Max Roach has five children: daughters Maxine, Ayo, and Dara, and sons Raoul and Daryl.

Mose

ENGLISH: Variation of Moses, savior
ROCK AND ROLL: Prolific, long-lived, innovative
RELATED ARTISTS/SONGS: Mose Allison
LINER NOTES: Blues legend Mose Allison inspired the Pixies' song "Allison." He has four children: Alyssa, Amy, John, and Janine, and two grandchildren, Kayley and Olivia.

Nat

ENGLISH: Form of Nathan, gift of God
ROCK AND ROLL: Smooth, accomplished, a snappy dresser
RELATED ARTISTS/SONGS: Nat Adderley, Nat King Cole, "Nat King Cole" by Adam Green
LINER NOTES: Nat King Cole was an avid baseball fan, keeping a regular seat at Dodgers games; he had five children: Carole and Nat Kelly, who were adopted, and Natalie, Casey, and Timolin.

Nathan

HEBREW: To give
ROCK AND ROLL: A heartbreaker, a poet
RELATED ARTISTS/SONGS: Nathan Beauregard, Nathan Berg, Nathan Connolly (Snow Patrol), "Nathan Jones" by The Supremes, "Nathan" by Vic Chesnutt, "Nathan" by Chris Conway
LINER NOTES: Nathan Beauregard sometimes was referred to as "King Tut of the Blues," thanks to his deeply sunken facial features.

Orville

FRENCH: Gold town
ROCK AND ROLL: Old-fashioned, inventive, formal
RELATED ARTISTS/SONGS: Orville Nash, Orville Johnson, Orville "Hoppy" Jones (The Ink Spots), "Old Orville Shop" by Sundance, "Orville the Duck" by Roy "Chubby" Brown
LINER NOTES: Before Orville Jones joined The Ink Spots, they were called "King, Jack, and Jester."

Pharaoh, Pharoah

EGYPTIAN: King
ROCK AND ROLL: Unique, creative, out there
RELATED ARTISTS/SONGS: The Pharaohs, Pharoah Sanders, Sam the Sham and the Pharaohs, "The Pharaoh Sails to Orion" by Nighthawk, "Pharaoh's Dance" by Miles Davis
LINER NOTES: Pharoah Sanders's birth name was Farrell Sanders; he changed his name at the suggestion of Sun Ra.

Ron

NORSE: Form of Ronald, royal advisor
ROCK AND ROLL: Conservative, buttoned-up, friendly
RELATED ARTISTS/SONGS: Ron Carter, Ron Hardy, Ron Sexsmith, "Ron" by Joy Zipper, "Ron" by Mary Lou Lords, "Ron" by Slint
LINER NOTES: Jazz double-bassist Ron Carter, who first gained fame as part of Miles Davis's early sixties quintet, appears on A Tribe Called Quest's album *The Low End Theory*.

Sal

ENGLISH: Variation of Salvatore, savior
ROCK AND ROLL: Tough, rugged, smooth-talking
RELATED ARTISTS/SONGS: Sal Salvador, "Sal" by Nightmares on Wax, "The Ballad of Sal Villanueva" by Taking Back Sunday
LINER NOTES: Bebop guitarist Sal Salvador was featured in the 1960 documentary *Jazz on a Summer's Day*.

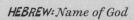

Samuel

HEBREW: Name of God

JASON UPTON:
"The whole world's in love with you baby."

PINK:
"You're so sweet, so coy."

BRADLEY HATHAWAY:
"He was wearing a brown button-up shirt and brown rope sandals."

LUNGFISH:
"We followed you, but you refused a trail."

Sandy

ENGLISH: Form of Sanford, sandy fort
ROCK AND ROLL: Old-fashioned, mellow, bright
RELATED ARTISTS/SONGS: Sandy Brown, Sandy Bull, Sandy Vee, "Hey Sandy" by Polaris, "Let's Get Sandy" by Be Your Own Pet
LINER NOTES: Jazz musician Sandy Brown was also an acoustic engineer at the BBC; his autobiography was called *The McJazz Manuscripts*.

Shelley, Shelly

ENGLISH: Meadow
ROCK AND ROLL: Free-spirited, youthful, loves baking
RELATED ARTISTS/SONGS: Shelley Bolman, Shelly Manne, Pete Shelley, "Shelley" by EKO, "Shelley" by Dance Hall Crashers, "Shelley" by Pyramis, "Shelley" by Will Dudley, "After Shelley" by Chumbawamba
LINER NOTES: West coast jazz impresario Shelly Manne tutored Frank Sinatra and assisted director Otto Preminger during the filming of *The Man with the Golden Arm*.

Sidney, Sydney

FRENCH: Saint-Denis
ROCK AND ROLL: Emotional, smooth, debonair
RELATED ARTISTS/SONGS: Sidney Bechet, Sidney Homer, Sidney DeParis, "Sidney" by Terence Blanchard, "Sidney" by Steve Spurgin, "Sydney" by David Bowie
LINER NOTES: Saxophonist Sidney Bechet inspired the character Pablo in Herman Hesse's novel *Steppenwolf*.

Skip

ENGLISH: Captain
ROCK AND ROLL: Amiable, cheerful, strong but silent
RELATED ARTISTS/SONGS: Skip Taylor, Skip Battin (The Flying Burrito Brothers), Skip Martin (Kool and the Gang), Skip James, "Skip" by Robby Krieger, "Skip" by The Rabies
LINER NOTES: Skip James, born Nehemiah Curtis James, gave up performing the blues during the Great Depression to become a Baptist minister.

Sven, Svend

NORSE: Young warrior
ROCK AND ROLL: Technologically adept, avant-garde, fashionable
RELATED ARTISTS/SONGS: Sven Barge (Royksopp), Svend Asmussen, Sven Vath, "Sven" by Bathtub Mary, "Sven" by Reinhard May
LINER NOTES: Danish Swing violinist Svend Asmussen played with both Fats Waller and Duke Ellington but was prevented from joining Benny Goodman's group by strict 1950s U.S. immigration laws.

Thelonious

LATIN: Version of Tillo, lord
ROCK AND ROLL: Cool, idiosyncratic, clever
RELATED ARTISTS/SONGS: Thelonious Monk, Thelonious Monster, "Thelonious" by Bud Powell, "Thelonious" by Steve Lacy
LINER NOTES: Thelonious Monk had two children, son Thelonious Jr., who continued to lead his band, and daughter Barbara.

Tito

SPANISH: Variation of Titus, to honor
ROCK AND ROLL: Fun, spunky, courageous
RELATED ARTISTS/SONGS: Tito Puente, Tito & Tarantula, Tito El Bambino, "Tito's Way" by The Juan Maclean, "Tito" by Louie Bellson, "Tito" by Groove Collective
LINER NOTES: King of Mambo Tito Puente's real name is Ernest; Tito was the nickname his parents gave him.

Uri

HEBREW: Form of Uriel or Uriah, God is my light
ROCK AND ROLL: Bright, dark-haired, beloved
RELATED ARTISTS/SONGS: Uri Caine, "Uri Is at It Again" by The Robocop Kraus, "Uri" by Angel Tears, "Akara (Uri)" by Noa
LINER NOTES: Jazz pianist Uri Caine collaborated with The Roots' Questlove on an album called *The Philadelphia Experiment*, blending hip-hop and experimental jazz.

Walt

GERMAN: Form of Walter, powerful warrior
ROCK AND ROLL: Strong, wealthy, a visionary
RELATED ARTISTS/SONGS: Walt Michael, Walt Dickerson, "Walt's First Trip" by The Ohio Player, "Walt's Dizzyland" by The Ex
LINER NOTES: Jazz vibraphonist Walt Dickerson recorded an album with Sun Ra called *Impressions of A Patch of Blue*.

Wilbur

GERMAN: Resolute
ROCK AND ROLL: Inventive, ahead of his time
RELATED ARTISTS/SONGS: Wilbur Ware, Wilbur Hart (The Delfonics), "Wilbur 10:30 am" by Grandaddy, "Wilbur" by Mark S. Greer
LINER NOTES: Jazz double-bassist Wilbur Ware pioneered "the Chicago Sound," a more laid-back hard bop method for jazz bassists.

Winton, Wynton

ENGLISH: Variation of Winston, friend's town
ROCK AND ROLL: Traditional, elegant, stately
RELATED ARTISTS/SONGS: Wynton Marsalis, Wynton Kelly, "Wynton" by Sonny Rollins, "Wynton" by Keystone Trio, "Winton" by Kubrick
LINER NOTES: Wynton Marsalis, whose father was the jazz great Ellis Marsalis, was named after jazz pianist Wynton Kelly; he got his first trumpet at age six from Al Hirt.

Musical Instrument-Inspired Names

For those looking to get creative in their naming choices, look no further than your local jazz band or orchestra section. Lots of instruments, both familiar and unfamiliar, double as great names—from Viola to Dobro.

BANJO: Actress Rachel Griffiths named her son this unusual, folksy name, traditionally a country music nickname.

BAYAN: The name of a traditional Ukrainian accordion, this would be an interesting variation on names like Bayard or Bay.

CALLIOPE: In Greek mythology, Calliope was the muse of epic poetry and the mother of Orpheus. As well it's an old-timey steam-powered organ, also known as a calliaphone.

DOBRO: A twist on Robert that means "goodness" in Slovak, Dobro is the kind of resonator guitar favored by Johnny Cash.

DULCIAN: Close to girl names like Dulcie and Dulcibella, Dulcian is an equally sweet choice, a Renaissance bass woodwind instrument that preceded the modern bassoon.

MELODICA: The so-dorky-it's-cool keyboard flute is another version of the popular girls' name Melody.

PIPA: A different spelling of the old-fashioned (but due for a comeback) English name Pippa that's also a four-stringed Chinese lute.

REBEC OR REBECK: Close to the popular name Rebecca, this name also refers to a pear-shaped stringed instrument developed in the middle ages.

SITAR: For those who wished the 1960s could come back again, this Indian instrument would be a quirky, innovative choice.

VIOLA: Latin for "violet," this stringed instrument is larger than a violin but smaller than a cello.

Jazz Nickname Etymology

The tradition of a quirky stage name, from Shadow to Cleanhead, was one begun in earnest by jazzmen. Not all of them may be appropriate nicknames for a baby— Cootie, for example, would probably come to haunt the child on the playground—but some of them would be cute alternatives for a more formal name.

NAME	WHERE'D THEY GET IT?
Louis "Satchmo" Armstrong	Satchmo is a variation of "Satchelmouth," a joke on Armstrong's legendarily large mouth.
William "Count" Basie	Count Basie gave himself the honorific "Count" as a play on Duke Ellington
Clarence "Gatemouth" Brown	Gatemouth came from "alligator mouth"; alligator was then the slang term for "dude" or "cat."
Kenny "Klook" Clarke	Clarke's nickname was short for "klook-mop"; the sound of a drum combination he immortalized in Dizzy Gillespie's "Oop Bop Sh'Bam."
Edward "Duke" Ellington	Ellington got the nickname from his family because of his serious manner and flashy dress sense.
John "Dizzy" Gillespie	Dizzy or Diz got his the nickname for his mischievous onstage antics and bubbly personality.
Charlie "Bird" Parker	Bird or Yardbird Parker came from the jazzman's love of fried chicken.
Jean "Django" Reinhardt	Django is Romani for "I awake." The jazz musician got that nickname from his Gypsy family.
Leroy "Stuff" Smith	Jazz fiddler was terrible with names; he got his nickname for his habit of addressing people as "Hey, Stuff!"
Eddie "Cleanhead" Vinson	Saxophonist Cleanhead Vinson got his nickname from his bald head, which he got from an accident with a straightening chemical.
Benjamin "Brute" Webster	Webster got this nickname from his raspy, growling vocal style.

Artists Who
Go by Their Initials

EEFFGGHHIIJJKKKLLMMNNOOPPQQRRSSTTUUVVWWXXYYZZ

As the famous story goes, Johnny Cash's birth name wasn't a name at all. His parents, unable to decide between names, settled on the initials J.R. The singer didn't adopt John as his first name until he was enlisting for the army. Here's hoping your decision won't quite come to that, but an initial can be a good jumping off point, particularly when you consider how many artists are known simply by a letter or two.

B.B. KING: B.B. King's nickname is a shortening of "Beale Street Blues Boy," a pseudonym he used as a radio DJ in Memphis.

C.C. DEVILLE: Born Bruce Anthony Johannesson, Poison guitarist C.C. adopted his nickname in honor of the Cadillac Coupe DeVille.

J. MASCIS: Dinosaur Jr.'s J. Mascis's birth name is Joseph Donald Mascis Jr. Fender made a guitar in honor of him, dubbed the J Mascis Jazzmaster.

GG ALLIN: Punk singer GG Allin's legal name is Jesus Christ Allen. His brother was unable to pronounce it, and called Allin JeJe, which he then stylized into "GG." Later in his childhood, his mother changed his legal name to Kevin Michael.

K.D. LANG: The k.d. stands for Kathryn Dawn, but the decision to not use capital letters in her name is a tribute to the poet e.e. cummings.

PJ HARVEY: Polly Jean Harvey got her sweet nickname from her mother, an artist, and her father, who worked in a quarry.

A.C. NEWMAN: Allen Carl Newman, sometimes known as Carl Newman, chose to go by A.C. once he struck out from indie band The New Pornographers.

Names That Make You Want to Sing

All names have theme songs of some sort, but some have instant song connections—think Roxanne, Sloopy, or Jude. Here are some great names with lullabies already built in.

"Alejandro" by Lady Gaga

"Brandy (You're a Fine Girl)" by Looking Glass

"Oh My Darling, Clementine" by Percy Montrose

"Delia's Gone" by Johnny Cash

"Jemima Surrender" by The Band

"Jesse's Girl" by Rick Springfield

"Hey Jude" by The Beatles

"Levon" by Elton John

"Dear Prudence" by The Beatles

"Help Me, Rhonda" by The Beach Boys

"Rosalita (Come Out Tonight)" by Bruce Springsteen

"Roxanne" by The Police

"My Sharona" by The Knack

"Sherry" by Frankie Valli and the Four Seasons

"Hang on Sloopy" by The McCoys

1960s:
From Bohemians to
The Beatles

The 1950s might be where rock and roll started, but the 1960s were when it reached full speed. Woodstock, Motown, the British Invasion, Bob Dylan . . . you get the picture. From "Lucy in the Sky with Diamonds" to Herman's Hermits, there's a range of catchy namesake tunes and artists. And who knows: your little one might be more popular than The Beatles.

GIRLS

Abilene

AMERICAN PLACE NAME
ROCK AND ROLL: Southern, charming, pretty
RELATED ARTISTS/SONGS: "Abilene" by George Hamilton IV, "Abilene" by Waylon Jennings, "Abilene" by Sheryl Crow, "Abilene on Her Mind" by Buddy Jewell
LINER NOTES: Songwriter Bob Gibson was inspired to write "Abilene" after watching the Randolph Scott film *Abeline Town*; the album George Hamilton IV recorded it for was titled *Hootenanny Hoot*.

Angela, Angie

GREEK: Divine messenger
ROCK AND ROLL: Righteous, a romantic
RELATED ARTISTS/SONGS: Angela Bowie, "Angela" by Mötley Crüe, "Angela" by John Vanderslice, "Angela" by John Lennon and Yoko Ono, "Angie" by The Rolling Stones, "Angie" by Tori Amos
LINER NOTES: Angela Bowie's ex-husband, David, wrote the songs "The Prettiest Star" and "Golden Years" for her.

Anka

ENGLISH: Form of Hannah, grace
ROCK AND ROLL: Magical, an old soul
RELATED ARTISTS/SONGS: Paul Anka, "Anka" by Dof, "Anka" by Brinaman, "Anka" by Łzy

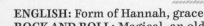
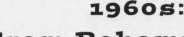

LINER NOTES: Sixties teen idol Paul Anka has five daughters, Anthea, Alicia, Amanda, Amelia, and Alexandra.

Bridget, Brigitte, Brigit

IRISH: Powerful
ROCK AND ROLL: Irresistible, loves to drive and smoke
RELATED ARTISTS/SONGS: Brigitte Bardot, Bridget Regan (Flogging Molly), Bridget St. John, "Bridget" by The Gourds, "Bridget Heat (Pt. 9)" by Swell Maps, "Bridget and Me" by The Jerrys, "Brigitte" by Stereolab
LINER NOTES: John Lennon and Paul McCartney idolized Brigitte Bardot, even making (unfulfilled) plans to make a movie with her and The Beatles.

Caroline, Carolyn

LATIN: The feminine form of Charles, joyous song
FRENCH: Little and strong
ROCK AND ROLL: A crush-worthy sweetheart, prefers short hair when she's older
RELATED ARTISTS/SONGS: "Caroline, No" by The Beach Boys, "Sweet Caroline" by Neil Diamond, "Caroline" by Concrete Blonde, "Caroline" by Wolfmother, "Caroline" by Harry Nilsson

"Sweet Caroline,
good times never seemed so good."
—NEIL DIAMOND

Cecilia, Cecillia, Cecille

LATIN: Blind
ROCK AND ROLL: Beautiful, bubby, but a capricious lover
RELATED ARTISTS/SONGS: "Cecilia Ann" by The Pixies, "Cecilia" by Simon & Garfunkel, "Cecilia" by Smokey Robinson & the Miracles, "Cecile" by The Wolfmen, "Cecilia" by Ace of Base
LINER NOTES: The Simon & Garfunkel song "Cecilia" is about Saint Cecilia, the patron saint of music and an inconstant muse.

Chelsea

ENGLISH: Chalk wharf
ROCK AND ROLL: Brave, sweet, cheerful, a little too cool
RELATED ARTISTS/SONGS: Chelsea, "Chelsea Morning" by Joni Mitchell, "(I Don't Want to Go to) Chelsea" by Elvis Costello, "Chelsea" by Counting Crows, "Chelsea Girls" by The Velvet Underground, "Chelsea Hotel No. 2" by Leonard Cohen
LINER NOTES: Chelsea Clinton was named for the Joni Mitchell song "Chelsea Morning."

Cynthia

GREEK: From Mount Cynthus
ROCK AND ROLL: Hard to get, nobody's fool
RELATED ARTISTS/SONGS: Cynthia Dall (Smog), Cynthia Lennon, Cynthia Weil, "Cynthia" by Lee Dorsey, "Cynthia" by Bruce Springsteen, "Cynthia" by Blue Rodeo, "Sarah Sylvia Cynthia Stout" by Tori Amos, "Cynthia" by MillionYoung

"I just like knowin', Cynthia,
you exist at all."
—BRUCE SPRINGSTEEN

Dee Dee

AMERICAN INVENTED
ROCK AND ROLL: Spunky, sweet, cheerful
RELATED ARTISTS/SONGS: Dee Dee Sharp, Dee Dee Warwick, "Dee Dee" by Dee Dee Bridgewater
LINER NOTES: Singer Dee Dee Sharp was the first black female idol, best known for her hit song "Mashed Potato Time" and creating the dance move "the mashed potato."

Denise

GREEK: Feminine form of Dennis, devoted to Bacchus

BOB DYLAN:
"I know you're laughin', what are you laughin' about?"

RANDY AND THE RAINBOWS:
"Denise, Denise, I've got a crush on you."

FOUNTAINS OF WAYNE:
"She listens to Puff Daddy."

OZMA:
"It's easy to love you."

Edie

ENGLISH: Variation of Edith, rich in war
ROCK AND ROLL: Glamorous, a youthquaker, the muse of the art scene
RELATED ARTISTS/SONGS: Edie Adams, Edie Brickell, "Edie (Ciao Baby)" by The Cult, "Edie" by Metallica, "Edie Is a Sweet Candy" by the 5.6.7.8's, "Edie" by The Fall

"Sweet little sugar talker/
Paradise dream stalker."
—THE CULTS

Eleanor

FRENCH: Variation of Helen, bright one
ROCK AND ROLL: Angelic, courageous, a dreamer, a bit of a loner
RELATED ARTISTS/SONGS: Eleanor Friedberger (The Fiery Furnaces), "Eleanor Rigby" by The Beatles, "Eleanor" by Jet, "Hey Eleanor" by Casiotone for the Painfully Alone, "Eleanor Put Your Boots On" by Franz Ferdinand, "Eleanor" by Dave Matthews Band
LINER NOTES: Though Paul McCartney originally got the name Eleanor from friend Eleanor Bron, an actress in The Beatles' movie *Help!*, a fan later found the grave of a woman named Eleanor Rigby in a graveyard in Liverpool close to where McCartney and John Lennon used to sunbathe.

Eva

HEBREW: Life
ROCK AND ROLL: Fearless, a pioneer, should avoid snakes
RELATED ARTISTS/SONGS: Eva Cassidy, Little Eva, "Eva" by Leadbelly, "Eva" by Serge Gainsbourg, "Eva" by Orgy, "Eve" by Sun Ra, "Eve" by The Statler Brothers
LINER NOTES: Little Eva, who was most famous for "The Loco-Motion," was Carole King's babysitter. King and Goffin wrote "the Loco-Motion" for King based on Eva's quirky dancing style.

Goldie

ENGLISH: Gold
ROCK AND ROLL: Precious, breezy, summery, and bright
RELATED ARTISTS/SONGS: Goldie, Goldie Hill, Goldie & the Gingerbreads, "Goldies" by Art Blakey, "Goldie" by Fannie Flagg, "Goldie" by Les Cowboys Fringant, "Acapulco Goldie" by Dr. Hook
LINER NOTES: Goldie Raven, born Genya Zelkowitz, founded Goldie & the Gingerbreads, the first all-girl group signed to a major label. They toured with The Beatles, The Rolling Stones, and The Yardbirds.

Hermione

GREEK: Messenger

ROCK AND ROLL: Whip-smart, tough, resourceful

RELATED ARTISTS/SONGS: "Letter to Hermione" by David Bowie, "The Wrath of Hermione" by Harry & the Potters, "Hermione" by Starless and Bible Black

LINER NOTES: David Bowie wrote "Letter to Hermione" about his former girlfriend Hermione Farthingale, who left him for musical star Stephen Reinhardt.

Jean, Jeane, Jeanne

FRENCH: Variation of Jane, God's grace

ROCK AND ROLL: Petite, sassy, a party animal

RELATED ARTISTS/SONGS: Jean & the Darlings, Jean Shepard, Jean Knight, "Oh Jean" by The Proclaimers, "String Bean Jean" by Belle & Sebastian, "Jeane" by The Smiths, "Jeanne" by Air, "Jeanne" by Georges Brassens

LINER NOTES: Songwriter and Kingston Trio member John Stewart, who wrote the Monkees' "Daydream Believer" with it's catchy chorus "cheer up, sleepy Jean," later became the official musician of the Democratic party, touring with John F. Kennedy's 1968 election campaign.

Jesamine

AMERICAN: Form of Jasmine

ROCK AND ROLL: Alluring, dreamy, a butterfly child

RELATED ARTISTS/SONGS: Spectrum & Jesamine, "Jesamine" by The Casuals, "Jesamine" by Squire, "When Jesamine Goes" by The Bystanders

LINER NOTES: The Casuals' famous "Jesamine" was a version of The Bystanders' "When Jesamine Goes," cowritten by rocker Marty Wilde under the alias Frere Mason.

Joan

FRENCH: Derived from Johanne, God is merciful

ROCK AND ROLL: A morning person, mysterious, elegant, loves nature

RELATED ARTISTS/SONGS: Joan Armatrading, Joan Baez, Joan Jett, "Joan" by Erasure, "Joan" by The Art Bears, "Good Morning Joan" by The Cardigans, "Joan" by Butch Walker

LINER NOTES: Joan Baez dated Apple computer cofounder Steve Jobs in the 1970s and 1980s.

Johanna, Joanna

HEBREW: God is gracious
ROCK AND ROLL: Unforgettable, loves the summer, sweet, shy
RELATED ARTISTS/SONGS: Joanna MacGregor, "Joanna" by Kool & the Gang, "Visions of Johanna" by Bob Dylan, "God Bless Joanna" by Neil Sedaka, "When Joanna Loved Me" by Tony Bennett, "Johanna" by The Stooges

"She's my girl and she's always on my mind."
—KOOL & THE GANG

Julia

LATIN: Youthful, downy-haired
ROCK AND ROLL: Gentle, loves the ocean, unlucky in love
RELATED ARTISTS/SONGS: "Julia" by The Beatles "Julia" by Our Lady Peace, "Julia" by Eurythmics, "Hey Julia" by Robert Palmer, "Julia Dream" by Pink Floyd
LINER NOTES: John Lennon wrote the song "Julia" for his mother, who died when he was seventeen.

Jura

LATIN: Just
ROCK AND ROLL: Decisive, smart
RELATED ARTISTS/SONGS: "Isle of Jura" by Skyclad, "Roll Over Jura" by Azra, "Jura (I Swear I Love You)" by Les Paul and Mary Ford, "Jura Secreta" by Simone
LINER NOTES: Les Paul and his wife Mary Ford, who cowrote "Jura (I Swear I Love You)," had four children, Lester, Gene, Robert, and Colleen.

Lily

ENGLISH FLOWER NAME
ROCK AND ROLL: Young starlet, nurturing, has lovely skin
RELATED ARTISTS/SONGS: Lily Allen, "Lily" by Joan Baez, "Lily Queen" by Scott Joplin, "Lily, Rosemary, and the Jack of Hearts," by Bob Dylan, "Pictures of Lily" by The Who, "Lily (My One and Only)" by The Smashing Pumpkins

"Lily was a princess, she was fair-skinned and precious as a child."
—BOB DYLAN

79

Lucy

LATIN: Variation of Lucille, light
ROCK AND ROLL: Mind-altering, has fantastic eyes
RELATED ARTISTS/SONGS: Juicy Lucy, Lucy Bardo, Lucy Wainwright Roche, "Lucy in the Sky with Diamonds" by The Beatles, "Lucy" by Nick Cave & the Bad Seeds, "Lucy Can't Dance" by David Bowie, "Lucy" by The Commodores, "Lucy" by Peter, Paul and Mary
LINER NOTES: Lucy Vodden, Julian Lennon's childhood friend, was the inspiration for The Beatles' "Lucy in the Sky with Diamonds."

Maggie

ENGLISH: Short for Margaret, pearl
ROCK AND ROLL: Tempting, capricious, a taskmaster
RELATED ARTISTS/SONGS: Maggie Parker, Maggie Roche, "Maggie May" by Rod Stewart, "When You and I Were Young, Maggie Blues" by Bing Crosby, "Maggie's Farm" by Bob Dylan, "Maggie M'gill" by The Doors, "Tantalizing Maggie" by The Nice
LINER NOTES: Bob Dylan's "Maggie's Farm" is a play on Silas McGee's Farm, where Dylan played at a civil rights protest.

Mallory

FRENCH: *Unlucky*

CHASE COY:
"I wanna have you with me all the time."

THE BRIGHTWINGS:
"Oh, Mallory, you move too fast for me."

SETTEVITE:
"Mallory walks without shoes and stockings."

TIGERCITY:
"We can have it all right now."

Marianne, Marian

FRENCH: Variation of Mary, beloved lady
ROCK AND ROLL: Impetuous, adorable, bright
RELATED ARTISTS/SONGS: Marianne Faithfull, Marian McPartland, "Marianne" by Harry Belafonte, "Marianne" by The Highwaymen, "So Long, Marianne" by Leonard Cohen, "Marianne" by Tori Amos, "Marianne" by The Human League
LINER NOTES: Marianne Faithfull's friend poet Allen Ginsberg called her "Professor of Poetics, Jack Kerouac School of Disembodied Parts."

Matilda

GERMAN: Mighty
ROCK AND ROLL: A great dancer, cute, rambunctious
RELATED ARTISTS/SONGS: "Matilda" by Harry Belafonte, "Matilda" by Marty Robbins, "Matilda" by Gritty Kitty, "Waltzing Matilda" by Banjo Paterson, "Matlida Mother" by Pink Floyd
LINER NOTES: Pink Floyd's Syd Barrett wrote "Matilda Mother" about a character in Edward Gorey's book of twisted fairy tales *Cautionary Tales for Children*.

Michelle

FRENCH: Feminine form of Michael, Who is like God?
ROCK AND ROLL: Beautiful, breezy, charming
RELATED ARTISTS/SONGS: Michel'le, Michelle Phillips (The Mamas & the Papas), Michelle Shocked, "Michelle" by The Beatles, "Michelle" by Clark Terry, "Michelle" by the Flat Duo Jets
LINER NOTES: In 1970, Michelle Phillips was married to Dennis Hopper for eight days.

Miriam

HEBREW: Wished-for child
ROCK AND ROLL: Quiet, powerful, sharp
RELATED ARTISTS/SONGS: Miriam Makeba, Miriam Stockley, "Miriam" by Johnny Mercer, "Miriam" by The Fugs, "Miriam" by Tracy Dratch, "Miriam" by King Diamond
LINER NOTES: South African singer Miriam Makeba was married to Black Panther Stokely Carmichael. They had one daughter, Bongi Makeba.

Pam

ENGLISH: Form of Pamela, sweet as honey
ROCK AND ROLL: Good-looking but tries too hard, glamorous
RELATED ARTISTS/SONGS: Pam Nestor, Pam Tillis, Pam Balam (The Cramps), "Polythene Pam" by The Beatles, "Pam Berry" by The Shins, "Pam's Tan" by Black Tambourine, "Pam V" by Super Furry Animals
LINER NOTES: The Beatles song "Polythene Pam" was named after one of the group's early fans, Pam Hodgett, who would routinely eat polythene.

Penny

GREEK: Form of Penelope, weaver
ROCK AND ROLL: Cute and sprightly but capricious
RELATED ARTISTS/SONGS: Pennywise, Penny Ford, "Penny Lane" by The Beatles, "Pretty Penny" by Stone Temple Pilots, "Bad Penny" by Big Black, "Penny and Me" by Hanson, "Penny Lover" by Lionel Richie
LINER NOTES: The lyric "very strange" in The Beatles' "Penny Lane" refers to the motor engineer firm Strange & Strange, which was then located at 51 Penny Lane in Liverpool.

Renée

LATIN: Form of Renatus, born again

ROCK AND ROLL: Talkative, smart, physically fit

RELATED ARTISTS/SONGS: Renée Geyer, Renee Olstead, "Walk Away Renée" by The Left Banke, "Renée" by Charlie Rich, "Renée" by Talk Talk, "Renee" by The Lost Boyz

LINER NOTES: Left Banke lead singer Michael Brown wrote "Walk Away Renée" about his unrequited love for bassist Tom Finn's girl-friend Renée.

Rita

HINDI: Brave, strong

ROCK AND ROLL: Lovely, chipper, youthful

RELATED ARTISTS/SONGS: Rita Lee, Rita Coolidge, Rita Marley, "Lovely Rita" by The Beatles, "Mrs. Rita" by the Gin Blossoms, "Rita Mae" by Eric Clapton, "Following Rita" by Train

LINER NOTES: Paul McCartney wrote the song "Lovely Rita" after get-ting a parking ticket from a warden outside of Abbey Road Studios.

Ronnie

ENGLISH: Pet form of Veronica, she who brings victory

ROCK AND ROLL: The original bad girl, sassy, bright

RELATED ARTISTS/SONGS: Ronnie Spector, "Ronnie" by The Four Seasons, "Ronnie" by Neil Sedaka

LINER NOTES: Ronnie Spector began the Ronettes with her sister and cousin, inspired by sessions of harmonizing to lullabies with their grandmother.

Rosalind

GERMAN: Red dragon

ROCK AND ROLL: Literary, fair, happy, electric

RELATED ARTISTS/SONGS: Rosalind Madison, Rosalind Ashford-Holmes (Martha Reeves and the Vandellas), Rosalind McAllister, "Rosalind" by Chuck Jackson, "Rosalind" by Meg Christian, "Rosa-lind" by Aunt Mary, "Rosalind and Orlando" by Barenaked Ladies

LINER NOTES: Before The Vandellas took off, Rosalind Ashford-Holmes and Annette Beard's girl group The DelPhis performed at Detroit-area YMCA functions.

Ruby

ENGLISH GEM NAME

ROCK AND ROLL: Innocent, dreamy, passionate

RELATED ARTISTS/SONGS: Ruby Braff, Ruby Starr, "Ruby Tuesday" by The Rolling Stones, "Ruby" by Ray Charles, "Ruby, Don't Take Your Love to Town" by Kenny Rogers, "Ruby's Arms" by Tom Waits, "Ruby Baby" by The Drifters

Sadie

ENGLISH: Variation of Sarah, princess
ROCK AND ROLL: A bombshell, loyal, friendly
RELATED ARTISTS/SONGS: Sadie Ama, "Sexy Sadie" by The Beatles, "Sadie" by Joanna Newsom, "Sadie" by Suede, "Sadie" by The Spinners, "Little Sadie" by Bob Dylan

"Sweeter than cotton candy, stronger than Papa's old brandy."
—R. KELLY

Sue

FRENCH: Form of Susan or Suzanne, lily
ROCK AND ROLL: Impetuous, lively, fun-loving, bright, a terrible name for a boy
RELATED ARTISTS/SONGS: Sue Fink, "Runaround Sue" by Dion and the Belmonts, "Ballad of Sister Sue" by Slowdive, "Sue" by Bobby Rush, "Sweet Sue, Just You" by Miles Davis, "A Boy Named Sue" by Johnny Cash
LINER NOTES: Doo-wop hit "Runaround Sue" inspired two answer songs: "I'm No Runaround Sue" by Ginger and the Snaps and "Stay-at-Home Sue" by Linda Laurie.

Twila, Twyla

ENGLISH: Woven with a double thread
ROCK AND ROLL: Light, breezy, creative
RELATED ARTISTS/SONGS: Twyla Herbert, Twila Paris, "I Love Twyla" by Mase, "Twyla Tharp" by Bob Dylan, "Twyla" by Richmond Fontaine
LINER NOTES: Songwriter Twyla Herbert, who cowrote many of Lou Christie's hits, like "Lightnin' Strikes," also claimed to be a clairvoyant with the ability to know ahead of time which songs would be hits.

Venus

LATIN: Roman goddess of love
ROCK AND ROLL: Stunning, sultry, chic
RELATED ARTISTS/SONGS: "Venus in Furs" by The Velvet Underground, "Venus" by Frankie Avalon, "Venus" by Television, "Venus" by Air, "Venus in Blue Jeans" by Jimmy Clanton
LINER NOTES: The Velvet Underground's "Venus in Furs" was inspired by a book of the same name by Leopold von Sacher-Masoch, the namesake of the term "masochism."

Yoko

JAPANESE: Ocean child
ROCK AND ROLL: A muse, artistic, might break up the band
RELATED ARTISTS/SONGS: Yoko Ono, "Oh Yoko!" by John Lennon, "Yoko" by Beulah, "Yoko" by The Cartoons, "Yoko" by The Eraserheads, "I Won't Be Your Yoko Ono" by Dar Williams
LINER NOTES: The first line of "Happy Christmas (War Is Over)" contains references to both Yoko Ono and John Lennon's children from different marriages; you can hear Yoko whisper "Happy Christmas, Kyoko" and John whisper "Happy Christmas, Julian."

BOYS

Alex, Alec

GREEK: Protector, variant of Alexander
ROCK AND ROLL: Pioneer, an original
RELATED ARTISTS/SONGS: Alex Chilton (Big Star, The Box Tops), Alex James (Blur), "Alec Eiffel" by Pixies, "Alex" by Ghostface Killah, "Alex" by The Jon Spencer Blues Explosion, "Alex Chilton" by The Replacements
LINER NOTES: Alex Chilton's band Big Star was originally called Rock City and then Ice Water; he had one son, named Timothee.

Art, Artie

AMERICAN: Variation of Arthur, stone
ROCK AND ROLL: Laid-back, mustachioed, smart
RELATED ARTISTS/SONGS: Art Garfunkel, Art Tatum, Art Blakey, "Art" by Steve Lacy, "Art" by The Meters, "Artie" by The Goo-Goo Dolls
LINER NOTES: Art Garfunkel is a serious bookworm; his Web site lists every book that he's read since 1968, including *The Random House Dictionary*.

Barclay

ENGLISH: Birch forest
ROCK AND ROLL: Traditional, athletic, handsome

RELATED ARTISTS/SONGS: Barclay James Harvest, Peter Barclay, "Barclay" by Amos Joy, "Barclay" by The Barmitzvah Brothers

LINER NOTES: Symphonic rock band Barclay James Harvest was founded by John Lees and Woolly Wolstenholme; they chose the band's name from a list by drawing straws.

Bill

ENGLISH: Short for William, protector

ROCK AND ROLL: Cowboy, a good storyteller, a big dude

RELATED ARTISTS/SONGS: Bill Berry (R.E.M.), Bill Callahan (Smog), Bill Haley, "Bill" by Talking Heads, "Lonesome Cowboy Bill" by The Velvet Underground, "Pecos Bill" by Nickel Creek, "The Continuing Story of Bungalow Bill" by The Beatles, "Buffalo Bill" by Garth Brooks

"He's the all-American bullet-headed Saxon mother's son."
—THE BEATLES

Bob

ENGLISH: Short for Robert, bright fame

ROCK AND ROLL: Beloved weirdo

RELATED ARTISTS/SONGS: Bob Dylan, Bob Marley, Bob Mould, "Bob" by NOFX, "Bob" by Drive-By Truckers, "Bob" by Primus

LINER NOTES: In tenth grade, Bob Dylan and his backup band were rejected from a high school talent show because the student council found his performance at the audition too shocking.

Brian, Bryan

ENGLISH: Strong, noble

ROCK AND ROLL: Experimental, brilliant, and bizarre

RELATED ARTISTS/SONGS: Brian Eno, Brian Jones (The Rolling Stones), Brian Wilson (The Beach Boys), "Brian Eno" by MGMT, "Brian the Vampire" by Xiu Xiu, "Brian Wilson" by Barenaked Ladies, "Brian" by Anita Carter

LINER NOTES: For the song "Good Vibrations," Brian Wilson recorded all the segments in different rooms in order to get contrasting echoes on the track.

Carlos

SPANISH: Manly

ROCK AND ROLL: Lady-killer, studious

RELATED ARTISTS/SONGS: Carlos Santana, Carlos Cavazo (Quiet

Riot), Carlos Montoya, "Carlos" by Floyd Dixon, "Carlos" by John Scofield, "Carlos" by Rick Wakeman, "Carlos" by Pete Yorn
LINER NOTES: Carlos Santana got his big break when a band canceled at the Fillmore West in 1966. The concert promoter assembled an impromptu group including Santana.

Charlie

GERMAN: Short for Charles, masculine
ROCK AND ROLL: Goofy, whimsical, fun
RELATED ARTISTS/SONGS: Charlie Feathers, Charlie Parker, Charlie Watts (The Rolling Stones), "Charlie" by Red Hot Chili Peppers, "Charlie" by Chumbawamba, "Charlie" by The Sharks, "Mister Charlie" by The Grateful Dead, "Sorry Charlie" by Ween
LINER NOTES: The Rolling Stones' Charlie Watts once published a cartoon called *Ode to a High Flying Bird* in honor of his hero, jazz great Charlie Parker.

Davey, Davy

HEBREW: Diminutive of David, beloved
ROCK AND ROLL: Patriotic, charming, great at cards
RELATED ARTISTS/SONGS: Davy Jones (The Monkees), Davy Graham, So Long Davey!, "Blackjack Davey" by Bob Dylan, "Davey Destroyed the Punk Scene" by Anti-Flag, "Davey" by Kate Bush, "Davey" by The Go Set
LINER NOTES: The Monkees' Davy Jones appeared with the Broadway cast of *Oliver!* on the same episode of *The Ed Sullivan Show* in which The Beatles made their debut.

Dennis, Denis

GREEK: Servant of Dionysus
ROCK AND ROLL: Ambitious, forward-thinking, a real catch
RELATED ARTISTS/SONGS: Dennis Brown, Dennis Thompson (The MC5), Dennis Wilson (The Beach Boys), "Dennis" by Badfinger, "You Can't Fool Me Dennis" by The Mystery Jets, "Denis" by Blondie, "Dennis" by R. Stevie Moore
LINER NOTES: Though all of the members of The Beach Boys sang about surfing, Dennis Wilson was the only one of them who actually surfed.

Eric

NORSE: Eternal leader
ROCK AND ROLL: Fair-haired, dashing, has prophetic visions
RELATED ARTISTS/SONGS: Eric Burdon (The Animals, War), Eric Clapton, Eric Kaz (Blues Magoos), "Eric" by Woody Shaw, "Eric's Trip" by Sonic Youth, "Eric's Interlude" by Modest Mouse, "Song for Eric" by Tori Amos, "Erroneous Escape into Eric Eckles" by Of Montreal
LINER NOTES: Eric Clapton is the only person who's been inducted

into the Rock and Roll Hall of Fame three times: once as a solo artist, once with The Yardbirds, and once with Cream.

Floyd

WELSH: Gray

ROCK AND ROLL: Bearded, resourceful, rough-hewn, cool, should avoid alligators

RELATED ARTISTS/SONGS: Floyd Council, Floyd Cramer, Pink Floyd, "Floyd" by Lynyrd Skynyrd, "Floyd the Barber" by Nirvana, "Floyd" by The Residents

LINER NOTES: Physicist Stephen Hawking makes a guest appearance on the Pink Floyd album *The Division Bell*, providing the robotic vocals on "Keep Talking."

Fritz

GERMAN: Often short for Frederick, peaceful ruler

ROCK AND ROLL: Chaotic, messy, psychedelic

RELATED ARTISTS/SONGS: Fritz Richmond, Fritz McIntyre (Simply Red), "The Fritz" by Say Hi to Your Mom, "Fritz the Blank" by Mannfred Mann's Earth Band, "Fritz" by Dick Cary

LINER NOTES: Washtub and jug player Fritz Richmond, known for his outrageous outfits and homemade granny glasses, came up with the name for the band The Lovin' Spoonful.

Graham, Gram

ENGLISH: Gravel homestead

ROCK AND ROLL: Moody, reflective, a cosmic guy, a DIY master

RELATED ARTISTS/SONGS: Graham Bond, Graham Colton, Gram Parsons (The Flying Burrito Brothers), "Graham" by Y'all, "Graham Greene" by John Cale

LINER NOTES: For a brief time in the 1970s, Gram Parsons and Keith Richards were housemates; Richards's girlfriend Anita Pallenberg kicked Parsons out after tiring of his hard-partying ways.

Jeremy

HEBREW: The Lord will uplift

ROCK AND ROLL: Shy, soft-spoken, decisive

RELATED ARTISTS/SONGS: Jeremy Finner (The Pogues), Jeremy Mills (Idlewild), Jeremy Spencer (Fleetwood Mac), "Jeremy" by Pearl Jam, "Jeremy" by Donna Summer, "Jeremy" by The Magnetic Fields, "Jeremy Bender" by Emerson Lake & Palmer

LINER NOTES: Fleetwood Mac guitarist Jeremy Spencer is known for his uncanny Elvis impersonation.

Jim

HEBREW: Form of James, he who supplants

ROCK AND ROLL: Unforgettable, strong, rowdy, a heartbreaker

RELATED ARTISTS/SONGS: Jim Fielder (Blood, Sweat & Tears), Jim Morrison (The Doors), Jim O'Rourke, "Jim" by Billie Holiday, "You Don't Mess Around with Jim" by Jim Croce, "Oh Jim" by Lou Reed, "Spring-Heeled Jim" by Morrissey

LINER NOTES: The Doors' Jim Morrison self-published two books of poetry, *The Lords/Notes on Vision* and *The New Creatures*.

John

HEBREW: God is gracious

ROCK AND ROLL: Good-hearted and friendly, peaceful and imaginative, has a cult following

RELATED ARTISTS/SONGS: John Cage, Joan Oates (Hall & Oates), John Lennon, "John Brown" by Bob Dylan, "John Riley" by The Byrds, "John, I'm Only Dancing" by David Bowie, "I, John" by Elvis Presley, "John the Revelator" by Son House

LINER NOTES: John Lennon's middle name is Winston, after Winston Churchill.

José

SPANISH: Form of Joseph, God will multiply

ROCK AND ROLL: Steadfast, honest, fun-loving

RELATED ARTISTS/SONGS: José Feliciano, José Alberto, "José" by Perez Prado, "José" by Clarence "Gatemouth" Brown, "José" by Lee Hazlewood

LINER NOTES: José Feliciano, best known for his Christmas song "Felice Navidad," caused widespread controversy for an anti-war version of "The Star-Spangled Banner" he played during the 1968 World Series.

Kyu

JAPANESE: Swift

ROCK AND ROLL: Mischievous, fun-loving

RELATED ARTISTS/SONGS: Kyu Sakamoto, Eye-Kyu, "Kyu" by Sansara, "Kyu" by Reigakusha

LINER NOTES: Teen idol Kyu Sakamoto, best known for his hit "Sukiyaki," had two daughters, Hanako and Maiko.

Lorne

ENGLISH: Form of Lawrence, from Laurentium

ROCK AND ROLL: Calm, trustworthy

RELATED ARTISTS/SONGS: Lorne Greene, Lorne Loomer, Lorna Padman, Lorne Balfe, "Lorne Blues" by Sun Dial

LINER NOTES: Lorne Greene, whose spoken ballad "Ringo" topped the charts in 1960, was born Lyon Hilman Green; his mother nicknamed him "Chaim."

Manfred

GERMAN: Man of peace
ROCK AND ROLL: Cerebral, boisterous, fun-loving
RELATED ARTISTS/SONGS: Manfred Mann, "Manfred" by Dave Stapleton, "Manfred" by Aramateix
LINER NOTES: South African keyboardist Manfred Mann, born Manfred Lebowitz, took his stage last name from jazz bandleader Shelley Manne.

Maxwell

SCOTTISH: Great stream
ROCK AND ROLL: Dangerous, skilled, spontaneous
RELATED ARTISTS/SONGS: Maxwell, Maxwell Demon, "Maxwell Murder" by Rancid, "Maxwell's Silver Hammer" by The Beatles, "Ballad of Maxwell Demon" by Shudder to Think, "Maxwell" by Red
LINER NOTES: Physicist James Clerk Maxwell's thought experiment "Maxwell's Demon" inspired the protagonist's name in "Maxwell's Silver Hammer."

Mitchell

ENGLISH: Variation of Michael, Who is like God?
ROCK AND ROLL: Cerebral, shy
RELATED ARTISTS/SONGS: Joni Mitchell, Blue Mitchell, Mitch Mitchell, "Mitchell" by Strangewax, "Mitchell" by Tishamingo, "Mitchell Bade" by Tech N9ne
LINER NOTES: Before drumming for the Jimi Hendrix Experience, Mitch Mitchell starred in a children's TV show called *Jennings and Derbyshire.*

Moon

ENGLISH NATURE NAME
ROCK AND ROLL: Nocturnal, luminous, bohemian
RELATED ARTISTS/SONGS: Moon Mullican, Moon Unit Zappa, "My Moon, My Man" by Feist, "Bad Moon Rising" by Creedence Clearwater Revival, "Pink Moon" by Nick Drake, "Fly Me to the Moon" by Frank Sinatra
LINER NOTES: Rockabilly star Moon Mullican, born Oscar, got the nickname "Moon" for his all-night performances and his love of moonshine.

Nicholas

GREEK: Victory
ROCK AND ROLL: Sharp, creative, charming
RELATED ARTISTS/SONGS: Nicholas Caldwell (The Whispers), Nicholas Gunn, Nick St. Nicholas (Steppenwolf), "Nicholas" by Forget Cassettes, "Nicholas" by Little Brazil, "Nicholas Prefers Dinosaurs" by Ghosts and Vodka

LINER NOTES: Steppenwolf bassist Nick St. Nicholas's real name is Klaus Karl Kassbaum.

Nilsson

SCANDINAVIAN: Son of Nils
ROCK AND ROLL: Wry, witty, quirky, original
RELATED ARTISTS/SONGS: Harry Nilsson, "Nilsson" by Monica Zetterlunch, "Nilsson" by Mr. Twit, "Nilsson" by James Kirk, "Nilsson" by Little Sue
LINER NOTES: At a press conference in 1968, both John Lennon and Paul McCartney were asked their favorite American singer. Both answered "Nilsson."

Octavio

LATIN: Eighth
ROCK AND ROLL: Suave, smooth-talking, handsome
RELATED ARTISTS/SONGS: Octavio Cruz, Octavio Mesa, "Octavio" by Viva Voce, "Octavio" by Moses Atwood
LINER NOTES: Jimi Hendrix named one of his guitar effects pedals Octavio. A later version, designed especially for him, was named Octavia by the manufacturer.

Oliver

LATIN: Olive tree
ROCK AND ROLL: Upbeat, in touch with nature, has a dark side
RELATED ARTISTS/SONGS: Oliver, King Oliver, Oliver Nelson, "Oliver James" by Fleet Foxes, "Moments with Oliver" by Rachel Yamagata, "Oliver's Army" by Elvis Costello, "Oliver Twister" by The Vaselines, "Oliver" by Björk
LINER NOTES: 1960s singer Oliver, known best for his song "Good Morning Starshine," briefly teamed up professionally with Karen Carpenter in the 1970s.

Paul

LATIN: Small
ROCK AND ROLL: A leader, beloved, solid, faithful
RELATED ARTISTS/SONGS: Paul McCartney, Paul Simon, Paul Wall, "Hey Paul" by The Pains of Being Pure at Heart, "Paul" by Bobby Bare, "Paul" by The Clash
LINER NOTES: Paul McCartney's pseudonyms include The Fireman, Paul Ramone, Bernard Webb, A. Smith, Apollo C. Vermouth, Country Hams, and Percy "Thrills" Thrillington.

Pete

GREEK: Form of Peter, rock
ROCK AND ROLL: Laid-back, rugged
RELATED ARTISTS/SONGS: Pete Townshend (The Who), Pete Brown

(Cream), Pete Seeger, "Pete Standing Alone" by Boards of Canada, "The Tale of Dusty and Pistol Pete" by The Smashing Pumpkins, "Pete" by Doris Day

LINER NOTES: Pete Townshend helped Eric Clapton kick his heroin addiction; in repayment Clapton agreed to appear in The Who's rock opera *Tommy*.

Phil

GREEK: Variation of Philip, lover of horses

ROCK AND ROLL: Ingenius, wild-eyed, has enormous hair

RELATED ARTISTS/SONGS: Phil Collins, Phil Woods, Phil Spector, Phil Lesh (The Grateful Dead), "Phil" by Tom Paxton, "Philthy Phil Philanthropist" by NOFX, "Phil" by Buck 65

LINER NOTES: As a young man, record producer Phil Spector claimed to have trained himself to sleep only two hours a night.

Quinn

GAELIC: Chief

ROCK AND ROLL: Hardy, magnetic, turns despair into celebration

RELATED ARTISTS/SONGS: Quinn Allman (The Used), "Quinn the Eskimo (The Mighty Quinn)" by Bob Dylan, "No Holly for Miss Quinn" by Enya

LINER NOTES: Quinn the Eskimo in Bob Dylan's song is based on Anthony Quinn's role in the movie *The Savage Innocents*.

Ravi

HINDU: Sun

ROCK AND ROLL: Masterful, spiritual, friends with The Beatles

RELATED ARTISTS/SONGS: Ravi Shankar, "Ravi" by Yves Robert, "Ravi" by Gerald Wilson, "Ravi" by Ugetsu

LINER NOTES: George Harrison's sitar playing on "Norwegian Wood (This Bird Has Flown)" was inspired by Ravi Shankar's musical style.

Rocky, Roky

ITALIAN: Form of Rocco, rest

ROCK AND ROLL: A fighter, creative, adventurous

RELATED ARTISTS/SONGS: Roky Erickson (The 13th Floor Elevators), Rocky Votolato, "Rocky" by Survivor, "Rocky Raccoon" by The Beatles, "Rocky Dennis in Heaven" by Jans Lekman

LINER NOTES: The title of The Beatles' "Rocky Raccoon" was originally "Rocky Sassoon," but Paul McCartney changed it so it would "sound more cowboy."

Scott

ENGLISH: Scottish

ROCK AND ROLL: Steadfast, loves dancing, handsome

RELATED ARTISTS/SONGS: Scott Joplin, Scott Walker, Scott Mescudi (Kid Cudi), "Scott" by Simian Mobile Disco, "Scott Farcas Takes It On the Chin" by Less Than Jake, "Scott" by Jack Wilkins, "Scott's a Dirk" by Reel Big Fish

LINER NOTES: Reclusive rock star Scott Walker, of The Walker Brothers, originally cut records under the name Scotty Engel; he once lived in a monastery for several months to study Gregorian chants for an album.

Serge, Sergio

FRENCH: Variation of Sergius, servant

ROCK AND ROLL: Jaunty, dashing, confident, provocative

RELATED ARTISTS/SONGS: Serge Gainsbourg, Sergio Mendes, Sergio Vargas, "Serge" by Pinback, "Serge" by The Folk Implosion, "Serge" by Split Enz, "Sergio" by Mike Tracy, "Sergio" by Al Stewart

LINER NOTES: Serge Gainsbourg and Bob Marley got into a prolonged argument over Serge Gainsbourg instructing Rita Marley to sing lyrics Bob judged to be too suggestive.

Shep, Shepherd

ENGLISH OCCUPATION NAME

ROCK AND ROLL: Loyal, watchful, a country boy

RELATED ARTISTS/SONGS: Shep & the Limelites, "Old Shep" by Elvis Presley, "Good Shepherd" by Jefferson Airplane

LINER NOTES: Elvis Presley's first performance was singing "Old Shep," an ode to a farm dog, at a State Fair when he was ten years old. He won fifth place.

Van

DUTCH: Descendent

ROCK AND ROLL: Confident, composed, mystical

RELATED ARTISTS/SONGS: Van Morrison, Van Halen, Van Cliburn, "Van Tango" by Franz Ferdinand, "Van" by The Descendents, "Van" by Pond

LINER NOTES: Van Morrison's "Brown Eyed Girl" was originally written about an interracial relationship and titled "Brown-Skinned Girl."

Virgil, Vergil

LATIN: Staff bearer

ROCK AND ROLL: A soldier, traditional, a hard worker

RELATED ARTISTS/SONGS: Virgil Webber (The Grass Roots), "Virgil" by Planet Love, "The Night They Drove Old Dixie Down" by The Band, "Me & Virgil" by Genesis, "Virgil" by Paul Simon

LINER NOTES: The Band's "The Night They Drove Old Dixie Down" refers to one of future California governor George Stoneman's Civil War raids.

The Beatles Baby Names

No one group defined the 1960s quite as much as The Beatles, from their bowl haircuts to their psychedelic explorations. If you love The Fab Four, then there are lots of options beyond John, Paul, George, and Ringo. (Though you might want to avoid Ringo.) From Apple to Yoko, here's a list of Beatles-inspired names:

GIRLS	BOYS
Abbey	Bill
Anna	Chuck
Apple	Dan
Bonnie	Dave
Clarabella	Desmond
Eleanor	Edgar
Joan	George
Julia	Gideon
Lane	Harrison
Lil	John
Lizzy	Johnny
Loretta	JoJo
Lucy	Jude
Madonna	Julian
Maggie	Lennon
Magill	Maxwell
Martha	Neil
Michelle	Paul
Molly	Ringo
Nancy	Robert
Ocean	Rocky
Pam	Teddy
Penny	Winston
Prudence	
Rita	
Sadie	
Starr	
Tangerine	
Vera	
Yoko	

Rock and Roll Royalty

Plenty of people take inspiration from the British royal family for their little tots, so why not take inspiration from a different and far more diverse hierarchy: rock and roll royalty. Though some of the titles are disputed—after all, rock is all about bravado—others have simply stuck.

Thin White Duke	David Bowie
The Crown Prince of Reggae	Dennis Brown
King of Soul	James Brown
Queen of Soul	Aretha Franklin
King of Britpop	Noel Gallagher
Prince of Motown	Marvin Gaye
Princess of Punk	Debbie Harry
King of Pop	Michael Jackson
Queen of Rockabilly	Wanda Jackson
King of Funk	Rick James
Queen of Rock and Roll	Janis Joplin
King of Ragtime	Scott Joplin
King of the Blues	B.B. King
Empress of Soul	Gladys Knight
Princess of Pop	Madonna
King of Reggae	Bob Marley
King of Rockabilly	Carl Perkins
King of Rock and Roll	Elvis Presley
His Purple Majesty	Prince
King of Western Swing	Bob Wills

Famous
Rock Couples

Lindsay and Stevie, June and Johnny, John and Yoko: Some things are just better in pairs. Rock music might be littered with broken hearts and wild nights, but some musician couples make unshakable duos, both on and off stage. Here are some of the most memorable rock power couples:

Benny Andersson & Anni-Frid Lyngstad (ABBA)

Bobby Brown & Whitney Houston

Britney Spears & Justin Timberlake

Britta Phillips & Dean Wareham (Luna)

Carly Simon & James Taylor

Claudette & Smokey Robinson (The Miracles)

Elizabeth Fraser & Robin Guthrie (Cocteau Twins)

Georgia & Ira Kaplan (Yo La Tengo)

Gwen Stefani & Gavin Rossdale

Ike & Tina Turner

Jack & Meg White (The White Stripes)

Janis Joplin & Stephen Stills

Jennifer Lopez & Sean "P. Diddy" Combs

John Lennon & Yoko Ono

Johnny Cash & June Carter

Kathleen Hanna (Le Tigre) & Ad-Rock (The Beastie Boys)

Kurt Cobain & Courtney Love

Lux Interior & Poison Ivy (The Cramps)

Mick Jagger & Marianne Faithfull

Pat Benatar & Neil Giraldo

Patti Smith & Fred "Sonic" Smith (The MC5)

Paul & Linda McCartney (Wings)

Ray Davies & Chrissie Hynde

Shawn "Jay-Z" Carter & Beyoncé Knowles

Sid Vicious & Nancy Spungen

Siouxsie Sioux & Budgie (Siouxsie & the Banshees)

Sonny Bono & Cher

Stevie Nicks & Lindsey Buckingham

Tammy Wynette & George Jones

Thurston Moore & Kim Gordon

Tim McGraw & Faith Hill

Tina Weymouth & Chris Frantz (Talking Heads)

Win Butler & Régine Chassagne (Arcade Fire)

WORLD TOUR: France

For those francophone rock fans, fear not: There are plenty of options beyond Pierre and Juju. Below, French names with rock cred:

GIRLS

Alisa, Elisa (*Pledged to God*/Special, passionate)
Desiree, Désirée (*Desired*/First love, has a thing for younger men)
Dominique (*My Lord*/ Delightful, kindhearted, polite)
Fifi (*God is all encompassing*/Fluffy, saccharine, a girly girl)
Françoise (*From France*/Elegant, sophisticated, hard to get)
Genevieve (*Woman of the people*/Sweet, gentle, a sophisticated lady)
Gigi (*Endearment*/Spunky, petite, friendly)
Kiki (*Endearment*/Energetic, bubbly, stylish)
Margot (*Precious pearl*/Angelic-looking but has a wild streak)
Mignon (*Cute*/Sweet, glamorous, flashy)
Noelle (*Christmas*/Lovely, innocent, fresh-faced)
Paulette (*Small*/Patriotic, grounded)
Solange (*Solemn*/Quirky, stylish, the underdog)

BOYS

Beau, Beauregard (*Handsome*/Fashionable, old-fashioned)
Bon (*Good*/The brains of the operation, acclaimed)
Bonham (*Good man*/Influential, has great rhythm, wild)
Claude (*Slow-moving*/Enigmatic, friendly, eccentric)
Dorsey (*From Orsay*/Innovative, determined)
Jacques (*He who supplants*/A lady-killer, sophisticated, debonair)
Lamar (*The ocean*/Precocious, loves to party)
Lavelle (*Valley*/Sophisticated, sensitive, style-conscious)
Pere (*Father*/Confident, bright)

Unplugged: Singer-songwriters and Folk

A guy, a gal, and a guitar: If that sounds like the perfect formula to you, then this is probably your chapter. Folk musicians and modern singer-songwriters draw inspiration from nature and Americana, which also happen to be great areas for finding a baby name. From rugged idol-inspired names, like Guthrie, to sweet classics, like Clementine, folk traditions are great places to look for names with Americana roots.

GIRLS

Anastasia

GREEK: Resurrection
ROCK AND ROLL: Beautiful stranger, summery
RELATED ARTISTS/SONGS: Anastasia Savage, Anastasia, Anastasia & John, "Yes, Anastasia" by Tori Amos, "Anastasia" by Voltaire, "Anastasia" by Pat Boone
LINER NOTES: Tori Amos's song "Yes, Anastasia" is a tribute to the late Anastasia Romanov, whose ghost Amos suspected was haunting her studio.

Angelina

GREEK: Diminutive of Angela, Angelic

THE BRAVERY: "You are the sun and the moon."

LOUIS PRIMA: "She is so nice, Angelina."

BOB DYLAN: "Farewell, Angelina, the night is on fire."

HALL & OATES: "Angelina, let my love be your life."

Betsy, Betsey

HEBREW: Form of Elizabeth, God's promise

ROCK AND ROLL: Energetic, outdoorsy, a pioneer; a nickname for inanimate objects

RELATED ARTISTS/SONGS: Betsy Olson, "Hurricane Betsy" by Lightnin' Hopkins, "Betsy" by The Squirrels, "Ballad of Ole Betsy" by The Beach Boys, "Sweet Betsy from Pike" by Johnny Cash, "Heavens to Betsy" by Johnny Cash

LINER NOTES: "Sweet Betsy from Pike" was written during the American Gold Rush and has since been sung by Pete Seeger, David Allan Coe, and Rosemary Clooney.

Bree, Brie

IRISH: Cheerful

ROCK AND ROLL: Cheesy but clever

RELATED ARTISTS/SONGS: Bree Sharp, Brie Larson, "Bree Bree" by Brokencyde, "Full Metal Bree" by Buck-O-Nine

LINER NOTES: Cult favorite songwriter Bree Sharp wrote a tribute to David Duchovny called "David Duchovny, Why Won't You Love Me?"

Buffy

AMERICAN: Derivative of Elizabeth, pledged to God

ROCK AND ROLL: A girly girl with some edge, spunky

RELATED ARTISTS/SONGS: Buffy Sainte-Marie, "The Buffy Conference" by Aaron Zigman, "Buffy" by Burnt by the Sun, "Buffy" by Buddy Childers, "Buffy" by Abby & Norm Group

LINER NOTES: Folk singer Buffy Sainte-Marie was a regular on *Sesame Street* in the mid-1970s; the show aired a week of shows from her home in Hawaii.

Celeste

LATIN: Heavenly

ROCK AND ROLL: Pretty, a great dancer, drives men wild

RELATED ARTISTS/SONGS: "Celeste" by Donovan, "Celeste" by The Telescopes, "Vox Celeste" by Deerhunter, "Celeste" by Project Pitchfork

LINER NOTES: Donovan named one of his children, Astrella Celeste, after the song "Celeste." He has two other daughters, Ione Skye and Oriole Nebula, and a son, Donovan Leitch.

Clementine

LATIN: Merciful

ROCK AND ROLL: Adorable, but awful at swimming

RELATED ARTISTS/SONGS: "Clementine" by The Decemberists, "Clementine" by Elliott Smith, "Clementine" by Johnny Cash, "Clementine Jam" by The Grateful Dead, "Clementine" by Pink Martini

*"Tell your mom to marry us ...
so sweet and hilarious."*
—THE DECEMBERISTS

Colbie, Colby

ENGLISH: Coal town
ROCK AND ROLL: Bubbly, optimistic, affable
RELATED ARTISTS/SONGS: Colbie Caillat, Colby O'Donis, "Colby" by Lake Trout, "Colby" by Dianogah, "Colby" by David Berkman
LINER NOTES: Colbie Caillat was inspired to become a singer after seeing Lauryn Hill's performance in *Sister Act 2*.

Corrina, Corina, Corinna, Corinne

GREEK: Maiden
ROCK AND ROLL: Beloved, flighty
RELATED ARTISTS/SONGS: "Corrina, Corrina" by Bob Dylan, "Corrina" by Black Francis, "Oh, Corrina" by Better Than Ezra, "Corina" by Uriah Heep, "Corinne" by Tom House
LINER NOTES: Bob Dylan's version of "Corrina, Corrina" is from blues singer Robert Johnson's song "Stones in My Passway."

Daisy

ENGLISH FLOWER NAME

THE MAINE:
"Sunlight, sunshine, all for you my Daisy."

HALFWAY TO HAZARD:
"Well I know she's an angel even though she ain't got wings."

XTC:
"I'll sing a song about you if no one else will."

AMERICA:
"Like the stars above me how I love you."

Dory, Dori

FRENCH: Golden
ROCK AND ROLL: Loves the beach, fun and funky
RELATED ARTISTS/SONGS: Dory Previn, "Dory" by Grizzly Bear,

"Dory Previn" by Camera Obscura, "Cape Dory" by Tennis, "Funky Dory" by Rachel Stevens

LINER NOTES: Singer-songwriter Dory Previn wrote the scathing "Beware of Young Girls" about Mia Farrow after Farrow had an affair with Previn's then husband Andre.

Frankie, Franky

LATIN: Diminutive of Frances, from France

ROCK AND ROLL: Cool, tough, favors leather jackets

RELATED ARTISTS/SONGS: Frankie Rose (Frankie and the Outs), "Frankie and Johnny" by Bob Dylan, "Frankie" by Bruce Springsteen, "Fuck Frankie" by Marilyn Manson, "Frankie" by Mississippi John Hurt

LINER NOTES: The blues standard "Frankie" or "Frankie and Johnny" inspired three movies, including Elvis's 1966 *Frankie and Johnny*.

Gillian, Jillian

LATIN: Youthful

ROCK AND ROLL: Sunny, an early riser, popular

RELATED ARTISTS/SONGS: Gillian Gilbert (New Order), Gillian Welch, Jillian Goldin, "Gillian" by The Waifs, "Jillian" by Within Temptation, "Gillian Was a Horse" by Damian Jurado, "Jillian" by Dave Rave

LINER NOTES: Gillian Welch was originally in a punk rock band; when a roommate played her an album by The Stanley Brothers, she had an epiphany and switched to folk music.

Greta, Gretta

GREEK: Variation of Margaret, pearl

ROCK AND ROLL: Independent, once a flower child, grows up to be tougher

RELATED ARTISTS/SONGS: Gretta Cohn (Cursive), Greta Matassa, Greta Salpeter (The Hush Sound), "Greta" by Stevie Nicks, "Greta" by Widespread Panic, "Greta" by Mylene Farmer, "Just Like Greta" by Van Morrison

"She's got her eyes wide open, and she's ready to stare you down."
—STEVIE NICKS

Guinevere

WELSH: White wave

ROCK AND ROLL: Green-eyed, fair-haired, a melancholy queen, a snappy dresser

RELATED ARTISTS/SONGS: "Guinevere" by Donovan, "Guinevere" by The Eli Young Band, "Guinnevere" by Crosby, Stills, & Nash, "Guinevere" by The Legendary Pink Dots, "Guinevere" by Rick Wakeman

LINER NOTES: David Crosby wrote the song "Guinnevere" about Joni Mitchell and his ex-girlfriend Christine Hinton.

Gwendolyn

WELSH: Fair-haired

ROCK AND ROLL: Curious, sweet, puts on a tough front

RELATED ARTISTS/SONGS: Gwendolyn Joy, Gwendolyn Sanford, "Gwendolyn Macrae" by The Frogs, "Gwendolyn" by Wolfie, "Gwendolyn" by The Mummies, "Gwendolyn" by The Badlees

LINER NOTES: Besides her solo work, Gwendolyn Sanford has recorded four children's albums under the name Gwendolyn and the Good Time Gang.

Ingrid

NORSE: Beautiful and nobly born

ROCK AND ROLL: A knockout, independent, has a mind of her own

RELATED ARTISTS/SONGS: Ingrid Bjoner, Ingrid Michaelson, Ingrid Weiss (The Raincoats), "Ingrid" by Mike Randle, "Ingrid" by Spalding Rockwell, "Ingrid Bergman" by Billy Bragg & Wilco

LINER NOTES: Raincoats drummer Ingrid Weiss sometimes plays drums in shows for Kitty, Daisy, & Lewis, a band made up of her three children.

Isis

EGYPTIAN: Goddess of the moon

ROCK AND ROLL: Beautiful, mysterious, untamed

RELATED ARTISTS/SONGS: Isis, "Isis" by Bob Dylan, "Isis" by Art Farmer, "Isis" by Alex North, "Isis" by Randy Weston, "Isis" by Hall of the Dead

"Faithful guide unfailing."
—HALL OF THE DEAD

Jeannie, Genie

SCOTTISH: Variation of Jane, God's grace
ROCK AND ROLL: Loving, a brunette, ethereal, chipper
RELATED ARTISTS/SONGS: Jeannie C. Riley, Jeannie Robertson, "Little Jeannie" by Elton John, "Jeannie" by Bud Powell, "Jeannie" by Donna Summer, "Jeannie's Diary" by The Eels, "Jeannie with the Light Brown Hair" by Stephen Foster
LINER NOTES: Spike Jones to release a parody of "I Dream of Jeannie with the Light Brown Hair" entitled "I Dream of Brownie with the Light Blue Jeans," about his pet terrier.

Jennifer

WELSH: Variation of Guinevere, white ghost
ROCK AND ROLL: Sultry, mysterious, wears flowers in her hair
RELATED ARTISTS/SONGS: Jennifer Finch (L7), Jennifer Hudson, Jennifer Lopez, "Jennifer" by Styx, "Jennifer" by Eurhythmics, "Jennifer" by The Blood Brothers, "Jennifer Louise" by of Montreal
LINER NOTES: Donovan wrote the song "Jennifer Juniper" about Jenny Boyd, sister of George Harrison's then-wife Pattie Boyd.

Joni, Joanie

FRENCH: Variation of Johanna, God is gracious
ROCK AND ROLL: Trustworthy, sincere, in touch with nature
RELATED ARTISTS/SONGS: Joni James, Joni Mitchell, "Joanie" by Tony Orlando, "Joni" by The Hudson Brothers
LINER NOTES: Joni Mitchell created the art for all of her album covers; Led Zeppelin wrote the song "Going to California" for her.

Juniper

AMERICAN PLANT NAME
ROCK AND ROLL: Flower child, bright, effervescent
RELATED ARTISTS/SONGS: Juniper Moon, "Jennifer Juniper" by Donovan, "Juniper" by Lindsey Buckingham, "Juniper" by Josh Joplin, "Juniper Suction" by T-Rex
LINER NOTES: Damien Rice played in an Irish rock band called Juniper, performing under the pseudonym Dodi Ma.

Kendall, Kendal

ENGLISH: River valley
ROCK AND ROLL: Earnest, spiritual, reflective, sweet
RELATED ARTISTS/SONGS: Kendall Payne, The Kendalls, "John Merrick and Mrs. Kendal" by John Morris, "Kendall" by Monkeysoop
LINER NOTES: Indie rocker Kendall Payne spent two years on the Lillith Fair circuit, touring with Sarah McLachlan and Dido.

Lalena

HAWAIIAN: Form of Laleini, heavenly girl
ROCK AND ROLL: Artistic, deep, melancholy
RELATED ARTISTS/SONGS: "Lalena" by Donovan, "Lalena" by Deep Purple, "Lalena" by Jane Olivor
LINER NOTES: Donovan wrote the song "Lalena" after the actress Lotte Lenya's role in the stage show and movie *The Threepenny Opera*.

Laura

ENGLISH: Crowned with laurels

JOHNNY MERCER:
"Laura is a face in the misty light."

SCISSOR SISTERS:
"Laura . . . don't you give me your love?"

FLOGGING MOLLY:
"Your beauty will never fade."

GIRLS:
"I really wanna be your friend forever."

Maddy, Maddie

ENGLISH: Variation of Madison or Madeleine, magnificent
ROCK AND ROLL: Reserved, cute, loves the autumn
RELATED ARTISTS/SONGS: Maddy Prior (Steeleye Span), "Maddy" by Talons, "Maddie" by The Descendents, "Here Comes Maddy" by Camille Jones, "Maddy & Archer" by James Newton Howard
LINER NOTES: English folk singer Maddy Prior's daughter, Rose, is also a professional singer.

Maria

HEBREW: Beloved

BLONDIE:
"Smooth as silk, cool as air."

GREEN DAY:
"She is the first voice of the last ones in the line."

RICKY MARTIN:
"Maria is an angel in disguise."

LUCINDA WILLIAMS:
"Maria, you're still wild and restless."

Maura

GAELIC: Form of Mary, beloved lady
ROCK AND ROLL: Elegant, agile, accomplished
RELATED ARTISTS/SONGS: Maura Kennedy (The Kennedys), Maura O'Connell, "Maura" by Luiz Melodia, "Maura on a Bicycle, Stout and Molasses, Way Back When" by Bela Fleck
LINER NOTES: Martin Scorsese cast Irish musician Maura O'Connell as a migrant street singer in his film *The Gangs of New York.*

Muriel

CELTIC: Bright sea
ROCK AND ROLL: Has beautiful eyes, a good friend, mischievous
RELATED ARTISTS/SONGS: Muriel Anderson, "Muriel" by Tom Waits, "Muriel" by Alton Ellis, "Muriel" by Judy Handler, "Muriel the Actor" by Cockney Rebel
LINER NOTES: Harp-guitarist Muriel Anderson's father played saxophone in John Philip Sousa's band.

Nerina, Narina

GREEK: Water
ROCK AND ROLL: Earthy, sassy, fun
RELATED ARTISTS/SONGS: Nerina Pallot, "Nerina" by Ambrogio Sparagna, "Narina" by Serart
LINER NOTES: Singer-songwriter Nerina Pallot, best known for her song "Everybody's Gone to War," taught herself how to play piano and wrote her first song at age thirteen.

Nettie

FRENCH: Gentle
ROCK AND ROLL: Skilled, modern, cute as a button
RELATED ARTISTS/SONGS: "Nettie Moore" by Bob Dylan, "Nettie" by Type O Negative, "Miss Nettie B." by Lee Morgan, "Nettie Teaches Celie" by Quincy Jones
LINER NOTES: Bob Dylan's "Nettie Moore" is based on the folk song "Gentle Nettie Moore," which was written by one of the songwriting team that coined "Jingle Bells."

Odette, Odetta

FRENCH: Wealthy
ROCK AND ROLL: Loves the nighttime, beautiful
RELATED ARTISTS/SONGS: Odetta Holmes, Odette Burger, "Odette" by Matthew Good, "Odette" by Django Reinhardt, "Odette" by Billy "Crash" Craddock
LINER NOTES: Martin Luther King Jr., dubbed Odetta Holmes "The Queen of American Folk Music."

Ola

SCANDINAVIAN: Form of Olaf, heritage
ROCK AND ROLL: Friendly, bright, open-minded
RELATED ARTISTS/SONGS: Ola Belle Reed, Ola Podrida, "Ola Kala" by I'm from Barcelona, "Ola" by Beenie Man, "Ola" by Glykeria, "Ola" by Brian Hirsch
LINER NOTES: Appalachian folk singer Ola Belle Reed played at a country music park for more than twenty-six years; she was the inspiration for the folk group Olabelle.

Ramona

SPANISH: Form of Ramone, protector
ROCK AND ROLL: Hardworking, a Southern beauty queen
RELATED ARTISTS/SONGS: "To Ramona" by Bob Dylan, "Ramona" by Guster, "Ramona" by The Ramones, "Ramona" by Jim Reeves, "Ramona" by Beck
LINER NOTES: Bob Dylan wrote the folk waltz "To Ramona" about his relationship with Joan Baez.

Rebecca

HEBREW: Stable
ROCK AND ROLL: Beautiful, mellow, a dreamer
RELATED ARTISTS/SONGS: Rebecca Hall, Rebecca Ryan, "Rebecca" by Lee Konitz, "Rebecca" by Big Joe Turner, "Rebecca" by The Pat McGee Band, "Rebecca" by PJ Harvey, "Rebecca" by The Bee Gees

*"Satin and lace,
she's so fine and mellow."*
—THE BEE GEES

Scarlet

ENGLISH: Red
ROCK AND ROLL: A night owl, gentle, spiritual
RELATED ARTISTS/SONGS: "Scarlet Begonias" by Sublime, "Scarlet" by U2, "Scarlet's Walk" by Tori Amos, "Scarlet Rose" by Edguy, "Sweet Scarlet" by Cat Stevens, "Scarlet" by Jars of Clay
LINER NOTES: Tori Amos's album *Scarlet's Walk* is about a cross-country trip taken by two friends.

Suzanne, Susanne

HEBREW: Form of Susan, joyful
ROCK AND ROLL: A quirky metalhead, nurturing, cool
RELATED ARTISTS/SONGS: Suzanne Vega, "Suzanne" by Weezer,

"Susanne" by The Audreys, "Suzanne" by Leonard Cohen, "Sorry Suzanne" by The Hollies

LINER NOTES: Suzanne Vega's song "Tom's Diner" is about the same restaurant in Manhattan where the characters in *Seinfeld* hang out.

BOYS

Albert

ENGLISH: Bright, distinguished

ROCK AND ROLL: A sweetheart who strays, a bluesman

RELATED ARTISTS/SONGS: Albert King, Albert Hammond Jr. (The Strokes), Albert Ayler, "Uncle Albert/Admiral Halsey" by Paul McCartney, "Frankie & Albert" by Bob Dylan, "Albert Goes West" by Nick Cave & the Bad Seeds

LINER NOTES: At least twenty different versions of the folk song "Frankie & Albert" have been recorded, including ones by Leadbelly, Lena Horne, and Stevie Wonder

Arlo

ENGLISH: Variation of Harlow, soldier's hill

ROCK AND ROLL: Rustic, cerebral, a social activist

RELATED ARTISTS/SONGS: Arlo Guthrie, Arlo West

LINER NOTES: Arlo Guthrie's daughter Cathy plays ukulele in Folk Uke, a band she formed with Willie Nelson's daughter Amy.

Carey, Cary

IRISH: Dark-haired

ROCK AND ROLL: Grumpy but affectionate

RELATED ARTISTS/SONGS: Carey Bell, Cary Brothers, Carey Ott (Torben Floor), Mariah Carey, "Carey" by Joni Mitchell

LINER NOTES: Though rumors abounded that Joni Mitchell wrote the song "Carey" about James Taylor, Mitchell said that she wrote it for a character she met during her travels to Crete.

Daniel

HEBREW: Judged by God

ROCK AND ROLL: Affectionate older brother, passionate

RELATED ARTISTS/SONGS: Daniel Johnston, Daniel Jones (Silverchair), Daniel Rossen (Grizzly Bear), "Daniel" by Elton John, "Daniel" by Bat for Lashes, "Daniel Cowman" by Regina Spektor, "Daniel Dolphin" by The Free Design, "Daniel Days" by Cloud Cult

LINER NOTES: Singer/songwriter Daniel Johnston first gained attention when Kurt Cobain was photographed wearing a T-shirt with his album art on it.

Devendra

HINDI: Refers to the god Indra

ROCK AND ROLL: Artistic, eccentric, spiritual

RELATED ARTISTS/SONGS: Devendra Banhart, Devendra Patel, "Devendra" by The Twilights

LINER NOTES: Indie folk artist Devendra Banhart was named for Indra, the Hindu god of thunder; his middle name is Obi, for the *Star Wars* character Obi-Wan Kenobi.

Dominic, Domenic

LATIN: Of God

ROCK AND ROLL: Poetic, charming, but can't commit

RELATED ARTISTS/SONGS: Dominic Costa, Dominic Howard (Muse), Domenic Troiano (The Guess Who), "Dominic" by Elvis Presley, "Saint Dominic's Preview" by Van Morrison, "Dominic" by The Legendary Pink Dots, "Dominic Christ" by Suicide

LINER NOTES: Van Morrison wrote "Saint Dominic's Preview" for a church in Northern Ireland.

Donovan, Donavon

IRISH: Dark

ROCK AND ROLL: Mellow, sensitive, a bit of a hippie

RELATED ARTISTS/SONGS: Donavon Frankenreiter, Donovan (Leitch), "Donovan" by The Happy Mondays, "Donovan Said" by The Brian Jonestown Massacre

LINER NOTES: One of Donovan's muses was Brian Jones's ex-girlfriend Linda Lawrence, for whom he wrote "Sunshine Superman" and "Legend of a Girl Child Linda."

Duncan

GAELIC: Chief

ROCK AND ROLL: Destined for greatness, flighty

RELATED ARTISTS/SONGS: Duncan Coutts (Our Lady Peace), Duncan James (Blue), Duncan Sheik, "Duncan" by Paul Simon, "Duncan" by Sarah Slean

LINER NOTES: Duncan Sheik and Lisa Loeb were in a band together at Brown University.

Dylan, Dillon

WELSH: Great sea

ROCK AND ROLL: Inscrutable, odd, but widely admired

RELATED ARTISTS/SONGS: Bob Dylan, Dylan Mills (aka Dizzee Rascal), "Dylan" by The Throwing Muses, "Dylan" by Good Riddance, "Like Dylan in the Movies" by Belle and Sebastian

LINER NOTES: Before adopting the name Bob Dylan, little Robert Zimmerman performed under the title Elston Gunn.

Gordon

SCOTTISH: Hill
ROCK AND ROLL: Clever, mellow, a nature-lover, resourceful
RELATED ARTISTS/SONGS: Gordon Lightfoot, Gordon Moakes (Bloc Party), Gordon Sumner (aka Sting), "Flash Gordon" by Talib Kweli, "Gordon" by Sonia Dada
LINER NOTES: Gordon Lightfoot was chosen as the honorary captain of the Toronto Maple Leafs in celebration of the NHL's seventy-fifth anniversary in 1991.

Irwin

ENGLISH: Friend of boar
ROCK AND ROLL: Old-fashioned, precise, a neatnik
RELATED ARTISTS/SONGS: Irwin Goodman, "Irwin" by Diego Moderna, "Irwin" by Mr. Heath
LINER NOTES: Irwin Goodman's folk protest songs were such a hit in his native Finland that "Irwin singalike" contests are held there every year.

Ivar

NORSE: Archer
ROCK AND ROLL: Forthright, loyal, outgoing
RELATED ARTISTS/SONGS: Ivar Haglund, "Ivar" by Svante Thuresson, "Ivar" by Margret Ornolfsdottir, "Ivar" by Adam Norden
LINER NOTES: Seattle folk musician Ivar Haglund opened Seattle's first aquarium, along with a chain of seafood restaurants.

Jeff, Geoff

GERMAN: Variation of Jeffrey, divine peace
ROCK AND ROLL: Sensitive, thoughtful, a guitar whiz
RELATED ARTISTS/SONGS: Geoff Barrow (Portishead), Jeff Beck, Jeff Buckley, "Jeff Wears Birkenstocks" by NOFX, "Jeff" by Nicolette, "Hey Geoff" by Dub Syndicate
LINER NOTES: Singer-songwriter Jeff Buckley's childhood name was Scotty, after his middle name and jazz musician Scotty Morehead.

Kyle

SCOTTISH: Channel
ROCK AND ROLL: A loyal friend, good company, athletic
RELATED ARTISTS/SONGS: Kyle Andrews, Kyle Gass (Tenacious D), Kyle Justin, "Kyle" by Spooky Tooth, "Sing Like Kyle" by The Blow, "Kyle Petty, Son of Richard" by Soundgarden, "Kyle's Song" by moe., "Calling Kyle" by Primus
LINER NOTES: Tenacious D's Kyle Gass sometimes goes by the name "Kage" or "Klip"; he appeared as an uptight lawyer in Good Charlotte's "Lifestyles of the Rich and the Famous" video.

Len

GERMAN: Variation of Leonard, brave lion
ROCK AND ROLL: Precocious, inspiring
RELATED ARTISTS/SONGS: Len Chandler, Len Barry, Len Faki, "Len"
by Dead Lane Cross, "Len" by Christos Dantis, "Len" by Mandrake
LINER NOTES: Folk singer and civil rights activist Len Chandler
toured the Pacific Rim as part of Jane Fonda's 1971 antiwar troupe.

Leo

LATIN: Lion
ROCK AND ROLL: Luminous, courageous, sharp
RELATED ARTISTS/SONGS: Leo Kottke, Leo Nocentelli (The Meters),
Leo Sayer, "Leo" by Mary Lou Williams, "Leo" by John Coltrane,
"Leo" by Roy Ayers, "Maybe I'm a Leo" by Deep Purple, "Stars of
Leo" by M. Ward
LINER NOTES: British singer-songwriter Leo Sayer's name, in cock-
ney rhyming slang, means an all-day drinking session or "all-
dayer."

Leonard

GERMAN: Strong as a lion
ROCK AND ROLL: Loves music, a West Coast boy, introspective
RELATED ARTISTS/SONGS: Leonard Chess, Leonard Cohen, Leon-
ard Hummer, "Leonard" by Randy Newman, "Leonard" by Merle
Haggard
LINER NOTES: Leonard Cohen named his daughter Lorca after his
favorite poet; she has a daughter, Viva, with Rufus Wainwright and
his partner Jorn Weisbrodt.

Loudon

GERMAN: From the low valley
ROCK AND ROLL: Idiosyncratic, funny, clever
RELATED ARTISTS/SONGS: Loudon Wainwright III, Loudon Thomas,
"Loudon III" by Amodio
LINER NOTES: The Wainwright family is famous for writing songs
about each other: Loudon's "Rufus Is a Tit Man" is about his son
learning how to breastfeed, Kate McGarrigle's "Blues in D" is about
Loudon, and Rufus Wainwright's "Dinner at Eight" is about an ar-
gument he once had with his father.

Murray

GAELIC: Sea settlement
ROCK AND ROLL: Sensitive, creative, loves television
RELATED ARTISTS/SONGS: Murray Low, Murray Head, Murray
McLauchlan, "Murray" by Uri Caine, "Murray" by Pete Yorn
LINER NOTES: Canadian singer-songwriter Murray McLauchlan is
also a bush pilot; he starred in a television documentary called
Floating Over Canada.

Neal, Neil

GAELIC: Cloud
ROCK AND ROLL: Creative, curious, a ladies' man
RELATED ARTISTS/SONGS: Neal Hefti, Neil Young, Neil Diamond, "Neil" by The Durutti Column, "Neil" by Johnny Love
LINER NOTES: Because of his influence on alternative rock, Neil Young has the nickname "The Godfather of Grunge"; he has three children, Zeke, Ben, and Amber Jean.

Theodore

GREEK: God's gift
ROCK AND ROLL: Jovial, athletic, warm
RELATED ARTISTS/SONGS: Theodore Bikel, Theodore Shapiro, "Theodore" by The Blue Note All-Stars, "Theodore" by Ghostface Killah
LINER NOTES: Folk singer and Newport Folk Festival founder Theodore Bikel originated the role of Captain von Trapp in the Broadway version of *The Sound of Music*.

Vic

LATIN: Form of Victor, champion
ROCK AND ROLL: Unconventional, a rogue, witty
RELATED ARTISTS/SONGS: Vic Chesnutt, Vic Damone, Vic Lewis, "Vic Acid" by Squarepusher, "Vic" by Throwing Muses, "Vic" by Kane & Abel
LINER NOTES: Singer-songwriter Vic Chesnutt made two albums with Widespread Panic under the band name brute.

Woody

ENGLISH: Form of Woodrow, houses by the forest
ROCK AND ROLL: Gritty, freewheeling, gallant
RELATED ARTISTS/SONGS: Woody Guthrie, Woody Evans, Woody Rock (Dru Hill), "Woody" by Arturo Sandoval, "Woody" by Leo Parker
LINER NOTES: Bob Dylan said that he moved to New York City just for the opportunity to meet folk singer Woody Guthrie.

Zachary

HEBREW: The Lord has remembered
ROCK AND ROLL: Precious, trusting, innocent
RELATED ARTISTS/SONGS: Zachary Richard, Zachary Breaux, "Zachary" by Sonia Dada, "Zachary" by Jonathan Hoffman, "Zachary" by Old Bull
LINER NOTES: Cajun singer-songwriter Zachary Richard has published three volumes of poetry and three children's books, all in French.

Bob Dylan Baby Names

If you're a diehard Dylan fan, then there are lots of options besides Dylan, Bobby, or Zimmerman. You could take inspiration from Dylan's idol, for example, and try Guthrie. There's also Beatrice, in honor of his mother, and Lybba, his maternal grandmother. Not to mention the wealth of names in Dylan's considerable song roster. Check out these Dylan suggestions below:

GIRLS	BOYS
Angelina	Billy
Beatrice	Blue
Bessie	Duncan
Cinderella	Durango
Corrina	Dylan
Delia	Floyd
Frankie	Guthrie
Hattie	Hezekiah
Isis	Huck
Johanna	Jack
Lily	Joe
Magdelena	Quinn
Maggie	Robert
Marie	Silvio
Mary Ann	Willie
Nadine	Woody
Rosemary	Zigman
Sara	
Suze	

Rock and Roll
Place Names

Bono named his daughter Memphis Eve, Ashlee Simpson named her son Bronx Mowgli, and Gwen Stefani dubbed her little boy Kingston. Place names are unusual yet familiar. Montana, Utah, and Cheyenne are cute names with a laid-back, country feel, while London, Rio, or Valencia hint of a life on international tour. Plus, they're clever ways to incorporate an element of musician fandom into a name without being too obvious. Devotees of Seattle's grunge scene could use Olympia or Washington, and hip-hop lovers could go for Brooklyn, Harlem, or Cali. (Though no matter how much you like The Beatles, we'd avoid Liverpool at all costs.)

Adelaide	Geneva	Reno
Africa	Harlem	Rio
Alabama	Indiana	Rochelle
Arizona	Jordan	Rochester
Asia	Kenya	Rome
Aspen	Kyoto	Sahara
Atlantis	Lodi	Savannah
Austin	London	Selma
Berlin	Mali	Sierra
Bronx	Memphis	Sydney
Brooklyn	Miami	Tallahassee
Calcutta	Montana	Tennessee
Cali	Montgomery	Tribeca
Cavan	Niagara	Tulsa
Cheyenne	Nolita	Utah
Cleveland	Odessa	Valencia
Dakota	Olympia	Virginia
Dallas	Orlando	Washington
Dixie	Paris	Wyoming
Eden	Peru	
Georgia	Phoenix	

Names That
Go Together in Songs

Having twins? Looking for a matching name for a little sister or brother to be? Some of the best songs are about two—or three—iconic names, not just one.

"Abraham, Martin & John" by Dion
"Bonnie & Clyde" by Serge Gainsbourg
"Charlie & Freddy" by of Montreal
"Ballad of Cleo & Joe" by Cyndi Lauper
"Dennis and Lois" by The Happy Mondays
"Duncan & Brady" by Leadbelly
"Eddie, Bruce, & Paul" by NOFX
"Frankie & Albert" by Bob Dylan
"Gene & Eddie" by Stray Cats
"Isaac & Abraham" by Joan Baez
"Ishmael & Maggie" by The Trews
"Jack & Ginger" by We Are Scientists
"The Return of Jackie & Judy" by Tom Waits
"Jean & Dinah" by Robert Mitchum
"Jocelyn & Greg" by Aaron Zigman
"John & Josie" by David Roth
"Julius & Ethel" by Zola Jesus
"Kim & Jessie" by M83
"Kristen & Jim" by Eric Clapton
"Lana & Stevie" by The Donnas
"For Leah & Chloe" by Lost in the Trees
"Little Lou, Prophet Jack, Uncle John" by Belle & Sebastian
"Manny, Moe & Jack" by The Dickies
"Millie & Billie" by Atmosphere
"Mykel and Carli" by Weezer
"Neal & Jack & Me" by King Crimson
"Ozzie & Harriet" by The Dust Brothers
"Rebecca & Romeo" by Blink-182
"Susie & Jeffrey" by Blondie
"Trudy & Dave" by John Hiatt
"Venus & Serena" by Super Furry Animals

Names Not Even
Rock Can Redeem

Rock and roll can make many seemingly terrible names cool, but there are a few that nothing can help. Below, names that almost no one can pull off:

Biff
Cain
Derf
Elgin
Elvira
Ernestine
Grizelda
Inger
Jebediah
Jezebel
Johnette
Judas
Mingue
Nezus
Olgita
Pirkle
Purvis
Reet
Spizz
Torquil
Werly
Yanni
Yngwie

1970s:
Disco, Glam Rock, and Arena Bands

The 1970s saw the rise of the rock star: big-haired shredders with banshee-like wails, lithe dancing queens, prog rock noodlers, and reactionary punk rockers (who there's a whole other chapter devoted to). The smorgasbord of names stretches from countercultural icons like Bowie and Zappa to girls next door like Donna and Kimberley.

GIRLS

Agnes, Agnetha

GREEK: Pure
ROCK AND ROLL: A poet, moody, introspective
RELATED ARTISTS/SONGS: Agnetha Fältskog (ABBA), "Alas Agnes" by Mystery Jets, "Saint Agnes and the Burning Train" by Sting, "Agnes, Queen of Sorrow" by Bonnie "Prince" Billy
LINER NOTES: Agnetha Fältskog has two children, Linda and Peter Christian.

Aja

HINDI: Goat, also refers to a Sudanese ethnic group
ROCK AND ROLL: A free spirit, happy
RELATED ARTISTS/SONGS: Aja Kim, "Aja" by Steely Dan, "Aja" by Christian McBride, "Aja" by Hal Galper
LINER NOTES: Rudy's Bar and Grill, which Steely Dan sings about on their album *Aja*, is a real place in Manhattan's Hell's Kitchen, where the members of the band used to go for their cheap beer and free hot dogs.

Amoreena, Amarena

AMERICAN: Derived from Amor, love
ROCK AND ROLL: Playful, loves the outdoors, sun-kissed

RELATED ARTISTS/SONGS: Project Amarena, "Amoreena" by Elton John, "Amarena" by Lucio Fabbri, "Amarena" by Stefano Sani
LINER NOTES: Elton John wrote "Amoreena" for his goddaughter.

Bijou

FRENCH: Jewel
ROCK AND ROLL: Precious, sweet, a tad spoiled
RELATED ARTISTS/SONGS: Bijou Phillips, Bijou, "Bijou" by Queen, "Bijou" by Django Reinhardt
LINER NOTES: Like "Delilah," Queen's song "Bijou" was named after one of Freddie Mercury's cats.

Camelia, Camellia, Camilia, Camille

ITALIAN: Flower
ROCK AND ROLL: Protective, nurturing, smells lovely
RELATED ARTISTS/SONGS: Camille, "Camellia" by Hall & Oates, "Camelia La Tejana" by Los Tigres Del Norte, "Camilia" by Basshunter, "Camelia" by Marty Robbins, "Camellia" by Verbena
LINER NOTES: Prince sometimes sings under the name of an alter ego named "Camille," using vocal filters to make his voice sound deep and slow à la Barry White.

Deanie

ENGLISH: Form of Dean, leader
ROCK AND ROLL: Summery, starry-eyed, beautiful
RELATED ARTISTS/SONGS: Deanie Parker, "Hey Deanie" by Shaun Cassidy, "Bud and Deanie" by My Bee's Garden, "Deanie Speaks" by Bloody Weather
LINER NOTES: Shaun Cassidy's "Deanie" is about Natalie Wood's character in the film *Splendor in the Grass*.

Donna

ITALIAN: Woman

10CC:
"Donna, I'd stand on my head for you."

RITCHIE VALENS:
"I love my girl Donna."

BOB MARLEY:
"You can hear me say that I need you."

FM STATIC:
"Come with me, oh I'm beggin' you please."

Dora

GREEK: God's gift
ROCK AND ROLL: Dances to her own tune, creative, spirited
RELATED ARTISTS/SONGS: "Revolving Dora" by Fountains of Wayne, "Cook That Dinner Dora" by Loudon Wainwright III, "Dora Goes to Town" by Andrew Bird, "Dora" by Gilberto Gil, "Dora" by The Alan Parsons Project
LINER NOTES: Singer-songwriter Loudon Wainwright III, who wrote "Cook That Dinner Dora" in 1971, composed the music for the Judd Apatow film *Knocked Up.*

Doreen, Dorine

IRISH: Serious
ROCK AND ROLL: A wild thing, rowdy, beautiful
RELATED ARTISTS/SONGS: "Doreen" by Frank Zappa, "Fair Doreen" by Tunng, "Doreen" by Old 97's, "Doreen Special" by The Skatalites
LINER NOTES: Doreen is a recurring character in Frank Zappa's work, appearing again in the song "Goblin Girl."

Elaine

FRENCH: Luminous
ROCK AND ROLL: Forgiving, delicate, sensitive
RELATED ARTISTS/SONGS: Elaine "Spanky" McFarlane (Spanky and Our Gang), Elaine Page, "Elaine" by ABBA, "Miss Elaine" by Run-DMC, "Days of Elaine" by The Decemberists, "Blue Eyed Elaine" by Ramblin' Jack Elliott, "Dear Elaine" by Roy Wood
LINER NOTES: ABBA's "Elaine" was the B-side of the ballad "The Winner Takes It All."

Elizabeth, Elisabeth

HEBREW: Pledged to God
ROCK AND ROLL: Pretty, warm, good-hearted, loves to dream, moody
RELATED ARTISTS/SONGS: Elizabeth Cotten, Elizabeth Fraser (Cocteau Twins), "Elizabeth" by Frank Sinatra, "Elizabeth" by The Statler Brothers, "Elizabeth, You Were Born to Play That Part" by Ryan Adams, "Elizabeth My Dear" by The Stone Roses, "Elizabeth, I Love You" by Michael Jackson

"Oh, Elizabeth, I long to see your pretty face."
—THE STATLER BROTHERS

Emily

LATIN: Rival, industrious

ROCK AND ROLL: A science-leaning woman, loves dancing, a great hostess

RELATED ARTISTS/SONGS: Emily Robinson (Dixie Chicks), Emily Sallers (Indigo Girls), Emily Sparks, "A Rose for Emily" by the Zombies, "For Emily, Whenever I May Find Her" by Simon & Garfunkel, "See Emily Play" by Pink Floyd, "Emily" by Elton John

LINER NOTES: Syd Barrett wrote "See Emily Play" about a girl he saw in a psychedelic dream.

Fanny

LATIN: Variation of Frances, French

ROCK AND ROLL: Tough, clever, responsible, and sweet, has an unfortunate derriere-related connotation

RELATED ARTISTS/SONGS: Fanny, "Fanny (Be Tender with My Love)" by the Bee Gees, "Jiving Sister Fanny" by The Rolling Stones, "Short Fat Fanny" by Little Richard, "Fanny Mae" by Dick Dale, "Fanny" by Pat Boone

LINER NOTES: The lyrics to The Rolling Stones' "Jiving Sister Fanny" were never finished; Mick Jagger just made them up as he went along.

Gail

HEBREW: Variation of Abigail, my father rejoices

ROCK AND ROLL: Innocent, fair-haired, has bad luck

RELATED ARTISTS/SONGS: Gail Davies, Gail Ann Dorsey (Tears for Fears), Gail Pappalardi, "Gail" by Alice Cooper, "Gail Loves Me" by Jonathan Richman and the Modern Lovers, "Gail with the Golden Hair" by The Handsome Family

LINER NOTES: Frank and Gail Zappa named their son Dweezil after Frank's pet name for one of Gail's pinky-toes.

Gloria

LATIN: Glory

ROCK AND ROLL: Always on the run, petite, a wild card

RELATED ARTISTS/SONGS: Gloria Estefan, Gloria Gaynor, "Gloria" by Laura Branigan, "Gloria" by Van Morrison, "Gloria" by Patti Smith, "Gloria" by U2, "Viva la Gloria" by Green Day

LINER NOTES: The only Grammy Award ever given for Best Disco Recording went to Gloria Gaynor for "I Will Survive."

Grace

ENGLISH: Virtuous

ROCK AND ROLL: Elegant, generous, always taking the blame, a sex symbol

RELATED ARTISTS/SONGS: Grace Jones, Grace Slick (Jefferson Airplane), "Grace" by Jeff Buckley, "Grace" by U2, "Grace" by Supergrass, "Grace Cathedral Hill" by The Decemberists, "Grace" by Jethro Tull

LINER NOTES: Grace Slick caused a media kerfuffle by jokingly commenting that she wanted to name her daughter "god" with a lowercase g to show humility.

Helen

GREEK: Torch

ROCK AND ROLL: Flirtatious, saucy, gorgeous, a heartbreaker

RELATED ARTISTS/SONGS: Helen Reddy, Helen Hooke, Helen Humes, "Helen Lundeberg" by Sonic Youth, "Helen" by Ariel Pink, "Helen Wheels" by Paul McCartney, "One for Helen" by Bill Evans, "Hey, Hey Helen" by ABBA

LINER NOTES: Helen Reddy is now a practicing hypnotherapist, acting as the patron of the Australian Society of Clinical Hypnotherapists.

Jessica

HEBREW: Foresight

JEWEL:
"He would shudder to think of what life would be like without his best friend and shrink Jessica."

RICK SPRINGFIELD:
"You're a lady of the world, you've been to Paris and London."

ELLIOT MINOR:
"She's good, she's bad, everything I need."

KAKI KING:
"Decorates her room with greeting cards."

Kimberley, Kimberly

ENGLISH, SOUTH AFRICAN PLACE NAME

ROCK AND ROLL: Beloved, starry-eyed, peppy

RELATED ARTISTS/SONGS: Kimberley Rew (The Soft Boys), Kimberley Walsh (Girls Aloud), Kimberley Wyatt (Pussycat Dolls), "Kimberly" by Patti Smith, "Kimberly Austin" by Porno for Pyros, "Somberly, Kimberly" by The Dirty Projectors, "Kimberley" by Clinic, "Kimberley" by Marques Houston

LINER NOTES: Patti Smith wrote the song "Kimberly" for her little sister.

Kristy, Christie

GREEK: Variation of Christine, anointed

ROCK AND ROLL: Mystical, fun, romantic

RELATED ARTISTS/SONGS: Christie Allen, Kristy Lee Cook, "Christie Road" by Green Day, "Christie Lee" by Billy Joel, "Christie" by Aqua-Nites, "Christie" by Gordon Thomas, "Kristy, Are You Doing Okay?" by The Offspring

LINER NOTES: Billy Joel wrote "Christie Lee" for his wife Christie Brinkley, whom he featured in his video for "Uptown Girl."

Lola

SPANISH: Variation of Dolores, sorrowful

ROCK AND ROLL: Provocative, voluptuous, likes to dress up, possibly a transvestite

RELATED ARTISTS/SONGS: Lola Albright, Lola Flores, "Lola" by The Coasters, "Lola" by The Kinks, "Pauvre Lola" by Serge Gainsbourg, "Lola, Lola" by Ricky Martin

LINER NOTES: The Kinks' song "Lola" prompted several parody songs, including The Madness's unreleased "Mistress, Mistress" and Weird Al Yankovic's "Yoda."

Lorelei

GERMAN: *Temptress*

STYX:
"As gentle as a butterfly, she moves without a sound."

THE POGUES:
"Lovesick men who caught her eye, and no-one knew but Lorelei."

COCTEAU TWINS:
"Covered by the sacred fire."

ELLA FITZGERALD:
"Her figure was divine."

Lorna

MODERN AMERICAN: Sprightly

ROCK AND ROLL: Angel child, not easily fazed, self-made

RELATED ARTISTS/SONGS: Lorna Bennett, Lorna Luft, Lorna Marshall, "Lorna" by Van Morrison, "Lorna" by The Mystery Jets, "Lorna" by 7 Year Bitch, "Lorna Doom" by Rocket from the Crypt, "Lorna Skank" by Lee "Scratch" Perry

LINER NOTES: Judy Garland's daughter Lorna Luft has two children, Jesse and Vanessa, with The Arrows' guitarist Jake Hooker.

Marie

LATIN: Star of the sea

ROCK AND ROLL: Looks like a princess, tender, sensitive

RELATED ARTISTS/SONGS: Marie Berard, Marie Osmond, "Marie" by Randy Newman, "Marie" by Joe Cocker, "Marie" by Otis Spann, "Absolutely Sweet Marie" by Bob Dylan, "(Marie's the Name) His Latest Flame" by Elvis Presley

LINER NOTES: Marie Osmond turned down the part of Sandy in the movie *Grease* because of what she deemed objectionable moral content.

Marjorie

ENGLISH: Variation of Margaret, pearl

ROCK AND ROLL: Fun-loving, gentle, spontaneous

RELATED ARTISTS/SONGS: Marjorie-Jean, "Marjorie" by Judy Collins, "Marjorie" by April Wine, "Marjorie (Margarine)" by Donovan, "Marjorie" by Counting Crows

LINER NOTES: Neil Diamond's song "Beautiful Noise" was inspired by his daughter Marjorie, who exclaimed "What beautiful noise, Daddy!" as the Puerto Rican Day Parade went by their window.

Melinda

GREEK: Dark honeysuckle

ROCK AND ROLL: Dreamy, sweet, a supportive wife

RELATED ARTISTS/SONGS: "Sweet Melinda" by John Denver, "Sweet Dream, Melinda" by Trey Anastasio, "Melinda was mine . . ." by Neil Diamond, "Come Away Melinda" by Judy Collins, "Melinda" by Tom Petty

LINER NOTES: The famous pirate radio station Radio Milinda, founded to escape the BBC's restrictions, took its name from Judy Collins's antiwar song "Come Away Melinda."

Mona

ITALIAN: My lady

ROCK AND ROLL: Precious, well cared for, a good friend

RELATED ARTISTS/SONGS: "Mona Bone Jakon" by Cat Stevens, "Mona" by James Taylor, "Mona Lisas and Mad Hatters" by Elton John, "Mona (I Need You Baby)" by Bo Diddley, "Barcelona Mona" by Bruce Hornsby

LINER NOTES: Elton John's song "Mona Lisas and Mad Hatters" was partially inspired by Ben E. King's song "Spanish Harlem." The song was inspiried by Bennie Taupin's experience in New York City during the 1970s, written after he heard a gun go off near his hotel window.

Poppy

ENGLISH FLOWER NAME

ROCK AND ROLL: Upbeat, sugary sweet, chipper

RELATED ARTISTS/SONGS: Poppy Jones, The Poppy Family, "Poppy" by TV on the Radio, "Poppy Day" by Siouxsie and the Banshees, "Poppy Nogood and the Phantom Band" by Terry Riley, "Poppy" by Mac Miller

LINER NOTES: The Poppy Family's Terry Jacks named his powerboat "Seasons in the Sun" after his hit solo number that paid for it.

Rhiannon

WELSH: Queen

ROCK AND ROLL: Beautiful, free, bewitching

RELATED ARTISTS/SONGS: Rhiannon Coppin, Rhiannon Alper, "Rhiannon" by Fleetwood Mac, "The Birds of Rhiannon" by Faith and the Muse

LINER NOTES: Stevie Nicks wrote the song Rhiannon after reading Mary Leader's novel *Triad*, about a witch named Rhiannon. After writing the song, rumors circulated that Nicks was practicing the dark arts.

Ricky, Rikki

ENGLISH: Variation of Frederica, peaceful ruler

ROCK AND ROLL: Independent, alluring

RELATED ARTISTS/SONGS: "Rikki Don't Lose That Number" by Steely Dan, "Ricky" by John Frusciante, "Rikki" by Mylo

LINER NOTES: Donal Fagen claims that the Rikki in Steely Dan's "Rikki Don't Lose That Number" is a girl he met in college; even though she was married and pregnant, Fagen insisted on giving her his number.

Sandy

ENGLISH: Form of Sandra, defender of mankind

ROCK AND ROLL: Rosy-cheeked, lovely, innocent

RELATED ARTISTS/SONGS: Sandy Denny, Sandy Duncan, Sandy Posey, "4th of July, Asbury Park (Sandy)" by Bruce Springsteen, "Sandy" by Dion, "Sandy" by The Hollies, "Sandy" by The Carpenters

LINER NOTES: The fortuneteller in Springsteen's "4th of July, Asbury Park" was a real person, named Madam Marie, who told Springsteen he would be a successful musician.

Thelma

GREEK: Strong-willed

ROCK AND ROLL: Sweet, youthful, free-spirited

RELATED ARTISTS/SONGS: Thelma Carpenter, Thelma Terry, Thelma Houston (Thelma & Jerry), "Thelma" by Paul Simon, "Thelma" by John Lee Hooker, "Thelma" by Larry Marshall

LINER NOTES: R&B singer Thelma Houston, best known for her song "Don't Leave Me This Way," costarred in the 1977 film *Game Show Models*.

Vera

LATIN: Truth

ROCK AND ROLL: Glamorous, optimistic, encouraging

RELATED ARTISTS/SONGS: Vera Lynn, "Vera" by Pink Floyd, "The Revenge of Vera Gemini" by Blue Oyster Cult, "Vera Lee" by Insane Clown Posse, "Vera" by Rosetta, "Vera" by Luther Wright & the Wrongs

LINER NOTES: Pink Floyd's "Vera" is about World War II chanteuse Vera Lynn; the film of *The Wall* opens with a clip of her singing "The Little Boy That Santa Claus Forgot."

Wilhelmina

GERMAN: Form of William, protector

ROCK AND ROLL: Beloved, trustworthy, pure

RELATED ARTISTS/SONGS: Impure Wilhelmina, "Wilhelmina" by Peter Hammill, "Wilhelmina" by Danny Kaye, "Wilhelmina" by Lawrence Welk

LINER NOTES: Peter Hammill wrote the song "Wilhelmina" as a lullaby for his daughter.

BOYS

Arnold

GERMAN: Powerful

ROCK AND ROLL: Eccentric, attentive

RELATED ARTISTS/SONGS: Eddy Arnold, Mac Arnold, "Arnold" by Austin Lounge Lizards, "Arnold" by The Kronos Quartet, "Arnold Layne" by Pink Floyd

LINER NOTES: "Arnold Layne," Pink Floyd's first single, is based on a real person who kept stealing from Syd Barrett and Roger Waters's mothers' clotheslines.

Arthur

CELTIC: Stone

ROCK AND ROLL: Fond of his mother, ambitious

RELATED ARTISTS/SONGS: Arthur Alexander, Arthur Kane (The New York Dolls), "Arthur" by Rick Wakeman, "Uncle Arthur" by David Bowie, "Arthur" by The Kinks

LINER NOTES: The Kinks' album *Arthur (Or the Decline and Fall of the British Empire)* was partially inspired by Ray Davies's older sister Rose, who moved to Australia with her husband Arthur.

Barnaby

ARAMAIC: Variant of Barnabas, son of comfort

ROCK AND ROLL: Studious, seriously hip, sometimes associated with the character Barnaby Tucker in *Hello, Dolly!*

RELATED ARTISTS/SONGS: Barnaby Bye, "Barnaby, Hardly Working" by Yo La Tengo

LINER NOTES: Andy Williams's record label was called Barnaby Records. He used it to release songs from the Cadence Records archives from 1970 to 1980, including some early Jimmy Buffett songs.

Benny

HEBREW: Variant of Benjamin, son of my right hand

ROCK AND ROLL: A tough guy, a renegade, rules the disco with an iron fist

RELATED ARTISTS/SONGS: Benny Andersson (ABBA), Benny Benassi, Benny Goodman, "Benny Bullfrog" by Madness, "Benny Got Blowed Up" by NOFX, "Benny the Bouncer" by Emerson Lake, & Palmer

LINER NOTES: Before ABBA, Benny Andersson was a member of pop band called The Hep Stars, widely known as "The Swedish Beatles."

Bowie

SCOTTISH: Blond

ROCK AND ROLL: Funky, glittery, glammed out

RELATED ARTISTS/SONGS: David Bowie, Lester Bowie, "Bowie" by Tenacious D

LINER NOTES: David Bowie's different-colored eyes are caused by an injury sustained during a childhood fight. His friend punched Bowie in the eye over a girl, giving Bowie a four-month stay in the hospital and one permanently dilated pupil.

Burke

FRENCH: From the fortress

ROCK AND ROLL: Serious, spiritual, sharp

RELATED ARTISTS/SONGS: Burke Shelley (Budgie), Solomon Burke, Alexandra Burke, "Burke" by Hans Zimmer

LINER NOTES: Budgie bassist Burke Shelley looks strikingly like Rush's Geddy Lee: Both have long hair, huge glasses, and trademark high-pitched vocal runs in their songs.

Chas

GERMAN: Form of Charles, free man

ROCK AND ROLL: An outdoorsman, good-natured

RELATED ARTISTS/SONGS: Chas Hodges (Chas & Dave), Chas Chandler (The Animals), "Chas" by Dolly Parton, "Chas" by Geoff Simkins

LINER NOTES: Chas Hodges, of the vocal duet Chas & Hodges, is now a beloved figure among the Tottenham Hotspur Football Club; he's written a number of Tottenham-dedicated songs, including "Spurs Are on Their Way to Wembley."

Cozy

ENGLISH: Form of Colin, cub
ROCK AND ROLL: Talented, warm, virtuosic
RELATED ARTISTS/SONGS: Cozy Powell, Cozy Cole, "Cozy" by The Bar-Kays, "Cozy" by Next, "Cozy" by Wanda Dee, "Cozy" by Goodness
LINER NOTES: Drummer Cozy Powell, who played with Black Sabbath and Jeff Beck, broke the world record for drums at once by playing four hundred on the children's program *Record Breakers*.

Crosby

IRISH: Town with crosses
ROCK AND ROLL: Laid-back, sharp, generous
RELATED ARTISTS/SONGS: David Crosby (Crosby, Stills & Nash), Bing Crosby, "Crosby" by Deke Leonard, "Crosby" by Kulte
LINER NOTES: David Crosby appeared in the movie *Hook* as a pirate and in *Thunderheart* as a bartender.

Derek

GERMAN: Ruler
ROCK AND ROLL: A man without a scene, a loyal friend
RELATED ARTISTS/SONGS: Derek and the Dominos, Derek Fudesco (Pretty Girls Make Graves), Derek Trucks (The Allman Brothers Band), "Derek" by Animal Collective, "Derek Fisher" by Trans Am, "Little Derek" by Sway
LINER NOTES: The origins of the band name "Derek and the Dominos" are disputed; one story claims that the name is a riff on Chubby Checker, another was that it was a mispronunciation of Eric and the Dynamos.

Dirk

SCOTTISH: Dagger
ROCK AND ROLL: Stylish, loves white socks
RELATED ARTISTS/SONGS: Dirk Leyers, Dirk Powell, "Dirk" by String Cheese Incident, "Devil and Dirk" by Natalie MacMaster, "Dirk Wears White Socks" by Adam and the Ants
LINER NOTES: In the joke band The Rutles (aka "The Prefab Four"), Eric Idle plays Paul McCartney equivalent Dirk McQuickly.

Donny, Donnie

SCOTTISH: Form of Donald, proud chief
ROCK AND ROLL: Upbeat, cute, fun-loving
RELATED ARTISTS/SONGS: Donny Osmond, Donnie Brooks, Donnie Iris, "Donny" by The Lorelei, "Donny" by Yah Supreme
LINER NOTES: Donny Osmond has six children: Brandon, Christopher, Glen, Jeremy, Joshua, and Donald.

Edgar

ENGLISH: Wealthy spearman

ROCK AND ROLL: Weaves a great tale, dark, haunted, has a voracious appetite

RELATED ARTISTS/SONGS: Edgar Meyer (Nickel Creek), Edgar Sampson, Edgar Winter (The Edgar Winter Group), "Edgar" by Butthole Surfers, "Edgar Allan Poe" by Lou Reed, "J. Edgar" by Ry Cooder, "Edgar" by Lunachicks

LINER NOTES: Edgar Winter arranged and performed *Planet Earth*, an album with lyrics and music written by Scientology founder L. Ron Hubbard.

Edward

ENGLISH: Wealthy guardian

ROCK AND ROLL: Quirky, vivacious, a good friend

RELATED ARTISTS/SONGS: Edward Bear, Edward Patten (Gladys Knight & the Pips), Edward Sharpe & the Magnetic Zeros, "Poor Edward" by Tom Waits, "Edward the Bear" by The Damned, "Jamming with Edward" by The Rolling Stones, "Edward" by Burl Ives

LINER NOTES: Canadian rock group Edward Bear is named for Winnie the Pooh, whose real name, according to A. A. Milne, is Edward Bear.

Ferdinand

GERMAN: Safe journey

ROCK AND ROLL: Intellectual, prim and proper, a master of disguise

RELATED ARTISTS/SONGS: Ferdinand "Jelly Roll Morton" Lamothe, Franz Ferdinand, "Ferdinand" by Caravan, "The Death of Ferdinand de Saussure" by The Magnetic Fields, "Ferdinand the Imposter" by The Band

LINER NOTES: The Band's song "Ferdinand the Imposter" refers to Ferdinand Demara, a master con man who was also the basis of the 1961 movie *The Great Imposter*.

Fernando

SPANISH: Adventurer

ROCK AND ROLL: Brave, a young soldier

RELATED ARTISTS/SONGS: Fernando Gama, Fernando Mon, "Fernando" by ABBA, "Fernando" by The Baseball Project

LINER NOTES: ABBA's "Fernando" is about two old army comrades telling stories, an idea Björn Ulvaeus came up with while at his summer house in Mexico.

Franklin

ENGLISH: Freeman, land owner

ROCK AND ROLL: A good influence, an optimist

RELATED ARTISTS/SONGS: Big Franklin, "Franklin" by Paramore,

"Joe Franklin" by David Isay, "Franklin" by Katell Keinig, "Franklin's Tower" by The Grateful Dead
LINER NOTES: There's a restaurant in Albany, New York, named "Franklin's Tower" after The Grateful Dead song.

Frederick

GERMAN: Peaceful ruler
ROCK AND ROLL: A stud, can rock a mustache, protective
RELATED ARTISTS/SONGS: Frederick Heath (Johnny Kidd and the Pirates), Frederick "Toots" Hibbert, "Frederick" by Patti Smith, "The Story of Cruel Frederick" by The Tiger Lillies, "Fisticuffs in Frederick Street" by The Toy Dolls
LINER NOTES: Patti Smith's song "Frederick" was dedicated to her husband, Fred "Sonic" Smith.

Gary

GERMAN: Spear-holder
ROCK AND ROLL: The class clown, doofy but lovable
RELATED ARTISTS/SONGS: Gary Glitter, Gary Moore (Thin Lizzy), Gary Numan, "Gary" by Phil Woods, "Gary" by Alter Ego, "Gary's Notebook" by Lee Morgan, "Gary's Theme" by Bill Evans
LINER NOTES: When Gary Glitter was developing a name for his persona, he worked backwards from Z—other options included Terry Tinsel and Vicky Vomit.

Giles

GREEK: Kid, young goat
ROCK AND ROLL: Old-fashioned, cautious, on the uptight side
RELATED ARTISTS/SONGS: Giles, Giles and Fripp; Giles Martin; "Giles Farnaby's Dream" by the Penguin Orchestra; "Giles" by Unearth; "Giles" by Evelyn Glennie
LINER NOTES: After Peter Giles left the band Giles, Giles and Fripp, the remaining members went on to form King Crimson.

Hamilton

ENGLISH: Treeless hill
ROCK AND ROLL: Formal, old-fashioned, amiable
RELATED ARTISTS/SONGS: Hamilton Bohannon, Chico Hamilton, Roy Hamilton, "Hamilton" by Chris Thompson, "Hamilton" by Cex
LINER NOTES: Disco producer Hamilton Bohannon dedicated his dance record "Dance Your Ass Off" to Jesus, noting that "the word 'ass' is not used here in the sense of profanity."

Jagger

ENGLISH: Carter
ROCK AND ROLL: Cool, glamorous, has serious swagger

RELATED ARTISTS/SONGS: Mick Jagger, "Jagger" by Shawn Lee, "Jagger '67" by Infadels

LINER NOTES: Mick Jagger auditioned for the role of Frank-N-Furter in the film adaptation of *The Rocky Horror Show*, but lost out to Tim Curry.

Jethro

HEBREW: Friend of God

ROCK AND ROLL: Attentive to detail, intelligent, has a country twang

RELATED ARTISTS/SONGS: Jethro Burns, Jethro Tull, Homer & Jethro, "Jethro" by Johnny Bush, "Jethro" by Josh Fix

LINER NOTES: The Jethro Tull song "Aqualung" was inspired by guitarist Ian Anderson's wife's amateur photography of homeless men.

Julio

SPANISH: Variation of Julius, young

ROCK AND ROLL: Mischevious, rambunctious, fun to have around

RELATED ARTISTS/SONGS: Julio Iglesias, "Me and Julio Down by the Schoolyard" by Paul Simon, "Julio" by Boom Boom Kid, "Julio Iglesias" by Butthole Surfers

LINER NOTES: Paul Simon made a video for "Me and Julio Down By the Schoolyard" in 1988, featuring a rap intro by Big Daddy Kane and Biz Markie and a cameo by baseball player Mickey Mantle.

Kashka

NIGERIAN: Friendly

ROCK AND ROLL: Brave, loving

RELATED ARTISTS/SONGS: "Kashka from Baghdad" by Kate Bush, "Kashka" by Ballycotton,

LINER NOTES: Kate Bush wrote "Kashka from Baghdad" about a gay couple who live together happily, despite vicious remarks sent their way.

Nash

ENGLISH: Near the ash tree

ROCK AND ROLL: Loyal, tuned-in

RELATED ARTISTS/SONGS: Graham Nash (Crosby, Stills & Nash), Kate Nash, "Nash" by Moby, "Nash" by Fairmount Girls

LINER NOTES: Graham Nash, who left The Hollies to join Crosby, Stills & Nash, wrote the song "Our House" about his love affair with Joni Mitchell.

Nigel

LATIN: Dark-haired

ROCK AND ROLL: Happy, quiet, hardworking

RELATED ARTISTS/SONGS: Nigel Dixon (Whirlwind), Nigel Douglas,

Nigel Kennedy, "Nigel" by the 88, "Making Plans for Nigel" by XTC, "Nigel" by Pavement, "Nigel" by Hepcat

LINER NOTES: Fictional heavy metal band Spinal Tap's Nigel Tufnel's insistence on having Oreos without frosting is inspired by Van Halen's rider, which required a bowl of M&M's "without the brown ones."

Ono

JAPANESE: Small field

ROCK AND ROLL: Artistic, aloof, controversial

RELATED ARTISTS/SONGS: Yoko Ono, "Ono" by R. Stevie Moore, "Ono" by King's X, "Ono" by Devo, "Ono" by Wasteland

LINER NOTES: John Lennon and Yoko's first personal interaction was when Ono handed Lennon a card that read "Breathe" at her art show.

Osmond

ENGLISH: Divine protector

ROCK AND ROLL: Sweet, wholesome, clean-cut

RELATED ARTISTS/SONGS: Osmond Wright, Donny Osmond, Marie Osmond, "The Osmonds" by Denim, "Hey Donny Osmond (Why Do You Walk That Way)" by The Seapods

LINER NOTES: The frenzy that the Osmonds inspired in their fans was called "Osmondmania" in the media; they originally started performing in order to raise money for hearing aids for fellow members of their church.

Pip

ENGLISH: Form of Phillip, lover of horses

ROCK AND ROLL: Cute, scrappy, bright

RELATED ARTISTS/SONGS: Pip Paxton, Pip Pyle (National Health), Gladys Knight & the Pips, "Pip" by The Freeze, "Cheerio & Toodle Pip" by The Toy Dolls

LINER NOTES: At his funeral, prog-rock drummer Pip Pyle's children decorated his coffin with the stickers of Pyle's favorite bands.

Quince

ENGLISH SPICE NAME

ROCK AND ROLL: Suave, witty, smart

RELATED ARTISTS/SONGS: Ian "Quince" Parker (The Tom Robinson Band), "Quince" by Count Basie, "Rinsing Quince" by Aphrodite, "Quince" by Sonny Stitt

LINER NOTES: After Quince Parker left The Tom Robinson Band, he went on to play keyboards in The Hollies.

Reginald

LATIN: Advisor

ROCK AND ROLL: Dextrous, multitalented, affable

RELATED ARTISTS/SONGS: Reginald Milton & the Soul Jets, Reginald Dixon, "Reginald's Groove" by Cosmic Kids, "The Leginald of Reginald" by Lords, "Reginald Denny" by Bill Hicks

LINER NOTES: Elton John's real name is Reginald Dwight. His stage name is in homage to musicians Elton Dean and Long John Baldry.

Rex

LATIN: King

ROCK AND ROLL: Intense, smart, powerful

RELATED ARTISTS/SONGS: Rex Gob, T-Rex, Rex Allen, "Rex" by Darkthrone, "Rex" by Kevin Henry, "Rex" by The Terrors

LINER NOTES: The wave of popularity inspired by the band T-Rex was known as "T-Rextasy."

Roger

GERMAN: Famous with a spear

ROCK AND ROLL: Unconventional, inventive

RELATED ARTISTS/SONGS: Roger Taylor (Duran Duran), Roger Daltrey (The Who), Roger Waters (Pink Floyd), "Roger" by Dag Nasty, "Roger" by The Mob, "Roger and Out" by Neil Young

LINER NOTES: When a Roger Waters–fronted Pink Floyd played at London's Crystal Bowl Palace in 1970, the volume was so loud that several fish in the lake nearby died.

Ross

GERMAN: Horse

ROCK AND ROLL: Strong, cerebral, theatrical

RELATED ARTISTS/SONGS: Diana Ross, James Ross, Ross Valory (Journey), "Ross" by Stuck in a Groove, "Ross" by Chris Lawhorn

LINER NOTES: Journey's bassist Ross Valory along with band members George, Neal, and Gregg originally performed as a backup band called The Golden Gate Rhythm Section.

Ry, Rye

ENGLISH: Variation of Ryland, rye field

ROCK AND ROLL: Philosophical, eccentric, has many interests

RELATED ARTISTS/SONGS: Ry Cooder, "Ry Ry's Song" by Glassjaw, "Ry Cooder" by Tortoise

LINER NOTES: Slide guitarist Ry Cooder first gained fame as a member of Captain Beefheart and the Magic Band; he later sat in as a session musician on The Rolling Stones' *Let It Bleed* album.

Shiloh, Shilo

HEBREW: He who is to be sent

ROCK AND ROLL: Friendly, a dreamer, playful

RELATED ARTISTS/SONGS: The Shilohs, Shiloh, Ras Shiloh, "Shiloh" by Magnolia Electric Co., "Shiloh Town" by Mark Lanegan, "Gone

to Shiloh" by Elton John and Leon Russell, "Shilo" by Neil Diamond, "Shiloh" by Buju Banton
LINER NOTES: Neil Diamond wrote the song "Shilo" in honor of his childhood imaginary friend.

Stu

ENGLISH: Variation of Stuart, guardian of the house
ROCK AND ROLL: Laid-back, fun, loves dancing
RELATED ARTISTS/SONGS: Stu Goldberg, Stu Cook (Creedence Clearwater Revival), Stu Boy King (The Dictators), "Stu" by Superdrag, "Boogie with Stu" by System of a Down, "Stu" by Chico Hamilton
LINER NOTES: The original title of Led Zeppelin's "Boogie with Stu" was "Sloppy Drunk"; it was named after road manager and pianist Ian Stewart's wacky dance moves.

Sylvester

LATIN: Woodland dweller
ROCK AND ROLL: Dramatic, brash, bright
RELATED ARTISTS/SONGS: Sylvester James, Sylvester Staline, "Sylvester" by Sly & the Family Stone, "Sylvester" by Supervixen
LINER NOTES: Disco singer Sylvester James, sometimes called "The Real Queen of Disco," sang backup for Aretha Franklin, Patti LaBelle, and Sarah Dash.

Timmy

ENGLISH: Variation of Timothy, honoring God
ROCK AND ROLL: Suave, spunky, a hustler
RELATED ARTISTS/SONGS: Timmy Thomas, Timmy Curran, "Timmy the Turtle" by NOFX, "Timmy" by The Residents, "Timmy" by Cowboy Mouth, "Forgot About Timmy" by Dr. Dre, "Timmy" by Meg & Dia
LINER NOTES: Before singer Timmy Thomas broke out with his 1972 hit "Why Can't We Live Together," he was part of a group called Phillip & the Faithfuls.

Tom

ARAMAIC: Form of Thomas, twin
ROCK AND ROLL: Sharp, witty, wiley
RELATED ARTISTS/SONGS: Tom Petty, Tom Waits, Tom Jones, "Tom Sawyer" by Rush, "Tom's Diner" by Suzanne Vega, "Tom" by Art Blakey, "Tom" by The Ids
LINER NOTES: Tom Waits is a close friend of the Coppolas: He met his wife, Kathleen Brennan, while working on the set of Francis Ford Coppola's *One from the Heart* and he performed at Sofia Coppola and Spike Jonze's wedding.

Tristan

CELTIC: Tumultuous
ROCK AND ROLL: Lively, troubled, beloved
RELATED ARTISTS/SONGS: Tristan Prettyman, "Tristan" by Patrick Wolf, "Tristan" by Dead Can Dance, "Tristan" by Pat Britt
LINER NOTES: Before forming Steely Dan, Donald Fagen played with Jay and the Americans under the pseudonym Tristan Fabiani.

Warren

GERMAN: Enclosure
ROCK AND ROLL: Witty, dry, smart
RELATED ARTISTS/SONGS: Warren Zevon, Warren Moore (The Miracles), Warren G, "Warren" by Slint, "Warren" by Gary Young, "Warren" by Jessica Bailiff
LINER NOTES: Canadian minor-league baseball team the Werewolves is named after Warren Zevon's song "Werewolves of London"; their mascot is named Warren Z. Von.

Wolfgang

GERMAN: Wolf of victory
ROCK AND ROLL: Eccentric, commanding, powerful
RELATED ARTISTS/SONGS: Wolfgang Flur (Kraftwerk), Wolfgang Van Halen, "Wolfgang" by Elliott Brood, "Wolfgang" by Pete Droge
LINER NOTES: Kraftwerk musician Wolfgang Flur built most of the group's stage equipment in his home workshop; he also published an autobiography in 2000 called *I Was a Robot*.

Zowie, Zowee

ENGLISH EXCLAMATION: Extraordainary
ROCK AND ROLL: Influential, interesting, eccentric
RELATED ARTISTS/SONGS: Zowie Fleury, "Wowie Zowie" by Frank Zappa, "Uncle Zowie" by Ill Bill, "Zowie Pop" by John Davis
LINER NOTES: David Bowie wrote the song "Kooks" for his son Duncan, who now goes by his middle name, Zowie.

Stage Name to Real Name Quiz

The most famous rock musicians didn't always start out with the commanding name that we know them best by. Take the quiz to see if you can figure out the name that appears on these rockers' birth certificates.

1. Bono
2. Alice Cooper
3. David Bowie
4. Sting
5. Joey Ramone
6. Joe Strummer
7. Meat Loaf
8. Elvis Costello
9. Jello Biafra
10. Billy Idol
11. Marilyn Manson

(a) Declan McManus
(b) Gordon Sumner
(c) John Mellor
(d) Vincent Furnier
(e) Brian Warner
(f) William Broad
(g) Paul Hewson
(h) David Jones
(i) Marvin Aday
(j) Jeffrey Hyman
(k) Eric Boucher

Rock Last Names as First Names

One way to commemorate your favorite rock star and give your baby a unique name in one fell swoop is going the last-name-as-first-name route. There's some instant swagger in choices like Byrne, Eno, or Gillespie, not to mention that your child would be in good company. Many celebrities have started going that way, from Oasis' Liam Gallagher, who named his son Lennon, to Tommy Lee and Pamela Anderson, who named one of their sons the double-whammy Dylan Jagger. Though they skew masculine, many of these can also make edgy girl's names. But the choices don't stop at Cash or Marley. Here are some musical last names ripe for consideration as first or middle names:

Albini	Donovan	Manzie	Reed
Baez	Ellington	Marley	Rollins
Barrett	Eno	Mayfield	Seeger
Basie	Everly	Mercury	Simone
Bechet	Garcia	Mingus	Spector
Bolan	Gillespie	Montgomery	Strummer
Bowie	Guthrie	Moore	Tatum
Buckley	Halen	Morrison	Taylor
Byrne	Harrison	Morrissey	Tillman
Cale	Hendrix	Orbison	Turner
Calloway	Holly	Page	Vega
Carter	Jagger	Palmer	Wainwright
Cash	Jett	Parker	Walker
Clapton	Joplin	Parton	Yorke
Coltrane	Judd	Pollard	Zappa
Costello	Kennedy	Presley	Zevon
Cyrus	Lennon	Prine	Zorn
Davis	Malkmus	Ramone	

Disco
Baby Names

Disco has long gotten a bad rap among rock fans, but nowadays those white suits and DISCO SUCKS T-shirts are long gone. Disco has gone so far out that it's in again, embraced by a new generation of hip-hop artists, dance punks, and indie bands for its opulent style and up-all-night spirit. Below, a list of disco names for a baby whose first shoes will be platforms.

GIRLS

Alicia	Melba
Alma	Merrilee
Anacostia	Narada
Anita	Odyssey
Asha	Persia
Celi	Rahni
Chanson	Retta
Cissy	Rozalin
Croisette	Samona
Dalida	Sharon
Esmerelda	Sheila
France	Sumeria
Gerri	Teena
Grace	Trini
Irena	Venise
Labelle	Yahna
Lavette	Zulema
Loleatta	

BOYS

Adriano	Idris
Apollo	Isley
Ashford	Jerry
Baker	Lew
Barry	Lionel
Bebu	Manu
Bruni	Maynard
Cedar	McRae
Cy	Moco
Dalton	Melvin
Dunn	Milan
Felipe	Ojay
Gibb	Patrick
Gino	Percy
Goody	Vince
Herb	Zager

WORLD TOUR: Spain

Spanish music—from Flamenco to Eurodisco—has long been influential on the shape of global pop music, so it only makes sense that Spanish names like Carmen, Javier, and Carlos have become favorites in the rock community. Check out the names below for something with a little spice to it:

GIRLS

Alicia (*Noble*/Determined, skillful)
Carmen (*Song*/Gentle, passionate)
Catalina (*Pure*/A sunny escape, a great hope)
Concha (*Conception*/Sultry, graceful)
Elvira (Fair/A bombshell, light on her feet)
Lolita (*Sorrowful*/Precocious, alluring, a VIP)
Matraca (*Noisemaker*/Intrepid, honest, passionate)
Mercedes (*Gracious lady*/Humble, has a big heart)
Vida (Life/Ebullient, amiable, happy)

BOYS

Cisco (*Freeman*/A rambler, politically active)
Garcia (*Strong*/Laid-back, earthy)
Lorenzo (*From Laurentium*/Adventurous, high-spirited, ebullient)
Manuel (*God is with us*/Responsible, friendly, punctual)
Otha (*Singer of spirituals*/Clever, kindhearted)
Pablo (*Small*/Artistic, suave, a ladies' man)
Perez (*To blossom*/Popular, magnetic)
Ramone (*Wise protector*/Rowdy, prefers tight pants)
Tico (*Little brother*/Mischievous, smart, curious)

Heavy Metal Heroes and Hard-Rockin' Honeys

Hard rock names tend to be on the more extreme end of the spectrum, more Ozzy and Blaze than John and William. But tucked in between those Lemmys and Slashes, there are more traditional choices, like Bon, Cooper, and Abigail, and unique names, like Azrael and Tarja, that have that heavy metal energy without the overly aggressive edge.

GIRLS

Abigail

HEBREW: Father's joy
ROCK AND ROLL: Intelligent, mysterious, ethereal
RELATED ARTISTS/SONGS: Abigail Williams, Abigail's Ghost, "Abigail" by King Diamond, "Abigail" by Motionless in White, "Abigail, Belle of Kilronan" by The Magnetic Fields, "Abigail" by Tryst, "Abigail" by The Corries
LINER NOTES: Black metal band Abigail Williams is named after the character of the same name in Arthur Miller's *The Crucible*.

Alice

GREEK: Honest
ROCK AND ROLL: Curious, adventurous, usually refers to the main character of Lewis Carroll's *Alice in Wonderland*
RELATED ARTISTS/SONGS: "Alice" by Tom Waits, "Alice" by Moby, "Alice" by Stevie Nicks, "All the Girls Love Alice" by Elton John, "Go Ask Alice" by Jefferson Airplane

"Baby, all I think about is Alice."
—TOM WAITS

Amber

ENGLISH: Gem
ROCK AND ROLL: Friendly but flighty, entrancing
RELATED ARTISTS/SONGS: "Amber" by 311, "Sweet Amber" by Metallica, "Amber Changing" by Rise Against, "At Amber" by Morrissey
LINER NOTES: Many fans surmise that the Metallica song "Sweet Amber" is about James Hetfield's past overindulgence with beer.

Anette, Annette

FRENCH: Variation of Ann, the Lord has favored me
ROCK AND ROLL: Innocent, lucky, elegant
RELATED ARTISTS/SONGS: Anette Olzon (Nightwish), Annette Hanshaw, Annette Funicello, "Anette" by Francis Lai, "Anette" by Margot Hielscher, "My Sweet Annette" by Drive-By Truckers, "Annette" by Tom Russell
LINER NOTES: Goth metal singer Anette Olzon has two children with Pain bassist Johan Husgafvel: Seth and Nemo.

Ash

ENGLISH PLANT NAME
ROCK AND ROLL: Sultry, wordly, clever
RELATED ARTISTS/SONGS: Ash, Ash Koley, Ash Bowie, "Only Ash Remains" by Necrophagist, "Ash & Debris" by Paradise Lost, "White Ash" by The Pillows
LINER NOTES: Before forming her self-titled band, singer Ash Koley sang with a Canadian ABBA tribute band called Supertroopers.

Asia

ENGLISH PLACE NAME
ROCK AND ROLL: Exotic, interesting, aloof
RELATED ARTISTS/SONGS: Asia, Asia Cruise, Asia Nitollano (Pussycat Dolls), "Asia" by Salem, "Asia" by Alex Neri, "Asia" by Paul Motian, "Asia" by Defunkt
LINER NOTES: Though Geoff Downes and John Payne are the most consistent members of supergroup Asia, the band has included twenty-six members over its thirty-year tenure, from bands like King Crimson, Yes, Uriah Heep, and Roxy Music.

Cherie

FRENCH: Variation of Cher, dear
ROCK AND ROLL: Sweet but saucy, a wild child
RELATED ARTISTS/SONGS: Cherie Currie (The Runaways), "Cherie" by Nat King Cole, "Cherie" by Bobby Rydell, "Cherie" by Billy Idol
LINER NOTES: The Runaways' lead singer Cherie Currie now works as a self-described "chainsaw artist."

Chevelle, Chevella

FRENCH: Form of Chevalier, horsewoman
ROCK AND ROLL: Trusty, powerful, glitzy
RELATED ARTISTS/SONGS: Chevelle, Chevela Vargas, The Mighty Chevelles, "Chevelle" by Drew Gress, "Chevelle" by The Curtains
LINER NOTES: Alternative metal trio Chevelle was named for the Chevrolet Chevelle, a car that the drummer's father wanted.

Christine, Christene

GREEK: Feminine variant of Christian, anointed follower
ROCK AND ROLL: Colorful, multifaceted, irresistible; a devil in disguise
RELATED ARTISTS/SONGS: Christine Lavin, Christine McVie (Fleetwood Mac), The Christines, "Christine Sixteen" by Kiss, "Christine" by Hall & Oates, "Meet Christine" by Elton John, "Christine's Tune" by The Flying Burrito Brothers, "Christine" by Motorhead

"She moves like a rattlesnake made out of razorblades."
—MOTORHEAD

Cinderella

FRENCH: Little ash girl
ROCK AND ROLL: A diamond in the rough, glamorous, a girly girl
RELATED ARTISTS/SONGS: Cinderella, "Cinderella" by The Sonics, "Cinderella" by Britney Spears, "Cinderella" by Firefall, "Cinderella" by Shakira, "Cinderella's Big Score" by Sonic Youth
LINER NOTES: Glam metal band Cinderella got their break when Jon Bon Jovi saw them play at a club in Philadelphia; he was so impressed that he called his record company after their set.

Clarissa, Clarisse, Clarice

ITALIAN: Variation of Clare, luminous
ROCK AND ROLL: Precocious, sharp, but has friends in low places
RELATED ARTISTS/SONGS: "Clarisse" by Venom, "Ode to Clarissa" by Queens of the Stone, "Sister Clarissa" by Michael Smith, "Spunky and Clarissa" by Bela Fleck and the Flecktones, "Clarice" by America
LINER NOTES: Clarissa of the Nickelodeon series *Clarissa Explains It All* had a They Might Be Giants poster hanging in her room. In one episode, she also ducks out of family dinner to go to a Pearl Jam concert.

Dana

ENGLISH: Dweller of the valley
ROCK AND ROLL: Literary, might have magic powers
RELATED ARTISTS/SONGS: Dana Fuchs, Dana Colley (Morphine), Dana Vicek (The Lounge Lizards), "Letter to Dana" by Sonata Arctica, "O, Dana" by Okkervil River, "Song for Dana Plato" by The Mountain Goats, "Dana" by Renata Zero, "O, Dana" by Big Star
LINER NOTES: The Mountain Goats' "Song for Dana Plato" was a tribute to the *Diff'rent Strokes* child star.

Darby

NORSE: Deer farm
ROCK AND ROLL: Independent, fierce, athletic
RELATED ARTISTS/SONGS: Darby Crash (The Germs), Darby Mills (Headpins), "Darby's Song" by Lucero, "Germs Burn for Darby Crash" by The Germs, "Darby's Castle" by Kris Kristofferson
LINER NOTES: While not out on tour, former Headpins vocalist Darby Mills is a tae kwon do teacher.

Delilah

HEBREW: Temptress
ROCK AND ROLL: Irresistible, sweet, loud, a city girl
RELATED ARTISTS/SONGS: Delilah Lee Lewis, "Delilah" by Queen, "Hey There Delilah" by Plain White T's, "Delilah" by Tom Jones, "Beautiful Delilah" by Chuck Berry, "Delilah" by The Dresden Dolls
LINER NOTES: Freddie Mercury wrote the song "Delilah" for his favorite cat.

Etty

ENGLISH: Form of Esther, star
ROCK AND ROLL: Petite, practical, saucy
RELATED ARTISTS/SONGS: Etty Farrell, Etti Ankri, "Etty" by Savage Progress, "Etty Paya" by Jamrud
LINER NOTES: Etty Farrell, who met her husband Perry while working as a dancer for Jane's Addiction, has two children, Hezron Wolfgang and Izzadore Bravo.

Felicity

ENGLISH: Happiness
ROCK AND ROLL: A great friend, dreamy, wishy-washy
RELATED ARTISTS/SONGS: Felicity Urquhart, "Felicity" by Fred Neil, "Felicity" by Orange Juice, "Misdemeanor Dream Felicity" by Skid Row, "Felicity" by The Wedding Present, "Felicity" by Cleaners from Venus
LINER NOTES: "Misdemeanor Dream Felicity" is the only Skid Row song on which Thin Lizzy's Phil Lynott appears.

Gitane

FRENCH: Gypsy woman
ROCK AND ROLL: Wild, a traveler, lovely
RELATED ARTISTS/SONGS: Gitane DeMone (Christian Death), "Gitane" by Dalida, "Gitane" by Terry Lee Brown Jr., "Gitane" by Luis Mariano
LINER NOTES: Christian Death's Gitane DeMone has two children with bandmate Valor Kand, Sevan and Zara; Zara plays with Gitane in her new band, The Crystelles.

Janie

ENGLISH: Form of Jane, God is merciful
ROCK AND ROLL: Free-spirited, outspoken, should keep away from firearms
RELATED ARTISTS/SONGS: "Janie's Got a Gun" by Aerosmith, "Janie Jones" by The Clash, "Janie Runaway" by The Clash, "Song for Janie" by Tim Buckley, "Janie" by Off with Their Heads
LINER NOTES: Steven Tyler wrote the song "Janie's Got a Gun" about a friend of his—the original title was "Danny's Got a Gun"—but changed the title to avoid embarrassing him.

Jenna

ENGLISH: Variation of Jennifer, fair spirit
ROCK AND ROLL: The cute girl next door, casual and clever
RELATED ARTISTS/SONGS: Jenna von Oy, Jenna Piccolo, Vains of Jenna, "Jenna Bush Army" by Nerf Herder, "Jenna Jenna" by The Chavos, "Jenna" by Riverboat Gamblers, "Jenna" by King's X, "Jenna" by John Frank
LINER NOTES: Before being recruited as the lead singer of Vixen, Jenna Piccolo sang with the bands NoNo BadDog and Belladonna.

Jett

AMERICAN: Fast
ROCK AND ROLL: Tough, brash, confident, independent
RELATED ARTISTS/SONGS: Joan Jett, Otis Jett, The Jetts, "Jett" by Plasma Blast
LINER NOTES: Joan Jett so idolized rocker Suzi Quatro that she used to wear wooden platform shoes with Quatro's name carved into the sides.

Kat, Cat

GREEK: Short for Catherine, unblemished
ROCK AND ROLL: Cool, detached, in the know
RELATED ARTISTS/SONGS: Kat Bjelland (Babes in Toyland), Kat Kraft (Vixen), Cat Power (Chan Marshall), "Honky Cat" by Elton John, "China Cat Sunflower" by The Grateful Dead, "Cat" by The Sugarcubes, "Cat" by Billy Joel
LINER NOTES: Babes in Toyland's Kat Bjelland is close friends with

Courtney Love; before Hole formed, the two started a band called Sugar Babydoll.

Kirsten

DANISH: Variation of Christina, faithful
ROCK AND ROLL: Willowy, loves nature and metal bands
RELATED ARTISTS/SONGS: Kirsten Easdale, Kirsten Rosenberg (The Iron Maidens), "Kirsten Dunst" by Pivot, "Kirsten Is a Machine" by Tiger Tunes, "Kirsten" by The Heaves
LINER NOTES: The Iron Maidens' singer Kirsten Rosenberg owned an all-vegan bakery in Washington, D.C., before striking out on a musical career.

Lee

ENGLISH: Pasture
ROCK AND ROLL: Glitzy, glamorous, a metal queen
RELATED ARTISTS/SONGS: Lee Aaron, "Lee" by The Detroit Emeralds, "Lee" by Vieux Diop, "Lee" by Moxy Fruvous
LINER NOTES: Heavy metal chanteuse Lee Aaron has two children, a daughter named Angella and a son named Jett Forrester Cody.

Lillian, Lilian

FRENCH: Lily
ROCK AND ROLL: A heartbreaker, sultry, sweet
RELATED ARTISTS/SONGS: Lillian Axe, "Lillian" by +44, "Lillan" by Depeche Mode, "Lillian" by Nat King Cole, "Lillian" by Link Wray
LINER NOTES: Lillian Axe was the first metal band inducted into the Louisiana Music Hall of Fame; their first album was produced by Ratt's Robbin Crosby.

Lita

ENGLISH: Form of Rosalita or Carmelita, little one
ROCK AND ROLL: A bombshell, talented, sultry
RELATED ARTISTS/SONGS: Lita Ford, "Lita" by Nurses, "Lita" by Lou Christie, "Lita" by Lars Hollmer, "Lita" by Sam Manning
LINER NOTES: Runaways guitarist Lita Ford's manager in the 1980s was Sharon Osborne.

Liv

ENGLISH: Form of Olivia, olive tree
ROCK AND ROLL: Cheerful, sweet, pretty
RELATED ARTISTS/SONGS: Liv Jagrell (Sister Sin), Liv Kristine, "Ret Liv Dead" by Teenage Fanclub, "Liv I Liv" by Mr. Brown
LINER NOTES: Steven Tyler's daughter Liv was named after the actress Liv Ullman; Bebe Buell, Liv's mother, was inspired by a picture of the actress on a cover of *TV Guide*.

Lorraine

FRENCH: From the province of Lorraine
ROCK AND ROLL: A fiery brunette, resourceful, kind
RELATED ARTISTS/SONGS: Lorraine Lewis (Femme Fatale), "Sweet Lorraine" by Nat King Cole, "Lorraine" by Bad Manners, "Sweet Lorraine" by Uriah Heep, "Darling Lorraine" by Paul Simon, "Lorraine" by Toto
LINER NOTES: After Femme Fatale, Lorraine Lewis formed a band with Vixen drummer Roxy Petrucci called Roktopus, labeling the duo "the desperate housewives of rock."

Lucretia

LATIN: Wealthy
ROCK AND ROLL: Eloquent, tail-shakin', a heartbreaker, party animal
RELATED ARTISTS/SONGS: "Lucretia" by Megadeth, "Lucretia" by Sisters of Mercy, "Lucretia Mac Evil" by Blood, Sweat & Tears, "Lucretia" by Lucid Nation
LINER NOTES: Megadeth's "Lucretia" is the story of the Roman historical figure Lucretia's ghost living in the singer's attic.

Maja

GERMAN: Variation of Mary, beloved lady
ROCK AND ROLL: Graceful, has a big heart
RELATED ARTISTS/SONGS: Maja Ivarsson (The Sounds), Maja Bladdan, "Maja's Song" by Sophie Zelmani, "Maja" by Cantoma, "Maja" by Michael Brecker
LINER NOTES: The Sounds' lead singer Maja Ivarsson has a tattoo of Modesty Blaise, a 1960s British comic character, on her right forearm; she is also an accomplished kickboxer.

Marta

FRENCH: Variation of Martha, lady
ROCK AND ROLL: Smart, well traveled, loves nature
RELATED ARTISTS/SONGS: Marta Peterson (Bleeding Through), Marta Sebestyen, "Marta's Song" by Deep Forest, "Marta" by Percy Faith, "Marta" by Placido Domingo
LINER NOTES: Keyboardist Marta Peterson's metalcore band Bleeding Through's name derived from the idea of universal equality because "we all bleed the same."

Mia

ENGLISH: Form of Maria, our lady
ROCK AND ROLL: Good-natured, cute, generous
RELATED ARTISTS/SONGS: Mia Rose, Mia Zapata (The Gits), "Me and Mia" by Ted Leo and the Pharmacists, "Mia" by Aerosmith, "Mia" by Gorki, "Mia" by Chevelle
LINER NOTES: Aerosmith's Steven Tyler wrote the lullaby "Mia" for his daughter.

Miri

HEBREW: Variation of Miriam, wished-for child
ROCK AND ROLL: A nature lover, naturally pretty, magnetic
RELATED ARTISTS/SONGS: Miri Milman (System Divide), Miri Ben-Ari, "Miri It Is" by Forefather, "Miri" by Alpha Blondy
LINER NOTES: Death metal band System Divide started out as a project by then-newlyweds Miri Milman and Sven de Caluwé.

Otep

EGYPTIAN: Creative offering
ROCK AND ROLL: Offbeat, artistic, fun-loving
RELATED ARTISTS/SONGS: Otep Shamaya, "Otep" by The Switch
LINER NOTES: Otep Shamaya, lead singer of the band Otep, is also a slam poet; she published her first poetry volume, *Little Sins*, in 2007.

Pearl

ENGLISH: Gem
ROCK AND ROLL: Beautiful but humble, loving, unstoppable
RELATED ARTISTS/SONGS: Pearl Jam, Pearl Aday, Pearl Bailey, *Pearl* by Janis Joplin, "Pearl" by Björk, "Pearl" by Stevie Wonder, "Pearl" by Flo & Eddie, "Pearl" by Katy Perry
LINER NOTES: Singer Pearl Aday, Meat Loaf's adopted daughter, is married to Anthrax guitarist Scott Ian.

Pia

LATIN: Devout
ROCK AND ROLL: Sensitive, loving, delicate
RELATED ARTISTS/SONGS: Pia Miaocco (Vixen), Pia Tassinari, Pia Toscano, "Pia" by Stanley Turrentine, "Pia" by Cousteau, "Pia" by Gunnar Johnson
LINER NOTES: Former Vixen bassist Pia Maiocco has two children with guitarist Steve Vai, Fire and Julian Angel.

Rosie

ENGLISH PLANT NAME: Variation of Rose
ROCK AND ROLL: Voluptuous, lovely, optimistic
RELATED ARTISTS/SONGS: Rosie (CocoRosie), "Rosie" by Tom Waits, "Rosie" by Rod Stewart, "Rosie" by Jackson Browne, "Rosie" by Eric Bogle, "Whole Lotta Rosie" by AC/DC
LINER NOTES: AC/DC's "Whole Lotta Rosie" is about Bon Scott's Australian fling with a larger woman.

Serena

LATIN: Tranquil
ROCK AND ROLL: Shy, a poet, courageous
RELATED ARTISTS/SONGS: Serena Maneesh, Serena Ryder, "Serena"

by James Galway, "Serena" by Rodney Jones, "Serena" by Duncan Sheik, "Serena" by Greg Burk Trio, "Oh Serena" by The Distillers

LINER NOTES: Norwegian group Serena Maheesh was named after the Norweigian words for "veil" and "audience," to describe their hazy, distortion-heavy sound.

Shirley

ENGLISH: Bright meadow

ROCK AND ROLL: A daredevil and intellectual, a good companion

RELATED ARTISTS/SONGS: Shirley Bassey, Shirley Collins, Shirley Manson (Garbage), "Shirley" by Billy Bragg, "Shirley" by L7, "Shirley" by The Strangers

LINER NOTES: Garbage's singer Shirley Manson played a Terminator in the short-lived television series *Terminator: The Sarah Connor Chronicles.*

Simone

HEBREW: Form of Simon, one who hears

ROCK AND ROLL: Sophisticated, stylish, elegant

RELATED ARTISTS/SONGS: Simone Denny, Simone Egeriis, Simone Simons (Epica), "Simone" by Elvin Jones, "Simone" by Archie Shepp, "Simone" by The Stone Roses, "Simone" by Oregon, "Simone" by Boz Scaggs, "Simone" by Frank Foster

"Oh, Simone, to hold you, dance you into the night."
—BOZ SCAGGS

Susie, Suzie, Suzi

HEBREW: Form of Susan, lily

ROCK AND ROLL: Multitalented, a heartbreaker, loves dancing

RELATED ARTISTS/SONGS: Suzi Quatro, "Susie" by John Lee Hooker, "Susie Q" by Creedence Clearwater Revival, "Wake Up Little Susie" by The Everly Brothers, "Suzy Lee" by The White Stripes, "Suzy Is a Headbanger" by The Ramones

LINER NOTES: Glam rock idol Suzi Quatro also starred in *Happy Days,* as Leather Tuscadero, Fonzie's girlfriend's younger sister.

Tashauna, Tishanna

AMERICAN: Form of Shawna, God is gracious

ROCK AND ROLL: One of a king, bohemian, dreamy

RELATED ARTISTS/SONGS: Tiashana Cobi, "Tashauna" by The Rossington-Collins Band

LINER NOTES: Though later incorporated into the Lynyrd Skynyrd repertoire, "Tashauna" was written by guitarist Allen Collins in the period between when the band broke up and when it re-formed, and it was released under the name The Rossington-Collins Band.

Valhalla

NORSE: Heaven
ROCK AND ROLL: A friendly headbanger, ambitious, gorgeous
RELATED ARTISTS/SONGS: Valhalla Vale, Gates of Valhalla, "Valhalla" by Black Sabbath, "Valhalla" by Manowar, "Valhalla" by Pantera, "Valhalla" by 30 Seconds to Mars
LINER NOTES: Vale Hamanka of Blue Cheer, also known as Valhalla, began the underground zine *Search & Destroy* with $1000 that he got from poet Allen Ginsberg.

Violet

ENGLISH FLOWER NAME
ROCK AND ROLL: Philosophical, colorful, bright
RELATED ARTISTS/SONGS: "Violet" by Hole, "Violet" by Seal, "Violet" by The Birthday Massacre, "Violet" by Savage Garden, "Violet" by Frank Black
LINER NOTES: Courtney Love wrote the song "Violet" about her ex-boyfriend, The Smashing Pumpkins' Billy Corgan.

Zephyr

GREEK: West wind
ROCK AND ROLL: Summery, optimistic, bright
RELATED ARTISTS/SONGS: Zephyr, The Zephyrs, "The Zephyr Song" by Red Hot Chili Peppers, "Rococo Zephry" by Bill Callahan
LINER NOTES: Members of the blues-rock band Zephyr went on to play with Gram Parsons, Carole King, and Deep Purple; Blues singer Otis Taylor also played bass with the band in the 1970s.

BOYS

Ace

ENGLISH: Highest rank, number one
ROCK AND ROLL: Eloquent, has a knack for theatrics, a risk-taker, too cool for any kind of school
RELATED ARTISTS/SONGS: Ace Frehley, Masta Ace, Johnny Ace, "The Ace of Spades" by Motorhead, "Ace" by The Descendents, "Ace" by Jimmy Buffett
LINER NOTES: Paul Frehley got the nickname "Space Ace"—later shortened to just "Ace"—because his stage persona in Kiss was "The Spaceman."

Angus

GAELIC: First choice
ROCK AND ROLL: Rowdy, fun, energetic
RELATED ARTISTS/SONGS: Angus Young (AC/DC), "Angus" by Iron Boss, "Angus" by Billy Dechand
LINER NOTES: AC/DC's Angus Young was the shortest member of the band at five-foot-two; he has a daughter named Caycey.

Artimus, Artemis

GREEK: Servant of the moon
ROCK AND ROLL: Lucky, mystical, loves the nighttime
RELATED ARTISTS/SONGS: Artimus Pyle (Lynyrd Skynyrd), "Artemis" by Sincola, "Artemis" by Stan Kenton
LINER NOTES: Artimus Pyle was one of the few survivors of the plane crash that killed fellow Lynyrd Skynyrd bandmates Ronnie Van Zant, Cassie Gaines, and Steve Gaines.

Blaze

ENGLISH: Fiery
ROCK AND ROLL: Hairy, loud, rowdy
RELATED ARTISTS/SONGS: Blaze Bayley (Iron Maiden), "Blaze of Glory" by Jon Bon Jovi, "A Blaze in the Northern Sky" by Darkthrone, "Blaze" by Junior Kelly
LINER NOTES: Wolfbane and Iron Maiden front man Blaze Bayley's favorite movie is *Dumb and Dumber*; he advocated for the film to get an Oscar when it first came out.

Boris

RUSSIAN: Fighter
ROCK AND ROLL: Intuitive and intense
RELATED ARTISTS/SONGS: Boris, Boris Grebenshikov (Aquarium), "Boris" by The Melvins, "Boris the Spider" by The Who, "Boris the Conductor" by Laika and the Cosmonauts
LINER NOTES: The Japanese doom-metal band Boris is named after The Melvins' song "Boris," the longest song in The Melvins' repertoire.

Bret, Brett

CELTIC: Breton
ROCK AND ROLL: Has great hair, glamorous, earnest
RELATED ARTISTS/SONGS: Brett Dennen, Bret Michaels (Poison), Brett Nelsom (Built to Spill), "Home (Bret's Story)" by Poison
LINER NOTES: Bret Michaels has two daughters, Raine Elizabeth and Jorja Bleu.

Caesar, Cesar

LATIN: Leader, long-haired

ROCK AND ROLL: Powerful but intemperate ruler, king

RELATED ARTISTS/SONGS: The Caesars, Little Caesar, "Caesar" by Iggy Pop, "Little Caesar" by Kiss, "Young Caesar 2000" by The Mountain Goats, "Black Caesar" by James Brown, "Caesar" by Ty Segall

LINER NOTES: "Little Caesar" is the only original song that Kiss drummer Eric Carr sang lead on.

Christopher

GREEK: Anointed one

ROCK AND ROLL: Tall, strong, courageous protector

RELATED ARTISTS/SONGS: Christopher Cross, Christopher Thorn (Blind Melon), Christopher Wallace (The Notorious B.I.G.), "Christopher" by Boyracer, "Christopher" by Dave Clarke, "Christopher" by Dungen, "Christopher, Mr. Christopher" by Styx

LINER NOTES: Prince, who was a fan of The Bangles, wrote the song "Manic Monday" for the band under the pseudonym Christopher.

Cooper

ENGLISH: Barrel-maker

ROCK AND ROLL: Nocturnal, glamorous, dark

RELATED ARTISTS/SONGS: Alice Cooper, The Cooper Brothers, "Cooper" by Roxette, "Cooper" by Deerhoof, "Cooper" by Fifty Foot Combo, "Dear Mr. Cooper" by Keziah Jones

LINER NOTES: Alice Cooper has three children, son Dash and daughters Calico and Sonora Rose.

Cory, Corey

IRISH: Hollow

ROCK AND ROLL: Enterprising, entertaining, but doesn't deal with celebrity well

RELATED ARTISTS/SONGS: Corey Taylor (Slipknot), Corey Hart, Corey Wells (Three Dog Night), "Darlin' Cory" by Burl Ives, "Part of Corey" by Akron/Family, "Corey, Corey" by The Kingston Trio

LINER NOTES: The mask that Slipknot lead singer Corey Taylor wears onstage is fashioned from a test dummy and his own cutoff dreadlocks; it was inspired by the movie *Halloween*.

Darrell

FRENCH: Loved one

ROCK AND ROLL: Fan favorite, lives hard

RELATED ARTISTS/SONGS: Darrell Evans, Darrell Barth (The Crybabys), Darrell Mansfield, Darrell Scott, Darrell Sweet (Nazareth), "Dimebag" Darrell (Pantera, Damageplan), "No-Name Darrell" by The Mother Hips, "Open Face Darrell" by Reeve Oliver, "I Cried (Tribute to Dimebag Darrell)" by Vic Anselmo

LINER NOTES: Dimebag Darrell had a tattoo of Kiss guitarist Ace Frehley on his chest.

Deron

WELSH: Bird
ROCK AND ROLL: Confident, hardworking, attention-hungy
RELATED ARTISTS/SONGS: Deron Miller (CKY), Deron Johnson, "El Deron" by The Loud Sounds
LINER NOTES: CKY's Deron Miller was a regular on MTV's *Jackass*, performing in such skits as "Heavy Metal Alarm Clock"; he has three children, Bianca Rose, Lola Marue, and Thomas Carver.

Drew

GREEK: Short for Andrew, manly
ROCK AND ROLL: Darling, honest, trustworthy
RELATED ARTISTS/SONGS: Kevin Drew (Broken Social Scene), Drew Forsyth (Quiet Riot), Drew Seeley, "Drew" by Rights of the Accused, "Drew" by Nick Reeder, "For Drew" by Say No More, "True Drew" by Diesel Boy, "Dearest Drew" by Cruiserweight
LINER NOTES: In the late 1970s, drummer Drew Forsyth and guitarist Randy Rhoads briefly changed the name of Quiet Riot to DuBrow.

Eddie, Eddy

ENGLISH: Variation of Edward or Edwin, prosperous guardian
ROCK AND ROLL: Ready to rock, wears his heart on his sleeve, everyone's friend
RELATED ARTISTS/SONGS: Eddie Money, Eddie Van Halen (Van Halen), Eddie Vedder (Pearl Jam), "Eddie" by Styx, "Eddie You Should Know Better" by Curtis Mayfield, "Eddie's Ragga" by Spoon, "Are You Ready Eddy?" by Emerson, Lake & Palmer
LINER NOTES: Eddie Van Halen's son is named Wolfgang; he replaced Michael Anthony as the bassist in Van Halen in 2006.

Eicca, Ecca, Ecco

FINNISH: Strong
ROCK AND ROLL: Aloof, worldly, suave
RELATED ARTISTS/SONGS: Eicca Toppinen (Apocalyptica), "Ecca" by Polar Luke, "Ecco" by Musique Noise, "Ecco" by Shantel
LINER NOTES: Apocalyptica founder Eicca Toppinen, born Eino, has two children with Finnish actress Kirsi Ylijoki: Eelis and Ilmari.

Felix

LATIN: Happy, lucky
ROCK AND ROLL: A chill cat, sly and hip
RELATED ARTISTS/SONGS: Felix Cavaliere, Felix da Housecat, Felix Pappalardi (Cream, Mountain), "Felix Partz" by Peaches, "Blues

for Felix" by John Williams, "Felix Felicis" by Harry and the Potters, "Agent Felix" by Blink-182

LINER NOTES: Felix Pappalardi was known for playing with amplifiers that he claimed had once belonged to Jimi Hendrix.

Freddie, Freddy

ENGLISH: Variation of Alfred or Frederick, wise

ROCK AND ROLL: Plugged in, hip, king of the streets

RELATED ARTISTS/SONGS: Freddie Jackson, Freddie Knuckles, Freddie Mercury (Queen), "Freddy" by Connie Francis, "Freddy" by Eartha Kitt, "Goodnight Freddy" by The Sounds, "Freddie Freeloader" by Miles Davis

LINER NOTES: Freddie Mercury was an avid stamp collector; his collection is exhibited at stamp shows under his birth name, Farrokh Bulsara.

Gene

GREEK: Noble

ROCK AND ROLL: Earnest, fun, has a flair for drama, a party animal

RELATED ARTISTS/SONGS: Gene Autry, Gene Simmons (Kiss), Gene Vincent, "Gene by Gene" by Blur, "Enemy Gene" by of Montreal, "Sweet Gene Vincent" by Ian Dury

LINER NOTES: Gene Simmons, whose birth name is Chaim Weitz, has had serious romantic relationships with both Cher and Diana Ross.

Ginger

ENGLISH: Red-haired

ROCK AND ROLL: A showman, grounded, clever

RELATED ARTISTS/SONGS: Ginger Baker (Cream), "Ginger" by Speedy J, "Ginger" by Neil Sedaka, "Ginger" by Martin Taylor

LINER NOTES: While drumming with Blues Incorporated, Ginger Baker auditioned a young Mick Jagger to sing with the band; Baker found Jagger whiny and worked to throw his singing off.

Izzy

AMERICAN: Diminuitve of Israel, Isaiah, or Isaac

ROCK AND ROLL: A hell-raiser, a car buff, prone to overindulging

RELATED ARTISTS/SONGS: Izzy Stradlin (Guns N' Roses), "Chillout Tent" by The Hold Steady, "Izzy" by Asian Persuasion

LINER NOTES: Izzy Stradlin, born Jeffrey Dean Isbell, started playing in a band with Axl Rose when he was fourteen years old.

Jason

GREEK: Healer

ROCK AND ROLL: Noble, young, loving, articulate

RELATED ARTISTS/SONGS: Jason DeRulo, Jason Molina (Magnolia Electric Co.), Jason Newsted (Metallica), "Jason" by Andy Williams, "Jason" by Atmosphere, "Jason" by Sufjan Stevens

LINER NOTES: Jason Newsted is Metallica's longest-serving bassist. He usually records under the pseudonym "Jasonic."

Jasper, Jesper

GREEK: Spotted stone

ROCK AND ROLL: Dark, dangerous, alluring

RELATED ARTISTS/SONGS: Jesper Kyd, Jesper Stromblad (In Flames), "Jasper" by Bobby Hutcherson, "Jasper" by Spiderbait, "Jasper" by Howard Shore

LINER NOTES: Death metal guitarist Jesper Stromblad is an avid World of Warcraft player, sometimes playing a guitar that carries the logo for the game.

Kirk

SCOTTISH: Church

ROCK AND ROLL: Spiritual, intense, smart

RELATED ARTISTS/SONGS: Kirk Franklin, Kirk Hammett (Metallica), Kirk Kelly, "The Kirk Pride" by Clannad, "Captain Kirk" by Master P, "Kirk" by Sixun

LINER NOTES: Between the Metallica albums *The Black Album* and *Load*, Kirk Hammett studied film at San Francisco State University. Hammett has two sons, Angel and Vincenzo.

Klaus

GERMAN: Form of Nicholas, victory

ROCK AND ROLL: Eccentric, hip, clever

RELATED ARTISTS/SONGS: Klaus Fluoride (The Dead Kennedys), Klaus Meine (The Scorpions), Klaus Nomi, "Klaus" by And One, "Claudia & Klaus" by Valley of the Giants, "Klaus Orbital" by Don Johnson Big Band, "Klaus Kombalad" by Magma

LINER NOTES: Klaus Voorman won a Grammy for designing the cover of The Beatles' *Revolver*.

Lars

NORDIC: Variation of Lawrence, from Laurentium

ROCK AND ROLL: Intense, edgy, but loves his mom

RELATED ARTISTS/SONGS: Lars Frederiksen (Rancid), Lars Ulrich (Metallica), MC Lars, "Lars" by Will Oldham, "Lars Von Sen" by Mr. Oizo

LINER NOTES: Before playing in Metallica, Lars Ulrich originally moved from Denmark to California to be a professional tennis player.

Lemmy

ENGLISH: Form of Lemuel, devoted to God

ROCK AND ROLL: A party animal, bold, outspoken

RELATED ARTISTS/SONGS: Lemmy Kilmister (Motorhead), "Lemmy" by The Axidentals, "Lemmy" by Radishes, "Lemmy" by Black Fiction
LINER NOTES: Lemmy Kilmister's legal name is Ian; he got the nickname Lemmy from his habit of asking people to "lemmy a quid till Friday" so that he could play the slot machines.

Linus

GREEK: Flax
ROCK AND ROLL: A poet, has his head in the clouds
RELATED ARTISTS/SONGS: "Linus and Lucy" by The Vince Guaraldi Trio, "Linus Spacehead" by Wavves, "Linus" by Deftones, "Linus" by The Silent League, "Linus" by Birdie
LINER NOTES: *(Like) Linus* was the name of the never officially released Deftones demo album.

Luke

GREEK: Bright
ROCK AND ROLL: Adept at technology, a hustler
RELATED ARTISTS/SONGS: Luke Bryan, Luke Kelly, Luke Slater, "Luke" by Iona, "Luke" by Long Beach Dub All-Stars, "War Pigs/Luke's Wall" by Black Sabbath
LINER NOTES: The outro to Black Sabbath's "War Pigs" is named "Luke's Wall" in homage to the band's roadies, Geoff "Luke" Lucas and Spock Wall.

Nikki, Nicky

GREEK: Form of Nicholas, victory
ROCK AND ROLL: Clever, intense, flashy
RELATED ARTISTS/SONGS: Nikki Sixx, Nicky Hopkins, "Nicky" by Momus, "Nicky" by Lafayette Hudson
LINER NOTES: Nikki Sixx was declared legally dead for two minutes after a heroin overdose in the late 1980s. He lived to have four children: Storm, Gunner, Frankie-Jean, and Decker.

Ollie

LATIN: Variation of Oliver or Olivia, olive tree
ROCK AND ROLL: Competitive, fun-loving, a good pal
RELATED ARTISTS/SONGS: Ollie & the Nightingales, Ollie & Jerry, Ollie Riedel (Ramstein), "Ollie Otson" by Dead Poetic, "Ollie North" by Gwar, "Ollie Ollie" by Flatfoot 56, "Ollie" by Phil Woods, "Rock Around with Ollie Vee" by Buddy Holly
LINER NOTES: Before he was in Rammstein, bassist Ollie Riedel played in a folk-fiddle punk band called The Inchtabokatables.

Perry

LATIN: Pilgrim
ROCK AND ROLL: Experienced, smooth-talking, but has some rough edges

RELATED ARTISTS/SONGS: Perry Como, Perry Farrell (Jane's Addiction), "Perry" by Butthole Surfers, "Perry" by Perfume Genius
LINER NOTES: Jane's Addiction's Perry Farrell, born Peretz Bernstein, took his stage name as a play on the word "peripheral."

Prairie

ENGLISH: Grassland
ROCK AND ROLL: A Westerner, breezy, rugged
RELATED ARTISTS/SONGS: Prairie Prince (Journey), Pure Prairie League, "Prairie Wind" by Neil Young, "Prairie" by Hawkwind, "Prairie" by Robin Spielberg
LINER NOTES: Journey drummer Prairie Prince has a line of children's T-shirts called Mouth Man Animated Hoodies, designed so that when you cross your arms, the pattern on the sleeves turns into an image.

Randall

IRISH: Wolf protector
ROCK AND ROLL: Famous, talented, goofy
RELATED ARTISTS/SONGS: Randall Hall (Lynyrd Skynyrd), Randall Lee, "Randall" by Wheatus, "Tony Randall" by Bikini Kill, "Lord Randall" by The Prodigals, "Randall's Attack" by Randy Newman, "The Randall Knife" by Guy Clark
LINER NOTES: When Lynyrd Skynyrd re-formed after a plane crash killed three members of the band, they christened their backup singers "The Honkettes."

Richie, Ritchie

ENGLISH: Form of Richard, powerful leader
ROCK AND ROLL: Dreamy, magnetic, easygoing
RELATED ARTISTS/SONGS: Richie McDonald, Richie Sambora (Bon Jovi), Ritchie Valens, "Richie" by Gloria Dennis, "Richie" by Larry John McNally, "Ritchie" by Johnny Respect
LINER NOTES: Before joining Bon Jovi, Richie Sambora auditioned unsuccessfully for both Kiss and Poison. He has one daughter, Ava Elizabeth, with actress Heather Locklear.

Robert

GERMAN: Famous
ROCK AND ROLL: Dresses well, wealthy, noble
RELATED ARTISTS/SONGS: Robert Plant (Led Zeppelin), Robert Smith (The Cure), Robert Johnson, "Robert" by Palomar, "Robert" by Dolly Parton, "Robert" by The Cannanes, "Robert" by Dark Dark Dark
LINER NOTES: Robert Plant's daughter Carmen is married to Charlie Jones, the bassist Robert Smith (of The Cure) uses on his solo tours.

Sasha, Sascha

SLAVIC: Defender
ROCK AND ROLL: Free-spirited, strong, centered
RELATED ARTISTS/SONGS: Sasha Bell, Sascha Konietzko (KMFDM), Sascha Sacket, "Sasha" by Ted Nugent, "Sasha" by La Ley, "Sasha" by Richie Hawtin, "For Sasha" by Joan Baez
LINER NOTES: KMFDM founder Sascha Konietzko also goes by the name Kapt'n K or Sascha K.

Sebastian

GREEK: Venerable
ROCK AND ROLL: Rebellious, dashing, music-obsessed
RELATED ARTISTS/SONGS: Belle & Sebastian, Sebastian Bach (Skid Row), "Sebastian" by Peter, Paul and Mary, "Sebastian" by Ernie Wilkens, "Sebastian" by Ruben Blades, "Sebastian" by Steve Harley
LINER NOTES: Sebastian Bach has three children: London Siddhartha Halford, Paris Francis Muir, and Sebastiana Maria Chantal.

Simon

HEBREW: He who hears the word of God
ROCK AND ROLL: Resilient, intellectual, merciful
RELATED ARTISTS/SONGS: Simon Wright (AC/DC), Simon Kirke (Bad Company), Simon Crowe (The Boomtown Rats), "Saint Simon" by The Shins, "Simon" by Liza Minnelli, "Simon" by Joan Armatrading, "Simon" by Lifehouse
LINER NOTES: Simon Crowe, drummer for The Boomtown Rats, originally was part of a group called The Velcro Files.

Ted

GREEK: Form of Theodore, gift of God
ROCK AND ROLL: Intelligent, friendly, resourceful
RELATED ARTISTS/SONGS: Ted Leo and the Pharmacists, Ted Nugent, Ted Fox, "Ted" by John Kirkpatrick, "Ted" by Benny Hill, "Ted" by Tandy
LINER NOTES: Hard rock guitarist and avid hunter Ted Nugent wrote a cookbook called *Kill It & Grill It: A Guide to Preparing and Cooking Wild Game and Fish*.

Tommy

ARAMAIC: Form of Thomas, twin
ROCK AND ROLL: A leader, determined, mellow
RELATED ARTISTS/SONGS: Tommy Lee (Mötley Crüe), Tommy Shaw (Styx), Tommy James, "Tommy Gun" by The Clash, "Tommy Can You Hear Me?" by The Who, "Tommy Gets His Tonsils Out" by The Replacements, "Tommy" by Connie Francis, "Tommy" by Peter Bellamy
LINER NOTES: After he broke up with Pamela Anderson, Tommy Lee was briefly engaged to Mayte Garcia, Prince's ex-wife.

Tony

LATIN: Form of Anthony, priceless

ROCK AND ROLL: Strong and silent, fierce, independent

RELATED ARTISTS/SONGS: Tony Bennett, Tony Iommi (Black Sabbath), Tony Rich, "Tony's Theme" by The Pixies, "Tony the Beat" by The Sounds, Tony the Tiger" by Manchester Orchestra, "Tony Randall" by Bikini Kill, "Tony the Pony" by Morrissey

LINER NOTES: Tony Iommi lost the tops of his two of his fingers in an accident at the sheet metal factory he worked at; he taught himself how to play the guitar using plastic tips.

Trent

ENGLISH: River-dweller

ROCK AND ROLL: A small town guy with big dreams, inventive, dark

RELATED ARTISTS/SONGS: Trent Reznor (Nine Inch Nails), Terence Trent D'Arby, "Trent" by Angel City Outcasts

LINER NOTES: Trent Reznor is a huge fan of David Bowie; he appeared in the music video of "I'm Afraid of Americans," as Bowie's stalker.

Trevor

GAELIC: Industrious

ROCK AND ROLL: Bright, witty, studious

RELATED ARTISTS/SONGS: Trevor Rabin (Yes), Trevor Horn, Trevor Bolder (Uriah Heep), "Trevor" by U2, "Trevor" by Bob Moses, "Trevor" by Thinking Fellers Union Local 282, "Clever Trevor" by Ian Dury and the Blockheads

LINER NOTES: Uriah Heep guitarist Trevor Bolder accidentally painted his face blue with semipermanent pigment, requiring a visit to a skin-peeling specialist in Switzerland; he still has traces of blue paint behind his ear.

Troy

GAELIC: Foot soldier

ROCK AND ROLL: Passionate, serious, romantic

RELATED ARTISTS/SONGS: Troy Sanders (Mastodon), Troy Van Leeuwen (Queens of the Stone Age), "Troy" by The Sugarhill Gang, "Troy" by Sinead O'Connor, "Troy" by Robin Holcomb

LINER NOTES: Troy Sanders, of Mastodon, has two children, a daughter named Haley and a son named Yuri.

Ulrich

GERMAN: Powerful heritage

ROCK AND ROLL: Cerebral, sophisticated, serious

RELATED ARTISTS/SONGS: Lars Ulrich (Metallica), Ulrich Krieger, Ulrich Roth (Scorpions), "Ulrich" by Luca Nostro, "Ulrich" by Fritz Zander

LINER NOTES: Scorpions' Ulrich Roth invented a guitar with up to forty-six frets—twenty-six more than an average acoustic guitar.

Vernon

ENGLISH: Place of alders
ROCK AND ROLL: Dependable, intelligent, warm
RELATED ARTISTS/SONGS: Vernon Burch, Vernon Dudley (The Bonzo Dog Band), Vernon Reid (Living Colour), "Vernon the Company Man" by Les Claypool, "Vernon" by The Libertines, "Vernon" by Intronaut
LINER NOTES: Heavy metal guitarist Vernon Reid, best known for his work in Living Colour, is also a prolific session musician, backing up artists like Santana, Mariah Carey, and Public Enemy.

Vince, Vinnie

LATIN: Variation of Vincent, conquering
ROCK AND ROLL: Mellow, a loner, a heartbreaker
RELATED ARTISTS/SONGS: Vinnie Vincent (Kiss), Vince Neil (Mötley Crüe), Vinny Appice (Black Sabbath), "Vince the Lovable Stoner" by The Fratellis, "Vince" by Bobby Bare, "Vince" by Newton Allen, "Vinnie" by Screaming Headless Torsos
LINER NOTES: Vince Neil has his own tattoo parlor in Las Vegas, dubbed Vince Neil Ink.

Zach, Zack, Zac

HEBREW: Form of Zachary, the Lord has remembered
ROCK AND ROLL: Sharp, industrious, bright
RELATED ARTISTS/SONGS: Zac Hanson, Zak Starkey (The Who), Zakk Wylde (Ozzy Osbourne), "Zach" by Keith Javors, "Zac" by Mudlow, "Zac" by Leisure Class, "Zack" by Sin Alley
LINER NOTES: Ozzy Osbourne's guitarist Zakk Wylde, born Jeffrey Phillip Wielandt, has three children: Hayley Rae, Hendrix, and Jesse.

Which Hard Rock Name Is Right for You?

Quirky and interesting names abound in the hard rock side of things, but finding one that keeps its cool without being too psychedelic can be a challenge. Sure, Viking Dawn ensures your child's status as a kickin' lead singer, but it might also mean some really embarrassing years in junior high. Try this handy quiz to figure out the right hard rock name for your future headbanger.

You're looking for a name that's . . .

a. subtle but cool, something that would look equally plausible on a poster and on the door of a law office.

b. fun, unique, and a little bit edgy; it's more important to have flair than to fit in.

c. traditional and solid but with solid rock and roll cred.

At a jukebox, you're most likely to play . . .

a. "The Boys Are Back in Town" by Thin Lizzy.

b. "I Love Rock and Roll" by Joan Jett.

c. "Smoke on the Water" by Deep Purple.

Your fashion tastes run toward . . .

a. jeans, black T-shirts, and shaggy hair.

b. studs, leather jackets, and rhinestone T-shirts.

c. well-worn band T-shirts on the weekends, dress shirts during the week.

In a band you would be . . .

a. the guitarist.

b. the singer.

d. the drummer.

Your tattoo is . . .

a. a favorite song lyric.

b. a flaming skull and roses, plus a winged V guitar.

c. easily concealed.

You got . . .

MOSTLY A'S

For a girl, try **Lita**, a sweet, old-fashioned name that still has some grit thanks to Runaways guitarist Lita Ford. Other options in the same realm: **Cherie**, **Marnie**, or **Lucia.**

For a boy, try **Vince**, a handsome, solid name that has metal cred from Mötley Crüe drummer **Vince Neil**. It has the nickname **Vinnie**, to boot, which has shredder Vinnie Moore and Pantera's Vinnie Paul as rock models. Other options in the same vein include **Ritchie**, **Eddie**, and **Perry.**

MOSTLY B'S

For a girl, try **Jett**, a hip homage to the grand lady of hard rock, Joan Jett. Other options: **Raven**, **Storm** (a la Nikki Sixx's daughter), or **Tesla.**

For a boy, what about another last-name-as-first-name with serious rock appeal—**Hendrix**? Less common than Jimi and has that sassy "x" already included. More names in that line: **Blaze, Rex, Bonham,** and **Sylvain.**

MOSTLY C'S

For a girl, the 1950s-turned-rock name **Suzi** is charming and old-fashioned with an edge, plus it has the strength of legendary Suzi Quatro. Other solid hard rock names with interesting musician ties include **Beth**, **Vicky**, and **Amanda.**

For a boy, **Ian** is a strong choice with a surprising wealth of pop culture history, including Fugazi front man **Ian MacKaye** and **Ian Astbury** of The Cult. Some other good names that aren't too out there are **Billy, Jimmy, Robert,** and **John Paul.**

The Worst Rock Nicknames

There are cool names, there are interesting and edgy names, and then there are those nicknames that make you wince a little. Avoid naming your children after these rock models at all cost, lest they be in a world of hurt on the grade school playground.

Buckethead

Virtuoso guitarist and Guns N' Roses contributor Buckethead might just win the prize for the worst rock name of all time. His real name is Brian Carroll, but the thing that most people know him for is the KFC bucket and creepy white mask he wears on stage.

Cannonball

Jazz saxophonist Cannonball Adderley, born Julian, originally had an even worse nickname: "Cannibal," a title bestowed upon him by his high school classmates for his impressive stomach capacity. Still, Cannonball is a little too roly-poly to be anything but the fat kid at the pool.

Chubby

Chubby Checker, who introduced the world to the Twist, was born with the toally acceptable and even alliterative name Ernest Evans. His nickname "Chubby" came from his boss at Fresh Farm Poultry, and "Checker" was a play on the name of his idol, Fats Domino. He could pull it off, but anyone else might just develop a complex.

Dimebag

Pantera frontman Dimebag Darrell is a beloved figure among metalheads, but this name pretty much guarantees your child to a life as a two-bit drug dealer. Go with Darrell instead.

The Edge

Even if you're the biggest U2 fan in the world, you still can't pull off a name with an article. On anyone but the permanently be-hatted David Evans, it just comes off as a dated macho title. Even Bono would be better.

Engelbert Humperdinck

He was born with the far more reasonable name Arnold Dorsey, but the crooner renamed himself Engelbert Humperdinck in honor of a German composer. It's the ultimate joke name, which no bundle of joy deserves to be the butt of.

Fats

Both Fats Domino and Fats Waller used this nickname with a certain amount of swagger—the former was born Antoine, the latter Thomas—but the same self-image problems exist as with Chubby. Nix it unless you're determined to raise an old-timey bluesman.

Geezer

Black Sabbath's Geezer Butler, born Terence Michael, got his nickname from a slang term he used all the time in childhood. Still, the first thing that comes to mind is a grumpy old man.

Munky

Korn frontman James Shaffer got this odd name from his toes, which apparently resemble monkey's hands when spread. The nontraditional spelling doesn't make it any less puzzling.

Pink Eyes

The ultimate bane of the playground, Pink Eyes is the pseudonym of hard-core band Fucked Up's Damian Abraham. Other band nicknames are just as terrible—Gulag and Mustard Gas—but those are beyond even the most adventurous naming possibilities. We hope.

Skunk

Guitarist Skunk Baxter of Steely Dan and The Doobie Brothers lends the nickname a touch of retro cool, but that won't mean that your kid will get out of the inevitable stinky jokes.

Bands Named After
Real People

Even if you're not in the band, it doesn't mean that you can't achieve musical fame and fortune. Real people, from celebrity artists to gym coaches, have inspired the names of some of the biggest rock acts.

Lynyrd Skynyrd took its name from a high school gym teacher named Leonard Skinner.

The California indie-punk band **Abe Vigoda** was named after the elderly cult actor of the same name.

Jethro Tull was named after a famous British agriculturalist who invented the seed drill.

Creedence Clearwater Revival was named after a friend of bandmember Tom Fogerty, Credence, whose favorite beer brand was Clearwater.

Kings of Leon is a band made up of extended relatives; Leon is the name of a family member.

Syd Barrett named **Pink Floyd** after two of his favorite bluesmen, Pink Anderson and Floyd Council.

Experimental noise band **Harvey Milk** was named after San Francisco's first openly gay supervisor.

Indie rocker group **Dale Earnhardt Jr. Jr.** took their name from famed Nascar racer Dale Earnhardt Jr.

Energetic dance-rock band **Franz Ferdinand** swiped their name from the archduke whose murder sparked World War I.

The Dandy Warhols are named after pop art legend Andy Warhol.

Famous Rock Star Muses

The partners of rock stars—girlfriends, boyfriends, and otherwise—are as indelibly a part of music history as the musicians they dated. Of course, it works both ways on the gender spectrum—Carole King wrote "Oh Neil" for Neil Sedaka and Rancid's Tim Armstrong inspired The Distillers' third album *Coral Fang*—but the list tends to skew female. From stately sweethearts like Pattie Boyd to fellow musicians like Marianne Faithfull and Cat Stevens, these musicians' muses might be as inspiring to your name hunt as they were to the rockers who loved them.

Pattie Boyd

IN A RELATIONSHIP WITH: George Harrison, whom she met filming *A Hard Day's Night*, and Eric Clapton, who fell in love with her while she was still married to Harrison

INSPIRED: "Something," "I Need You," "For You Blue," and "Isn't It a Pity" by George Harrison/The Beatles, and Eric Clapton's "Layla," "Wonderful Tonight," and "Bell Bottom Blues"

Patti D'Arbanville

IN A RELATIONSHIP WITH: Cat Stevens, whom she met while modeling in London

INSPIRED: "Lady D'Arbanville" and "Wild World"

Bob Dylan

IN A RELATIONSHIP WITH: Joan Baez, who dated Dylan off and on for two years

INSPIRED: Baez's songs "To Bobby" and "Diamonds & Rust"

Marianne Faithfull

IN A RELATIONSHIP WITH: Mick Jagger. The couple's antics and party-going became the stuff of rock legend, including an incident where the police found Faithfull wearing nothing but a fur rug.

INSPIRED: "You Can't Always Get What You Want," "Wild Horses," and "I Got the Blues" by The Rolling Stones, and "And Your Bird Can Sing" by The Beatles

Anna Gordy

IN A RELATIONSHIP WITH: Marvin Gaye
INSPIRED: Gaye's album *Here, My Dear* was written after his acrimonious divorce from Gordy and was inspired at least partially by the portion of royalties from the LP that he had to set aside for her.

Mutt Lange

IN A RELATIONSHIP WITH: Shania Twain, with whom he had a son, Eja
INSPIRED: Twain's song "You're Still the One"

Sarah Lownds

IN A RELATIONSHIP WITH: Bob Dylan, with whom she had four children: Jesse, Anna, Samuel, and Jakob
INSPIRED: The album *Blood on the Tracks* and Dylan's "Sara" and "Sad Eyed Lady of the Lowlands"

Yoko Ono

IN A RELATIONSHIP WITH: John Lennon. The most famous—and controversial—rock girlfriend of all brought an avant-garde edge to John Lennon's music, even if she might have broken up The Beatles.
INSPIRED: "Oh Yoko," "Julia," "The Ballad of John and Yoko" by John Lennon/The Beatles

Claudette Orbison

IN A RELATIONSHIP WITH: Roy Orbison
INSPIRED: "Pretty Woman" and "Claudette" by Roy Orbison. "Pretty Woman" came from a quip of Claudette's that "a pretty woman don't need no money."

Anita Pallenberg

IN A RELATIONSHIP WITH: Brian Jones and Keith Richards. She and Richards had three children: Marlon, Angela, and Tara.
INSPIRED: "You Got the Silver" by The Rolling Stones

Claudette Robinson

IN A RELATIONSHIP WITH: Smokey Robinson, of the Miracles, with whom she had two children: Berry William Borope and Tamla Claudette
INSPIRED: The Miracles' "My Girl"

Edie Sedgwick

IN A RELATIONSHIP WITH: The Velvet Underground's John Cale, who met her through Andy Warhol
INSPIRED: "Femme Fatale" by The Velvet Underground

Cat Stevens

IN A RELATIONSHIP WITH: Carly Simon for a year, in 1970

INSPIRED: Simon's song "Anticipation," which she wrote about waiting for a date with Stevens.

Punk Rockers
and Riot Grrrls

Sure, mohawks are cute, but the name Sid Vicious outside of the context of a band just sounds like a playground bully. Yet punk rock's core philosophy is all about self-reliance, creativity, and thinking outside the box, values that most parents want to instill in their children. Punk, proto-punk, and post-punk names can be both traditional (Lou, Joey, Jane, and Kathleen) and quirky (Dez, Riff, Kembra, and Mignon), but if you're looking for something unique and modern, punks past and present have always been the standard-bearers of cool, avant-garde, and artistic names.

GIRLS

Anna, Ana

HEBREW: Gracious
ROCK AND ROLL: Charming, a heartbreaker
RELATED ARTISTS/SONGS: Anna McGarrigle, Ana da Silva (The Raincoats), "Anna" by Bad Company, "Anna's Song" by Marvin Gaye, "Ana" by The Pixies, "Anna" by The Jesus Lizard, "Anna (Go to Him)" by The Beatles

"She's my fave."
—THE PIXIES

Ari

HEBREW: Lion
ROCK AND ROLL: Confident, brash, loves reggae
RELATED ARTISTS/SONGS: Ari Hest, Ari Up (The Slits), "Ari" by Naum, "Ari" by Deuter, "Ari" by Lily Maase
LINER NOTES: Ari Up learned guitar from The Clash's Joe Strummer; her stepfather is The Sex Pistols' John Lydon.

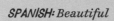

Belinda

SPANISH: Beautiful

CHRIS ANDREWS:
"Her eyes were exciting her hair was golden."

EURYTHMICS:
"Belinda your mind is dreaming."

ROY ORBISON:
"You're as strong as any human can be."

EDISON LIGHTHOUSE:
"I can't face tomorrow if you're not here with me."

Brix

ENGLISH: Form of Brixton, place name
ROCK AND ROLL: Spunky, bright, chic
RELATED ARTISTS/SONGS: Brix Smith (The Fall), "Brix" by Crossbreed, "Brix" by Diario, "Brix" by Rhamsis Ali
LINER NOTES: After leaving The Fall, Brix Smith started a boutique in East London; she's appeared as a fashion expert on several British television shows.

Caitlin, Caitlyn, Katelyn

IRISH: Pure
ROCK AND ROLL: Bouncy, bright, and beautiful
RELATED ARTISTS/SONGS: Caitlin Cary, Caitlin O'Riordan (The Pogues), Caitlyn Lynn (Caitlin & Will), "Caitlin" by The Irresponsibles, "Caitlin" by Sandra Bell, "Kaitlyn" by Blake Thomas, "Caitlyn Is Great" by Bouncing Souls
LINER NOTES: Caitlin O'Riordan—better known as Cait—was married to Elvis Costello for sixteen years.

Candy, Candace

LATIN: Pure

THE STRANGLERS: "I know a girl who's soft and sweet."

CAMEO: "You're so dandy."

IGGY POP: "Beautiful girl from the north."

THE CARS: "Candy-O, I need you so."

Cathy, Kathy

GREEK: Short for Catherine, genuine

ROCK AND ROLL: Inspiration, beloved muse, a little moody

RELATED ARTISTS/SONGS: Cathy Carr, Kathy Valentine (The Go-Gos), "Kathy's Song" by Paul Simon, "Cathy's Clown" by The Everly Brothers, "Carrying Cathy" by Ben Folds Five, "Kathy with a K's Song" by Bright Eyes, "Kathy-O" by Neil Diamond

LINER NOTES: Kathy Chitty, Paul Simon's muse and early girlfriend, is the inspiration for "Kathy's Song." She's also referred to in his song "America."

Chrissy, Chrissie

GREEK: Variation of Christina or Christine, follower of Christ

ROCK AND ROLL: Pretty, kind, but prone to bad habits

RELATED ARTISTS/SONGS: Chrissie Hynde (The Pretenders), "Chrissy Kiss the Corpse" by of Montreal, "Chrissy Reid" by Percy Hill, "Chrissie" by The Make-Ups, "I Love You Chrissy" by The Police

LINER NOTES: In the early 1970s, Chrissie Hynde worked part-time at Vivienne Westwood and Malcolm McLaren's clothing boutique.

Corin

LATIN: Spear

ROCK AND ROLL: Literate, likes to do things herself

RELATED ARTISTS/SONGS: Corin Cole, Corin See, Corin Tucker (Sleater-Kinney), "Corin" by Charles Law, "Corinne" by Tom House, "Corinne" by Frankie "Half-Pint" Jaxon

LINER NOTES: Sleater-Kinney drummer Corin Tucker sometimes played in the band Cadallaca under the name Kissy; she has a son named Marshall and a daughter named Glory.

Debbie, Debby

HEBREW: Short for Deborah, honeybee

BILL EVANS:
"In her own sweet world . . . lives my favorite girl."

THE B-52'S:
"Oh, Debbie, queen of the underground/ carrying a golden guitar."

SUGARCULT:
"She wore black round her eyes just to scare all the normal guys."

BLUE OYSTER CULT:
"She kept the light open, all night long."

Dika

NORDIC: Leader
ROCK AND ROLL: A bookworm, precocious, literate
RELATED ARTISTS/SONGS: Dika Newlin, "Ina Meena Dika" by Timid Tiger, "Dika Energia" by Ruslana
LINER NOTES: Punk rock singer Dika Newlin earned a Ph.D. from Columbia when she was twenty-two years old; her mother named her after an Amazon in one of Sappho's poems.

Eloise

GERMAN: In high spirits
ROCK AND ROLL: Capricious but sweet, attractive, romantic
RELATED ARTISTS/SONGS: Eloise Laws, "Dear Eloise" by The Hollies, "Sweet Eloise" by Glenn Miller, "Walking in the Park with Eloise" by Wings, "Eloise the Eloquent" by The Extraordinaires, "Eloise" by Bruce Springsteen
LINER NOTES: The children's book *Eloise*, about a little girl who lives at the Plaza, was based on author Kay Thompson's niece, Liza Minnelli.

Gee

ITALIAN: Form of Geeta, pearl
ROCK AND ROLL: Passionate, creative, enigmatic
RELATED ARTISTS/SONGS: Gee Vaucher (Crass), "Ess Gee" by Underworld, "Wendell Gee" by R.E.M., "Gee" by Phil Woods, "Gee" by The Moonglows
LINER NOTES: Crass's Gee Vaucher, who designed many of the band's album sleeves and flyers, published two books of her anarchist collages, *Animal Rites* and *Crass Art and Other Pre Post-Modernist Monsters*.

Gina, Geena

ITALIAN: Variation of Regina, queen
ROCK AND ROLL: Bouncy, a knockout with a tough side
RELATED ARTISTS/SONGS: Gina Birch (The Raincoats), Gina Glocksen, Gina Schock (The Go-Go's), "Mama Gina" by Shellac, "Gina" by Johnny Mathis, "Gina" by Blues Traveler, "Lunch with Gina" by Steely Dan, "Gina" by Michael Bolton
LINER NOTES: Go-Go's drummer Gina Schock cowrote the title song for the Miley Cyrus album *Breakout*.

Honey

ENGLISH: Sweet

ERYKAH BADU:
"Honey, you're so sweet."

THE JESUS & MARY CHAIN:
"Listen to the girl as she takes on half the world."

THE HUSH SOUND:
"Honey, honey, you are the first one."

LADY ANTEBELLUM:
"Steady as a preacher, free as a weed."

Imani

ARABIC: Faith

ROCK AND ROLL: Graceful, buoyant, strong

RELATED ARTISTS/SONGS: Imani Coppola, "Imani" by Dewy Redman, "Imani" by Nick Jones, "Imani" by Alfonzo Blackwell

LINER NOTES: Imani Coppola named her band Little Jackie from the song "Little Jackie Wants to Be a Star" by Lisa Lisa and Cult Jam.

Ivy

ENGLISH PLANT NAME

ROCK AND ROLL: Glamorous, a risk-taker, wild and dangerous

RELATED ARTISTS/SONGS: Operation Ivy, Poison Ivy Rorschach (The Cramps), "Ivy" by Hoagy Carmichael, "Ivy" by Screaming Trees, "Poison Ivy" by The Coasters, "For the Love of Ivy" by the Mamas & the Papas

LINER NOTES: Though The Coasters recorded the first version of "Poison Ivy," The Rolling Stones, The Hollies, and Manfredd Mann have all recorded versions of the song.

Jane

HEBREW: God is merciful

ROCK AND ROLL: Sweet, likes to play hard to get, has a dazzling smile

RELATED ARTISTS/SONGS: Jane Siberry, Jane Wiedlin (The Go-Go's), Jane's Addiction, "Jane" by Barenaked Ladies, "Jane" by Ben Folds Five, "Sweet Jane" by The Velvet Underground, "Hazey Jane I" by Nick Drake, "How Come You're Such a Hit with the Boys, Jane?" by Dolly Mixture

LINER NOTES: Go-Go's Jane Wiedlin played the voice of Bruce Wayne's girlfriend in an episode of *The New Batman Adventures*.

Judy

HEBREW: Form of Judith, woman of Judea
ROCK AND ROLL: Hip, fun-loving, a daydreamer, a little flakey
RELATED ARTISTS/SONGS: Judy Collins, Judy Clay, Judy Nylon, "Judy" by Art Tatum, "Judy" by Al Green, "Judy and the Dream of Horses" by Belle & Sebastian, "Back in Judy's Jungle" by Brian Eno, "Judy Is a Punk" by The Ramones

"Since I met Judy,
my life has been one sweet melody."
—AL GREEN

Kaia, Kaya

GREEK: Earth
ROCK AND ROLL: A good listener, understanding, loves nature
RELATED ARTISTS/SONGS: Kaia Wilson (Team Dresch), Kaya Project, "Kaya" by Bob Marley, "Good Morning Kaia" by BT, "Kaya Kayooka" by Adiemus, "Kaia" by Keith Canisius
LINER NOTES: Team Dresch founder Kaia Wilson is a competitive ping-pong player; her table tennis alter ego is named "the Spin Slayer."

Kathleen

GREEK: Variation of Katherine, pure
ROCK AND ROLL: Independent, brainy, great at dancing
RELATED ARTISTS/SONGS: Kathleen DeLuna, Kathleen Hanna (Le Tigre), "Kathleen" by David Gray, "Kathleen" by Josh Ritter, "Kathleen" by Townes Van Zandt

"All the other girls are stars, you are the
Northern Lights."
—JOSH RITTER

Kembra, Kembara

AMERICAN: Derived from Kemuel, helper of God
ROCK AND ROLL: Creative, bold, artistic
RELATED ARTISTS/SONGS: Kembra Pfahler (The Voluptuous Horror of Karen Black), "Kembara" by Seha & Freedom, "La Kembra" by Madame X
LINER NOTES: Musician and artist Kembra Pfahler follows the phi-

losophy of availablism, constructing her costumes, art, and even instruments from whatever found objects she has at hand; her brother is Jawbreaker drummer Adam Pfahler.

Kira, Kyra

RUSSIAN: Sunlight
ROCK AND ROLL: Fair-skinned, sunny, literate
RELATED ARTISTS/SONGS: Kira Roessler (Black Flag), Kira Willey, "One for Kyra" by New Cool Collective, "Kira" by Fred Frith, "Kira" by PC Synergy, "Kira" by Glassjaw
LINER NOTES: Black Flag bassist Kira Roessler now works as a dialogue editor in Los Angeles on such films as *Sucker Punch* and *The Twilight Saga: New Moon*.

Kirstie, Kirsty

DANISH: Variation of Christina, faithful
ROCK AND ROLL: Affable, a free spirit, works well with others
RELATED ARTISTS/SONGS: Kirstie Hawkshaw, Kirsty MacColl, "Kirstie" by Ben Reynolds, "Kirsty" by Milk
LINER NOTES: Kirsty MacColl, best known for her work with The Pogues, also often sang on tracks produced by her husband Steve Lillywhite for bands like The Smiths and Talking Heads.

Laurie

LATIN: Variation of Lauren or Laura, laurel tree
ROCK AND ROLL: Avant-garde, quirky, inventive, cool
RELATED ARTISTS/SONGS: Laurie Anderson, Laurie Berkner, Laurie Freelove, "Laurie (Stranger Things Happen)" by Dickey Lee, "Laurie" by Datarock, "Laurie's Theme" by John 5, "Laurie" by Daniel Johnston, "Laurie" by Bill Evans
LINER NOTES: Experimental musician Laurie Anderson, who married Lou Reed in 2008, was NASA's first and only artist in residence.

Lydia

GREEK: From the kingdom of Lydia
ROCK AND ROLL: Urbane, artistic, mysterious
RELATED ARTISTS/SONGS: Lydia Lunch, Lydia Pense, Lydia Wong, "Lydia" by Her Space Holiday, "Lydia" by The Butchies, "Donald and Lydia" by John Prine, "Lydia" by Jonathan Richman
LINER NOTES: Poet and musician Lydia Lunch—born Lydia Koch—earned the surname "Lunch" from her habit of stealing lunches for her impoverished artist friends.

Marguerite

FRENCH: Form of Margaret, pearl
ROCK AND ROLL: Shy, smart, tells a good joke
RELATED ARTISTS/SONGS: Marguerite Conti, Marguerite Van Cook

(The Innocents), "Marguerite" by Oregon, "Moon Marguerite" by The Pillows, "Lullaby for Marguerite" by Autumn

LINER NOTES: The Innocents' lead singer Marguerite Van Cook works as a graphic novel illustrator, most notably for the book *Seven Miles a Second*.

Maureen

IRISH: Variation of Mary, our lady

ROCK AND ROLL: Popular, a good friend, a bit of an over-sharer

RELATED ARTISTS/SONGS: Maureen Herman (Babes in Toyland), Maureen "Moe" Tucker (The Velvet Underground), "Maureen" by Nick Lowe, "Maureen" by Jim Reeves, "Maureen" by Sade, "Maureen" by The Jon Spencer Blues Explosion, "Maureen" by Vetiver

"My Maureen,
don't ever dream I could be leaving you."
—VETIVER

Molly

ENGLISH: Form of Mary or Margaret, beloved

ROCK AND ROLL: Approachable, lovely, fresh-faced, youthful

RELATED ARTISTS/SONGS: Molly Hatchet, Mollie Kind (The Saturdays), Flogging Molly, "Molly's Chambers" by Kings of Leon, "Molly's Lips" by The Vaselines, "Good Golly Miss Molly" by Little Richard, "Handsome Molly" by Bob Dylan, "Molly" by Ween

LINER NOTES: The Vaselines song "Molly's Lips" was about Scottish actress Molly Weir, whose signature look included emphatic blood-red lips.

Nomy, Nomi

HEBREW: Form of Naomi, my delight

ROCK AND ROLL: Eccentric, sassy, brash

RELATED ARTISTS/SONGS: Nomy Lamm, Klaus Nomi, Nomi Ruiz (Hercules and Love Affair), "Nomi" by Alex Britti, "Nomi" by Nicole Milner, "Nomi" by Sweet Thunder

LINER NOTES: The Need's Nomy Lamm is famous for her lectures on feminism at Western Washington University, which she often gives while wearing fairy wings and waving a magic wand.

Nico

ITALIAN: Variation of Nicola, victorious

ROCK AND ROLL: Ethereal, blond, bohemian

RELATED ARTISTS/SONGS: Nico, "Nico" by the Space Twins, "Nico" by Fay Victor

LINER NOTES: Velvet Underground chanteuse Nico, born Christa

Päffgen, got her nickname from photographer Hebert Tobias, who named her after his ex-boyfriend Nico Papatakis.

Paloma

SPANISH: Dove

ROCK AND ROLL: Energetic, fashionable, forward-thinking

RELATED ARTISTS/SONGS: Paloma Faith, Paloma Romero (aka Palmolive), "Paloma Negra" by Lita Downs, "Paloma" by Carbon Leaf, "Paloma" by Jesse Cook

LINER NOTES: After leaving punk band The Raincoats, Paloma Romero—better known as Palmolive—formed a cover band called Hi-Fi, which rewrites the lyrics of punk hits to be more Christian-friendly.

Patti, Patty

LATIN: Variation of Patricia, nobly born

ROCK AND ROLL: Creative, scrappy, endearingly messy

RELATED ARTISTS/SONGS: Patti Smith, Patti LaBelle, Patti LuPone, "Patty Lee" by Les Savy Fav, "Patty" by Half Japanese, "Patty" by The Moments

LINER NOTES: Before gaining fame as a solo artist, Patti Smith was in the running to be the lead singer in Blue Öyster Cult.

Pauline

LATIN: Variation of Paul, petite

ROCK AND ROLL: Graceful, leads a charmed life, cute

RELATED ARTISTS/SONGS: Pauline Murray (Penetration), Pauline Black (The Selecter), Pauline Black (Hard Top), "Margaret vs. Pauline" by Neko Case, "Hermann Loves Pauline" by Super Furry Animals, "Pauline" by Screeching Weasel

"Everything's so easy for Pauline."
—NEKO CASE

Penelope

GREEK: Weaver

ROCK AND ROLL: Intrepid, a daredevil, loves to travel

RELATED ARTISTS/SONGS: Penelope Houston (The Avengers), "Penelope" by Pinback, "Penelope" by of Montreal, "Penelope" by Saosin, "Le Voyage de Penelope" by Air

LINER NOTES: San Francisco–based punk band The Avengers, helmed by Penelope Houston, opened at The Sex Pistols' last show at Winterland. After The Avengers broke up, Houston went on to lead the neo-folk movement on the West Coast.

Rizzo

ITALIAN: Curly-haired
ROCK AND ROLL: Gun-snapping, sassy, rebellious
RELATED ARTISTS/SONGS: Rizzo, "Rizzo" by Michael Foreman, "Rizzo" by Left Alone, "Rizzo" by The Caldwells
LINER NOTES: Riot grrrl band Rizzo was originally called Mopar; band members Sarah Dale and Jen Abercrombie changed it when they realized that they had both played Rizzo in their respective high school productions of *Grease*.

Sheena

IRISH: Version of Jane, God is gracious
ROCK AND ROLL: A headbanger, fun-loving, friendly
RELATED ARTISTS/SONGS: Sheena Easton, "Sheena Is a Punk Rocker" by The Ramones, "Sheena Is a Parasite" by The Horrors, "Lean on Sheena" by The Bouncing Souls
LINER NOTES: Joey Ramone based the character Sheena in "Sheena Is a Punk Rocker" on the heroine of the film *Sheena: Queen of the Jungle*.

Siouxsie

ENGLISH: Form of Susan, lily
ROCK AND ROLL: A loner, glamorous, calm
RELATED ARTISTS/SONGS: Siouxsie Sioux (Siouxsie and the Banshees), "Siouxsie Sioux" by Mike Macharyas, "Too Late for Siouxsie" by Jamie Sheriff, "Siouxsie Please Come Home" by Blue Skies for Black
LINER NOTES: Siouxsie Sioux turned down the role of Catwoman in *Batman Returns*, which later went to Michelle Pfeiffer.

Tamara

HEBREW: Palm tree
ROCK AND ROLL: Tough, chic, spontaneous
RELATED ARTISTS/SONGS: Tamara Barnett-Herrin, Tamera Lyndsay (Chalk Circle), "Tamara Is a Punk" by The Queers, "Tamara" by Warren Hill, "Tamara" by Phoenix
LINER NOTES: The Queers wrote "Tamara Is a Punk" in tribute to Chalk Circle bassist Tamera Lyndsay.

Tessa

ENGLISH: Form of Theresa, gatherer
ROCK AND ROLL: A risk-taker, brassy, independent
RELATED ARTISTS/SONGS: Tessa Pollitt (The Slits), Tessa Drummond, "Tessa" by Edmundo Rivero, "Tessa" by The Shame Idols, "Tessa" by Chicken Bone
LINER NOTES: The Slits' bassist Tessa Pollitt has a daughter, Phoebe, with Rip Rag bassist Sean Oliver.

Theo

ENGLISH: Variation of Theodora, God's gift
ROCK AND ROLL: Assertive, clever, a great dancer
RELATED ARTISTS/SONGS: Theo Kogan (Lunachicks), "Theo" by Darlington
LINER NOTES: Lunachicks' vocalist Theo Kogan has a cosmetics line called Armour Beauty and models for Calvin Klein and Kenneth Cole.

Tobi

ENGLISH: Variation of Tobias, the Lord is good
ROCK AND ROLL: Laid-back, a tomboy, capable
RELATED ARTISTS/SONGS: Tobi Vail (Bikini Kill), Tobi Tob, "Tobi" by Ninos Mutantes, "Tobi" by Rhythmo Loco, "Tobi" by Reto Suhner.
LINER NOTES: Bikini Kill drummer Tobi Vail dated Kurt Cobain in 1990 while the two of them were collaborating on a side band called The Bathtub Is Real.

Una

LATIN: One
ROCK AND ROLL: Affable, lighthearted, artistic
RELATED ARTISTS/SONGS: Una Baines (The Fall), Una Mia, "Una" by Inkuyo, "Una" by Lucio Battisti, "Una" by Excerpts
LINER NOTES: The Fall's keyboardist Una Baines was originally supposed to be the group's drummer but could not afford a drum kit. The first few shows she played with the band were with a Snoopy toy keyboard.

Vi

ENGLISH: Form of Violet or Vivian, lively
ROCK AND ROLL: Radical, a chamelon, an activist
RELATED ARTISTS/SONGS: Vi Subversa (Poison Girls), Vi Ann, "Vi" by Kid Loco
LINER NOTES: Vi Subversa's first appearance with a punk band was when she was forty-four years old; her children, Daniel and Gemma, are also punk musicians.

Vicky, Vicki

LATIN: Form of Victoria, a champion
ROCK AND ROLL: Creative, independent, edgy
RELATED ARTISTS/SONGS: Vicki Anderson, Vicki Peterson (The Bangles), Vicki Blue (The Runaways), "Vicky's Box" by Throwing Muses, "Vicky" by Trace, "Vicky" by Brute Force, "Vicky" by Johnny Reno
LINER NOTES: Violinist Vicky Aspinall joined The Raincoats when she saw a flyer in a bookstore that read: "female musician wanted: no style but strength."

Wendy

WELSH: Form of Gwendolyn, a fair woman

ROCK AND ROLL: An affable, hometown heartbreaker whom all the boys love

RELATED ARTISTS/SONGS: Wendy Wild, Wendy O. Williams (Plasmatics), Wendy Wilson, "Wendy" by The Beach Boys, "Wendy Time" by The Cure, "Tomorrow, Wendy" by Concrete Blonde, "Wendy Said" by Kim Wilde

LINER NOTES: After leaving Plasmatics, punk provocateur Wendy O. Williams gave up her stage life to work as an animal rehabilitator and natural food activist.

BOYS

Andrew

GREEK: Manly

ROCK AND ROLL: The cool kid at the party

RELATED ARTISTS/SONGS: Andrew Bird, Andrew W.K., Andrew Lloyd Webber, "St. Andrew (This Battle Is In the Air)" by The White Stripes, "Andrew" by Crystal Antlers, "Andrew" by Bowling for Soup

LINER NOTES: In addition to penning hard rock party anthems, Andrew W.K. is a motivational speaker.

Baz

SWEDISH: Form of Sebastian, from Sebastia

ROCK AND ROLL: Flashy, rich, affable

RELATED ARTISTS/SONGS: Baz Warne (The Stranglers), Maher Shalal Hash Baz, "Baz" by Pako Parisi

LINER NOTES: Baz Warne's bands aside from punk outfit The Stranglers include The Toy Dolls, The Sun Devils, and The Troubleshooters.

Bernard, Bernie

GERMAN: Brave, stalwart

ROCK AND ROLL: Well connected, the behind-the-scenes guy

RELATED ARTISTS/SONGS: Bernard Sumner (Joy Division, New Order), Bernie Taupin, "Bernard Jenkins" by Eric Clapton, "Bernie" by The Jon Spencer Blues Explosion, "Bernie" by Failure

LINER NOTES: New Order's Bernard Sumner is known by his bandmates as Barney and sometimes credited in recordings by the name "Barney Rubble."

Calum, Calumn

SCOTTISH: Dove

ROCK AND ROLL: Tough, capable, close to the land

RELATED ARTISTS/SONGS: Calum Marshall, Calumn MacKay (The Scars), Calum Stewart, "Calum Sgaire" by The Bothy Band

LINER NOTES: Scars' drummer Calumn MacKay is now an engineer and play in a blues group called The Pinetop's Boogiemen.

Danny

HEBREW: Short for Daniel, judged by God

ROCK AND ROLL: A rambunctious troublemaker, well loved

RELATED ARTISTS/SONGS: Danny Davis, Danny Elfman, Danny Wood (NKOTB), "Danny the Dog" by Massive Attack, "Danny" by Elvis, "Danny Vapid" by The Queers, "Danny's Chant" by Fleetwood Mac, "Danny Says" by The Ramones

"He's rough, he's tough, he's fun to have around."
—THE QUEERS

Dee Dee

AMERICAN INVENTED: Fun-loving

ROCK AND ROLL: Prolific, fierce

RELATED ARTISTS/SONGS: Dee Dee Bridgewater, Dee Dee Ramone, "Dee Dee Forever" by Nelly

LINER NOTES: Dee Dee Ramone had a brief, failed stint as a hip-hop artist, recording "Funky Man" as Dee Dee King.

Dexter

LATIN: Right-handed

ROCK AND ROLL: Cerebral, inventive, skilled

RELATED ARTISTS/SONGS: Dexter Freebish, Dexter Gordon, Dexter Holland (The Offspring), "Dexter" by Ricky Ford, "Dexter" by Ricardo Villalobos, "Dee Dee and Dexter" by They Might Be Giants, "Dexter" by Tiger Tunes

LINER NOTES: Offspring's guitarist Dexter Holland is a certified flight instructor.

Dez

IRISH: Variation of Desmond, Southerner

ROCK AND ROLL: Energetic, spiritual, a fan favorite

RELATED ARTISTS/SONGS: Dez Cadena (Black Flag), Dez Dickerson (Prince and the Revolution), "Dez" by Seu Cuca, "Dez" by Pimenta Nativa

LINER NOTES: Black Flag's third vocalist Dez Cadena's hoarse, raw singing style was later adopted by many hard-core bands; his father was renowned jazz producer Ozzie Cadena, whom the bachelor in the comic strip *Mutts* is named after.

Ethan

HEBREW: Steadfast
ROCK AND ROLL: Sweet, long-suffering, cool, off-kilter
RELATED ARTISTS/SONGS: Ethan James (Blue Cheer), "Ethan Sequence" by R. Stevie Moore, "Ethan Allen" by Jejune, "Ethan" by Lords, "Hey Ethan" by The Gyros
LINER NOTES: After leaving Blue Cheer, Ethan James engineered several iconic L.A. punk albums, including The Minutemen's *Double Nickels on the Dime*.

Eugene

GREEK: Well born
ROCK AND ROLL: Melancholy, a bit unbalanced, a heartbreaker
RELATED ARTISTS/SONGS: Eugene Hutz (Gogol Bordello), Eugene Kelly (The Vaselines), Eugene McGuinness, "Hey Eugene" by Pink Martini, "Eugene" by Andrew Bird, "Eugene's Lament" by The Beastie Boys, "Careful with That Axe, Eugene" by Pink Floyd
LINER NOTES: Eugene Hutz, singer for Gogol Bordello, starred in the Madonna-directed film *Filth and Wisdom*.

Grant

SCOTTISH: Large
ROCK AND ROLL: Neat, professional, dashing
RELATED ARTISTS/SONGS: Grant Hart (Husker Du), Grant McLennan (The Go-Betweens), Grant Lee Buffalo, "Grant" by Curd Duca, "Grant" by Kurt Rosenwinkel
LINER NOTES: Husker Du's Grant Hart met bandmate Bob Mould while working at the same record store; Hart's main inspiration is film scores from the 1950s and 1960s.

Greg, Gregg

GREEK: Short for Gregory, watchmen
ROCK AND ROLL: Ambitious, intense, a good childhood friend
RELATED ARTISTS/SONGS: Gregg Allman (The Allman Brothers Band), Greg Ginn (Black Flag), Greg Lake (Emerson, Lake & Palmer), "Greg Street Stuntin'," by Big Tymers, "Go-Getter Greg" by Ludo, "Greg" by Eminem, "Greg's Last Day" by The Starting Line
LINER NOTES: Black Flag's songwriter Greg Ginn's brother Raymond designed the band's iconic logo, as well as several of their album covers.

Henry

GERMAN: Powerful ruler
ROCK AND ROLL: Literate, politically conscious, smart, sarcastic

RELATED ARTISTS/SONGS: Henry "Red" Allen, Henry Mancini, Henry Rollins (Black Flag), "Henry Lee" by Nick Cave & the Bad Seeds, "Henry" by Rod Stewart, "Henry" by Dick Cary, "Henry" by New Riders of the Purple Sage, "Don't Ya Tell Henry" by The Band

LINER NOTES: Henry Garfield adopted the last name Rollins as a result of a joke with Fugazi singer Ian MacKaye, who would write Henry mysterious notes signed "ROLLINS."

Howard

ENGLISH: Watchman

ROCK AND ROLL: Inventive, intense, a little wild

RELATED ARTISTS/SONGS: Howard Devoto (Buzzcocks, Magazine), Howard Levy (Bela Fleck and the Flecktones), Howard Shore, "Howard" by Rickie Lee Jones, "Howard" by The Residents, "Howard" by The String Cheese Incident

LINER NOTES: The Buzzcocks' Howard Devoto had a small role as a janitor in the movie *24 Hour Party People*.

Hugo

LATIN: Variation of Hugh, high-minded

ROCK AND ROLL: Complicated, a hopeless romantic, organized

RELATED ARTISTS/SONGS: Hugo Burnham (Gang of Four), "Hugo" by Paper Tiger, "Hugo" by The Tellers, "Hugo" by Terumesa Hino

LINER NOTES: Gang of Four drummer Hugo Burnham is an associate professor at the New England Institute of Art.

Ian

GAELIC: God is gracious

ROCK AND ROLL: Original, independent, a cult hero

RELATED ARTISTS/SONGS: Ian Anderson (Jethro Tull), Ian Astbury (The Cult), Ian Curtis (Joy Division), "Ian" by Rainier Maria, "Ian" by Withered Earth, "Ian" by The Horror

LINER NOTES: U2's song "A Day Without Me" is a tribute to Joy Division's Ian Curtis.

Iggy

LATIN: variation of Ignatius, Fiery

ROCK AND ROLL: Wild, glamorous, often shirtless, puts on a great show

RELATED ARTISTS/SONGS: Iggy Pop, "Iggy" by Afrika Corps

LINER NOTES: Iggy Pop, born James Osterberg, took his name from his high school band, The Iguanas.

Jad

ARABIC: Benevolent

ROCK AND ROLL: Confident, prolific, high-spirited

RELATED ARTISTS/SONGS: Jad Fair (Half Japanese), Jad Abumrad, "Jad" by Anthony Cox

LINER NOTES: Jad Fair started the group Half Japanese with his brother David; he began making paper collages as a distraction while on the road and has since published four books of his art and designed most of the band's album covers.

Joe

HEBREW: Form of Joseph, God will increase

ROCK AND ROLL: Handsome, strong, fearless, but has a temper

RELATED ARTISTS/SONGS: Joe Strummer (The Clash), Joe Tex, Big Joe Williams, "Joe the Lion" by David Bowie, "Hey Joe" by Jimi Hendrix, "Joe's Head" by Kings of Leon, "Joe" by PJ Harvey, "Cotton-Eyed Joe" by Rednex

"His eyes were his tools and his smile was a gun."
—REDNEX

Joey

HEBREW: Variation of Joseph, God multiplies

ROCK AND ROLL: Leader of the pack, lucky, resourceful

RELATED ARTISTS/SONGS: Joey Catillo (Queens of the Stone Age), Joey Fatone ('N Sync), Joey Ramone (The Ramones), "Joey" by Bob Dylan, "Joey" by Bon Jovi, "Joey" by Concrete Blonde, "Joey" by Nick Drake, "Joey" by Sugarland

LINER NOTES: The "Joey Ramone Place" sign at the corner of Bowery and East Second Street in Manhattan is the most stolen sign in New York City.

Jonathan

HEBREW: God has given

ROCK AND ROLL: Sensitive, goofy, inventive, thoroughly modern

RELATED ARTISTS/SONGS: Jonathan Donahue (The Flaming Lips), Jonathan King, Jonathan Richman (The Modern Lovers), "Jonathan" by Nerf Herder, "Jonathan David" by Belle & Sebastian, "Jonathan" by Korn

LINER NOTES: Jonathan Richman and The Modern Lovers recorded their first demos in 1972 with The Velvet Underground's John Cale.

Lou

GREEK: Variation of Louis, brave warrior

ROCK AND ROLL: Stylish, a world traveler, sophisticated

RELATED ARTISTS/SONGS: Lou Barlow (Dinosaur Jr.), Lou Christie, Lou Reed, "Caribou Lou" by Tech N9ne, "Lou" by Adam & the Ants, "Lou" by Sanford & Townshend

LINER NOTES: Lou Reed invented an alternative kind of guitar tuning called "Ostrich guitar," named after the pre-Velvet Underground song "The Ostrich" by Lou Reed and the Primitives.

Malcolm

SCOTTISH: Follower of Saint Columba

ROCK AND ROLL: Eccentric, innovative, brainy

RELATED ARTISTS/SONGS: Malcolm McLaren, Malcolm Mooney (Can), Malcolm Young (AC/DC), "Malcolm" by Ghostface Killah, "Malcolm" by The Arrogant Worms, "Malcolm" by Charles Sullivan

LINER NOTES: Legendary manager Malcolm McLaren and girlfriend Vivienne Westwood ran a London punk rock boutique, where he outfitted The Sex Pistols and New York Dolls.

Manny

SPANISH: Variation of Manuel, God is with us

ROCK AND ROLL: Artsy, prefers to dress in black, suave

RELATED ARTISTS/SONGS: Manny Martinez (The Misfits), Manny Manuel, Manny Moch, "Manny with Lunchbox" by John Lurie, "Manny's Bones" by Los Lobos, "Manny, Moe, & Jack" by The Dickies, "Manny's Song" by Stroke 9, "Manny" by Nobodys

LINER NOTES: Manny Martinez, The Misfits' original drummer, helped give the band their name, which was taken from Marilyn Monroe's last movie.

Melvin

SCOTTISH: Variation of Melville, protector

ROCK AND ROLL: Boisterous, funny, laid-back

RELATED ARTISTS/SONGS: The Melvins, Melvin Ragin, Melvin Sparks, "I, Melvin" by NOFX, "Melvin's Interlude" by The Temptations, "Melvin" by The Pandoras, "Melvin" by The Belles, "Melvin" by Thee Headcoatees

LINER NOTES: Kurt Cobain tried out to be the bassist of The Melvins but was so nervous that he forgot the songs.

Milo

GERMAN: Peaceful

ROCK AND ROLL: Nerdy but cool, loves food, dextrous

RELATED ARTISTS/SONGS: Milo Aukerman (The Descendents), "Milo, Sorghum & Maiz" by Meat Puppets, "Interlude (Milo)" by Modest Mouse, "Milo" by Bowling for Soup

LINER NOTES: The Descendents' Milo Aukerman has a doctorate in biochemistry; his academic research has caused the band to take several extended hiatuses.

Monty

ENGLISH: Form of Montgomery, manpower
ROCK AND ROLL: Jaunty, a handsome rogue
RELATED ARTISTS/SONGS: Monty Alexander, Monty Oxymoron (The Damned), Monty Norman, "Monty" by Spiderbait, "Monty Got a Raw Deal" by R.E.M., "Hands Off My Cash, Monty" by Two Door Cinema
LINER NOTES: Befored he joined The Damned, Monty Oxymoron played in a Pink Floyd cover band called Punk Floyd and Dr. Spacetoad Experience.

Noko

JAPANESE: Form of Kinoko, mushroom
ROCK AND ROLL: Zany, literate, a risk-taker
RELATED ARTISTS/SONGS: Noko Fisher-Jones (Magazine), "Noko" by Molotov, "Noko" by Torso, "Noko" by Aggas Zokoko
LINER NOTES: Magazine guitarist Noko's first band was called Alvin the Aardvark & the Fuzzy Ants.

Riff

ENGLISH: A melodic phrase
ROCK AND ROLL: Improvisational, funny, popular
RELATED ARTISTS/SONGS: Riff Regan (London), Riff Raff, "Riff Raff" by AC/DC, "Riff Wraiths" by Lightning Bolt, "Big Riff" by Cave In
LINER NOTES: London singer Riff Regan, real name Miles Treddinick, is a Broadway buff; his stage name was taken from the character in *West Side Story*.

Rob

GERMAN: Variation of Robert, famous
ROCK AND ROLL: A hustler, smooth, adapts easily
RELATED ARTISTS/SONGS: Rob Zombie, Rob Thomas (Matchbox Twenty), Rob Tyner (The MC5), "Rob" by Ray Street Park
LINER NOTES: The MC5's Rob Tyner, born Robert Derminer, took the last name Tyner in honor of jazz pianist McCoy Tyner.

Rory

IRISH: Red king
ROCK AND ROLL: Introspective, mischievous, youthful
RELATED ARTISTS/SONGS: Rory Lee Feek, Rory Storm, Rory Block, Rory Gallagher, "Rory Rides Me Raw" by The Vaselines, "Rory" by Black 47

Shane

IRISH: Variation of John, God's grace

ROCK AND ROLL: Brave, tough, virile

RELATED ARTISTS/SONGS: Shane MacGowan (The Pogues), Shane Filan (Westlife), "Shane" by Liz Phair, "Shane, She Wrote This" by Television, "The Shane Song" by Charles Bronson, "Shane" by Kim Wilde

LINER NOTES: Before helming The Pogues, Shane MacGowan fronted the band The Nipple Erectors under the name Shane O'Hooligan.

Sid, Syd

FRENCH: Variation of Sidney, Saint-Denis

ROCK AND ROLL: A visionary, magnetic, spontaneous

RELATED ARTISTS/SONGS: Syd Barrett (Pink Floyd), Sid Vicious (The Sex Pistols), Sid Wilson (Slipknot), "Sid's Ahead" by Miles Davis, "Jumpin' with Symphony Sid" by Lester Young

LINER NOTES: Sid Vicious was born John Simon Ritchie; John Lydon (aka Johnny Rotten) named him Sid after Lydon's ornery pet hamster.

Sterling

ENGLISH: Of the highest quality

ROCK AND ROLL: Glamorous, stylish, engaging

RELATED ARTISTS/SONGS: Sterling Morrison (The Velvet Underground), Sterling Simms, Sterling Knight, "Sterling" by Strand of Oaks, "Sterling" by Hungry John, "Sterling" by Plankeye

LINER NOTES: The Velvet Underground's Sterling Morrison met Lou Reed while they were both studying English at Syracuse University.

Sylvain

FRENCH: Spirit of the woods

ROCK AND ROLL: Bold, dramatic, fashion-forward

RELATED ARTISTS/SONGS: Sylvain Sylvain (New York Dolls), Sylvain Chauveau, "Sylvain" by Prince Mabiala Youlou, "Sylvain" by Bernard Rambaud, "Sylvain" by Jean-Marc Jafet

LINER NOTES: Before joining New York Dolls, Sylvain Sylvain and drummer Billy Murcia ran a glam rock clothing company called Truth and Soul.

Terry

LATIN: Variation of Terentius, clan name

ROCK AND ROLL: Experimental, creative, eccentric

RELATED ARTISTS/SONGS: Terry Riley, Terry Hall (The Specials), "Terry's Song" by Bruce Springsteen, "Terry" by Pat Boone, "Terry" by Kirsty MacColl, "Terry" by The Ladybug Transistor, "Terry" by Twinkle

LINER NOTES: The Specials' Terry Hall cowrote The Go-Go's' "Our Lips Are Sealed"; it was a hit for both The Go-Go's and Hall's band Fun Boy Three.

Theo

GREEK: God-like

ROCK AND ROLL: Modest, talented

RELATED ARTISTS/SONGS: Theo Van Rock, Theo Peoples (The Temptations), Theo Parrish, "Theo B" by Sunny Day Real Estate, "Theo" by Vodka Collins, "Theo" by Alan Merrill

LINER NOTES: The Rollins Band's live sound engineer, Theo Van Rock, is always credited on recordings as a full member of the band; his birth name is Theo van Eenbergen.

Thor

NORSE: Thunder

ROCK AND ROLL: Studious, intense, dedicated

RELATED ARTISTS/SONGS: Thor, Thor Eisentrager (The Cows), "Thor Arise" by Amon Amarth, "Thor" by Manowar

LINER NOTES: Cows founder Thor Eisentrager now works as a director of security for the Minneapolis Institute of Arts.

Walter, Wally

GERMAN: Warrior

ROCK AND ROLL: Kind, a heartbreaker in his youth, a good friend

RELATED ARTISTS/SONGS: Walter Lure (The Heartbreakers), Walter Becker (Steely Dan), Wally Palmer (The Romantics) "Walter's Walk" by Led Zeppelin, "Do You Remember Walter?" by The Kinks, "Uncle Walter" by Ben Folds, "Walter" by Petula Clark, "Wally" by Joe Gilman

LINER NOTES: After punk band The Heartbreakers broke up, guitarist Walter Lure became a Wall Street stockbroker.

Zander, Xander

GREEK: Form of Alexander, defending warrior

ROCK AND ROLL: Quirky, dark, bold

RELATED ARTISTS/SONGS: Zander Schloss, Xander Venema, MC Xander, Frank Zander, "Xander" by Antonino Di Leva, "Zander Two" by Boards of Canada, "Zander" by James Morrison

LINER NOTES: Thelonious Monster and Circle Jerks bassist Zander Schloss acts in independent films, playing the role of Kevin in *Repo Man* and a heavy metal fan in *Tapeheads*.

Zoran

BASQUE: Cosmic

ROCK AND ROLL: Clever, skillful

RELATED ARTISTS/SONGS: Zoran Predin, Zoran Vanev, Zoran Sztevanovity (Metro), "Zoran" by Zoran Terzic

LINER NOTES: Metro front man Zoran Sztevanovity has two children, Zoltan and Sandra.

The Best Punk Names
for Girls

A punk-inspired little girl's name needn't just be one with a lot of extra X's and Z's. Punk, hardcore, and riot grrrl bands also have plenty of role models for strong, independent women with a little edge to them. Try one of these, inspired by lady punk band members. She'll be learning how to distort a power chord in no time.

NAME	INSPIRATION
Arianna	Ari Up, lead singer of The Slits
Betsy	Riot grrrl band Heavens to Betsy
Corin	Sleater-Kinney's Corin Tucker
Debbie	Blondie's Debbie Harry
Donna	Team Dresch bassist Donna Dresch
Iggy	Yes, Iggy Pop's a boy—but this would make a fresh, tomboyish choice for a little girl
Kathy	Go-Go's drummer Kathy Valentine
Lydia	Punk poet Lydia Lunch
Moe	Velvet Underground drummer Maureen Tucker
Nomi, Nomy	Shock rockers Nomy Lamm and Klaus Nomi
Sheena	Ramones song "Sheena Is a Punk Rocker"
Vivienne	Punk fashion designer Vivienne Westwood

Real or Fake
Punk Name Quiz

Outrageous stage names are standard fare in punk bands, but some of them seem too bizarre to be true. Can you sort the real punk rockers from the fictional ones?

1. Pat Smear
2. Klaus Fluoride
3. Billy Blade
4. 6025
5. Rex Everything
6. Cheetah Chrome
7. Poly Styrene
8. Rat Scabies
9. Fat Mike
10. Manny Ramone
11. Tazzie Bushweed
12. Chris Hate
13. Lorna Doom
14. Lux Interior
15. Captain Sensible

ANSWER: All are real except for 3 and 10.

The Punk
Name Machine

The name Johnny Rotten or Richard Hell gets a little awkward come standardized test time, but that doesn't mean you, too, can't have a nickname with some in-your-face attitude. For that safety pin–pierced Mohawk-sporting punk in all of us, here's an easy guide to making your punk name.

First: Take your childhood nickname as your first name, preferably something that ends in "y" or "i." If you didn't have one, spell your first name backwards. So Tom becomes "Tommy" or "T-bird" or "Mot."

Step Two: To find your punk surname, follow these steps:

Who are you in the band?

a. The crazy one! It's not a good night if I don't end up with a new piercing.

b. The nice one. I've bailed a lot of people out in my day.

c. The brains behind the operation. No one would even own an instrument if not for me.

IF YOU CHOSE A

Add the name of the weapon you would use in a duel (Tommy Knuckles).

IF YOU CHOSE B

Add the name of your favorite holiday (Tommy Christmas).

IF YOU CHOSE C

Add a word you would use to describe garbage (Tommy Nasty).

So Margaret would be Maggie Valentine, Maggie Tanks, Maggie Vile, Teragram Putrid, or Teragram Independence.
Bonus points for alliteration!

1980s:
New Wavers,
Jangle Pop, and the
Age of Big Hair

T he dawn of MTV launched a whole new wave of teen pop, while at college radio stations across the country, alternative rock groups were also gaining steam. There's a second Elvis, the beginning of Madonna's reign, and a slew of great name songs.

GIRLS

Allison, Alison

SCOTTISH: Truth
ROCK AND ROLL: The girl who got away
RELATED ARTISTS/SONGS: Alison Brown, Alison Moyet, Allison Moorer, "Alison" by Elvis Costello, "Allison," by The Pixies
LINER NOTES: The chorus of Elvis Costello's "Alison" is based on the song "Ghetto Child" by The Spinners.

Amanda

LATIN: Worthy of love
ROCK AND ROLL: Girl next door, a reluctant beauty queen
RELATED ARTISTS/SONGS: Amanda Overmyer, Amanda Palmer, "Amanda" by Waylon Jennings, "Amanda," by Boston, "Miss Amanda Jones" by The Rolling Stones, "Crazy Amanda" by Sum 41

"Amanda, light of my life, you should have been a gentleman's wife."
—WAYLON JENNINGS

Carnie, Carni, Carny

LATIN: Horn

ROCK AND ROLL: A celebrity, eccentric, might work at a carnival

RELATED ARTISTS/SONGS: Carnie Wilson, "The Carny" by Nick Cage, "Baby Carni Bird" by Camille, "Carny Town" by Elvis Presley

LINER NOTES: Carnie Wilson has two children, Lola and Luciano.

Cindy, Cyndi

GREEK: Short for Cynthia or Lucinda, moon goddess

ROCK AND ROLL: Sweet but capricious hometown girl, high school sweetheart

RELATED ARTISTS/SONGS: Cindy Birdsong (The Supremes), Cyndi Lauper, Cindy Wilson (The B-52's), "Cindy, Cindy" by Elvis Presley, "Taste of Cindy," by Jesus and Mary Chain, "Hurricane Cindy" by Liz Phair, "Cindy, Oh Cindy" by The Beach Boys, "Cindy of a Thousand" by Billy Bragg

LINER NOTES: Cyndi Lauper was the musical director for the film *The Goonies*.

Claire, Clare

FRENCH: Bright, clear

CHEAP TRICK:
"You're much stronger than I'd ever hoped to be."

THE B-52'S:
"She drove a Plymouth Satellite faster than the speed of light."

MATT POND PA:
"Claire, you do it perfectly."

PAUL SIMON:
"A strange young smile, as warm as I have known."

Danielle, Daniella

HEBREW: Variant of Daniel, judged by God

ROCK AND ROLL: A great dancer, a free spirit

RELATED ARTISTS/SONGS: Danielle Dax, Danielle Howle, Danielle Peck, "Danielle" by Vic Lewis, "Danielle" by Juice, "Danielle" by Mick Jones, "Daniella" by Shack, "Danielle's Breakfast" by Chris Rea

LINER NOTES: Experimental musician Danielle Dax of The Lemon Kittens is an interior designer who makes occasional appearances on the TV show *Homefronts*.

Darlene

ENGLISH: Darling
ROCK AND ROLL: Alluring, wild, sweet
RELATED ARTISTS/SONGS: Darlene Love, "Darlene" by Slint, "Darlene" by Led Zeppelin, "Darling Darlene" by Farewell
LINER NOTES: Darlene Love, who first rose to fame with the girl group The Blossoms, played Danny Glover's wife in the *Lethal Weapon* movies.

Diane

GREEK: Variation of Diana, devine
ROCK AND ROLL: Laid-back, a fresh-faced sweetheart; should be careful around strangers
RELATED ARTISTS/SONGS: Diane Stewart, Diane Warren, "Jack & Diane" by John Mellencamp, "My Diane" by The Beach Boys, "Oh Diane" by Fleetwood Mac, "Diane" by Hüsker Dü, "Little Diane" by Dion
LINER NOTES: John Mellencamp was inspired to write "Jack & Diane" after watching the 1961 film *Splendor in the Grass*.

Eileen

FRENCH: Bright, shining
ROCK AND ROLL: Haunting, can really work a dress
RELATED ARTISTS/SONGS: Eileen Rose (Daisy Chain), "Eileen" by Keith Richards, "Come On, Eileen" by Dexy's Midnight Runners, "Eileen" by Skid Row, "Eileen" by Bing Crosby, "Eileen" by The Hush Sound
LINER NOTES: "Come On, Eileen" is about a childhood sweetheart of Kevin Rowland; the band's name is slang for the drug Dexadrine.

Elise

FRENCH: Dedicated to God
ROCK AND ROLL: A beautiful singer, a heartbreaker
RELATED ARTISTS/SONGS: Elise Estrada, "A Letter to Elise" by The Cure, "A Perfect Day Elise" by PJ Harvey, "Elise" by Toro y Moi, "Elise Affair" by Thievery Corporation, "Elise" by Don Williams
LINER NOTES: The Cure's song "A Letter to Elise" was inspired by Jean Cocteau's *The Holy Terrors* and David Bowie's "A Letter to Hermione."

Erin

GAELIC: Ireland
ROCK AND ROLL: Mischievous, a fun friend, keeps to herself
RELATED ARTISTS/SONGS: Erin McCarley, "Erin O'Connor" by The Long Blondes, "The Greenhorn/Exile of Erin/Glasgow Reel" by Andrew Bird, "Erin" by Sister Hazel, "Erin with an 'E'" by The Impossibles
LINER NOTES: The Everly Brothers' Don Everly's daughter Erin Everly was briefly married to Axl Rose. She appeared in the music video for "Sweet Child O' Mine."

Evelyn

FRENCH: Radiant
ROCK AND ROLL: Lovely, desired but fickle
RELATED ARTISTS/SONGS: Evelyn "Champagne" King, Evelyn Laye, Evelyn Thomas, "Evelyn" by Sun Ra, "Evelyn Is Not Real" by My Morning Jacket, "Evelyn, a Modified Dog" by Frank Zappa, "Evelyn" by The Tragically Hip, "Evelyn" by The Silhouettes
LINER NOTES: Disco singer Evelyn "Champagne" King's nickname is a variation of a nickname she had as a child, "Bubbles."

Genevieve

FRENCH: Woman of the people
ROCK AND ROLL: Sweet, gentle, a sophisticated lady
RELATED ARTISTS/SONGS: Genevieve McGuckin (The Birthday Party), Genevieve Waite, "Genevieve" by The Kingsmen, "Genevieve" by John Phillips, "Genevieve" by Grand Funk Railroad, "Sweet Lady Genevieve" by The Kinks, "Genevieve" by Sugarland

*"She's my only love,
she's my favorite sinner."*
—SUGARLAND

Gypsy

ENGLISH: Wanderer
ROCK AND ROLL: A sultry bohemian, free-spirited
RELATED ARTISTS/SONGS: Gypsy Eden, "Gypsy Eyes" by Jimi Hendrix, "Gypsy" by Fleetwood Mac, "Gypsy" by Suzanne Vega, "Gypsy" by Shakira, "Gypsy" by Van Morrison
LINER NOTES: Stevie Nicks wrote the song "Gypsy" partially in tribute to her late friend Robin Anderson.

Henrietta

ENGLISH: Feminine form of Henry, ruler of the home
ROCK AND ROLL: Crush-worthy, flirtatious, magnetic
RELATED ARTISTS/SONGS: "Henrietta" by The Fratellis, "Henrietta" by The Trashmen, "Henrietta" by John Fogerty, "Henrietta" by Chris King, "Henrietta" by Tracy & the Plastics

*"You got me so shook up,
I never ever wanna leave."*
—JOHN FOGERTY

Jeanette, Jeannette

HEBREW: Form of Jean, God is gracious

ROCK AND ROLL: Leads the way, has a dark side, boisterous

RELATED ARTISTS/SONGS: Jeanette Baker, Jeanette Biedermann, Jeanette Hutchison (The Emotions), "Jeanette" by Mando Diao, "Jeanette" by The English Beat, "Jeannette" by Gus Viseur, "Jeanette" by The Monroes, "Bring a Torch, Jeanette, Isabella" by Tori Amos

LINER NOTES: The English Beat song "Jeanette" was inspired by a friend of the band who habitually wore her hair in a beehive hairdo.

Jenny

WELSH: Variation of Guinevere or Jennifer, white wave

ROCK AND ROLL: A great dancer, sweet and delicious, uninhibited

RELATED ARTISTS/SONGS: Jenny Berggren (Ace of Base), Jenny Lewis (Rilo Kiley), "Jenny" by The Mountain Goats, "Jenny Jenny" by Little Richard, "867-5039/Jenny" by Tommy Tutone, "Jenny Was a Friend of Mine" by The Killers, "Jenny" by Sleater-Kinney

LINER NOTES: Inspired by the Tommy Tutone song, a man auctioned off the phone number 867-5039 for $80,000 on eBay.

Juliet

ENGLISH: Variation of Julia, youthful

ROCK AND ROLL: Beautiful but dangerous, star-crossed

RELATED ARTISTS/SONGS: Juliet Richardson, "Juliet of the Spirits" by The B-52's, "Juliet" by The Bee Gees, "Romeo and Juliet" by Dire Straits, "Juliet" by Neil Diamond, "Juliet" by Stevie Nicks

LINER NOTES: Guitarist Mark Knopfler wrote Dire Straits' "Romeo and Juliet" about his split from Holly Vincent, of Holly and the Italians; the line "I used to have a scene with him" came from an interview Holly gave about the breakup.

Kate, Cate

GREEK: Form of Catherine, pure

ROCK AND ROLL: Breaks all the rules, a great drummer, cool and laid-back

RELATED ARTISTS/SONGS: Kate Bush, Kate Pierson (The B-52's), Moonshine Kate, "Kate" by Ben Folds Five, "Klondyke Kate" by Suzi Quatro, "Kate" by Johnny Cash, "Kate" by Linda Rondstadt

LINER NOTES: Kate Bush's fans celebrate July 30, her birthday, as "Katemas."

Katrina

GREEK: Form of Katherine, pure

ROCK AND ROLL: Flirty, fun, but dangerous

RELATED ARTISTS/SONGS: Katrina and the Waves, Katrina Elam, Katrina Ford, "O Katrina" by Black Lips, "Katrina" by Bing Crosby, "Katrina Blues" by Ronnie Earl & the Broadcasters

LINER NOTES: The band Katrina and the Waves, best known for their song "Walking on Sunshine," was cofounded by Kimberley Rew, who had previously played guitar with The Soft Boys.

Leah, Lea

HEBREW: Delicate
ROCK AND ROLL: Popular, charming, a blue-eyed beauty
RELATED ARTISTS/SONGS: Leah Dizon, Leah Haywood, Lea Michele, "Leah" by Bruce Springsteen, "Leah" by Roy Orbison, "Ah! Leah" by Donnie Iris, "My Beautiful Leah" by PJ Harvey, "Lea" by Toto
LINER NOTES: Donnie Iris' song "Ah! Leah!" was about a former girl-friend of a bandmate of his; he later referenced it in his albums *Ah! Live!* and *Ah! Leluiah!*

Leila, Leela

ARABIC: Born at night
ROCK AND ROLL: Tempting, a rambler, a free spirit
RELATED ARTISTS/SONGS: Leila and the Snakes, Leela Floyd, "Leila" by Jesse Cook, "Leila" by ZZ Top, "Leila" by Wes Montgomery, "Leila" by Dolly Dots

"She had a look in her eye that could make you melt."
—ZZ TOP

Leonora, Lenora

ENGLISH: Variation of Eleanora, bright one
ROCK AND ROLL: Noctural, patient, alluring
RELATED ARTISTS/SONGS: Lenora Lafayette, "Leonora" by Emma Shapplin, "Leonora" by Hercules and the Love Affair, "Leonora" by The Gin Club
LINER NOTES: Stevie Ray Vaughan wrote the track "Lenny" for his wife Lenora; she claimed that she never listened to it without crying.

Madge

ENGLISH: Form of Margaret, pearl
ROCK AND ROLL: Old-fashioned, pretty, tidy
RELATED ARTISTS/SONGS: "Madge Speaks" by The Prodigy, "Fight-ing for Madge" by Fleetwood Mac, "Madge" by Stephen Bishop, "Harry, You're a Beast" by Frank Zappa
LINER NOTES: The British press nicknamed Madonna "Madge"—short for both Madonna and "Her Majesty."

Margarita

SPANISH: Variation of Margaret, pearl
ROCK AND ROLL: Intoxicating, mellow, exotic
RELATED ARTISTS/SONGS: "Margarita" by The Traveling Wilburys, "Margarita" by Spin Doctors, "Margarita" by Sleepy Brown
LINER NOTES: Classic rock supergroup The Traveling Wilburys was made up of George Harrison, Tom Petty, Roy Orbison, Bob Dylan, and Jeff Lynne, who all wrote under aliases. Charlie T. Wilbury Jr., better known as Tom Petty, wrote "Margarita."

Nikita

RUSSIAN: Unconquered
ROCK AND ROLL: Beautiful, aloof
RELATED ARTISTS/SONGS: "Nikita" by Elton John, "Oh Nikita" by The Guggenheim Grotto
LINER NOTES: Elton John wrote "Nikita" about the Cold War; George Michael provided backing vocals on the song.

Pat

LATIN: Variation of Patricia, wealthy
ROCK AND ROLL: Slick, tough, polished, powerful
RELATED ARTISTS/SONGS: Pat Benatar
LINER NOTES: The character Pat Bernardo in *Fast Times at Ridgemont High* was inspired by Pat Benatar, who has two daughters, Hana and Haley.

Peaches

ENGLISH FRUIT NAME
ROCK AND ROLL: Brash, bold, soulful, glamorous
RELATED ARTISTS/SONGS: Peaches, Peaches & Herb, "Peaches" by The Stranglers, "Peaches" by The Presidents of the United States of America
LINER NOTES: Peaches Geldof, daughter of The Boomtown Rats' Bob Geldof, is legally named Peaches Honeyblossom Michelle Charlotte Angel Vanessa Geldof. Geldof's other daughters' names are Little Pixie, Fifi Trixabelle, and Heavenly Hiraani Tiger Lily Hutchence.

Roxy, Roxie

PERSIANI: Form of Roxanne, dawn
ROCK AND ROLL: Glowing, saucy, a golden child
RELATED ARTISTS/SONGS: Roxy Music, "Roxy" by Supergrass, "Roxy" by Sons of the Subway, "Roxy" by Concrete Blonde, "Roxy" by Ludo
LINER NOTES: Before Bryan Ferry formed Roxy Music, he lost his job teaching ceramics at a girls' school for holding record listening sessions instead of class.

Sabrina

WELSH: River-dweller
ROCK AND ROLL: Sprightly, pretty, bright
RELATED ARTISTS/SONGS: Sabrina Bryan (Cheetah Girls), Sabrina Salerno, "Sabrina" by Einstürzende Neubaten, "Sabrina" by The Hanson Brothers, "A Song for Sabrina" by Kero One
LINER NOTES: Sabrina Salerno's video for "Boys (Summertime Love)" was initially banned from the United Kingdom for the scantiness of her bikini.

Samantha

SANSKRIT: Universal
ROCK AND ROLL: Elegant, fashionable, loving
RELATED ARTISTS/SONGS: Samantha Cole, Samantha Jade, Samantha Mumba, "Samantha" by Hole, "Samantha" by the Village People, "Samantha" by Madness, "Lady Samantha" by Elton John, "Goodbye Sam Hello Samantha" by Cliff Richard
LINER NOTES: The Smashing Pumpkins' Billy Corgan co-wrote Hole's "Samantha" with Courtney Love.

Sandra

ENGLISH: Form of Alessandra, defender of mankind
ROCK AND ROLL: Cheeky, kindhearted, affable
RELATED ARTISTS/SONGS: Sandra, Sandra Nasic, "Golly Sandra" by Eisley, "Sandra's Theme" by Danny Elfman, "Sandra" by Gilberto Gil, "Sandra" by Barry Manilow, "Sandra" by Byron Lee and the Dragonaires
LINER NOTES: Eighties pop sensation Sandra has twins named Nikita and Sebastian.

Shannon

GAELIC: Small, wise one
ROCK AND ROLL: A swimmer, dreamy, well loved
RELATED ARTISTS/SONGS: Shannon Greene, Shannon Wright, "Shannon" by Henry Gross, "Shannon" by Geoffrey Castle, "Shannon" by The Sinatras
LINER NOTES: Shannon Greene, best known for her hit 1980s single under the mononym just Shannon "Let the Music Play," cut the track as a single while singing with The New York Jazz Ensemble.

Siobhan

IRISH: God's grace
ROCK AND ROLL: The life of the party, sunny, luminous
RELATED ARTISTS/SONGS: Siobhan Donaghy (Sugababes), Siobhan Fahey (Bananarama), Siobhan Dillon, "Hang On, Siobhan" by The Walkmen, "This Beard Is for Siobhan" by Devendra Banhart, "Siobhan" by The Tossers

LINER NOTES: Siobhan Fahey met the other members of Bananarama while in a fashion journalism class; they began playing with help from The Sex Pistols' Paul Cook.

Susan

HEBREW: Joyful
ROCK AND ROLL: Clued in, a good listener, luscious
RELATED ARTISTS/SONGS: Susan Boyle, Susan Ann Sulley (The Human League), "Susan's House" by The Eels, "Susan" by Aimee Mann, "To Susan on the West Coast Waiting" by Donovan, "Wake Up Susan" by The Spinners, "Susan" by Dean Martin

"Susan has got that certain air the boys call supersonic."
—DEAN MARTIN

Susanna, Susannah

HEBREW: Form of Susan, joyous
ROCK AND ROLL: Folksy, beloved, dedicated
RELATED ARTISTS/SONGS: Susanna Hoffs (The Bangles), "Susannah's Still Alive" by The Kinks, "Oh Sweet Susanna" by The Mooney Suzuki, "Oh! Susanna" by Stephen Foster
LINER NOTES: Susanna Hoffs, Vivi Peterson, and Debbi Peterson originally named their band The Colours, The Supersonic Bangs, and then The Bangs. The "les" got added to avoid legal complications with another group called The Bangs.

Theodora

GREEK: God's gift
ROCK AND ROLL: Elegant, sophistacted, hip
RELATED ARTISTS/SONGS: Theodora Morse, "Theodora" by Wes Montgomery, "Theodora" by Billy Taylor, "Theodora" by Tim Moore, "Theodora" by Rick Strauss
LINER NOTES: Theodora Richards, Keith Richards's daughter, is a model and designer, most recently designing a line of jeans inspired by her mother, Patti Hansen.

Tiffany

GREEK: Born on Epiphany
ROCK AND ROLL: Happy, breezy, bubbly
RELATED ARTISTS/SONGS: Tiffany Darwish, Tiffany Evans, Tiffany Villareal, "Tiffany Queen" by The Byrds, "Tiffany Hall" by The Coup, "Tiffany" by Bill Evans

LINER NOTES: Pop singer Tiffany Darwish, best known for her 1980s cover of Tommy James & the Shondells' "I Think We're Alone Now," has one son, Elijah Bulmaro Garcia.

Tracy

FRENCH: Form of Theresa, of Thracia
ROCK AND ROLL: Interesting, charismatic, dangerous
RELATED ARTISTS/SONGS: Tracy Chapman, Tracy Byrd, Tracy Lawrence, "Tracy" by Mogwai, "Tracy Jacks" by Blur, "Tracy" by 8th Day
LINER NOTES: Tracy Chapman was one of rapper Tupac's favorite musicians; he repeatedly called her "a true poet."

Veronica

GREEK: She who brings victory
ROCK AND ROLL: Forgetful, sweet, lovely
RELATED ARTISTS/SONGS: Veronica Finn, The Veronicas, Veronica Maggio, "Veronica" by Elvis Costello, "Veronica" by Bert Jansch, "Veronica" by Christy Moore, "Veronica" by Paw, "Veronica" by Dave Evans
LINER NOTES: Elvis Costello's song "Veronica," which focuses on a woman who is losing her memory, was inspired by his grandmother.

BOYS

Adrian, Adrien

GERMAN: Dark-skinned, wealthy
ROCK AND ROLL: Fearless, clever, friendly
RELATED ARTISTS/SONGS: Adrian Belew, Adrian Young (No Doubt), "Adrian" by Jewel, "Adrian," by Mason Jennings, "Adrian" by Eurythmics
LINER NOTES: King Crimson leader Adrian Belew also toured with Frank Zappa, David Bowie, Nine Inch Nails, and Talking Heads.

Benjamin

HEBREW: Son of my right hand
ROCK AND ROLL: Restless, a rugged cowboy type
RELATED ARTISTS/SONGS: Breaking Benjamin, Benjamin Orr (The Cars), "Song to Benjamin" by Lil' Kim, "Benjamin" by James Taylor, "Benjamin" by Martha Reeves, "Benjamin" by Celine Dion, "Benjamin" by Veruca Salt
LINER NOTES: Before they formed The Cars, Benjamin Orr played in a folk band called Milkwood with Ric Ocasek and Jas Goodkind.

Eno

GERMAN: Strong
ROCK AND ROLL: Avant-garde, bold, inventive
RELATED ARTISTS/SONGS: Brian Eno, "Eno" by The Generals
LINER NOTES: Brian Eno's full name is Brian Peter George St. John le Baptiste de la Salle Eno.

Finn

ENGLISH: Finnish
ROCK AND ROLL: Strong, likely Irish, a brave warrior
RELATED ARTISTS/SONGS: The Finn Brothers, Jerry Finn, Tim Finn (Split Enz), "The Legend of Finn MacCumhail" by Dropkick Murphys, "John Finn's Wife" by Nick Cave & the Bad Seeds, "Finn" by Tori Amos
LINER NOTES: Split Enz's lead singer Tim Finn altered the spelling of the band's name to reference his home country, New Zealand (NZ); he has two children, Son and Ellie.

Francis

LATIN: Free
ROCK AND ROLL: An adventurer, fond of the ocean
RELATED ARTISTS/SONGS: Francis Dunnery, "Francis" by Coeur de Pirate, "Francis" by Uncle Wiggly, "Francis" by Califone, "Francis" by Peel
LINER NOTES: The Pixies' Black Francis, born Francis Black, has two children, Jack Errol and Lucy Berlin.

Gavin

WELSH: White hawk
ROCK AND ROLL: Eccentric, lyrical, prolific
RELATED ARTISTS/SONGS: Gavin DeGraw, Gavin Friday (The Virgin Prunes), Gavin Rossdale (Bush), "Gavin" by Pain, "Gavin's Song" by Marc Broussard
LINER NOTES: Gavin Friday and the rest of The Virgin Prunes were childhood friends of U2's Bono; Friday and bandmate Guggi were the ones who bestowed Bono's stage name "Bono Vox" on him.

Geddy

ENGLISH: Variation of Gary, strong
ROCK AND ROLL: Serious, jazzy, a wailer
RELATED ARTISTS/SONGS: Geddy Lee (Rush), "Stereo" by Pavement
LINER NOTES: Geddy Lee's real name is Gary; his nickname "Geddy" came from the way his Polish mother pronounced his name.

Hal

ENGLISH: Form of Harold, army ruler
ROCK AND ROLL: Easygoing, the class cutup
RELATED ARTISTS/SONGS: Hal Lindes (Dire Straits), Hal Cragin (They Might Be Giants), "Hal" by Phil Asher, "Hal" by Ahura, "Hal" by Trans-Am
LINER NOTES: They Might Be Giants began as a band called Dial-A-Song, recording their music using only an answering machine.

Hector

GREEK: Steadfast
ROCK AND ROLL: Modest, virtuosic, bubbly
RELATED ARTISTS/SONGS: Hector Rivera, Hector Lavoe, Hector Torres, "Hector" by The Village Callers, "First of the Gang to Die" by Morrissey
LINER NOTES: Salsa singer Hector Lavoe was born Hector Martinez; his stage name is a play on *La Voz* ("The Voice").

Horatio

ENGLISH: Variation of Horace, timekeeper
ROCK AND ROLL: Poetic, adventurous, outgoing
RELATED ARTISTS/SONGS: Horatio Lee Jenkins, Horatio Hernandez, Horatio Hornblower (The Darts), "Horatio" by King Kurt, "Horatio" by Ashley Hutchings, "Oh Horatio" by Tiger Lou, "Horatio" by The Genders
LINER NOTES: The Darts' Horatio Hornblower—real name Nigel Trubridge—took his stage name from the Gregory Peck film *Captain Horatio Hornblower*.

Huey

GERMAN: Variation of Hugh, intellectual
ROCK AND ROLL: Cool, bouncy, loves a good time
RELATED ARTISTS/SONGS: Huey Lewis, Huey Long, Huey Morgan (Fun Lovin' Criminals), "Baby Huey" by Dim Stars, "Free Huey" by The Boo Radleys
LINER NOTES: Huey Lewis's band was originally The American Express; he changed it to The News to avoid confusion with the credit card company.

Ivan

SLAVIC: Variation of John, God is gracious
ROCK AND ROLL: Clever, prolific, lucky
RELATED ARTISTS/SONGS: Ivan Doroschuk (Men Without Hats), Ivan Julian (The Voodoos), Ivan Kraal, "Ivan Meets G.I. Joe" by The Clash, "Ivan" by Kid Dakota, "Ivan" by Shelly Manne, "Ivan" by Byron Lee & the Dragonaires
LINER NOTES: At the age of thirteen, punk rocker Ivan Julian played in a Led Zeppelin cover band.

Jeffrey, Geoffrey

GERMAN: Divine peace
ROCK AND ROLL: Mellow, an explorer, blue-blooded
RELATED ARTISTS/SONGS: Jeffrey Gaines, Geoffrey Downes (The Buggles), "Running Through the Fields with Jeffrey" by Sister Hazel, "Song for Jeffrey" by Jethro Tull, "Geoffrey Ingram" by Television Personalities, "Love Song for Jeffrey" by Helen Reddy
LINER NOTES: Keyboardist Geoffrey Downes, who also played for Yes and Asia, was once listed in the *Guinness Book of World Records* for playing twenty-eight keyboards at one time.

Joel

HEBREW: God is good
ROCK AND ROLL: Emotional, dramatic, rambunctious
RELATED ARTISTS/SONGS: Billy Joel, Joel Chernoff (Lamb), Joel Dorn, Joel Madden (Good Charlotte), Joel Plaskett, "Joel's Theme" by Shiny Toy Guns, "Song for Mark and Joel" by The Mountain Goats, "Joel" by The Boo Radleys
LINER NOTES: Billy Joel has one daughter, Alexa Ray; her middle name is in honor of the singer Ray Charles.

Jules

LATIN: Youthful
ROCK AND ROLL: Kindhearted, spiritual, intuitive
RELATED ARTISTS/SONGS: Jules Shear, "Jules" by Novembre, "Jules" by Stephen Mercer, "Jules Lost His Jules" by Ariel Pink's Haunted Graffiti, "J for Jules" by 'Til Tuesday
LINER NOTES: "J for Jules" is about singer-songwriter Jules Shear and his relationship with 'Til Tuesday's lead singer, Aimee Mann.

Luca, Luka

ITALIAN: Light
ROCK AND ROLL: A quiet neighbor, introverted, sophisticated
RELATED ARTISTS/SONGS: Luca Turilli, Luka Bloom, "Luca" by Brand New, "Luca" by Divididos, "Luka" by Suzanne Vega
LINER NOTES: Blue Oyster Cult made an unreleased parody of Suzanne Vega's "Luka" called "My Name is Loofa," told from the perspective of a sponge.

Marc, Mark

LATIN: Warlike
ROCK AND ROLL: Emotional, bright, savvy
RELATED ARTISTS/SONGS: Marc Bolan (T-Rex), Mark Hoppus (Blink-182), Mark Mothersbaugh (Devo), "Mark on the Bus" by The Beastie Boys, "Mark" by Red Rodney, "Mark" by Glassjaw, "Marc" by Louis XIV
LINER NOTES: Devo's Mark Mothersbaugh hosts a segment of the Nickelodeon show *Yo Gabba Gabba!* called "Mark's Magic Pictures," in which he teaches children how to draw simple cartoons.

Martin

LATIN: Devotee of war
ROCK AND ROLL: Tough, pioneering, an outdoorsman
RELATED ARTISTS/SONGS: Martin Atkins (Public Image Ltd.), Martin Gore (Depeche Mode), Medeski, Martin, and Wood, "Martin" by Zac Brown Band, "Martin" by Soft Cell, "Martin" by Tom Robinson
LINER NOTES: Depeche Mode songwriter Martin Lee Gore has three children: Viva Lee, Ava Lee, and Calo Leon.

Morten, Morton

ENGLISH: Town near the moor
ROCK AND ROLL: Traditional, honest
RELATED ARTISTS/SONGS: Marten Harket (a-ha), Mark Morton (Lamb of God), "Morton" by Ennio Morricone, "Morton" by God Is My Co-Pilot
LINER NOTES: A-ha frontman Morten Harket has four children: Jakob Oscar, Jonathan Henning, Anna Katharina, and Karmen Poppy.

Myron

GREEK: Perfume
ROCK AND ROLL: Gruff but kind, quirky
RELATED ARTISTS/SONGS: Myron Grombacher (Pat Benatar), Myron Hill, Myron Yules, "Echoss Myron" by Guided by Voices, "Myron" by The Ocean Blue, "Myron" by Unjust
LINER NOTES: Pat Benatar's drummer Myron Grombacher regularly makes cameos in her music videos, notably as the crazy dentist in the video for "Get Nervous."

Ned

ENGLISH: Derived from Edward, prosperous guard
ROCK AND ROLL: Introverted, artistic, innocent
RELATED ARTISTS/SONGS: Ned Lagin, Ned the Band, Ned's Atomic Dustbin, "Young Ned of the Hill" by The Pogues, "Ned's Shanty" by The Rambling Sailors, "Ned" by Offbeats
LINER NOTES: Ned's Atomic Dustbin took their name from an episode of the British comedy program *The Goon Show*. Their fans called the band "The Neds" for short.

Nick

ENGLISH: Form of Nicholas, victory
ROCK AND ROLL: Quirky, shy, interesting
RELATED ARTISTS/SONGS: Nick Carter (The Backstreet Boys), Nick Cave, Nick Drake, "Little Saint Nick" by The Beach Boys, "Nick" by Marc Blitzstein, "Nick & Chico" by The Deadly Snakes
LINER NOTES: At the request of his friend Russell Crowe, Nick Cave wrote a sequel to *Gladiator*, but the script was rejected.

Paddy

LATIN: Variation of Patrick, nobleman

ROCK AND ROLL: A rogue, handsome, conservative

RELATED ARTISTS/SONGS: Paddy O'Brien, Paddy McAloon, "Paddy McCarthy" by The Corrs, "Paddy's Lament" by Flogging Molly, "Paddy" by Roger Cooper, "Paddy" by The Chad Mitchell Trio, "P is for Paddy" by Cara Dillon

LINER NOTES: Prefab Sprout front man Paddy McAloon wrote Kylie Minogue's song "If You Don't Love Me" and Cher's song "The Gunman."

Peter

GREEK: Rock, foundation

ROCK AND ROLL: Powerful, suave, open-minded

RELATED ARTISTS/SONGS: Peter Gabriel, Peter Frampton, Peter Tosh, "Peter Piper" by Run-DMC, "Peter Gunn" by Duane Eddy, "Peter" by Josh White, "Peter" by The Pretty Things, "Peter's Song" by Elton John

LINER NOTES: The apartheid government of South Africa banned Peter Gabriel's recordings after he released the song "Biko" about the civil rights leader Stephen Bantu Biko.

Rupert

GERMAN: Variation of Robert, bright fame

ROCK AND ROLL: Cuddly, warm, laid-back

RELATED ARTISTS/SONGS: Rupert Hine, Rupert Holmes, Rupert Huber, "Rupert the Riley" by David Bowie, "Rupert the Bear" by The Toy Dolls, "Rubert White" by Eternity's Children

LINER NOTES: Rupert Holmes, best known for his hit "Escape (The Piña Colada Song)," was also a playwright; he won a Tony for his musical *The Mystery of Edwin Drood*.

Sanjay, Sanjaya

HINDI: Victorious

ROCK AND ROLL: Peaceful, cerebral, virtuosic

RELATED ARTISTS/SONGS: Sanjay Mishra, Sanjaya Malakar, "Sanjay" by Walter Trout, "Sanjay" by Rock Four

LINER NOTES: Composer and guitarist Sanjay Mishra was good friends with members of The Grateful Dead, recording an album, *Blue Incantation*, with Jerry Garcia.

Seth

HEBREW: Placed

ROCK AND ROLL: Goofy, caring, cute

RELATED ARTISTS/SONGS: Seth Justman (The J. Geils Band), Seth Horan (Vertical Horizon), Seth Lakeman, "Seth" by Big Black, "Seth" by The Brentwoods, "Congratulations Seth" by Quiet Company, "Seth and the Fly" by Howard Shore

LINER NOTES: Before setting out on a solo career, Seth Lakeman played in a band with his brothers, Sam and Sean.

Sirius

LATIN: Burning
ROCK AND ROLL: Starry-eyed, philosophical, smart
RELATED ARTISTS/SONGS: "Sirius" by The Alan Parsons Project, "To Sirius" by Gojira, "Sirius" by Mike Oldfield, "The Death of Sirius" by Nicholas Hooper, "Sirius" by Clannad
LINER NOTES: The Alan Parsons Project's "Sirius" was Michael Jordan's entry song when he was with the Chicago Bulls.

Thomas

GREEK: Twin
ROCK AND ROLL: Dependable, hardworking, smart
RELATED ARTISTS/SONGS: Thomas Dolby, Thomas Newman, "Thomas" by A Perfect Circle, "St. Thomas" by Sonny Rollins, "Thomas" by Jacques Dutronc, "Thomas" by Richard Jobson, "Thomas" by The Tree People
LINER NOTES: Thomas Dolby, best known for his song "She Blinded Me with Science," composes soundtracks for video games and movies, including the eighties film *Howard the Duck*.

Tucker

ENGLISH: Fabric pleater
ROCK AND ROLL: Optimistic, rustic, courageous
RELATED ARTISTS/SONGS: Tucker Martine (My Morning Jacket), The Marshall Tucker Band, "Tucker's Town" by Hootie & the Blowfish, "Tucker" by Wayne Benson, "Tucker" by The Corner Street Band
LINER NOTES: The Marshall Tucker Band was named after a Spartanburg, South Carolina, piano tuner whose name was inscribed on the key for the band's practice space.

Victor

LATIN: Conqueror
ROCK AND ROLL: Literate, erudite, passionate
RELATED ARTISTS/SONGS: Victor Willis (Village People), Victor Feldman, Victor Jara, "Victor" by Blondie, "The Hands of Victor Jara" by Chuck Brodsky, "Victor's Deception" by Danny Elfman, "Victor and Carolyn" by Caribou
LINER NOTES: Singer-songwriter and activist Victor Jara inspired Chuck Brodsky's "The Hands of Victor Jara," The Clash's "Washington Bullets," and U2's "One Tree Hill."

William

GERMAN: Protector

ROCK AND ROLL: Good-hearted, friendly, articulate

RELATED ARTISTS/SONGS: will.i.am, William "Bootsy" Collins, William Goldsmith (Sunny Day Real Estate), "William, It Was Really Nothing" by The Smiths, "William, Clap Your Hands" by The Unicorns, "William's Last Words" by Manic Street Preachers

LINER NOTES: Morrissey wrote the song "William, It Was Really Nothing" as a warning against marriage.

Ziggy

GERMAN: Variation of Sigmund, victorious peace

ROCK AND ROLL: Ambitious, dramatic, mellow

RELATED ARTISTS/SONGS: Ziggy Marley, Ziggy Sigmond (Econoline Crush), "Ziggy Stardust" by David Bowie, "Ziggy" by Celine Dion, "Ziggy" by Aphex Twin

LINER NOTES: Ziggy Marley made his recording debut with his father and his siblings Cedelia, Stephen, and Sharon on the track "Children Playing in the Streets"; the four siblings then formed a group called The Melody Makers.

The Weirdest Rocker
Baby Names

There's unusual, there's interesting, there's unique . . . and then there are rocker baby names. Rock stars borrow from all over—numbers, greetings, terms they seem to find on cereal boxes—to come up with their children's names. Some turn out cute, and others, well, you hope they have a good nickname.

NAME	PARENT
Bronx Mowgli	Ashlee Simpson & Pete Wentz
Calico	Alice Cooper
D'lila Star	P. Diddy
Denim & Diezel	Toni Braxton
Dweezil, Moon Unit, & Diva Thin Muffin Pigeen	Frank Zappa
Fifi Trixabelle & Tiger Lily	Bob Geldof
Fuchsia	Sting
Gunner	Nikki Sixx
Ikhyd	M.I.A.
Jazz Domino	Joe Strummer
Jermajesty	Jermaine Jackson
Pirate Houseman	Jonathan Davis (Korn)
Puma	Erykah Badu
Speck Wildhorse	John Mellencamp

Great Rock Double Names

Double names, though now mostly the province of the American South, have an old-fashioned charm about them that's worth reviving. Try one of these combinations for a name with a unique retro feeling, or just to honor some of the great songs in rock and roll history. Where would we be without Peggy Sue?

GIRLS

Anna Lee ("Anna Lee" by Elmore James)

Barbara Ann ("Barbara Ann" by The Beach Boys)

Billie Jean ("Bille Jean" by Michael Jackson)

Bobby Jean ("Bobby Jean" by Bruce Springsteen)

Christie Lee ("Christie Lee" by Billy Joel)

Leslie Anne ("Leslie Anne Levine" by The Decemberists)

Lindy Lou ("My Lindy Lou" by Bubba Ford)

Maggie May ("Maggie May" by Rod Stewart)

Mary Lou (Williams)

Mary Susan ("Mary Susan" by Blood on the Wall)

Norma Jean ("Candle in the Wind" by Elton John)

Peggy Sue ("Peggy Sue" by Buddy Holly)

Phyllis Ruth ("Phyllis Ruth" by 16 Horsepower)

Ruby Ann ("Ruby Ann" by Marty Robbins)

Sally Ann ("Sally Ann" by Bobby Wayne)

Sarah Beth ("Sarah Beth" by Rascal Flatts)

BOYS

Billie Joe (Armstrong, Green Day)

Billy Ray (Cyrus)

David Allan (Coe)

Frankie Lee ("The Ballad of Frankie Lee and Judas Priest" by Bob Dylan)

Jeffrey Lee (Pierce, The Gun Club)

Jerry Lee (Lewis)

Jimmie Dale (Gilmore, The Flatlanders)

Jimmy Carl (Black, The Mothers of Invention)

John Lee (Hooker)

Stevie Ray (Vaughan)

WORLD TOUR: Ireland

Ireland has its share of lovely, Celtic-rooted names that also happen to make great rocker names (think Sinead O'Connor and Fiona Apple). Here is a list of angels, scallywags, and rogues that might inspire your naming process:

GIRLS

Ciara (*Dark-haired*/sassy, boisterous, a bombshell)

Deirdre (*Full of sorrows*/A redhead, wise when she's older, reckless when she's young)

Fiona (*Light-skinned*/Edgy, brassy)

Kitty (*Virtuous*/Strong, pioneering, warm, capricious in love)

Shanne (*Blessed*/Saucy, a tomboy, loves to party)

Sinead (*God is gracious*/Fiery, principled, a feminist)

Tegan (*Fair*/Sprightly, quirky, chic)

BOYS

Cavan (*The hollow*/Stylish, dashing)

Clancy (*Red-haired, lively*/Dynamic, a trickster, doesn't have much of a singing voice)

Delaney (*Dark challenger*/A lovable rogue, funny)

Duff (*Swarthy*/Slick, rambunctious, impulsive)

Feargal, Fergal (*Valorous*/A party animal, good with money)

Garrett (*Brave*/Rough-and-ready, a cowboy)

O'Shea (*Hawklike*/Mischievous, boisterous)

Riley (*Courageous*/Fun, lucky, pampered)

Country:
Cowpokes and
Honky-tonkers

I f you're looking for a name with a rustic, down-home feeling, you couldn't do much better than glancing at CMT these days. From frilly Southern charmers like Loretta, Dolly, and Dixie to hip unisex urban cowpokes like Ashton and Aubrey, country music has much to offer on the naming front.

GIRLS

Anita

SPANISH: Version of Ana, gracious
ROCK AND ROLL: A traditional lady
RELATED ARTISTS/SONGS: Anita Baker, Anita Carter, Anita Pallenberg, "Anita" by Fats Waller, "Anita" by Neva Dinova, "Anita" by Clem Snide, "Anita, You're Dreaming" by Waylon Jennings
LINER NOTES: Anita Carter was the first to record the song "Ring of Fire," but Johnny Cash added the horn section after hearing them in a dream.

Audrey

ENGLISH: Noble strength
ROCK AND ROLL: A good listener
RELATED ARTISTS/SONGS: "Audrey" by Say Hi to Your Mom, "Audrey" by Bud Powell, "Audrey's Prayer" by Angelo Badalamenti
LINER NOTES: Faith Hill, born Audrey Faith Perry, helms a literacy project inspired by her father, dedicated to donating children's books to hospitals and day care centers.

Beatrice, Bea

LATIN: Blessed
ROCK AND ROLL: Stargazer, filled with childlike wonder
RELATED ARTISTS/SONGS: Beatrice McCartney, "Beatrice" by Chet Atkins, "May I Call You Beatrice" by The Wild Strawberries, "Bea"

by Throwing Muses, "Bea's Song" by Cowboy Junkies, "Beatrice" by Daniel Lanois

LINER NOTES: Beatrice Milly McCartney was named for Heather Mills's mother Beatrice and Paul's aunt Milly.

Becky

ENGLISH: Form of Rebecca, loyal

ROCK AND ROLL: A caretaker, summery, courageous, but can be a fickle friend

RELATED ARTISTS/SONGS: Becky Hobbs, "Becky" by Be Your Own Pet, "Becky" by Jupiter Coyote, "Becky" by All Girl Summer Fun Band

LINER NOTES: Besides her work as a solo country singer, Becky Hobbs has also written songs for Loretta Lynn and George Jones.

Bobbie, Bobbi, Bobby

AMERICAN: Short for Roberta, bright flame

ROCK AND ROLL: An old-fashioned lady. Usually part of a double name.

RELATED ARTISTS/SONGS: Bobbie Gentry, "Dear Bobbie" by Yellowcard, "For Baby (For Bobbie)" by John Denver, "Bobby Jean" by Bruce Springsteen, "Bobbie Sue" by The Oak Ridge Boys

LINER NOTES: Bobbie Gentry's first album, *Ode to Billie Joe*, knocked The Beatles' *Sgt. Pepper's Lonely Hearts Club Band* off the top of the U.S. charts.

Carlene

ENGLISH: Variation of Carl, free

ROCK AND ROLL: A math whiz and a model, clever, beautiful

RELATED ARTISTS/SONGS: Carlene Carter, "Carlene" by Phil Vassar, "Carlene" by Westbound Train, "Carlene" by Tad Marks, "Carlene" by Brian Piper

"Girl, you glitter like Hollywood."
—PHIL VASSAR

Cordelia

LATIN: Warm-hearted

ROCK AND ROLL: Sweet, Southern, polite, and stubborn

RELATED ARTISTS/SONGS: Cordelia's Dad, "Cordelia" by The Tragically Hip, "Cordelia" by David Blue, "Cordelia" by Hoodoo Drugstore, "Cordelia Brown" by Harry Belefonte, "Cordelia" by Boris

LINER NOTES: Cordelia's Dad were pioneers of the "No Depression" genre, also known as alternative country music.

Crystal

GREEK: Ice
ROCK AND ROLL: Luminous, fragile, and expensive
RELATED ARTISTS/SONGS: Crystal Castles, Crystal Gayle, Crystal Taliefero (Billy Joel Band), "Crystal" by Fleetwood Mac, "Crystal" by Elton John, "Crystal" by New Order
LINER NOTES: Country musician Crystal Gayle is Loretta Lynn's sister.

Dottie, Dotty, Dot

GREEK: Short for Dorothy, gift of the gods
ROCK AND ROLL: Cool, smart, and sensible
RELATED ARTISTS/SONGS: Dottie Danger, Dottie Peoples, Dottie West, "I'm a Loner Dottie, a Rebel" by The Get Up Kids, "Dot" by Jurassic 5, "Dotty" by The Refreshments, "Dear Dottie" by Lunachicks, "Dottie" by Tommy Roe
LINER NOTES: Country singer Dottie West's composition "Country Sunshine" so impressed the Coca-Cola company that they signed her to a lifetime contract as a jingle writer.

Emmylou

AMERICAN: Variation of Emma, whole
ROCK AND ROLL: Visionary, wise, earthy
RELATED ARTISTS/SONGS: Emmylou Harris, "Emmylou" by the Oak Ridge Boys
LINER NOTES: Emmylou Harris is a staunch supporter of animal rights; she runs a small dog shelter in Nashville.

Evangeline

LATIN: Gospel

BAD RELIGION:
"Evangeline, conspirator so fine."

LITTLE BIG TOWN:
"Evangeline, you're a hard one."

MATTHEW SWEET:
"She's some kind of angel."

THE JULIANA THEORY:
"You sent me up to the sky."

Felice

LATIN: Happy
ROCK AND ROLL: Colorful, witty, magnetic
RELATED ARTISTS/SONGS: Felice Bryant, "Felice" by Jay Hoggard,

"Felice" by Ron Kavana, "Felice" by Manticora, "Felice" by Rosario Di Bello

LINER NOTES: Songwriting husband-and-wife team Felice and Boudleaux Bryant wrote hits for The Everly Brothers, Roy Acuff, and The Grateful Dead among others, including "Wake Up Little Susie" and "Rocky Top."

Gretchen

GERMAN: Variation of Margaret, pearl

ROCK AND ROLL: Fetching, flirtatious, confident

RELATED ARTISTS/SONGS: Gretchen Parlato, Gretchen Phillips, Gretchen Wilson, "Gretchen Ross" by Michael Andrews, "Gretchen" by Jandek, "Gretchen" by Nina Hagen

LINER NOTES: "Redneck Woman" singer Gretchen Wilson customized a version of her song "Work Hard, Play Harder" for the Nashville Predators hockey team.

Hillary, Hilary

LATIN: Cheerful

ROCK AND ROLL: Mellow, eccentric, the life of the party

RELATED ARTISTS/SONGS: Hilary Duff, Hillary Lindsey, Hillary Scott (Lady Antebellum), "Hillary" by The Normals, "Hillary Dresser" by Piebald, "Hilary" by The Fall, "Hilary" by The Durutti Column, "Hey, Hey Hillary" by Dean Friedman

"And though she's got her share of quirks/Living with her has got its perks."
—DEAN FRIEDMAN

Jan

HEBREW: Variation of John, God is gracious

ROCK AND ROLL: A philanthropist, compassionate, looks good in hats

RELATED ARTISTS/SONGS: Jan & Dean, Jan Howard, Jan Wayne, "The Beginning: Jan" by Marvin Gaye, "Jan" by Scott Hamilton, "Jan" by Little Brother Montgomery, "Jan" by Lambchop, "Jan" by The Intruders

LINER NOTES: Singer Jan Howard became fast friends with Patsy Cline after she stood up to one of Cline's notorious tongue-lashings.

Jolene

AMERICAN INVENTED

ROCK AND ROLL: An auburn-haired green-eyed looker, a heartbreaker

RELATED ARTISTS/SONGS: "Jolene" by Dolly Parton, "Jolene" by Bob Dylan, "Jolene" by Ray LaMontagne
LINER NOTES: The song "Jolene" was inspired by a beautiful ginger-haired girl who asked for Dolly Parton's autograph at a concert.

Juanita

SPANISH: *Diminutive of Juana, she who supplants*

SHANIA TWAIN:
"She rides without the reins."

IRON MAIDEN:
"I just know I gotta get you back."

DAVID ALLAN COE:
"I promise I'll make you my wife."

JIM REEVES:
"Thy dark eyes' splendor where the warm light loves to dwell."

Julianne

LATIN: Youthful
ROCK AND ROLL: Long-haired, frilly, well dressed
RELATED ARTISTS/SONGS: Julianne Hugh, Julianne Regan (All About Eve), "Julianne" by Ben Folds Five, "Julianne" by The New Christy Minstrels, "Julianne" by George Jones, "Julianne" by The Everly Brothers
LINER NOTES: Ballroom dancer and singer Julianne Hugh appeared in the music video for Snoop Dogg's "My Medicine."

Kelsey, Kelsi

ENGLISH: Ship's island
ROCK AND ROLL: Popular, a great friend
RELATED ARTISTS/SONGS: Kelsey Brown, Kelsi Osborn (SHeDAISY), "Kelsey" by Metro Station, "Kelsey" by Still Remains, "Kelsey" by Dominique Vouk
LINER NOTES: Kelsi Osborn has twin daughters named Savannah Marie and Adyson Amilia.

LaWanda

AMERICAN: Form of Wanda, shepherdess
ROCK AND ROLL: Saucy, bright, fun-loving
RELATED ARTISTS/SONGS: LaWanda Lindsey, "Lawanda" by Skillet & Leroy
LINER NOTES: Lawanda Lindsey's track "Pickin' Wild Mountain Ber-

ries" was considered so risqué that several Midwestern radio stations refused to play it.

Leann, Lee Ann

LATIN: Close to Leandra, lioness-like
ROCK AND ROLL: Fresh-faced, exuberant, earnest, youthful
RELATED ARTISTS/SONGS: LeAnn Rimes, Lee Ann Womack, "Leann" by Impediments, "Leanne" by Kurt Hagardorn
LINER NOTES: By the age of nine, LeAnn Rimes was on the road with her father, often singing "The Star-Spangled Banner" at the opening of Dallas Cowboys games.

Loretta

ENGLISH: Variation of Laura, laurel by the river
ROCK AND ROLL: Always youthful, tough, opinionated, a role model
RELATED ARTISTS/SONGS: Loretta Lynn, "Loretta" by Townes Van Zandt, "Loretta's Scars" by Pavement, "Loretta Young Silks" by Sneaker Pimps
LINER NOTES: Loretta Lynn had four children before she turned nineteen. She learned guitar at the age of twenty-four, after her husband gave her one as an anniversary present.

Lucinda

LATIN: Luminous
ROCK AND ROLL: Starry-eyed, has a sly grin, adventurous
RELATED ARTISTS/SONGS: Lucinda Williams, "Lucinda" by The Knack, "Lucinda" by Randy Newman, "Lucinda" by A Certain Ratio, "Lucinda" by Tom Waits, "Dancing Lucinda" by The Nadas
LINER NOTES: Lucinda Williams was kicked out of high school for refusing to say the Pledge of Allegiance.

Lynn, Lynne

CELTIC: Waterfall
ROCK AND ROLL: Sweet, capable, practical
RELATED ARTISTS/SONGS: Lynn Anderson, Lynn Miles, Lynn Morris, The Lynns, "Lynn" by Ramsey Lewis, "Lynn" by Mark Winkler
LINER NOTES: Bluegrass pioneer Lynn Morris was the first woman to win the National Banjo Championship.

Margaret

GREEK: Pearl
ROCK AND ROLL: Flighty, brave, a good listener
RELATED ARTISTS/SONGS: Margaret Ross, "Dear Margaret" by The Kinks, "Stand Down Margaret" by The English Beat, "Margaret vs. Pauline" by Neko Case, "Tell Me Margaret" by Johnny Reid, "Come Back, Margaret" by Camera Obscura

LINER NOTES: The Everly Brothers' mother, Margaret, and father, Ike, were both country musicians. The brothers got their start singing on their parents' radio show.

Martina

LATIN: Feminine variation of Martin, bellicose
ROCK AND ROLL: Affable, bubbly, trustworthy
RELATED ARTISTS/SONGS: Martina McBride, Martina Topley-Bird, "Martina" by Bill Evans, "Martina" by Tim Fast
LINER NOTES: Martina McBride and her husband, sound engineer John McBride, have three daughters: Delaney Katharine, Emma Justine, and Ava Rose.

Maybelle

ENGLISH: Variation of Mabel, friendly
ROCK AND ROLL: Warm, loving, a leader
RELATED ARTISTS/SONGS: Big Maybelle, Maybelle Carter, "Maybelle" by Chet Atkins
LINER NOTES: Carter family matriarch Maybelle Carter was Johnny Cash's mother-in-law and a regular performer on his late 1960s variety TV show.

Mindy

ENGLISH: Form of Melinda, honey
ROCK AND ROLL: Old-fashioned, sweet but has some spark
RELATED ARTISTS/SONGS: Mindy McCready, Mindy Smith, "Mindy" by Andy Pratt, "Her Name Rhymes with Mindy" by All-American Rejects
LINER NOTES: Country singer Mindy McCready has a son named Zander Ryan.

Minnie

AMERICAN: Form of Amelia or Mary, beloved
ROCK AND ROLL: Sophisticated, slender, thinks on her feet
RELATED ARTISTS/SONGS: Memphis Minnie, Minnie Riperton, Minnie Pearl, "Skinny Minnie" by Bill Haley & His Comets, "Minnie the Moocher" by Cab Calloway, "Minnie" by Big Jay McNeeley
LINER NOTES: Minnie Pearl and gospel singer Mahalia Jackson briefly owned a chain of Nashville fried chicken restaurants.

Miranda

LATIN: Worthy of admiration
ROCK AND ROLL: Brave, charming, a little lonely
RELATED ARTISTS/SONGS: Miranda Chartrand, Miranda Lambert, Miranda Lee Richards, "Miranda" by Phil Ochs, "Miranda" by Wu-Tang Clan, "Miranda" by Fleetwood Mac, "Miranda" by Doug White
LINER NOTES: Miranda Lambert is married to fellow country singer

Blake Shelton. Guests at their wedding included Reba McEntire, Martina McBride, and Cee Lo Green.

Naomi

HEBREW: Pleasure
ROCK AND ROLL: Angelic, shimmering, soulful
RELATED ARTISTS/SONGS: Naomi Judd, Naomi Phoenix, Naomi Yang (Galaxie 500), "Naomi" by Neutral Milk Hotel, "Naomi" by Loudon Wainwright III, "Naomi" by Ralph McTell, "Naomi" by The Boo Radleys
LINER NOTES: Naomi Judd's birth name is Diana Ellen Judd; her daughter, known by the name Wynonna Judd, was born Christina Ciminella.

Patsy

LATIN: Variation of Patricia, noble
ROCK AND ROLL: Sweet, vulnerable, pretty
RELATED ARTISTS/SONGS: Patsy Cline, Patsy Montana, "Patsy" by Jack Scott, "Patsy" by Hank C. Burnette, "Patsy" by Keith Marks
LINER NOTES: Patsy Cline's Nashville living room has been recreated in the Opryland Museum, complete with a bar engraved with "Patsy & Charlie" (Charlie Dick, her second husband).

Rachel

HEBREW: Pure

LIL CHRIS:
"She's my angel."

KEVIN AYERS:
"She's safe from the darkness."

BASSHUNTER:
"Rachel's hair is dancing in the wind."

SEALS & CROFTS:
"Rachel comes to dry my tears away."

Ralna, Rana

ARABIC: Queenly
ROCK AND ROLL: Sophisticated, smart, loves to cook
RELATED ARTISTS/SONGS: Ralna English, "Rana" by Ilya, "Rana" by Fat Jon
LINER NOTES: In high school, Ralna English won a battle of the bands with her group Ralna and the Ad-Libs; one of her competitors was fellow Lubbock native Buddy Holly.

Reba

HEBREW: Form of Rebecca, fourth born

ROCK AND ROLL: Honest, bubbly, affable, good-natured

RELATED ARTISTS/SONGS: Reba McEntire, "Reba" by Phish, "Reba" by Pepper McGowan

LINER NOTES: Reba McEntire was James Cameron's first choice to play the unsinkable Molly Brown in *Titanic*, but her touring schedule made the filming too difficult.

Rosa

LATIN: Rose

ROCK AND ROLL: Beautiful, rare, has a strong moral center

RELATED ARTISTS/SONGS: Rosa Lee Carson (aka Moonshine Kate), Rose Lee Hill, Rosa Lee Hawkins (The Dixie Cups), "Rosa" by Devendra Bandhart, "Rosa Morena" by The Thermals, "Rosa's Cantina" by Deep Purple, "Rosa Blue" by Planet Funk

LINER NOTES: Rosa Lee Carson, better known as Moonshine Kate, got her nickname from a music executive who wanted to capitalize on the Prohibition-era thirst.

Rosanne, Roseanne

ENGLISH: Combination of Rose and Anne, graceful

ROCK AND ROLL: Delicate, sweet, mischievous

RELATED ARTISTS/SONGS: Rosanne Cash, "Rosanne" by Nick & Simon, "Roseanne" by The Toasters, "Roseanne" by Vic Damone, "Roseanne" by Cherry Poppin' Daddies, "Sweet Roseanne" by Kristin Hersh

LINER NOTES: Rosanne Cash occasionally teaches classes in songwriting; her advice to her students is to put furniture in their songs rather than focusing on abstract themes.

Shania

OJIBWAY: I'm on my way

ROCK AND ROLL: Confident, popular, cheerful

RELATED ARTISTS/SONGS: Shania Twain, "Shania" by Paul Moore, "Shania" by Andy LaVerne

LINER NOTES: Shania Twain's German shepherd is named Tim after her hometown of Timmins, Ontario.

Sonja, Sonia, Sonya

HINDI: Golden

ROCK AND ROLL: Lucky, fashionable, beautiful

RELATED ARTISTS/SONGS: Sonia Dada, Sonya Isaacs, Sonya Kitchell, "Sonia" by The Gladiators, "Sonia" by Robert Wyatt, "Sonya" by The Sonny Clark Trio, "Sonya" by Miles Davis, "I Married Sonja" by The Wrens

LINER NOTES: Country singer Sonia Isaacs is part of a gospel music group, The Isaacs, with her mother Lily, sister Becky, and brother Ben.

Tammy

ENGLISH: Variatior of Tamara, palm tree
ROCK AND ROLL: The sweetheart next door, loyal
RELATED ARTISTS/SONGS: Tammy Wynette, Tammy Lucas, "Tammy" by Debbie Reynolds, "For Tammy Rae" by Bikini Kill, "Jim & Tammy's Upper Room" by Frank Zappa
LINER NOTES: Tammy Wynette's birth name was Virginia Wynette Pugh; she got the nickname Tammy because she reminded a record producer of Debbie Reynolds in the movie *Tammy and the Bachelor*.

Tanya

RUSSIAN: Praiseworthy
ROCK AND ROLL: Clever, bubbly, luminous
RELATED ARTISTS/SONGS: Tanya Tucker, Tanya Donelly (Throwing Muses), Tanya Stephens, "Tanya" by Dexter Gordon, "Tanya" by Jimmy Witherspoon, "Tanya" by Cal Tjader, "Tanya" by King Curtis, "Tanya" by Willie Mitchell
LINER NOTES: Country singer Tanya Tucker has two children, daughter Presley Tanita and son Beau Grayson.

Taylor

ENGLISH: One who cuts cloth
ROCK AND ROLL: A good girl, sweet, cute as a button
RELATED ARTISTS/SONGS: Taylor Swift, "Taylor" by Jack Johnson
LINER NOTES: Country singer Taylor Swift grew up on a Christmas tree farm; her childhood job was to rake praying mantis pods off the trees.

Tricia, Trisha

LATIN: Form of Patricia, noble
ROCK AND ROLL: Chipper, magnetic, lively
RELATED ARTISTS/SONGS: Trisha Yearwood, "Trisha" by Paul Cavins, "Tricia" by Ted Snyder, "(I'm Stuck in a Pagoda) with Tricia Pagoda" by The Dickies,
LINER NOTES: Trisha Yearwood collects cookbooks as a hobby.

Wilma

ENGLISH: Variation of Wilhelmina, resolute
ROCK AND ROLL: Virtuous, old-fashioned, warm
RELATED ARTISTS/SONGS: Wilma Burgess, Wilma Lee Cooper, "Wilma's Rainbow" by Helmet, "Wilma" by Anchor, "Wilma" by Travis Larson, "Wilma" by Sunshine Club
LINER NOTES: Country singer Wilma Burgess was a great poker player; on tours with Ernest Tubbs, she routinely cleaned out both Tubbs and his bus driver.

Wynonna, Winona

SIOUX: First-born daughter

ROCK AND ROLL: Popular, faithful, a chameleon

RELATED ARTISTS/SONGS: Wynonna Judd, "She's My Winona" by Fall Out Boy, "Winona" by Matthew Sweet, "Winona" by The Pillows, "Winona" by Quickspace

LINER NOTES: Wynonna Judd, who sometimes goes by the nickname Sweet Tater thanks to her auburn hair, has two children, Elijah and Grace Pauline.

Zella

AFRICAN: One who knows the way

ROCK AND ROLL: Quirky, athletic, a stargazer

RELATED ARTISTS/SONGS: Zella Lehr, "Zella" by Dax, "Zella" by D.Y.C.R., "Zella Zella" by Giles Apap

LINER NOTES: Zella Lehr was a regular on *Hee Haw* as "the unicycle girl."

BOYS

Abner

HEBREW: Cheerful leader

ROCK AND ROLL: A storyteller, traditionalist, and old soul

RELATED ARTISTS/SONGS: Abner Jay, "Abner Brown," by Johnny Cash, "Why Did I Fall for Abner?" by Merle Travis, "Fire 'em Up, Abner" by Guided by Voices

LINER NOTES: Blues multi-instrumentalist Abner Jay was known to use bleached cow bones to create percussion on his recordings.

Aubrey

FRENCH: King of the elves

ROCK AND ROLL: Extraordainary, beloved, well traveled

RELATED ARTISTS/SONGS: Aubrey O'Day, Aubrey Haynie, "Aubrey" by Bread, "Aubrey" by Grover Washington Jr., "Aubrey" by Perry Como

LINER NOTES: Fiddler Aubrey Haynie is one of the most prolific session players in Nashville, appearing on recordings with George Jones, Porter Wagoner, and Trisha Yearwood, among others.

Blaine

IRISH: Slender

ROCK AND ROLL: Trustworthy, rugged, an outdoorsman

RELATED ARTISTS/SONGS: Blaine Larsen, "Blaine Osborne" by Transfer, "Requiem for Joseph Blaine Cooper" by John Fahey

LINER NOTES: Blaine Larsen bought his first guitar at age thirteen with the profits he scraped together from selling homemade birdhouses.

Buck, Bucky

ENGLISH: Male deer

ROCK AND ROLL: Industrious, strong, tough

RELATED ARTISTS/SONGS: Buck Clayton, Buck Owens, Young Buck, "Buck's Boogie" by Blue Oyster Cult, "Buck" by Nina Simone, "Buck Rogers" by Feeder, "Bucky Done Gun" by M.I.A., "Bucky Little Wing" by Islands

LINER NOTES: Buck Owens's given name is Alvis, but he changed it to "Buck" as a child in honor of his favorite donkey.

Chet

ENGLISH: Short for Chester, walled fort

ROCK AND ROLL: Inspirational, virtuosic

RELATED ARTISTS/SONGS: Chet Atkins, Chet Baker, "Chet" by The Pushers, "Chet" by Chet Baker, "Ode to Chet" by Clint Black, "Chicken Chet" by Brad Paisley

LINER NOTES: Chet Atkins's first instrument was a ukulele. When he was nine, he traded his brother a pistol for his first guitar.

Clay

ENGLISH: Form of Clayton, place with good earth

ROCK AND ROLL: Traditional, lovable, understanding

RELATED ARTISTS/SONGS: Clay Cook (Zac Brown Band), Clay Aiken, Clay Walker, "Clay" by Echo & the Bunnymen, "Clay" by Wire, "Clay" by Lamb, "Clay" by Exene Cervenka

LINER NOTES: Clay Walker has four children, MaClay and Skylor with rodeo queen Lori Anne Lampson, and William and Mary Elizabeth with model Jessica Craig.

Clint

ENGLISH: Variation of Clinton, hilltop town

ROCK AND ROLL: Rugged, tough, a cowboy

RELATED ARTISTS/SONGS: Clint Black, Clint Daniels, Clint Eastwood, "Clint" by Sad Lovers and Giants, "Clint" by Vanilla Ice, "Clint Eastwood" by Gorillaz

LINER NOTES: Clint Black dropped out of high school to play music full-time, supporting himself with a job as a fishing guide.

Colt

ENGLISH: Young horse

ROCK AND ROLL: Athletic, resourceful, sure of himself

RELATED ARTISTS/SONGS: Colt Ford, "Colt" by The Kittens, "Colt" by Glass Harp, "Colt" by Scala

LINER NOTES: Before his country career, Colt Ford was a professional golfer and golf instructor.

Conway

IRISH: Hound of the plain
ROCK AND ROLL: Dependable, honest, has a mischievous streak
RELATED ARTISTS/SONGS: Conway Twitty, Conway Savage, "Conway" by Reel 2 Real
LINER NOTES: Conway Twitty was a dedicated baseball player; he turned down a bid from the Philadelphia Phillies to join the army.

Dan

HEBREW: Form of Daniel, judged by God
ROCK AND ROLL: An outsider, an outdoorsman, a bit of a loner
RELATED ARTISTS/SONGS: Dan Deacon, Dan Fogelberg, Steely Dan, "Song for Dan Treacy" by MGMT, "Cowboy Dan" by Modest Mouse, "Dan Abnormal" by Blur, "Old Dan Tucker" by Bruce Springsteen, "Dan Dare" by Art of Noise

> *"Cowboy Dan's a major player in the cowboy scene."*
> **—MODEST MOUSE**

Doug

SCOTTISH: Diminutive of Douglas, black stream
ROCK AND ROLL: Fresh, interesting, not a great driver
RELATED ARTISTS/SONGS: Doug Dillard, Doug Sahm (Texas Tornados), Doug Yule (The Velvet Underground), "How's My Driving, Doug Hastings?" by Less Than Jake, "Doug" by The Coolies, "Doug" by The Cosmopolitans
LINER NOTES: Country rock guitar prodigy Doug Sahm played on stage with Hank Williams at Williams's last concert.

Dudley

ENGLISH: Rich, from the field
ROCK AND ROLL: Dashing, smooth-talking, confident
RELATED ARTISTS/SONGS: Dudley Connell, Dudley Hill, Dudley Perkins, "Dudley" by The Yeah Yeah Yeahs, "Then Comes Dudley" by The Jesus Lizard, "Dave Dudley" by Tosca, "Funky Dudley" by Madlib, "Dudley's Kitchen" by the String Cheese Incident
LINER NOTES: Bluegrass musician Dudley Connell helped forge the Washington, D.C., "newgrass" scene with his group The Johnson Mountain Boys in the 1970s.

Dwight

GERMAN: Blond
ROCK AND ROLL: Introverted but makes friends easily
RELATED ARTISTS/SONGS: Dwight Tilley, Dwight Yoakam, "Ballad of Dwight Fry" by Alice Cooper, "The Speed of Dwight" by The Polish Ambassador, "Dwight Spitz" by Count Bass D
LINER NOTES: Crossover country star Dwight Yoakam toured with grunge bands Husker Du and The Meat Puppets in the early 1990s.

Earnest, Ernest

ENGLISH: Honest
ROCK AND ROLL: Innocent, trustworthy, a good orator
RELATED ARTISTS/SONGS: Ernest Ranglin, Ernest Tubb, Ernest Wright Jr. (Little Anthony and the Imperials), "Earnest" by Starling, "Ernest" by Llama Tsunami & the Without Helmet, "Ernest" by The Ambassadors, "Talking Ernest" by Kimya Dawson
LINER NOTES: Honky-tonk troubadour Ernest Tubbs contacted Jimmie Rodgers's wife for a signed photo of the country pioneer. She became a close friend and introduced Tubbs to executives at RCA.

Faron

ENGLISH: Handsome servant
ROCK AND ROLL: A dreamboat with a Southern accent
RELATED ARTISTS/SONGS: Faron Young, "Faron" by Prefab Sprout
LINER NOTES: When he started out, Faron Young was billed as "the Singing Sheriff" and "the Hillbilly Heartthrob" for his rustic good looks.

Garth

NORSE: Groundskeeper
ROCK AND ROLL: A family man, a great friend
RELATED ARTISTS/SONGS: Garth Brooks, Garth Hudson (The Band), "Garth" by Dan Freeme
LINER NOTES: Garth Brooks earned an athletic scholarship to Oklahoma State University for javelin throwing.

George

GREEK: Farmer
ROCK AND ROLL: Funky, emphatic, reflective
RELATED ARTISTS/SONGS: George Clinton (Parliament Funkadelic), George Harrison, George Jones, "George" by Petula Clark, "Oh, George" by Foo Fighers, "Yo George" by Tori Amos, "George Fell into His French Horn" by The Beach Boys, "Duffer St. George" by Fiery Furnaces
LINER NOTES: George Jones was nicknamed "The Possum" for the shape of his nose.

Glen, Glenn

SCOTTISH: Valley

ROCK AND ROLL: Jaunty, unshakably calm, a sophisticated cowboy

RELATED ARTISTS/SONGS: Glen Campbell, Glen Hansard, Glenn Miller, "Glenn" by Slint, "Glenn" by The Accelerators

LINER NOTES: Guitarist Glen Campbell was a touring member of The Beach Boys in the mid-1960s, replacing an ailing Brian Wilson; he's also golfing buddies with Alice Cooper.

Hank

GERMAN: Variation of Henry, home ruler

ROCK AND ROLL: Gritty, rustic, a honky-tonk guy

RELATED ARTISTS/SONGS: Hank Cochran, Hank Mobley, Hank Williams, Hank Snow, "Hank" by Jay Bennett, "Hank" by Johnny Paycheck, "Hank" by Big Heavy Stuff

LINER NOTES: Hank Williams learned guitar from a blues street performer named Rufus "Tee-Tot" Payne, who gave Williams lessons in exchange for food.

Harlan

GERMAN: Rocky land

ROCK AND ROLL: Steadfast, prolific, sensitive

RELATED ARTISTS/SONGS: Harlan Howard, "Harlan" by Freakwater, "Harlan" by The Jazz Butcher, "Harlan" by Michelle Nixon

LINER NOTES: Songwriter Harlan Howard was sometimes known as "the Irving Berlin of country music" for his enormous output.

Johnny

HEBREW: Variation of John, God is gracious

ROCK AND ROLL: Lovable outlaw, a charmer with attitude

RELATED ARTISTS/SONGS: Johnny Cash, Johnny Otis, Johnny Paycheck, "Johnny Ryall" by The Beastie Boys, "Johnny B. Goode" by Chuck Berry, "Johnny Thunder" by The Kinks, "Johnny Born Bonny" by Link Wray, "Johnny Sunshine" by Liz Phair

LINER NOTES: Johnny Cash met his first wife, Vivian Liberto, at a roller skating rink. During his time in the air force, Cash wrote her hundreds of love letters, all in green ink.

Kix

AMERICAN INVENTED

ROCK AND ROLL: Laid-back, inventive, interesting

RELATED ARTISTS/SONGS: Kix Brooks (Brooks & Dunn), "Kix" by Miles Davis, "Kix" by The Motels

LINER NOTES: Kix Brooks, of Brooks & Dunn, began his career by singing at ski resorts; he currently co-owns a vineyard outside of Nashville.

Lester

ENGLISH PLACE NAME
ROCK AND ROLL: Lucky, strong, well educated
RELATED ARTISTS/SONGS: Lester Bangs, Lester Bowie, Lester Flatt, "Looking for Lester" by David Bowie, "Lester Left Town" by Art Blakey & the Jazz Messengers, "Lester" by David Murray, "Lester" by Crowded House, "Doctor Lester" by Toots & the Maytals
LINER NOTES: After Flatt & Scruggs split up, Lester Flatt formed the group The Nashville Grass and toured until shortly before his death in 1979.

Lyle

FRENCH: From the isle
ROCK AND ROLL: Friendly, charismatic, has a great sense of humor
RELATED ARTISTS/SONGS: Lyle Lovett, Lyle Mays, Lyle Preslar (Minor Threat), "Lyle Lovette" by Atmosphere, "Lyle" by Delaney
LINER NOTES: Lyle Lovett met his first wife, Julia Roberts, while he was filming the movie *The Player*.

Mason

ENGLISH: Brick worker
ROCK AND ROLL: Clever, boisterous, friendly
RELATED ARTISTS/SONGS: Mason Jennings, Mason Williams, "Free Mason" by Rick Ross, "Mason" by Crystal Bowersox
LINER NOTES: Singer-songwriter Mason Williams was the head writer of *Saturday Night Live* for a brief time in 1980.

Merle

FRENCH: Blackbird
ROCK AND ROLL: An outlaw cowboy, practical, has a good smile
RELATED ARTISTS/SONGS: Merle Haggard, Merle Kilgore, "Merle" by Bianca DeLeon
LINER NOTES: Growing up during the Great Depression, Merle Haggard and his family lived in a converted train boxcar.

Norman

ENGLISH: Northerner
ROCK AND ROLL: A heartthrob with a Southern twang
RELATED ARTISTS/SONGS: Norman Blake, Norman Granz, "Norman" by Sue Thompson, "Norman" by Max Romeo & the Upsetters, "Norman 3" by Teenage Fanclub
LINER NOTES: Country musician Norman Blake played backup on both Bob Dylan's *Nashville Skyline* and Johnny Cash's *Orange Blossom Special*.

Owen

WELSH: Nobly born

ROCK AND ROLL: Eccentric, talented, has excellent taste

RELATED ARTISTS/SONGS: Owen Bradley, Owen Pallett, "Owen Down" by Gary Jules, "Owen Meaney" by Lagwagon, "Owen" by Tom Kitt

LINER NOTES: Country music producer Owen Bradley has a public park in Nashville named in his honor, at the northern end of Music Row.

Porter

ENGLISH: Doorkeeper

ROCK AND ROLL: Levelheaded leader, patient

RELATED ARTISTS/SONGS: Porter Wagoner, "Hey Porter" by Johnny Cash, "King Porter Stomp" by Benny Goodman, "Porter" by George Lewis

LINER NOTES: Porter Wagoner had the word "Hi!" embroidered on the inside of all his suits and threw the jacket open whenever someone snapped his picture.

Randy

ENGLISH: Shield-wolf

ROCK AND ROLL: Beloved, good-hearted, quirky

RELATED ARTISTS/SONGS: Randy Jackson, Randy Newman, Randy Travis, "Randy" by Dolly Parton, "Randy" by Cat Stevens, "Randy" by The Happenings, "Randy" by Blue Mink

LINER NOTES: Before becoming a professional musician, Randy Travis was a professional cook.

Red

ENGLISH COLOR NAME

ROCK AND ROLL: Warm, dependable, kindhearted but knows how to have fun

RELATED ARTISTS/SONGS: Red Foley, Red Norvo, Red Garland, "Infra-Red" by Placebo, "Red House" by Jimi Hendrix, "Red Rabbits" by The Shins

LINER NOTES: Country star Red Foley hosted *Ozark Jubilee*, the first country music television show, from 1955 to 1960.

Reno

ENGLISH PLACE NAME: Lucky

ROCK AND ROLL: A risk-taker, a wheeler-dealer, a charmer

RELATED ARTISTS/SONGS: Reno & Smiley, Mike Reno (Loverboy), Tony Reno (Europe), "Reno Dakota" by The Magnetic Fields, "Reno" by Bruce Springsteen, "Reno" by R.E.M.

LINER NOTES: Country singer Don Reno had two sons, Don Wayne and Dale.

Rich

ENGLISH: Variation of Richard, powerful leader
ROCK AND ROLL: Laid-back, rugged, boisterous
RELATED ARTISTS/SONGS: Buddy Rich, Rich Mullins, John Rich
(Big & Rich), "Baby You're a Rich Man" by The Beatles, "Rich Girl"
by Hall & Oates, "Rich" by The Yeah Yeah Yeahs
LINER NOTES: Country musician John Rich and his wife Joan named
their son Cash Rich.

Rodney

ENGLISH: Island near the clearing
ROCK AND ROLL: Traditional, bubbly, honest
RELATED ARTISTS/SONGS: Rodney Crowell, Rodney Sheppard
(Sugar Ray), Rodney Atkins, "Rodney" by the Bollweevils, "Little
Rodney" by Brother Ali, "Rodney" by The G.T.O.'s
LINER NOTES: Country singer Rodney Crowell was married to
Rosanne Cash for thirteen years; they have three daughters: Caitlin, Chelsea, and Carrie.

Slim

AMERICAN: Slender
ROCK AND ROLL: Rugged, laid-back, resourceful
RELATED ARTISTS/SONGS: Slim Smith, Memphis Slim, Slim Whitman, "Slim Slow Slider" by Van Morrison, "Slim Jenkin's Joint" by
Booker T & the MG's
LINER NOTES: Michael Jackson and George Harrison both cited
country musician Slim Whitman as one of their biggest influences.

Stanley

ENGLISH: Stony meadow
ROCK AND ROLL: A problem-solver, honorable, a good friend
RELATED ARTISTS/SONGS: Stanley Turrentine, The Stanley Brothers, Stanley Clarke, "Stanley" by The Basement Jaxx, "Stanley" by
Antietam, "Stanley Climbfall" by Lifehouse, "My Man Stanley" by
Baha Men
LINER NOTES: The bluegrass duo The Stanley Brothers featured
Ralph Stanley, who won a Grammy for his role in the soundtrack
for *O Brother, Where Art Thou?*

Steve

ENGLISH: Form of Stephen, crowned with victory
ROCK AND ROLL: Loves the beach, laid-back, a survivor
RELATED ARTISTS/SONGS: Steve Miller, Steve Earle, Steve Young,
"Steve Biko (Stir It Up)" by A Tribe Called Quest, "Steve" by Pere
Ubu, "Steve" by Shelly Manne
LINER NOTES: Outlaw country singer Steve Young wrote the Eagles'
1980s hit song "Seven Bridges Road."

Tex

AMERICAN: Texan
ROCK AND ROLL: Rootin-tootin', rough, a party animal
RELATED ARTISTS/SONGS: Tex Perkins (The Cruel Sea), Tex Ritter, Tex Williams, "Tex" by NRBQ, "Tex" by Jack Logan, "Tex" by The Orange Peels
LINER NOTES: Tex Ritter, sometimes known as the singing cowboy, is the father of actor John Ritter and the grandfather of actor Jason Ritter.

Tim

ENGLISH: Form of Timothy, honoring God
ROCK AND ROLL: Adventurous, loves the finer things, powerful
RELATED ARTISTS/SONGS: Tim McGraw, Tim O'Brien, Tim Buckley, "I'm Telling Tim" by NOFX, "Tim I Wish You Were Born a Girl" by of Montreal
LINER NOTES: Country singer Tim McGraw was salutatorian of his high school class.

Toby

HEBREW: Variation of Tobias, God is good
ROCK AND ROLL: Patient, sweet, ambitious
RELATED ARTISTS/SONGS: Toby Keith, Toby Lightman, TobyMac, "Toby, Take a Bow" by Casiotone for the Painfully Alone, "Toby" by The Chi-Lites, "Toby" by VietNam
LINER NOTES: Before making it big, Toby Keith played in a honky-tonk group called The Easy Money Band; he has three children: Shelley, Krystal, and Stelen.

Townes

ENGLISH: Domestic
ROCK AND ROLL: Honest, uncomplicated, folksy
RELATED ARTISTS/SONGS: Townes Van Zandt, Carol Lynn Townes, "Townes" by Early Day Miners, "Townes' Blues" by Cowboy Mouth
LINER NOTES: Country musician Townes Van Zandt was an idol of both Bob Dylan and Willie Nelson; Steve Earle once called him "the best songwriter in the whole world and I'll stand on Bob Dylan's coffee table in my cowboy boots and say that."

Travis

FRENCH: Tollgate-keeper
ROCK AND ROLL: Rambunctious, sentimental, faithful
RELATED ARTISTS/SONGS: Travis Tritt, Travis, Travis Barker (Blink-182), "Travis" by Scientists, "Travis" by Altered States, "Travis" by Monique Berry
LINER NOTES: When he first began playing music, Travis Tritt was working at an air-conditioning company. Tritt's three children are named Tyler, Tristan, and Tarian.

Waylon

ENGLISH: Land beside the road
ROCK AND ROLL: A rule-bender, a risk-taker, lucky, laid-back
RELATED ARTISTS/SONGS: Waylon Jennings, "Waylon" by Chuck Barnes, "Waylon" by Rebel State, "Waylon" by Phillips & Surrency
LINER NOTES: Waylon Jennings narrowly escaped death in the plane crash that killed Buddy Holly; he gave his seat to The Big Bopper, who had been feeling ill with the flu.

Willie, Willy

GERMAN: Variation of William, protector
ROCK AND ROLL: Compact, hardworking, courageous
RELATED ARTISTS/SONGS: Willie Nelson, Boxcar Willie, Willie Dixon, "Willie" by Elizabeth Cotton, "Willie" by Sammi Smith, "Willie" by Cat Power, "Willy" by Joni Mitchell
LINER NOTES: Willie Nelson is a staunch advocate for the environment; his tour bus, Honeysuckle Rose IV, runs on biodiesel.

Wynn, Win

WELSH: Fair
ROCK AND ROLL: A straight shooter, kind, resourceful
RELATED ARTISTS/SONGS: Win Butler (Arcade Fire), Wynn Stewart, "Sarah Wynn" by Alien Ant Farm, "Wynn's Boogie" by Jim Wynn
LINER NOTES: During a stint in the 1960s, Merle Haggard subbed for Wynn Stewart while Stewart was out of town, and he was soon hired by Stewart as a regular player.

Zeke

HEBREW: Form of Ezekial, God is my strength
ROCK AND ROLL: Idiosyncratic, effervescent, rowdy
RELATED ARTISTS/SONGS: Zeke Clements, Zeke Manners, Zeke Carey (The Flamingos), "Zeke" by REO Speedwagon, "Zeke" by Ruby Likes Red, "Zeke the Freak" by Isaac Hayes
LINER NOTES: Country singer Zeke Clements did the voice for Bashful, the yodeling dwarf, in Disney's *Snow White and the Seven Dwarfs*.

Children of
Country Stars

From Shooter to Carlene to Sunday Rose, country musicians have some interesting, inspiring, and just plan bizarre choices when it comes to naming their children.

BABY NAME	COUNTRY PARENT(S)
Allie	Garth Brooks
August	Garth Brooks
Christos James	Crystal Gayle
Cissie	Loretta Lynn
Eja D'Angelo	Shania Twain
Faith	Keith Urban
Georgette	Tammy Wynette & George Jones
Lukas Autry	Willie Nelson
Marty	Merle Haggard
Mikha	Emmylou Harris
Paula Carlene	Willie Nelson
Roy	Roy Acuff
Shelby	Reba McEntire
Shooter	Waylon Jennings
Sunday Rose	Keith Urban
Tamala	Tammy Wynette
Tara	Johnny Cash
Taylor	Garth Brooks
Tomi Lynn	Waylon Jennings

Musical Families

The Von Trapps aren't the only sibling-only musical group. Check out these bands that keep it all in the family:

The Andrews Sisters	LaVerne, Maxene, & Patty
The Bee Gees	Barry, Robin, & Maurice
The Carpenters	Karen & Richard
The Carter Family	A.P., Sarah, Maybelle, Anita, June, Helen, Joe, & Janette
Death	Bobby, David, & Dannis
The Dixie Cups	Barbara Ann, Rosa Lee, & Joan Marie
The Emotions	Pamela, Sheila, Wanda, & Jeanette
The Everly Brothers	Don & Phil
Gladys Knight & the Pips	Gladys, Bubba, Brenda, William, & Eleanor
The Isley Brothers	O'Kelly, Rudolph, Ronald, Vernon, Chris, Marvin, & Ernie
The Jacksons	Jackie, Tito, Jermaine, Janet, Marlon, Michael, & Randy
Kings of Leon	Caleb, Ivan, Michael, & Cameron
The Louvin Brothers	Ira & Charlie
The McGarrigle-Wainwrights	Kate & Anna, Loudon, Rufus, & Martha
The Ronettes	Veronica, Estelle, & Nedra
The Shaggs	Dot, Betty, Helen, & Rachel
Sister Sledge	Kim, Debbie, Joni, & Kathy
The Staple Singers	Roebuck, Mavis, Cleotha, Pervis, & Yvonne
Trachtenburg Family Slideshow Players	Jason, Tina, & Rachel

Johnny Cash
Baby Names

The Man in Black inspires country musicians and parents alike—his last name has become a fashionable choice for rock star parents like Slash from Guns N' Roses and John Rich, of Big & Rich. But the prolific cowboy left a wealth of options beyond Johnny, Cash, and J.R. Just avoid naming your little boy Sue.

GIRLS		BOYS	
Annie	Irene	Abner	Luther
Apache	Jenny-Jo	Casey	McGee
Barbara	Jeri	Cisco	Ned
Calilou	June	Cotton	Nicodemus
Cana	Kate	Custer	Noel
Cindy	Kathleen	Flint	Porter
Clementine	Magdala	Garfield	Rob
Delia	Nina	Harley	Rusty
Dolorosa	Pocohontas	Hiawatha	Shep
Dorraine	Rosanne	Ira	Tiger
Galway	Ruby	J.R.	Willie
Grace	Vivian	Jack	Woody
Halsy		Jackson	Woolly
		Jessie	Yuma
		Lee	

1990s:
Grunge, Post-Punk, and Alternative

T he 1990s saw the emergence of alternative rock and grunge into the mainstream, inspiring a chart takeover by the likes of Nirvana, R.E.M., Alanis Morrissette and Red Hot Chili Peppers. Though it might seem too early for 1990s nostalgia, it's a safe bet that by the time your baby is in high school, some of these names will have attained a sheen of retro cool.

GIRLS

Ada, Aida, Adia

GERMAN: Noble
ROCK AND ROLL: Sensitive, quiet, insightful
RELATED ARTISTS/SONGS: Ada Lee, Ada Dyer, "Ada" by The National, "Fucking Ada" by Ian Drury and the Blockheads, "Aida" by Miles Davis, "Adia" by Sarah McLachlan
LINER NOTES: Sarah McLachlan's song "Adia" is an apology to her best friend, whose ex-boyfriend she had started dating.

Andrea

GREEK: Lady

MXPX:
"Your beautiful face—like God's amazing grace."

JOE PURDY:
"Oh, Andrea, honey I want you around."

RX BANDITS:
*"I know the answer to this riddle:
It's Andrea every time."*

CITY SLEEPS:
"If looks could kill you'd be a murderer."

Charlotte

FRENCH: Petite and womanly
ROCK AND ROLL: Cool, calm, and collected
RELATED ARTISTS/SONGS: The Charlottes, Good Charlotte, Charlotte Gainsbourg, "Charlotte" by Slint, "Charlotte Sometimes" by The Cure, "Charlotte" by Kittie, "Charlotte" by Air Traffic, "Charlotte" by The Macc Lads
LINER NOTES: The band Good Charlotte took its name from *Good Charlotte: The Girls of Good Day Orphanage*, a children's book by Carol Beach York.

Cheryl, Sheryl

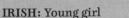

FRENCH: Variation of Cher, beloved
ROCK AND ROLL: Sunny, gorgeous, bouncy
RELATED ARTISTS/SONGS: Cheryl Cole, Sheryl Crow, Cheryl Lynn, "Cheryl" by Chet Baker, "Cheryl Tweedy" by Lily Allen, "Cheryl" by Charlie Parker, "Sheryl" by The Wrenfields, "Cheryl's Going Home" by Cher
LINER NOTES: Sheryl Crow often eats four or five donuts after a show.

Colleen

IRISH: Young girl
ROCK AND ROLL: An optimist, blessed, worldly
RELATED ARTISTS/SONGS: Colleen Fitzpatrick (aka Vitamin C), "Colleen" by The Heavy, "Colleen" by Joanna Newsom, "Colleen" by Ted Leo & the Pharmacists, "Colleen" by Half Japanese, "Colleen" by Glen Campbell

"Colleen, the outcast rebel queen."
—TREATY OF PARIS

Courtney

LATIN: Short
ROCK AND ROLL: Wild, unpredictable, strong-willed
RELATED ARTISTS/SONGS: Courtney Jane, Courtney Love, Courtney Pine, "Courtney" by Nerf Herder, "Courtney" by The Clarks, "Courtney" by The Cynics, "He's Courtin' Courtney" by The Dickies
LINER NOTES: When she was twelve, Courtney Love auditioned for and was rejected by the Mickey Mouse Club. She read a Sylvia Plath poem for her tryout.

Dani

HEBREW: Variant of Danielle, God is my judge
ROCK AND ROLL: Spirited, reckless, lives life to its fullest
RELATED ARTISTS/SONGS: Dani Filth (Cradle of Filth), Dani Siciliano, "Dani California" by Red Hot Chili Peppers, "Dani" by Buddy Greco
LINER NOTES: Dani California is a recurring character in many Red Hot Chili Peppers songs, a composite based on Anthony Kiedis's ex-girlfriends.

Donita

LATIN: Form of Domina, lady of the house
ROCK AND ROLL: Dependable, dreamy, energetic
RELATED ARTISTS/SONGS: Donita Sparks (L7), "Donita Havabomb" by The Narcicyst, "Donita" by Knut Bell
LINER NOTES: Donita Sparks and L7 played in a fake rock group called Camel Lips in John Waters's film *Serial Mom*.

Enid

WELSH: Purity
ROCK AND ROLL: One who got away, long-lost love
RELATED ARTISTS/SONGS: The Enid, Enid Cumberland, "Enid" by Barenaked Ladies, "Enid" by All Future
LINER NOTES: The Barenaked Ladies song "Enid" is about singer Steven Page's ex-girlfriend, but the name is taken from Enid Leger, a waitress at Spanky's Pub, the band's New Brunswick hangout.

Gaea, Gaia

GREEK: Earth goddess
ROCK AND ROLL: Fresh-faced, generous, nurturing, a hippie chick
RELATED ARTISTS/SONGS: "Gaea" by Pentangle, "Gaia" by James Taylor, "Gaia" by Olivia Newton-John, "Gaia" by Jeff Johnson
LINER NOTES: The lyrics for Olivia Newton-John's song "Gaia" came to her in a dream; the album *Gaia* was the first one of tracks Newton-John penned entirely by herself.

Harriet

ENGLISH: Variation of Henry, powerful ruler
ROCK AND ROLL: Spunky, patriotic, a beautiful, bright star
RELATED ARTISTS/SONGS: Harriet Roberts, Harriet Wheeler (The Sundays), "Harriet's Got a Song" by Ben Kweller, "Harriet Tubman" by Wynton Marsalis, "For the Love of Harriet" by Map, "Harriet Thugman" by Rah Digga
LINER NOTES: The Sundays' Harriet Wheeler and David Gavurin have two children, daughter Billie and son Frank.

Hazel

ENGLISH: Hazlenut tree

ROCK AND ROLL: The girl next door, pretty, a little rough around the edges

RELATED ARTISTS/SONGS: Hazel Dickens, Hazel Scott, Sister Hazel, "Hazel" by Bob Dylan, "Hazel" by Cocteau Twins, "Hazel" by Junior Boys, "Hazel" by Ken Nordine, "Slow Fast Hazel" by Stereolab

LINER NOTES: Sister Hazel was named for a nun, Sister Hazel Williams, who ran a homeless shelter near the group's hometown of Gainesville, Florida.

Heidi

GERMAN: Of noble birth

ROCK AND ROLL: Wild, "a cool kind of crazy," an endearing character

RELATED ARTISTS/SONGS: Heidi Berry, Killing Heidi, "Heidi Is a Headcase" by the Ramones, "Heidi Breuhl" by Tosca, "Heidi" by Ruby, "Heidi" by Kingfisher

LINER NOTES: Australian rock band Killing Heidi formed around then-teenage brother-sister duo Ella and Jessie Hooper.

Indigo

ENGLISH COLOR NAME: Blue-eyed

ROCK AND ROLL: Bohemian, nature-lover, a free spirit

RELATED ARTISTS/SONGS: Indigo Girls, "Mood Indigo" by Duke Ellington, "Indigo Children" by Puscifer, "Indigo" by Peter Gabriel, "Indigo" by The Shadows

LINER NOTES: The two members of Indigo Girls met during elementary school and began playing together during high school.

Iris

GREEK: *Rainbow*

THE GOO GOO DOLLS:
"You're the closest to heaven that I'll ever be."

THE BREEDERS:
"When Iris sleeps over, It'll be all right."

SPLIT ENZ:
"Ooh, Iris, the girl with the lovely name."

HERCULES & THE LOVE AFFAIR:
"Bearer of peace with a message for all."

Josie

HEBREW: Variation of Josephine, the Lord increases
ROCK AND ROLL: Smart, independent, the life of the party
RELATED ARTISTS/SONGS: Josie and the Pussycats, "Josie (Everything's Going to Be Fine)" by Blink-182, "Josie" by Donovan, "Josie Anderson" by John Vanderslice, "Josie" by Kris Kristofferson, "Josie" by Steely Dan

"I've been chasing after Josie since the day I could run."
—STEELY DAN

Judith

HEBREW: Woman of Judea
ROCK AND ROLL: Inspiring, independent-minded, a warrior
RELATED ARTISTS/SONGS: Judith Holofernes, Judith LeClair, Judith Durham (The Seekers), "Judith" by A Perfect Circle, "Judith" by The Cult, "Judith" by Pat Boone, "Judith" by Serge Gainsbourg
LINER NOTES: A Perfect Circle's "Judith" is about vocalist Maynard James's mother, whose unwavering faith after being paralyzed with a stroke inspired him to write the song.

Kristen, Kristin

NORWEGIAN: Variation of Christina, servant of God
ROCK AND ROLL: Easygoing, a dreamer, loving
RELATED ARTISTS/SONGS: Kristin Hersh (Throwing Muses), Kristen Pfaff (Hole), "Kristen" by Rooney, "Kristen Said" by Howie Day, "Kristen" by Jessica Williams
LINER NOTES: Throwing Muses' Kristin Hersch published a children's book titled *Toby Snax* for her two sons, Dylan and Ryder James.

Leigh

ENGLISH: Variation of Lee, clearing
ROCK AND ROLL: Clever, beguiling, delightful
RELATED ARTISTS/SONGS: Leigh Fox, Leigh Jones, Leigh Nash (Sixpence None the Richer), "Leigh" by Nathan Angelo, "Leigh" by The New Monarchs, "Anna Leigh" by The Sadies
LINER NOTES: Leigh Nash named the band Sixpence None the Richer from a line in C. S. Lewis's book *Mere Christianity*.

Marilyn

ENGLISH: Variation of Mary, beloved lady
ROCK AND ROLL: Sultry, blond, a star

RELATED ARTISTS/SONGS: Marilyn Crispell, "Marilyn" by Nat King Cole, "Marilyn" by John Fahey, "Marilyn" by Jackie Gleason
LINER NOTES: Nat King Cole recorded the song "Smile" as a tribute to his friend Marilyn Monroe.

Melanie

GREEK: Dark
ROCK AND ROLL: Spunky, cheerful, disciplined, has a great smile
RELATED ARTISTS/SONGS: Melanie Brown (Spice Girls), Melanie Chisholm (Spice Girls), Melanie Thornton (La Bouche), "Melanie" by Donna Summer, "Melanie" by Guster, "Melanie" by Celine Dion, "Melanie" by John Zorn
LINER NOTES: Spice Girls collectively have eight children: Brooklyn, Romeo, Cruz, and Harper (Victoria Beckham); Phoenix and Angel (Mel B.); Bluebell (Geri Halliwell); and Scarlet (Mel C.).

Melissa

GREEK: Honeybee
ROCK AND ROLL: Worldly, kindhearted, loves to travel
RELATED ARTISTS/SONGS: Melissa Etheridge, Melissa Manchester, "Melissa" by The Allman Brothers Band, "Melissa" by Al Hirt, "Melissa" by Chet Atkins
LINER NOTES: Melissa Etheridge played rock band with neighborhood kids at an early age, using tennis rackets, pots, and pans.

Meredith

WELSH: Great ruler
ROCK AND ROLL: The life of the party, strong, bright
RELATED ARTISTS/SONGS: Meredith Andrews, Meredith Brooks, "Meredith" by The Servants, "Meredith" by Oceansize, "Meredith" by The Bled
LINER NOTES: In 2008, Meredith Brooks released a children's album called *If I Could Be . . .* ; she has one son named Troy.

Olga

RUSSIAN: Holy
ROCK AND ROLL: Ambitious, outgoing, organized
RELATED ARTISTS/SONGS: Olga Guillot, Olga Samaroff, Olga Tanon, "Olga" by King Oliver, "Olga" by Daniel Santos, "Blue Green Olga" by Jon Spencer Blues Explosion, "Olga Crack Corn" by The Toy Dolls
LINER NOTES: Latin singer Olga Tanon is known to her fans as the *Mujer de Fuego* or "Woman of Fire."

Paula

LATIN: Small
ROCK AND ROLL: Bright, peppy, strong
RELATED ARTISTS/SONGS: Paula Abdul, Paula DeAnda, Paula Cole,

"When Paula Sparks" by Copeland, "Paula" by Duke Jordan, "Paula" by Phil Woods, "Hey Paula" by Paul & Paula

LINER NOTES: Paula Abdul choreographed the scene where Tom Hanks dances on a giant piano in the movie *Big*.

Phoebe

GREEK: Bright, shining

ROCK AND ROLL: Gentle, talented, introspective

RELATED ARTISTS/SONGS: Phoebe Snow, "Phoebe" by Eddie Baccus, "Phoebe" by Spirit, "Phoebe" by Glenn Phillips

LINER NOTES: Phoebe Snow performed at Howard Stern's wedding in 2008.

Sarah, Sara

HEBREW: Ruler

ROCK AND ROLL: Luminous, angelic, one of a kind

RELATED ARTISTS/SONGS: Sara Bareilles, Sarah McLachlan, Sarah Vaughan, "Sara" by Bob Dylan, "Sara" by Fleetwood Mac, "Sarah" by Ween, "Sarah" by Ray LaMontagne, "Sara Smile" by Hall & Oates

LINER NOTES: Singer Sarah McLachlan has two daughters, India Ann and Taa-Jah Summer; Taa-Jah is the Hindi word for crown.

Selena

GREEK: Variation of Selene, moon goddess

ROCK AND ROLL: Fierce, dramatic, has a big personality

RELATED ARTISTS/SONGS: Selena Quintanilla-Perez, Selena Gomez, "Selena" by Wyclef Jean, "Selena" by Bobby Sky, "Selena" by Ray Pillow

LINER NOTES: The late Selena Quintanilla-Perez, the Queen of Tejano Music and the subject of the Jennifer Lopez movie *Selena*, loved Pizza Hut. Her favorite was double pepperoni.

Sophia, Sofia

GREEK: Wisdom

ROCK AND ROLL: A poet, introverted, lovely, honest

RELATED ARTISTS/SONGS: Sophia the Ocean, Sofia Bernston, "Sophia" by Good Shoes, "All for You, Sophia" by Franz Ferdinand, "Song of Sophia" by Dead Can Dance, "Sophia" by Nerina Pallot, "Jewels for Sophia" by Robyn Hitchcock

LINER NOTES: The Soft Boys' Robyn Hitchcock's solo album *Jewels for Sophia* featured an appearance by soundtrack maestro Jon Brion.

Tabatha, Tabitha

HEBREW: Gazelle

ROCK AND ROLL: Sassy, a thrill-seeker

RELATED ARTISTS/SONGS: Tabitha's Secret, Tabitha Roy, "Tabitha" by Marry Me Jane, "Tabatha's Song" by Philip Wesley, "Tabatha" by Jad Fair & Jason Willett

LINER NOTES: Tabitha's Secret's lead vocalist, Rob Thomas, went on to found the nineties rock group Matchbox Twenty.

Tori

LATIN: Form of Victoria, conqueror
ROCK AND ROLL: Sultry, sharp, has a mind of her own
RELATED ARTISTS/SONGS: Tori Amos, "Tori" by John Mayer, "Tori" by Craig Handy, "Tori" by Ananda Shankar, "Tori" by Steven Brown
LINER NOTES: Tori Amos was voted her high school's Homecoming Queen, as well as Choir Flirt and Most Likely to Succeed.

Ursula

LATIN: Bear
ROCK AND ROLL: Assertive, levelheaded, calm
RELATED ARTISTS/SONGS: Ursula 1000, Ursula Rucker, "Ursula" by Miles Davis, "Ursula" by Larry Coryell
LINER NOTES: DJ Ursula 1000, born Alex Gimeno, took his name as a tribute to Swiss Bond girl Ursula Andress.

Virginia

ENGLISH: Pure
ROCK AND ROLL: Innovative, quirky, warm, happy
RELATED ARTISTS/SONGS: "Virginia" by Tori Amos, "Meet Virginia" by Train, "Sweet Virginia" by The Rolling Stones, "Virginia" by Clipse, "Virginia" by Chin Up Chin Up

"She doesn't own a dress, her hair is always a mess."
—TRAIN

Zoe, Zoey

GREEK: Life
ROCK AND ROLL: Sweet, cheerful, doe-eyed
RELATED ARTISTS/SONGS: Zoe Pollock, Gorilla Zoe, "Flowers for Zoe" by Lenny Kravitz, "Zoe" by Tony Trischka, "Zoe" by Brooks William
LINER NOTES: Lenny Kravitz's song "Flowers for Zoe" was a tribute to his then three-year-old daughter.

BOYS

Anthony, Antony

LATIN: Praiseworthy
ROCK AND ROLL: Upwardly mobile
RELATED ARTISTS/SONGS: Little Anthony & the Imperials, Anthony Kiedis (Red Hot Chili Peppers), Anthony Hamilton, "Anthony" by Nickel Creek, "Anthony" by Tonéx, "Movin' Out (Anthony's Song)" by Billy Joel
LINER NOTES: Under the stage name Cole Dammett, Anthony Kiedis of Red Hot Chili Peppers, appeared in the movies *Point Break* and *The Chase*.

Bart, Bartholomew

HEBREW: Steadfast
ROCK AND ROLL: Mischievous
RELATED ARTISTS/SONGS: Dave Bartholomew, Bart Coen, "Bartholomew" by Frank Black, "Bartholomew" by Adam Green, "Do the Bart" by The 2 Live Crew, "Bayou Bartholomew" by the Weeks, "Dissolution: The Dream of Bartholomew" by Clinic
LINER NOTES: Michael Jackson wrote the *Simpsons* song "Do the Bartman" but didn't appear in the credits because he was under contract for a different record company.

Brendan

IRISH: Prince
ROCK AND ROLL: Moody, smart
RELATED ARTISTS/SONGS: Brendan Benson (The Raconteurs), Brendan Hines, Brendan Reed (Arcade Fire), "Brendan #1" by Fugazi, "Brendan's Boogie" by Brendan Power
LINER NOTES: Music producer Brendan O'Brien was one of the most notable sound engineers of the 1990s, working with The Black Crowes, Pearl Jam, and Stone Temple Pilots.

Calvin

LATIN: Bald
ROCK AND ROLL: Curious, quirky, a party animal
RELATED ARTISTS/SONGS: Calvin Broadus (aka Snoop Dogg), Calvin Harris, Calvin Johnson, "For Calvin" by Frank Zappa, "Calvin" by The Jon Spencer Blues Explosion
LINER NOTES: K Records founder Calvin Johnson was so influential on Kurt Cobain that Kurt had the record's symbol (a K inside a shield) tattooed on his arm.

Chad

WELSH: Warrior
ROCK AND ROLL: Unassuming, introverted

RELATED ARTISTS/SONGS: Chad Mitchell (The Chad Mitchell Trio), Chad Smith (Red Hot Chili Peppers), Chad Channing (Nirvana), "Chad" by Smoke, "Chad" by Lee Konitz

LINER NOTES: Red Hot Chili Peppers drummer Chad Smith bears an uncanny resemblance to Will Ferrell, so much so that when he appeared on *The Tonight Show* with his side project Chickenfoot, he wore a T-shirt that read "I Am Not Will Ferrell."

Dale

ENGLISH: Valley

ROCK AND ROLL: Intimidating, a daredevil

RELATED ARTISTS/SONGS: Dale Bozzio (Missing Persons), Dale Hawkins, Dale Norris (The Champs), "The Ring (Hypnotic Seduction of Dale)" by Queen, "Dale" by Digger

LINER NOTES: Dale Nixon is a pseudonym used by both Gregg Ginn of Black Flag and Foo Fighters' Dave Grohl, who was credited as such on The Melvins' album *King Buzzo*.

Damian, Damien

GREEK: Conqueror

ROCK AND ROLL: Mellow, mystical, loyal

RELATED ARTISTS/SONGS: Damien Jurado, Damian Marley, Damien Rice, "Damian" by Frost, "Habanos Days/Damien" by Thievery Corporation, "Damian" by Mike Harrison, "Damien" by The Legendary Pink Dots, "Damien" by DMX

LINER NOTES: Damian Marley's nickname, Junior Gong, is derived from his father Bob Marley's nickname, Tuff Gong.

Dave

HEBREW: Variation of David, beloved

ROCK AND ROLL: Laid-back, affable, destined for greatness

RELATED ARTISTS/SONGS: Dave Grohl (Foo Fighters), Dave Matthews (Dave Matthews Band), Dave Navarro (Jane's Addiction), "Dave" by Kool & the Gang, "Dave" by The Boomtown Rats, "Dave" by The Bears, "For Dave" by Peter Broderick, "Big Dave" by David Anthony

LINER NOTES: Dave Matthews once broke two ribs trying to catch a grape with his mouth.

Ed

ENGLISH: Variation of Edward or Edwin, happy

ROCK AND ROLL: An artist and a decent guy, unfortunately rhymes with "dead"

RELATED ARTISTS/SONGS: Ed O'Brien (Radiohead), Ed Robertson (Barenaked Ladies), Ed Sanders (The Fugs), "Ed Is Dead" by The Pixies, "Ed Is a Portal" by Akron/Family, "Ed" by King Missile, "Presuming Ed (Rest Easy)" by Elbow

LINER NOTES: At six-foot-five, Ed O'Brien is the tallest member of Radiohead. (None of the other members crack six feet.)

Flynn

GAELIC: Red

ROCK AND ROLL: A powerful leader, a courageous warrior, up for anything

RELATED ARTISTS/SONGS: Jim Flynn, Matt Flynn (Maroon 5), "Flynn" by Ratatat, "Flynn" by Tricky, "The Son of Flynn" by Daft Punk, "In Like Flynn" by Girls Against Boys, "Flynn Lives" by Daft Punk

LINER NOTES: Matt Flynn, drummer for Maroon 5, has also played for The B-52's and Gavin DeGraw.

Gerard

GERMAN: Brave, spear-bearer

ROCK AND ROLL: Bookish, clever, introverted

RELATED ARTISTS/SONGS: Gerard Dott (The Incredible String Band), Gerard Love (Teenage Fanclub), Gerard Way (My Chemical Romance), "Gerard" by Peggy Lee, "Gerard" by Das Pop, "Gerard" by Boss Hog

LINER NOTES: Before forming My Chemical Romance with his brother, Gerard Way worked as an intern at the Cartoon Network.

Harvey

ENGLISH: Blazing iron

ROCK AND ROLL: Rambunctious, rowdy, tough

RELATED ARTISTS/SONGS: Harvey Brooks, Harvey Danger, Harvey Mandel (Canned Heat), "Harvey" by Hoagy Carmichael, "Harvey" by Ambrosia

LINER NOTES: The band Harvey Danger got their name from some graffiti on the University of Washington newspaper office wall.

Hiro

JAPANESE: Widespread

ROCK AND ROLL: Playful, witty

RELATED ARTISTS/SONGS: Hiro Yamamoto (Soundgarden), "Hiro" by Blame, "Hiro" by Ingrid Karklins, "Hiro" by Sadao Watanabe

LINER NOTES: Bassist Hiro Yamamoto left Soundgarden to form psychedelic indie band Truly with former Screaming Trees members Robert Roth and Mark Pickerel.

Jake

HEBREW: Variation of Jacob, he who supplants

ROCK AND ROLL: Spontaneous, fearless, should be careful around whiskey

RELATED ARTISTS/SONGS: Less Than Jake, Jake Owen, "Jake Leg" by Baroness, "Jake" by Lynyrd Skynyrd, "Jake" by Lisa Loeb

LINER NOTES: Less Than Jake's name was inspired by drummer Vinnie Fiorello's dog, whose lush treatment made everyone else in the family feel "less than Jake."

Jaron

HEBREW: Sing out
ROCK AND ROLL: An optimist, bright, clear-eyed
RELATED ARTISTS/SONGS: Evan & Jaron, "Halling Jaron" by Garmana, "Last Smile for Jaron" by Tera Melos
LINER NOTES: After splitting from the duo Evan & Jaron, which he formed with his twin brother, Jaron Lowenstein named his solo act Jaron and the Long Road to Love.

Jonas

GREEK: Variation of Jonah, dove
ROCK AND ROLL: Courteous, handsome, serious
RELATED ARTISTS/SONGS: Jonas Field, Jonas Hellborg, The Jonas Brothers, "Jonas" by Binary Mind, "The Bike of Jonas" by Peter and the Wolf, "My Name Is Jonas" by Weezer, "Jonas" by Jean Derome
LINER NOTES: Rivers Cuomo wrote "My Name Is Jonas" for Weezer after his younger brother got into a car accident and was having difficulties with health insurance.

Kenneth

SCOTTISH: Born of fire
ROCK AND ROLL: Clever, in a world of his own, smiley
RELATED ARTISTS/SONGS: Kenneth Cooper, Kenneth Edmonds (aka Babyface), Kenneth & the Knutters, "What's the Frequency, Kenneth?" by R.E.M., "Kenneth" by Jonas Hellborg
LINER NOTES: Michael Stipe wrote "What's the Frequency, Kenneth?" about "a guy who's desperately trying to understand what motivates the younger generation"; the title came from an incident where news anchor Dan Rather was attacked and heard one of the assailants ask, "What's the Frequency, Kenneth?"

Kurt, Curt

ENGLISH: Full of wisdom
ROCK AND ROLL: A wry, troubled genius
RELATED ARTISTS/SONGS: Kurt Cobain (Nirvana), Curt Smith (Tears for Fears), Kurt Vile, "Kurt" by Electric Dragon, "Kurt's Rejoinder" by Brian Eno, "Kurt" by Dan Bern, "Kurt Vonnegut" by Born Ruffians
LINER NOTES: Kurt Cobain's imaginary childhood friend was named "Boddah."

Lenny

GERMAN: Form of Leonard, brave
ROCK AND ROLL: A cutup and a poet, experienced
RELATED ARTISTS/SONGS: Lenny Kaye (Patti Smith Group), Lenny Kravitz, "Lenny" by Supergrass, "Lenny" by John Mayer, "Lenny" by The Buggles, "Lenny" by Umphrey's McGee, "Lenny Bruce" by Bob Dylan

LINER NOTES: In his early career, Lenny Kravitz performed under the name Romeo Blue; Kravtiz also went to high school with Guns N' Roses' Slash.

Liam

IRISH: Protector
ROCK AND ROLL: Eccentric, confident, distinguished
RELATED ARTISTS/SONGS: Liam Gallagher (Oasis), Liam Howlett (The Prodigy), Liam O'Moanlai (Hothouse Flowers), "Liam" by Evan Lurie, "Liam" by Colin Reid, "Liam" by In Extremo
LINER NOTES: Oasis's Liam Gallagher is banned for life from Cathay Pacific airlines, owing to a tantrum he threw over a scone.

Patrick

LATIN: Upper class
ROCK AND ROLL: Hardy, tough, soulful
RELATED ARTISTS/SONGS: Patrick Park, Patrick Olive (Hot Chocolate), Patrick Monahan (Train), "Patrick" by June, "Patrick" by Kirsty MacColl, "Patrick" by Goblin
LINER NOTES: Train's lead singer Patrick Monahan is the voice of Driver Dan on the PBS kids' show *Driver Dan's Story Train*.

Rico

SPANISH: Form of Ricardo, ruler
ROCK AND ROLL: Smooth, dapper
RELATED ARTISTS/SONGS: "Rico Suave" by Gerardo, "Born in Puerto Rico" by Paul Simon, "Rico" by Goodie Mob, "Rico" by Barrio Boyzz
LINER NOTES: Weird Al Yankovic recorded a parody of "Rico Suave" called "Taco Grande."

Rivers

ENGLISH NATURE NAME
ROCK AND ROLL: Nerdy but cool, quirky, brainy
RELATED ARTISTS/SONGS: Rivers Cuomo (Weezer), "I Follow Rivers" by Lykke Li, "By the Rivers Dark" by Leonard Cohen, "Rivers" by Sugar Ray
LINER NOTES: Weezer's frontman Rivers Cuomo's mother named him Rivers because he was born between the East and Hudson rivers in Manhattan; "Weezer" was Cuomo's childhood nickname.

Rooney

IRISH: Red name
ROCK AND ROLL: Fresh-faced, practical, sunny
RELATED ARTISTS/SONGS: Rooney Roon (Ultramagnetic MCs), Rooney, "Rooney" by Roger Whittaker, "Rooney" by Michael Holliday, "Rooney" by Akhenaton
LINER NOTES: Alternative rock band Rooney is named for Ed Rooney, the principal in *Ferris Bueller's Day Off*.

Ryan

IRISH: Little king
ROCK AND ROLL: Confident, aloof, literate
RELATED ARTISTS/SONGS: Ryan Adams, Ryan Cabrera, "Ryan" by Casey Scott, "Ryan" by Jami Lunde, "Ryan" by Chris Conway, "Ryan" by Manu Military
LINER NOTES: Before meeting his current wife, Mandy Moore, singer-songwriter Ryan Adams was in serious relationships with Parker Posey and Leona Naess.

Seal

ENGLISH WORD NAME
ROCK AND ROLL: Smooth, good-natured
RELATED ARTISTS/SONGS: Seal, "Seal Jubilee" by Bat for Lashes, "Grey Seal" by Elton John, "Seal Eyeing" by Animal Collective
LINER NOTES: Seal's full name is Seal Henry Olusegan Olumide Adeola Samuel; he and Heidi Klum have four children, Leni, Henry, Johan, and Lou Sulola.

Tad

ENGLISH: Form of Thaddeus, courageous
ROCK AND ROLL: Clean-cut, traditional, has a dark side
RELATED ARTISTS/SONGS: Tad Doyle (TAD), Tad Morose, Tad Kinchla (Blues Traveler), "Tad" by Pushing Red Buttons, "Tad" by The Pseudo Superheroes
LINER NOTES: Grunge pioneer Tad Doyle and his band TAD were dropped from their first major label deal because their album poster for *Inhaler* featured a picture of Bill Clinton smoking a joint.

Waldo

GERMAN: To rule
ROCK AND ROLL: Intelligent, quick, enigmatic
RELATED ARTISTS/SONGS: Waldo's People, Terry Waldo, Waldo Val, "Waldo" by Granfaloon Bus, "Waldo" by Lyman Enloe, "Waldo" by The Short Sisters
LINER NOTES: Despite his Finnish ancestry, Eurodance musician Waldo, born Marko Reijonen, sings all his songs in a faux Jamaican accent.

Wes

ENGLISH: Form of Wesley, dweller by the woods
ROCK AND ROLL: Studious, talented, plays by his own rules
RELATED ARTISTS/SONGS: Wes Montgomery, Wes Borland (Limp Bizkit), Wes Scantlin (Puddle of Mudd), "Wes" by Melvin Rhyne, "Wes" by Jimmy Stewart, "Wes" by Martin Rev
LINER NOTES: Limp Bizkit guitarist Wes Borland is known for wearing black contacts and elaborate face paint while performing.

Children's Books
Written by Musicians

Rock and roll parents and parents-to-be, take note: Once that sweet child of yours is on to the picture book stage, there are plenty of music-related options. In fact, many musicians have taken it upon themselves to write spunky alternatives to *Goodnight Moon*, among them LeAnn Rimes, Dionne Warwick, and Sting.

The Jolly Man by Jimmy Buffett

Over the Rainbow by Judy Collins

Man Gave Names to All the Animals by Bob Dylan

The Magically Mysterious Adventures of Noelle the Bullfrog by Gloria Estefan

There Ain't No Bugs on Me by Jerry Garcia

The English Roses series by Madonna

My Little Girl by Tim McGraw

Coat of Many Colors by Dolly Parton

Broadway Barks by Bernadette Peters

Jag by LeAnn Rimes

Abiyoyo by Pete Seeger

Amy the Dancing Bear by Carly Simon

Rock Steady: A Story of Noah's Ark by Sting

Say a Little Prayer by Dionne Warwick

Nature Names

The outdoors is often as much an inspiration for rock songs as any heartbreak or gritty party-filled tour. There are some beautiful, simple, and familiar names to be found in the world of nature.

Acacia	Hyacinth
Aurora	June
Autumn	Lake
Azure	Marigold
Basil	Meadow
Bay	Misty
Birch	Nile
Brooke	Rain
Cayenne	Rowan
Cerise	Sequoia
Cherry	Sky
Cliff	Spruce
Cougar	Star
Dahlia	Stone
Dawn	Stormy
Dew	Summer
Fern	Thunder
Flint	West
Fox	Willow
Gemma	Winter
Heather	

Kickin' It Old School: Hip-hop and Rap

Looking for something with more of a beat to it? Hip-hop, rap, afrobeat, reggae, and dancehall music present a whole spectrum of choices, from the African-inspired Ashanti and Fela to the traditional-but-cool Carter and Eve. The more adventurous namer will find plenty of fodder here, but even if Ludacris's gold-plated swagger isn't your thing, remember that Jay-Z started out as just plain Shawn.

GIRLS

Aaliyah, Aliya

HEBREW: Moving up
ROCK AND ROLL: Baby girl, R&B princess
RELATED ARTISTS/SONGS: Aaliyah, "Aliyah" by Lucky Thompson
LINER NOTES: Aaliyah, whose full name is Aaliyah Haughton, had a dove tattooed on her lower back in tribute to her grandmother, Dana.

Anquette, Anquet
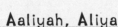

AMERICAN: Form of Annette, hospitable
ROCK AND ROLL: Witty, introspective
RELATED ARTISTS/SONGS: Anquette Allen, "Anquet" by The Drastics
LINER NOTES: Miami booty bass musician Anquette Allen, head of the group Anquette, wrote a dance song in tribute to then Florida DA Janet Reno, congratulating her for throwing the book at deadbeat dads.

Antonia

LATIN: Priceless
ROCK AND ROLL: Fair-skinned, loves to eat cereal
RELATED ARTISTS/SONGS: Antonia Reed (Bahamadia), "Antonia" by Motion City Soundtrack, "My Antonia" by Emmylou Harris, "Antonia" by Tony Bennett
LINER NOTES: Hip-hop lyricist Bahamadia came up with her pseud-

onym through the combination of the Arabic words *badia*, meaning "original creation," and *hamd'allah*, which translates to "thankful to God."

Apollonia

GREEK: Form of Apollo, goddess
ROCK AND ROLL: Exotic, sultry
RELATED ARTISTS/SONGS: Apollonia Kotero, Apollonia 6, "St. Apollonia" by Beirut, "Apollonia" by Nino Rota, "Apollonia" by Team Sleep
LINER NOTES: Singer and *Purple Rain* star Apollonia was romantically linked to Prince and David Lee Roth.

Charlene, Charlena, Sharlene, Sharlena

FRENCH: Petite
ROCK AND ROLL: A sweetheart, a honky-tonk gal, flighty
RELATED ARTISTS/SONGS: Sharlene Flores, Charlene Keys (aka Tweet), "Charlene" by Carl Perkins, "Charlene" by Björk, "Sharlena" by Frank Zappa, "Charlena" by Ritchie Valens
LINER NOTES: Missy Elliott discovered Tweet when she auditioned for her girl group Sugar.

Erica, Erykah

NORSE: Ruler of the people
ROCK AND ROLL: Majestic, secretive, rebellious
RELATED ARTISTS/SONGS: Erykah Badu, "Erica Kane" by Aaliyah, "Erica" by Project Wyze, "The Lying Lies and Dirty Secrets of Miss Erica Court" by Coheed and Cambria, "Erica" by The Cynics, "Erica the Beautiful" by Rhett Miller
LINER NOTES: Erykah Badu was charged with disorderly conduct for stripping nude in public while shooting the music video for her song "Window Seat."

Foxy

AMERICAN: Slang for sexy
ROCK AND ROLL: Alluring, assertive
RELATED ARTISTS/SONGS: Foxy Brown, Foxy Shazam, "Foxy Lady" by Jimi Hendrix, "Foxy Foxy" by Rob Zombie, "You're So Foxy" by No Doubt, "Foxy Girl" by Daniel Johnston
LINER NOTES: When Foxy Brown suffered hearing loss for a time in 2005, she opted to have someone tap beats on her shoulder while she recorded rather than get a hearing aid.

Hester, Hesta

PERSIAN: Form of Esther, star
ROCK AND ROLL: Courageous, dramatic, literate
RELATED ARTISTS/SONGS: Hester Prynne, Hesta Prynn (Northern

State),"Hester" by Beyond the Pale, "Hester" by Erin McCamley, "Hester" by Gordon McLeod

LINER NOTES: Hip-hop group Northern State began when Hesta Prynn, Correne Spero, and Robyn "Sprout" Goodmark were in high school; Hesta Prynn, born Julie Potash, took her pseudonym from *The Scarlet Letter*, one of their required reading books.

Hortense

LATIN: Gardener
ROCK AND ROLL: Hip, free-spirited, flighty
RELATED ARTISTS/SONGS: Hortense Ellis, "Hortense" by Tabu Ley Rochereau, "Hortense" by Hum
LINER NOTES: Before achieving success under her own name in the late seventies, reggae singer Hortense Ellis recorded under the name Mahalia Saunders.

Jade

ENGLISH GEM NAME
ROCK AND ROLL: The girl of the hour, luminous, quick to laugh
RELATED ARTISTS/SONGS: Jade, Jade Castrinos (Edward Sharpe and the Magnetic Zeros), Ms. Jade, "Jade" by Edward Sharpe and the Magnetic Zeros, "Jade" by The Razorcuts, "Jade" by Metro, "Jade" by The Untouchables, "Goodnight Jade" by Squarepusher
LINER NOTES: Rapper Ms. Jade, born Chevon Young, used to work as a beautician between her touring gigs.

Jentina, Jantine

DUTCH: Generous
ROCK AND ROLL: Worldy, clever
RELATED ARTISTS/SONGS: Jentina Chapman, "Jantine" by Eltjo Haselhoff
LINER NOTES: Gypsy rapper Jentina Chapman is now a professional model, representing Wonderbra and Cadbury; she has a son, Ralph, and a daughter, Annie.

Kelis

AMERICAN INVENTED
ROCK AND ROLL: Sultry and sweet, a firecracker
RELATED ARTISTS/SONGS: Kelis Rogers
LINER NOTES: Kelis's name is a combination of her father's name, Kenneth, and her mother's name, Eveliss.

Lana

IRISH: Form of Alana, harmony

ROY ORBISON:
"The sweetest and the neatest girl in the whole world."

THE BEACH BOYS:
"Lana come with me, oh Lana dear."

THE EXCENTRICS:
"Tell Lana that I really love her."

THE DONNAS:
"She's a teenage runaway."

Latifah

ARABIC: Delicate
ROCK AND ROLL: A powerhouse, funny, brassy
RELATED ARTISTS/SONGS: Queen Latifah, "Latifah" by Shelly Snow, "Latifah" by Organic Akusticks, "Latifa" by Kenny Garrett
LINER NOTES: Queen Latifah, born Dana Owens, got her stage name from her cousin when she was eight.

LaToya, La Toya, LeToya

AMERICAN INVENTED
ROCK AND ROLL: Fresh, jazzy, modelesque
RELATED ARTISTS/SONGS: LaToya London, La Toya Jackson, Letoya Luckett, "LaToya" by Just-Ice
LINER NOTES: La Toya Jackson suffers from ailurophobia, a deadly fear of cats.

Lauren, Lauryn

LATIN: Victory of wisdom
ROCK AND ROLL: A great negotiator, passionate and playful
RELATED ARTISTS/SONGS: Lauryn Hill, Lauren O'Connell, Lauren Wood, "Lauren" by Johnny Pate, "Lauren Marie" by Girls, "Lauren London" by Clipse, "Lauren's Cathedral" by Mando Diao, "Lauren & I" by Celtic Thunder
LINER NOTES: Lauryn Hill has five children with Rohan Marley: Zion, Selah, Joshua, John, and Sarah.

Lisa

ENGLISH: Variation of Elizabeth, God's promise
ROCK AND ROLL: Emotional, mesmerizing, has an enigmatic smile
RELATED ARTISTS/SONGS: Lisa Loeb, Lisa "Left Eye" Lopes (TLC), Lisa Origliasso (The Veronicas), "Lisa" by Burt Bacharach, "Losing Lisa" by Ben Folds, "Lisa Says" by The Velvet Underground, "Lisa" by Prince, "O Lisa" by Weezer

"She's my best friend and more."
—BEN FOLDS

Louise, Louisa

GERMAN: A mighty warrior
ROCK AND ROLL: Very kind but plain, melodramatic, loves breakfast in bed
RELATED ARTISTS/SONGS: Louise Harman (Lady Sovereign), "Louise Louisa" by Mew, "Louisa" by Weeping Willows; "Louise" by John Lee Hooker, "Louise" by Orange Juice, "Louise" by The Human League
LINER NOTES: Rapper Lady Sovereign, born Louise Harman, picked up her stage name after she began wearing a sovereign ring.

Magnolia

ENGLISH PLANT NAME
ROCK AND ROLL: A sassy Southern belle
RELATED ARTISTS/SONGS: Magnolia Electric Company, Magnolia Shorty, "Magnolia" by Jorge Ben, "Sugar Magnolia" by The Grateful Dead, "Magnolia" by Jon Brion, "Magnolia Mountain" by Ryan Adams
LINER NOTES: "Queen of Bounce" Magnolia Shorty, born Renetta Lowe-Bridgewater, got her nickname from fellow rapper Soulja Slim, whom she grew up with in New Orleans.

Maia, Maya, Mya

GREEK: Mother
ROCK AND ROLL: Creative, elegant, joyful
RELATED ARTISTS/SONGS: Maia Sharp, Maya Arulpragasm (aka M.I.A.), Mya, "Maya" by The Incredible String Band, "Maya" by Wayne Shorter, "Maia" by Louis Osbourne, "Maya" by Sugababes, "Maya" by M.I.A.
LINER NOTES: Singer Mya was named after the poet Maya Angelou.

Makeba

XHOSA: Princess
ROCK AND ROLL: Humble, serious, politically active
RELATED ARTISTS/SONGS: Miriam Makeba, Makeba Riddick, "Makeba" by Actis Band, "Makeba" by Aceyalone, "Makeba" by Carla Fischi
LINER NOTES: Songwriter Makeba Riddick, who has penned songs for Rihanna, Mariah Carey, and Beyoncé, got the nickname "Girl Wonder" from P. Diddy for her knack for writing hit songs.

Mary

GREEK: Beloved lady
ROCK AND ROLL: Loving, forgiving, laid-back
RELATED ARTISTS/SONGS: Mary Chapin Carpenter, Mary J. Blige, Mary Wells, "Proud Mary" by Creedence Clearwater Revival, "Now Mary" by The White Stripes, "The Wind Cries Mary" by Jimi Hendrix, "Mary" by Sublime, "Help Me, Mary" by Liz Phair
LINER NOTES: Mary J. Blige has three stepchildren from her husband Kendu's first marriage: Brianna, Jordan, and Nas.

Missy

ENGLISH: Variation of Melissa, honeybee
ROCK AND ROLL: Bold, independent, sassy
RELATED ARTISTS/SONGS: Missy Elliott, Missy Higgins, "Missy" by Pee Wee Russell, "Missy" by Sidney Bechet, "Missy" by Red Monkey
LINER NOTES: In the video for Missy Elliott's "Work It," Missy commemorated friends Aaliyah and Lisa "Left Eye" Lopes by having their images airbrushed on a car that she stands in front of.

Monie, Mony

AMERICAN: Form of Simone, wise
ROCK AND ROLL: Fun-loving, brainy, outgoing
RELATED ARTISTS/SONGS: Monie Love, "Stop by Monie's" by Liquid Soul, "Mony Mony" by Tommy James & the Shondells, "Monie" by Kanda Bongo Man
LINER NOTES: Rapper and radio personality Monie Love was a member of positive-minded hip-hop crew Native Tongues, along with Q-Tip, De La Soul, and Queen Latifah; she has a weekly radio show named after Queen Latifah's hit "Ladies First."

Natia, Niatia, Nasha

SPANISH: Miracle
ROCK AND ROLL: Introspective, exotic, pretty
RELATED ARTISTS/SONGS: Niatia Kirkland (aka Lil Mama), "Natia" by Death in Vegas, "Terra Natia" by Bruno Tassone, "Nasha" by Alisha Chinai, "Nasha" by The Evolution Control Committee
LINER NOTES: Rapper Niatia Kirkland got the nickname Mama from her mother.

Nicki, Nicky, Nikki

GREEK: Variation of Nicole, victory
ROCK AND ROLL: Sultry, wild, a free spirit
RELATED ARTISTS/SONGS: Nicki Minaj, "Darkling Nikki" by Prince, "Tricky Nicky" by Mike Pinto, "Watching Nicky" by Pulp
LINER NOTES: Nicki Minaj's full name is Onika Tanya Maraj; she was born in Trinidad and moved to Queens when she was five years old.

Olive

ENGLISH PLANT NAME
ROCK AND ROLL: Old-fashioned, sweet but reserved
RELATED ARTISTS/SONGS: Olive, DJ Olive, "An Olive Grove Facing the Sea" by Snow Patrol, "Olive" by Ken Nordine, "Olive" by Isobella, "Olive" by Alison Crockett
LINER NOTES: Ken Nordine was Linda Blair's vocal coach for her role in *The Exorcist*.

Pepper, Pepa

ENGLISH SPICE NAME
ROCK AND ROLL: Makes things more interesting, sharp, spunky
RELATED ARTISTS/SONGS: Sandra "Pepa" Denton (Salt-N-Pepa), Art Pepper, Red Hot Chili Peppers, "Pepper" by Butthole Surfers, "Pepper" by Millencolin, "Pepper Tree" by Cocteau Twins
LINER NOTES: Pepa Denton has two children, son Tyran and daughter Egypt.

Rasheeda, Rashida

SWAHILI: Righteous
ROCK AND ROLL: Adorable, magnetic, intelligent
RELATED ARTISTS/SONGS: Rasheeda Buckner, "Rashida" by John Lucien, "Rashida" by Paveier, "Rasheeda" by Smoked Out Society
LINER NOTES: Atlanta's Rasheeda Buckner is sometimes known as "Queen of Crunk," thanks to her pioneering lyrics and brassy vocal style.

Rashia, Rasha

ARABIC: Feminine form of Rashas, having good judgment
ROCK AND ROLL: Talented, persuasive, affable
RELATED ARTISTS/SONGS: Rashia Fisher (Rah Digga), Nasha Rasha, Rasha Shaheen, "The Story of Rasha & Dhara" by Bobby Callender, "Rasha" by Flam, "Rasha" by Rux
LINER NOTES: MC Rah Digga was the only female member of Busta Rhyme's Flipmode Squad, collaborating with the likes of Lauryn Hill and A Tribe Called Quest.

Remy

LATIN: Oarsman
ROCK AND ROLL: Tough, capable, clever
RELATED ARTISTS/SONGS: Remy Zero, Remy Ma, Remy Shand, "Remy" by Wolverines, "Remy Red" by Angie Stone, "Remy" by Ludwig Von 88
LINER NOTES: Rapper Remy Ma's real name is Reminisce Smith. She's the only female member of the Fat Joe–fronted group Terror Squad.

Rye, Ryeisha

ENGLISH: Feminine variation of Ryland, farmer
ROCK AND ROLL: Flashy, patriotic, friendly
RELATED ARTISTS/SONGS: Ryeisha Berrain (Rye Rye), "Catcher in the Rye" by Guns N' Roses, "Waves of Rye" by Department of Eagles, "Rye" by Sounds from the Ground
LINER NOTES: Rapper and M.I.A. protégée Rye Rye has a daughter, Kennidi Malaysia.

Shaniqua

MODERN INVENTED: Beautiful
ROCK AND ROLL: Enigmatic, talented
RELATED ARTISTS/SONGS: Shaniqua Williams, "Shaniqua" by Little T and One Track Mike, "Shaniqua" by Whitehead Bros.
LINER NOTES: Rapper 50 Cent and his on-again off-again girlfriend Shaniqua Tompkins have one child, a boy named Marquise Jackson.

Shante, Chanté, Shawntae

AMERICAN: Variation of Shantal, singer
ROCK AND ROLL: Lyrical, spiritual, charming
RELATED ARTISTS/SONGS: Shawntae Harris (Da Brat), "Shante Prashante" by Deva Premal, "Shante" by Mass Production, "Chanté" by Petula Clark
LINER NOTES: Shawntae Harris chose her stage name Da Brat because she considered herself "a spoiled only child." She's the stepsister of actress LisaRaye McCoy.

Sharissa, Charissa, Charisse

GREEK: Form of Charis, grace
ROCK AND ROLL: Literate, rowdy, sweet
RELATED ARTISTS/SONGS: Sharissa, Sharisse "Shar" Jackson, "Charissa" by Margaret Slovak, "Charissa" by AM Taxi, "Charisse" by Xavier Cugat, "Charisse" by David Burns
LINER NOTES: When rapper Sharissa was growing up, her enthusiasm for singing was so infectious that her dad nicknamed her "Little Stevie Wonder."

Shawna, Shawnna, Shauna

IRISH: Faminine variation of Sean, God's grace
ROCK AND ROLL: Tough, sassy, witty
RELATED ARTISTS/SONGS: Shauna Davis, Shauna Burns, Shawnna, "Shauna" by Spookey Ruben, "Shauna Made Me Cry" by Gary Wilson, "Shauna" by Big Bad Shakin', "Shawna" by the Street-walkin' Cheetahs
LINER NOTES: Rapper Shawnna, born Reshawnna Guy and known for her collaborations with Lil Kim and Ludacris, is the daughter of blues musician Buddy Guy.

Syleena, Seleena

AMERICAN: Form of Selene, moon goddess
ROCK AND ROLL: Loves the nighttime, smart, a hard worker
RELATED ARTISTS/SONGS: Syleena Johnson, "Syleena" by Blueshift Signal, "Seleena" by Padame Om
LINER NOTES: Syleena Johnson's brother is the football player Chad Ochocinco; her two sons are name Kiwane and Kingston.

Sylvia, Silvia

LATIN: Woodland nymph
ROCK AND ROLL: Ethereal, independent, free-spirited
RELATED ARTISTS/SONGS: Sylvia Jane Kirby, Sylvia Robinson (Mickey & Sylvia), Sylvia Tyson (Ian & Sylvia), "Silvia" by Jens Lekman, "Silvia" by Marissa Nadler, "Sylvia" by Pulp, "Sylvia Plath" by Ryan Adams, "Sylvia" by The Antlers
LINER NOTES: R&B singer and record executive Sylvia Robinson masterminded the formation of The Sugarhill Gang and released their first hit, "Rapper's Delight."

Tionne, Tion

AMERICAN: Variation of Tatiana, snow queen
ROCK AND ROLL: Beautiful, resilient, ambitious
RELATED ARTISTS/SONGS: Tionne "T-Boz" Watkins (TLC), Words of Tione, "Tion" by Nils Petter Molvaer, "Tion" by Jackhead, "Tion" by Blood of Abraham
LINER NOTES: TLC's Tionne Watkins owns a children's boutique called Chase's Closet, named after her daughter Chase Anela.

Tiye, Tey

EGYPTIAN: Form of Nefertari, pharaoh queen
ROCK AND ROLL: Elegant, spiritual, empowered
RELATED ARTISTS/SONGS: Tiye Phoenix, Tiye Giraud, "Tey" by Andrew Cyrille, "Solo Tiye" by John Cale
LINER NOTES: Underground hip-hop femcee Tiye Phoenix, best known for her work with the group The Polyrhythm Addicts, is a classically trained pianist.

Trina

LATIN: Triple
ROCK AND ROLL: Sassy, bubbly, sharp
RELATED ARTISTS/SONGS: Trina, "Trina" by Native Roots, "Trina" by Yowie, "Trina" by Mad Machinery
LINER NOTES: Rapper Trina's self-invented nicknames are "The Diamond Princess" and "The Baddest Bitch"; those are also the titles of her two albums.

Vinia, Vina

SANSKRIT: To wish
ROCK AND ROLL: Whip-smart, always one step ahead, romantic
RELATED ARTISTS/SONGS: Vinia Mojica, Vina Morales, "Vina" by TW, "Vina" by Obroke
LINER NOTES: Reclusive rapper Vinia Mojica, sometimes known as "the First Lady of Soulful Hip-Hop" has appeared on tracks by Talib Kweli, Mary J. Blige, and Pete Rock.

Yolanda

GREEK: Violet
ROCK AND ROLL: Soulful, philosophical, urbane
RELATED ARTISTS/SONGS: Yolanda Adams, Yolanda del Rio, Yolanda Whittaker (Yo-Yo), "Yolanda" by Fred Astaire, "Yolanda" by Nana Mouskouri, "Yolanda" by Bobby "Blue" Bland, "Yolanda" by Robert Wyatt
LINER NOTES: Hard-core rapper and feminist Yo-Yo made cameo appearances in the films *Boyz n the Hood*, *Who's the Man?*, and *Sister Act 2*.

BOYS

Africa, Afrika

ENGLISH PLACE NAME
ROCK AND ROLL: Strong, independent, an old soul
RELATED ARTISTS/SONGS: Afrika Bambaataa, "Africa" by Toto, "Africa Unite" by Bob Marley & the Wailers, "Mama Africa" by Akon, "Thank You for Talkin' to Me Africa" by Sly & the Family Stone
LINER NOTES: Hip-hop pioneer Afrika Bambaataa, born Kevin Donovan, took his stage name from Zulu chief Bambatha, whose activism against oppression was a precursor to the anti-apartheid movement.

Andre

FRENCH: Form of Andrew, man
ROCK AND ROLL: Creative, intelligent, suave

RELATED ARTISTS/SONGS: Andre Young (Dr. Dre), Andre 3000, Andre Nickatina, "Andre" by Buddy Collette, "Andre" by Louis Hayes, "Andre" by David Becker

LINER NOTES: Andre "3000" Benjamin wrote the OutKast song "Ms. Jackson" as an apology to then girlfriend Erykah Badu's mother; his son with Badu is named Seven.

Antoine, Antwan

FRENCH: Variation of Anthony, praiseworthy

ROCK AND ROLL: Rambunctious, good-natured, funny

RELATED ARTISTS/SONGS: Antoine Domino (Fats Domino), Antoine Dufour, Antwan Patton (Big Boi), "Cher Antoine" by Los Hermanos, "Antoine" by The Incredible String Band, "Antoine" by Garage a Trois

LINER NOTES: Big Boi's nickname and song "Daddy Fat Sax" is in tribute to a White Castle employee and OutKast fan who would slip extra sliders into his take-out bag.

Artis

LATIN: Art

ROCK AND ROLL: Laid-back, a poet, passionate

RELATED ARTISTS/SONGS: Artis Ivey Jr. (Coolio), D.D. Artis, "Artis" by Brad Mehldau Trio, "Arcana Artis" by Ador Dorath

LINER NOTES: Coolio published a cookbook in 2009, *Cookin' with Coolio*, which includes recipes for "Tricked-out Westside Tilapia" and "Chili Mac Pimp."

Camaron, Cameron

GAELIC: Crooked nose

ROCK AND ROLL: Wealthy, a close friend

RELATED ARTISTS/SONGS: Cameron Giles (aka Cam'ron), "Camaron" by Freddy Fender, "Cameron" by The Actual

LINER NOTES: Rapper Cam'ron started his career in a group called Children of the Corn.

Clifford

ENGLISH: Ford by a cliff

ROCK AND ROLL: Mellow, friendly, unassuming

RELATED ARTISTS/SONGS: Clifford Brown, Clifford Davies (Ted Nugent), Clifford Harris (T.I.), Clifford Smith (Method Man), "I Remember Clifford" by Ray Charles, "Clifford" by The Changes, "Clifford" by Chip White

LINER NOTES: In 2010, T.I. helped talk a suicidal man down from jumping off a building.

Drake

ENGLISH: Dragon
ROCK AND ROLL: Precocious, clever
RELATED ARTISTS/SONGS: Drake, Nick Drake, Drake Bell, "Drake" by Beth Gibbons, "Drake" by Afro Celt Sound System
LINER NOTES: Before his rapping career began, Drake starred as Jimmy Brooks on the Canadian teen show *Degrassi: The Next Generation*.

Duane, Dwayne

IRISH: Dark one
ROCK AND ROLL: Wise elder, revered
RELATED ARTISTS/SONGS: Duane Allman (The Allman Brothers Band), Dwayne Carter (Lil Wayne), Duane Eddy, "For Duane" by Frank Zappa, "Nub" by The Jesus Lizard, "Duane" by Lamb of God, "Duane Joseph" by The Juliana Theory, "Dwayne" by Red Rat
LINER NOTES: Lil Wayne is said to have more than 360 tattoos, including several visible only under ultraviolet light.

Earl

ENGLISH: Nobleman
ROCK AND ROLL: A gentleman, should avoid black-eyed peas
RELATED ARTISTS/SONGS:, Earl Hooker, Earl Palmer, Earl Simmons (aka DMX), "Goodbye Earl" by The Dixie Chicks, "Duke of Earl" by The Platters, "Earl" by E-40, "The Earl of Suave" by Thee Headcoatees, "Cousin Earl" by The Dead Milkmen
LINER NOTES: DMX, born Earl Simmons, has four children, Xavier, Tocoma, Shawn, and Praise Mary Ella; he also has nine dogs.

Farrell, Ferell, Pharrell

IRISH: Courageous
ROCK AND ROLL: Lucky, easygoing, kind
RELATED ARTISTS/SONGS: Pharrell Williams, "Farrell" by Eddie Daniels, "Farell Blues" by Eileen Ivers, "Ferell" by Stanley Cowell
LINER NOTES: The Neptunes' Pharrell Williams is a big-time trekky, often using the Vulcan salute to signify his label, Star Trak.

Fela

WEST AFRICAN: Warlike
ROCK AND ROLL: An activist, innovative, a leader
RELATED ARTISTS/SONGS: Fela Kuti, "Time Travelin' (A Tribute to Fela)" by Common, "Fela" by Hugh Masekela, "Fela" by Frank London
LINER NOTES: Afrobeat trailblazer Fela Kuti, born Olufela Olusegun Oludotun Ransome-Kuti, married twenty-seven women at once to commemorate the attack on the Kalakuta Republic; he later adopted a rotation system, keeping only twelve wives simultaneously.

Femi, Olufemi

WEST AFRICAN: God loves me
ROCK AND ROLL: Attentive student
RELATED ARTISTS/SONGS: Femi Kuti, Femi Fem, Femi B, Olufemi Ajasa, "Olufemi" by Demola Adepoju
LINER NOTES: Femi Kuti has one child, Omrinmade or "Made", and an ex-wife, Funke.

Gil

HEBREW: Happiness
ROCK AND ROLL: Dapper, devious, a mad genius with a past full of secrets
RELATED ARTISTS/SONGS: Gil Evans, Gil Ofarim, Gil Scott-Heron, "Wicked Gil" by Band of Horses, "Gil Sleeping" by The Horrors, "Gil" by Captain Beefheart, "Gil" by Mo Foster
LINER NOTES: Poet and hip-hop legend Gil Scott-Heron has a master's degree in creative writing from Johns Hopkins University, despite never finishing college.

Jamie, Jaime

SPANISH: Variation of James, replacement
ROCK AND ROLL: Edgy, aloof, popular
RELATED ARTISTS/SONGS: Jamie Cullum, Jamie Foxx, Jaime Gomez (aka "Taboo," The Black Eyed Peas), "Jaime" by Carolyn Hester, "Jamie" by The Jackson Five, "Jamie" by Mouse
LINER NOTES: At Taboo's wedding, fellow Black Eyed Peas will.i.am and apl.de.ap served as groomsmen.

Jermaine, Germaine

LATIN: Sprout
ROCK AND ROLL: Innovative, from a powerful family
RELATED ARTISTS/SONGS: Jermaine Clement, Jermaine Dupri, Jermaine Jackson, "Germaine" by Sinead O'Connor, "Germaine" by Renaud
LINER NOTES: Jermaine Jackson's two sons are name Jermajesty Jermaine and Jaafer Jeremiah.

King

ENGLISH: Leader
ROCK AND ROLL: Suave, a great dancer, but a little immature
RELATED ARTISTS/SONGS: King Crimson, King Curtis, King Oliver, "King Back" by T.I., "King" by UB40, "Sun King" by The Beatles, "King of the Rodeo" by Kings of Leon, "King of Pain" by The Police, "King" by Weezer
LINER NOTES: King Curtis led Aretha Franklin's backup band, the Kingpins.

Lex

AMERICAN: Variation of Alexander, ruler

ROCK AND ROLL: Bewitching, thinks on his feet

RELATED ARTISTS/SONGS: Lex Luger, "Lex" by Ratatat, "Lex" by Donald Byrd, "Lex Tallionis" by Sol Invictus, "Lex" by Duke Pearson

LINER NOTES: Hip-hop producer Lex Luger, born Lexus Lewis, began making beats using his PlayStation before selling them to Snoop Dogg, Slim Thug, and Soulja Boy, among others.

Lonnie

SPANISH: Form of Alonzo, enthusiastic

ROCK AND ROLL: Well-bred, original, innovative

RELATED ARTISTS/SONGS: Lonnie Brooks, Lonnie Donegan, Lonnie Lynn (Common), "Lonnie" by John Ellis, "Lonnie's Lament" by McCoy Tyner, "Lonnie" by Godley & Creme

LINER NOTES: Lonnie Lynn, aka Common, regularly tours with his entire family in tow.

Lucas

GREEK: From Luciana

ROCK AND ROLL: Well traveled, philosophical, urbane

RELATED ARTISTS/SONGS: Lucas Prata, Lucas Secon, "Lucas" by Dalida, "Lucas" by John Hughes, "Mad Lucas" by The Breeders, "Chewin' George Lucas' Chocolate" by Butthole Surfers

LINER NOTES: Danish-American rapper Lucas Secon's father is the cofounder of Pottery Barn and was a songwriter for Nat King Cole.

Lupe

LATIN: Wolf

ROCK AND ROLL: Feisty, philosophical, ebullient

RELATED ARTISTS/SONGS: Lupe Fiasco, "Little Latin Lupe Lu" by The Righteous Brothers, "Lupe" by Sphere, "Lupe Brown" The Fratellis

LINER NOTES: Rapper Lupe Fiasco's real name is Wasalu Muhammad Jaco. He got his stage name from his childhood nickname "Lu" and The Firm's song "Fiasco."

Mac, Mack

SCOTTISH: Diminuitive form of "Mc" names, friendly

ROCK AND ROLL: A lady-killer, smooth, dangerous

RELATED ARTISTS/SONGS: Craig Mack, Mac Dre, "The Story of Mack" by Moses Cleveland, "Who's the Mack?" by Ice Cube, "Return of the Mack" by Mark Morrison, "The Mack Is Back" by Kool Keith, "Mac" by Lotus

LINER NOTES: Mark Morrison's "Return of the Mack" samples Tom Tom Club's "Genius of Love" and the Kool & the Gang's "K.T."

Marley

ENGLISH: Seaside meadow
ROCK AND ROLL: Laid-back, has an ear for the beat
RELATED ARTISTS/SONGS: Bob Marley, Marley Marl, "Marley" by Lazy K
LINER NOTES: Bob Marley, born Nesta Robert Marley, has eleven children acknowledged by the Marley estate: Sharon, Cedella, Ziggy, Stephen, Robbie, Rohan, Karen, Stephanie, Julian, Ky-Mani, and Damian.

Mike

ENGLISH: Form of Michael, Who is like God?
ROCK AND ROLL: Easygoing, waggish, pleasant to be around
RELATED ARTISTS/SONGS: Mike D (The Beastie Boys), Mike Love (The Beach Boys), "Mike" by Django Reinhardt, "Mike" by Xiu Xiu, "Mike Mills" by Air
LINER NOTES: The Beastie Boys' Mike D has two sons, Skyler and Davis.

Moe

HEBREW: Variation of Moses, savior
ROCK AND ROLL: A free spirit, fun-loving, good-natured
RELATED ARTISTS/SONGS: Moe Jaffe, Kool Moe Dee, moe., "Dinah-Moe Humm" by Frank Zappa, "Moe's Luv Theme" by Ultramagnetic MC's, "Moe Tucker" by The Jesus and Mary Chain, "Moe" by David Wilcox
LINER NOTES: Since 2008, Kool Moe Dee has hosted his own online hip-hop talk show called *SpitFire with Kool Moe Dee.*

Morgan

IRISH: Magnanimous
ROCK AND ROLL: Upbeat, debonair, fussy
RELATED ARTISTS/SONGS: Morgan Heritage, Morgan Fichter (Camper Van Beethoven), "Morgan" by Alan Stivell, "Morgan" by Charles Earland, "Morgan" by Cloud Nothings
LINER NOTES: Reggae group Morgan Heritage is composed of five children of the singer Denroy Morgan: Una, Roy, Peter, Nakhamyah, and Memo.

Nasir, Nas

ARABIC: Variation of Nasser, the winner
ROCK AND ROLL: Loyal, magnanimous
RELATED ARTISTS/SONGS: Nas Jones, "Nas" by Seventh Sign, "Nasir" by Saweh, "Nasir de Nuevo" by Chieli Minucci
LINER NOTES: Rappers Nas and Kelis have one son, Knight; Nas has a daughter, Destiny, from another relationship.

Nathaniel, Nate

HEBREW: God's gift

ROCK AND ROLL: A good friend, has swagger, smart

RELATED ARTISTS/SONGS: Nathaniel Glover (aka The Kidd Creole), Nathaniel "Jerry" Matthias (Toots and the Maytals), Nate Dogg, "Nathaniel" by OuKast, "Nathaniel" by O'Death

LINER NOTES: Furious Five member Kidd Creole coined the hip-hop staple phrase "yes, yes y'all."

Omar, Omari

ARABIC: Long-lived

ROCK AND ROLL: Earthy, sultry, has a great sense of humor

RELATED ARTISTS/SONGS: Omar Rodriguez-Lopez (The Mars Volta), Omari Grandberry (Omarion), Omar Santana, "Omar" by J. D. Allen, "Omar" by Chuck Coleman, "Omar Bay" by State Radio

LINER NOTES: Omarion has six siblings, O'Ryan, Amira, Ariella, Tymon, Ukil, and Kira; his mother, Leslie, was the stylist for his band B2K.

Rick

ENGLISH: Variation of Richard or Patrick, ruler

ROCK AND ROLL: Confident, wealthy, bold

RELATED ARTISTS/SONGS: Rick Springfield, Rick Ross, Slick Rick, "Meanwhile, Rick James . . ." by Cake, "Rick" by Cheap Trick

LINER NOTES: Rapper Rick Ross's real name is William Roberts. His stage name is taken from the notorious drug trafficker "Freeway" Ricky Ross, who later sued the rapper for using his name.

Romeo

LATIN: A pilgrim to Rome

ROCK AND ROLL: An idealist, dedicated, star-crossed

RELATED ARTISTS/SONGS: Romeo Miller, MC Romeo, Michael Romeo (Symphony X), "Romeo" by Petula Clark, "Romeo" by The Wipers, "Romeo" by Sublime, "Romeo" by Donna Summer, "Romeo" by Dolly Parton

LINER NOTES: Rapper Romeo is the son of Master P and the nephew of the rappers C-Murder and Silkk the Shocker.

Russell

FRENCH: Red-haired

ROCK AND ROLL: Conscientious, witty, intelligent

RELATED ARTISTS/SONGS: Russell Lissack (Bloc Party), Russell Simmons, Russell Jones (ODB, Wu-Tang Clan), "Russell" by The Happy Mondays, "Russell" by Balloon Guy

LINER NOTES: Reverend Run, member of Run-DMC and Russell Simmons's brother, officiated the wedding between Kimora and Russell Simmons.

Sage

ENGLISH: Wise
ROCK AND ROLL: Cerebral, witty, a bohemian
RELATED ARTISTS/SONGS: Sage Francis, "Wild Sage" by The Mountain Goats, "The Sage" by Emerson, Lake & Palmer, "Sage" by The Yellowjackets, "Sage" by Cloud Cult
LINER NOTES: Rapper Sage Francis majored in journalism in college; his birth name is Paul Francis.

Sean, Shaun, Shawn

IRISH: Variation of John, God is gracious
ROCK AND ROLL: Dedicated, persistant, loyal
RELATED ARTISTS/SONGS: Sean Paul, Shawn Carter (Jay-Z), Sean Combs (P. Diddy), "Sean" by The Proclaimers, "Sean" by Tony Trischka, "Shaun" by Kreidler
LINER NOTES: Sean Combs got his first nickname, "Puffy," for the hissy fits he threw as a child when he would huff and puff until he got his way.

Shad, Shadrach

HEBREW: Brave
ROCK AND ROLL: Boisterous, loves a good time
RELATED ARTISTS/SONGS: Shad Moss (Bow Wow), Shadrach Kabango, "Shad Thames" by Saint Etienne, "Shadrach" by The Beastie Boys
LINER NOTES: Bow Wow began rapping at age six under the name "Kid Gangsta."

Talib

ARABIC: Student
ROCK AND ROLL: Politically conscious, wry, literate
RELATED ARTISTS/SONGS: Talib Kweli (Black Star), "Talib" by Africanism, "Talib" by Nasrin
LINER NOTES: Talib Kweli has two daughters, Amani Fela and Diyani Eshe.

Tariq

ARABIC: He who hammers
ROCK AND ROLL: Strong, witty, politically aware
RELATED ARTISTS/SONGS: Lord Tariq, Tariq "Black Thought" Trotter (The Roots), "Tariq" by Abaji, "Tariq" by Dollar Brand, "Tariq" by AF1
LINER NOTES: Tariq Trotter became friends with Ahmir "Questlove" Thompson in high school, forming The Square Roots, later just The Roots.

Tupac

AZTEC: Warrior
ROCK AND ROLL: Confident, clever, a poet
RELATED ARTISTS/SONGS: Tupac Shakur, "Tupac" by Noah Beck, "Tupac" by Butterfinger, "Tupac" by Big Stick Friday
LINER NOTES: Tupac Shakur's mother, Afeni, named him after the Peruvian revolutionary Tupac Amaru II.

Wiley

SCOTTISH: Form of William, protector
ROCK AND ROLL: Sly, hip, has swagger
RELATED ARTISTS/SONGS: Wiley, MC Wiley, "Wiley" by Basher
LINER NOTES: British grime rapper Wiley, born Richard Cowie, got his pseudonym from Wiley Kat, a character in the cartoon *Thundercats*.

Will

GERMAN: Variation of William, protector
ROCK AND ROLL: Multifaceted, bouncy, fresh, witty
RELATED ARTISTS/SONGS: Will Oldham, Will Smith, Will Sergeant (Echo & the Bunnymen), "Will" by The Weather Report, "Will" by Boyz II Men, "Will" by Bill Nelson, "Will" by Common Factor
LINER NOTES: Will Smith met Jada Pinkett when she unsuccessfully auditioned for the role of his girlfriend on *The Fresh Prince of Bel-Air*.

Winston

ENGLISH: Friend's town
ROCK AND ROLL: Laid-back, cool
RELATED ARTISTS/SONGS: Winston Dale, Winston Rodney (aka Burning Spear), Winston MacIntosh (aka Peter Tosh), "Winston" by Bound Stems, "Winston" by Vicious Circles, "Winston" by Infected Mushroom
LINER NOTES: Peter Tosh, born Winston MacIntosh, was a committed unicyclist and knitter, often beginning shows by riding out on stage.

Young

ENGLISH: Youthful
ROCK AND ROLL: Articulate, spontaneous, athletic
RELATED ARTISTS/SONGS: Young MC, Young Jeezy, Young Money, "Young" by Kenny Chesney, "Young" by Rancid, "Young" by Frankie Lymon & the Teenagers
LINER NOTES: Red Hot Chili Peppers' Flea contributed the bass line on rapper Young MC's hit song "Bust a Move."

Zion

HEBREW: Homeland

ROCK AND ROLL: Strong, courageous, loyal

RELATED ARTISTS/SONGS: "Zion" by David Bowie, "Iron Lion Zion" by Bob Marley, "Road to Zion" by Damian Marley, "To Zion" by Lauryn Hill

LINER NOTES: Lauryn Hill and Rohan Marley named their first son Zion David-Nesta Marley.

Hip-Hop Power Children

Wordplay is on the forefront of every hip-hop artist's mind, so it's only natural that the names they choose for their children are on the creative end. From the wacky but charming Bamboo to the can-I-buy-a-vowel Kaydnz, if there's anything you take from the list of hip-hop power children it's that where choosing a name is concerned, as Biggie Smalls said, the sky's the limit.

BABY NAME	HIP-HOP PARENT(S)
A'keiba	MC Hammer
Bamboo	Big Boi
Blue Ivy	Beyoncé & Jay-Z
Christian Casey	P. Diddy
Cordel	Snoop Dogg
Cross	Big Boi
Deyjah Imani	T.I.
Dusti Rain	Vanilla Ice
Ikhyd Edgar Arular	M.I.A
Jeremiah	MC Hammer
Jordan	Ja Rule
Karma Bridges	Ludacris
Kaydnz Kodah	T-Pain
KeeLee Breeze	Vanilla Ice
Lennox	50 Cent
Lyriq	T-Pain
Major Philant	T.I.
Marquise	50 Cent
Mars Makeda	Erykah Badu & Jay Electronica
Messiah Ya' Majesty	T.I.
Muziq	T-Pain
Praise Mary Ella	DMX
Reginae	Lil Wayne
Seven	Erykah Badu & Andre 3000
Shayne	Coolio
Story	Sol & Ginuwine
Tenzin Losel	Adam Yauch (The Beastie Boys)
Tocoma	DMX
Truly	Dr. Dre

Reggae Baby Names

For fans of rocksteady and reggae, there are a world of naming options beyond Bob and Marley. From Lee (for pioneer Lee "Scratch" Perry) to Cedella (one of Bob Marley's daughters), the Jamaican-rooted genres have a wealth of inspiration.

GIRLS	INSPIRATION
Althea	Althea Forrest, of the reggae group Althea & Donna
Bredda	Wailing Souls song "Bredda Gravalicious"
Carolina	Shaggy song "Oh Carolina"
Cedella	Marley's eldest daughter
Guava	"Guava Jelly" by Bob Marley
Kingston	Kingston, Jamaica
Macka	Dancehall DJ Macka Diamond
Marcia	Reggae artist Marcia Griffiths
Nadine	Bob Marley protégée Nadine Sutherland
Nancy	Sister Nancy, dancehall DJ
Nyanda	Sister Nyanda, of reggae duo Brick & Lace
Rita	Marley's wife's name

BOYS	INSPIRATION
Augustus	Reggae melodica player Augustus Pablo
Buju	Dancehall ambassador Buju Banton
Coxsone	Reggae producer Celement "Coxsone" Dodd
Dennis	Crown prince of reggae Dennis Brown
Desmond	Jamaican ska singer Desmond Dekker
Ini	"Here Comes the Hotstepper" artist Ini Kamoze
Lee	Pioneer Lee "Scratch" Perry
Natty	U-Roy song "Natty Don't Fear"
Nesta	Bob Marley's given first name
Norval	Marley's father's name
Shabba	Dancehall star Shabba Ranks
Tosh	Peter Tosh
Ziggy	Oldest son of Bob Marley

Rappers' Real Names

With a few exceptions, notably Kanye and Tupac, the names you know rappers by aren't the ones their family knows them by. They might be full of swagger now, but once Chingy was baby Howard, and Coolio was just little Artis. Check out the names that their mamas gave 'em.

STAGE NAME	REAL NAME
50 Cent	Curtis Jackson
Big Daddy Kane	Antonio Hardy
Biz Markie	Marcel Hall
Bubba Sparxxx	Warren Matthis
Busta Rhymes	Trevor Tahlem Smith
Cee Lo Green	Thomas Callaway
Chamillionaire	Hakeem Seriki
Chuck D	Carlton Ridenhour
Flavor Flav	William Drayton
Ginuwine	Elgin Baylor Lumpkin
Gucci Mane	Radrick Davis
Ice-T	Tracy Morrow
Jadakiss	Jayson Phillips
Juvenile	Terius Gray
Kid Cudi	Scott MesCudi
LL Cool J	James Todd Smith
Ludacris	Christopher Brian Bridges
MC Hammer	Stanley Kirk Burrell
MF Doom	Daniel Dumile
Mystikal	Michael Tyler
Ne-Yo	Shaffer Chimere Smith
The Notorious B.I.G.	Christopher George Latore Wallace
Pitbull	Amando Christian Perez
Redman	Reggie Noble
Sir Mix-a-Lot	Anthony Ray
Snoop Dogg	Calvin Cordazer Broadus
Soulja Boy	DeAndre Ramone Way
Swizz Beatz	Kaseem Dean
T-Pain	Faheem Najm
Wake Flocka Flame	Juaquin Malphurs
Wiz Khalifa	Cameron Jibril Thomaz
Young Jeezy	Jay Jenkins

Soul Sisters and Funk Brothers

Soul names, like the music itself, run from smooth and urbane to fun and bouncy, with pretty much everything in between. There are pioneers like Ray and Sly and out-there boogie fiends like Bootsy and Zapp, not to mention the instant classics like Curtis and Otis.

GIRLS

Ann, Anne

LATIN: Grace
ROCK AND ROLL: A strong woman, a keeper
RELATED ARTISTS/SONGS: Anne DeMarinis (Sonic Youth), Anne Murray, Ann Peebles, "Anne" by Santogold, "Anne with an E" by The Pains of Being Pure at Heart, "Gift for Melody Anne" by The Avett Brothers, "Ann" by The Stooges, "Ann" by The Kingston Trio

"I know I'll never meet another hunk o'woman like Ann."
—THE KINGSTON TRIO

Bernadette

FRENCH: Brave
ROCK AND ROLL: Stylish, affectionate, high-maintenance
RELATED ARTISTS/SONGS: Bernadette Peters, "Bernadette" by Paul Simon, "Bernadette" by The Four Tops, "Bernadette" by The Kinks, "Hey Bernadette" by Russ Ballard, "Pictures of Bernadette" by Talk Talk

"A girl I can't forget/whoa, you're the smile of the moon, Bernadette."
—PAUL SIMON

Carla

GERMAN: Feminine form of Charles, free woman
ROCK AND ROLL: Spunky, unique, but bad with relationships
RELATED ARTISTS/SONGS: Carla Bley, Carla Bruni, Carla Thomas, "Carla" by Daniel Lanois, "Carla" by Todd Snider, "Carla Came Home" by Chris Knight, "Dro Loving Carla" by Savage Garden
LINER NOTES: Carla Thomas, the Queen of Memphis Soul, wrote the hit single "Gee Whiz (Look at His Eyes)" when she was only fifteen years old.

Deborah, Debra

HEBREW: Bee
ROCK AND ROLL: Loves zebras, a fun date, a witch goddess
RELATED ARTISTS/SONGS: Deborah Allen, Deborah Cox, "Debra" by Beck, "Deborah's Theme" by Ennio Morricone, "Deborah" by T-Rex, "Debra Kadabra" by Frank Zappa, "Debra Jean" by The Queers
LINER NOTES: R&B singer Deborah Cox has three children, Isaiah, Sumayah, and Kaila.

Della

ENGLISH: Variation of Adela, noble
ROCK AND ROLL: Vivacious, high-spirited, inviting
RELATED ARTISTS/SONGS: Della Reese, "Della Brown" by Queensrÿche, "Della" by Elizabeth Cotton, "Della" by Blind Willie McTell, "Della" by Mal Waldron
LINER NOTES: Della Reese, born Delloreese Early, was ordained as a minister in 2010; she has one daughter, Deloreese Daniels.

Desdemona

GREEK: Star-crossed
ROCK AND ROLL: Beautiful, bright, a worrywart
RELATED ARTISTS/SONGS: "Desdemona" by John's Children, "Desdemona" by The Allman Brothers Band, "Desdemona" by Jimmy Buffett, "Desdemona" by Eddie Murphy, "Desdemona" by The Searchers

*"She's got a passion for cookies,
a crew full of rookies."*
—JIMMY BUFFETT

Divine

ENGLISH WORD NAME: Holy
ROCK AND ROLL: Sassy, outgoing
RELATED ARTISTS/SONGS: Divine Brown, "Divine" by Korn, "Love's

Divine" by Seal, "Divine Hammer" by The Breeders, "Heavenly Divine" by Jedi Mind Tricks

LINER NOTES: Singer Divine Brown also goes by the name Divine Earth Essence; her biggest influence is reggae singer Dennis Brown, for whom she recorded the tribute "Sitting & Watching."

Dorothy

GREEK: Gift of the gods
ROCK AND ROLL: Lively, fierce, a dreamer
RELATED ARTISTS/SONGS: Dorothy Fields, Dorothy Linell, Dorothy Shay, "Dorothy at Forty" by Cursive, "The Ballad of Dorothy Parker" by Prince, "Dorothy" by Alkaline Trio, "Dorothy Mae" by Howlin' Wolf, "Dorothy" by Lou Donaldson

"Dishwater blonde, tall and fine."
—PRINCE

Duffy

IRISH: Dark
ROCK AND ROLL: Spunky, stylish, quirky
RELATED ARTISTS/SONGS: Duffy, "Duff" by Venetian Snares, "Duffy" by Asleep, "Duffy" by Los Dragos
LINER NOTES: Welsh soul diva Duffy, born Aimée Ann Duffy, has a variation of a daffodil named after her, the "Duffydil."

Eartha

ENGLISH: Of the earth
ROCK AND ROLL: Stylish, sultry, and slinky, a city girl
RELATED ARTISTS/SONGS: Eartha Kitt, Eartha Moore
LINER NOTES: Eartha Kitt's first starring role was as Helen of Troy in Orson Welles's production of *Dr. Faustus*; Welles called her "the most exciting woman in the world."

Ebony

ENGLISH: Dense black wood
ROCK AND ROLL: Beautiful, harmonious, proud
RELATED ARTISTS/SONGS: Ebony Lake, The Ebonys, "Ebony Eyes" by Stevie Wonder, "Ebony and Ivory" by Paul McCartney and Stevie Wonder, "Ebony Jam" by Tower of Power, "Ebony" by Kim Fowley, "Ebony Eyes" by Rick James
LINER NOTES: Of all Paul McCartney's work after The Beatles, "Ebony and Ivory" had the longest run at the top of the *Billboard* charts, spending seven weeks in the number one spot.

Estelle, Estella

FRENCH: Star

ROCK AND ROLL: Effervescent, magnetic, entrancing

RELATED ARTISTS/SONGS: Estelle Axton, Estelle Bennett (The Ronettes), Estelle (Swaray), "Estelle" by A Man Called Adam, "Estelle" by The Beltones, "Estella" by Uzi & Ari, "Estella" by Ace Troubleshooter

LINER NOTES: Memphis soul record label Stax was named by combining Estelle Axton and her brother Jim Stewart's last names.

Geraldine

GERMAN: Feminization of Gerald, spear-bearer

ROCK AND ROLL: Dark-haired, nurturing, warm, kind, carefree

RELATED ARTISTS/SONGS: Geraldine, Geraldine Halliwell (Spice Girls), Geraldine Hunt, "Geraldine" by Glasvegas, "Geraldine" by Chuck Ragan, "Ballad of Geraldine" by Donovan, "Geraldine" by Jack Scott, "Geraldine" by The Rattles

"I was born with the name Geraldine, with hair coal black as a raven."
—DONOVAN

Irma

GERMAN: Universal, of the whole world

ROCK AND ROLL: Practical, powerful, deep

RELATED ARTISTS/SONGS: Irma Curry, Irma Thomas, "Irma" by The Magnetic Fields, "Irma" by Tex Williams, "Irma" by John Greaves, "Irma Jackson" by Merle Haggard

LINER NOTES: Irma Thomas, the Soul Queen of New Orleans, had four children by the time she was nineteen and launched her singing career in her mid-twenties; The Rolling Stones covered her song "Time Is on My Side."

Issa

ENGLISH: Form of Isabel, God-loving

ROCK AND ROLL: Bouncy, sweet, friendly

RELATED ARTISTS/SONGS: Issa Pointer, Issa Bagayoyo, "Issa" by Dobet Gnahoré, "Issa" by Al Tanner, "Issa" by Mich Gerber, "Issa" by Kanal

LINER NOTES: Issa Pointer, late member of The Pointer Sisters, is the daughter of Ruth Pointer and The Temptations' Dennis Edwards; she has one son, Bailan.

Jada

SPANISH: Jade
ROCK AND ROLL: Young, sharp, in control
RELATED ARTISTS/SONGS: Jadakiss, "Jada" by The Four Seasons, "Jada" by Art Tatum, "Jada" by Joe Turner, "Jada" by The Pointer Sisters, "J-A-D-A" by Jadakiss
LINER NOTES: The Pointer Sisters' song "Jada" is dedicated to Anita Pointer's only daughter, Jada.

Jill

LATIN: Youthful
ROCK AND ROLL: Honest, beloved, earthy
RELATED ARTISTS/SONGS: Jill Emery (Hole), Jill Scott, "Tongue-Tied Jill" by Charlie Feathers, "Jill" by Harry Connick Jr., "Pumpin' for Jill" by Iggy Pop, "Jill" by Gary Lewis & the Playboys, "Jill" by the Riptones
LINER NOTES: Singer Jill Scott learned to read when she was just four years old; She has one son, Jett Hamilton.

Jocelyn

GERMAN: Merry
ROCK AND ROLL: Exuberant, loves to sparkle, optimistic
RELATED ARTISTS/SONGS: Jocelyn Brown, Jocelyn Poor, Jocelyn Stoker (aka Joss Stone), "Jocelyn" by Adam Marano, "Jocelyn" by McRad
LINER NOTES: The 1990 Snap song "The Power" sampled the line "I've got the power!" from Jocelyn Brown's "Love's Gonna Get You."

Joss, Jossy

ENGLISH: Variation of Jocelyn, joyful
ROCK AND ROLL: A tomboy, rambunctious but sweet
RELATED ARTISTS/SONGS: Joss Stone, "Joss" by Milton Sting, "Jossy" by The Motet, "Jossy" by Moses Kayeska
LINER NOTES: Joss Stone, born Jocelyn, dated Beau Dozier, son of the legendary Motown songwriter Lamont Dozier of Holland-Dozier-Holland; she has two dogs named Dusty and Missy.

Joyce

FRENCH: Lord
ROCK AND ROLL: Spritely, boisterous, in touch with nature
RELATED ARTISTS/SONGS: Joyce Cooling, Joyce Sims, "Joyce's Hut" by Spiderbait, "Hey Joyce" by Lou Courtney, "Joyce" by Carl Cox
LINER NOTES: R&B singer Joyce Sims is best known for her 1980s hits "Come into My Life" and "All and All."

Kendra

SCOTTISH: Champion
ROCK AND ROLL: Experimental, eccentric, independent
RELATED ARTISTS/SONGS: Kendra Ross, Kendra Smith (The Dream Syndicate), Kendra Springer, "Major Kendra Shaw" by Bear McCreary, "Hey Kendra" by Jason Robert Brown, "Kendra McCormick" by They Might Be Giants
LINER NOTES: Kendra Ross provided session vocals for Talib Kweli, Kanye West, and Faith Evans, most notably on Kweli's single "Get By."

Laverne, LaVern

FRENCH: Springlike
ROCK AND ROLL: Trusty, magnetic, earthy
RELATED ARTISTS/SONGS: LaVerne Andrews (The Andrews Sisters), LaVern Baker, "Laverne" by Tommy Tutone, "Laverne" by The Melroys, ""Laverne (Why Do You Treat Me So Mean?)" by Muddy Waters, "Laverne Walk" by Stan Getz
LINER NOTES: When R&B singer LaVern Baker started singing in Chicago clubs, she was billed as "Little Miss Sharecropper."

Macy

FRENCH: Weapon
ROCK AND ROLL: Sassy, soulful, witty
RELATED ARTISTS/SONGS: Macy Gray, "Macy" by Steve Moakler, "Macy" by Count Basie
LINER NOTES: Macy Gray's children are named Aanisha, Tahmel, and Cassius. She has a tattoo on her right wrist featuring all three of their names.

Marge

ENGLISH: Variation of Margaret, Greek
ROCK AND ROLL: Strong, loving, delightful
RELATED ARTISTS/SONGS: Marge Ganser (The Shangri-Las), "Marge" by Monty Alexander, "Dear Marge" by Stereolab, "My Marge" by ELO
LINER NOTES: Marge Ganser's twin sister, Mary Ann, also sang in The Shangri-Las. The girls named their group after a restaurant in Queens.

Martha

ARAMAIC: Mistress of the house
ROCK AND ROLL: Sweet, patient, silly, a great sibling, loves poetry.
RELATED ARTISTS/SONGS: Martha Reeves, Martha Wainwright, "Martha, My Dear" by The Beatles, "Martha" by Tom Waits, "Ms. Martha" by Curtis Mayfield, "Martha" by Rufus Wainwright, "For Martha" by The Smashing Pumpkins

Mavis

FRENCH: Songbird
ROCK AND ROLL: Powerful, passionate, high-spirited
RELATED ARTISTS/SONGS: Mavis Staples, "Mexican Mavis" by Boy & Bear, "Mavis" by Eden
LINER NOTES: Bob Dylan once asked soul singer Mavis Staples's father, Roebuck, for her hand in marriage. He declined.

Millie

ENGLISH: Form of Emily or Millicent, high-born power
ROCK AND ROLL: The fun girl next door, has a dark side, a little clumsy
RELATED ARTISTS/SONGS: Millie Small, Millie Good, Millie Jackson, "Millie Fell Off the Fire Escape" by Atmosphere, "Millie" by Ikonika, "Millie Brown" by Al Stewart, "U.S. Millie" by Theoretical Girls, "Millie" by The Four Seasons
LINER NOTES: Soul singer Millie Jackson is famous for her outlandish album covers, including one that has her pictured on the toilet.

Natalie

LATIN: Christmas Day
ROCK AND ROLL: Fashionable, a disco queen, a big city girl
RELATED ARTISTS/SONGS: Natalie Cole, Natalie Imbruglia, Natalie Merchant, "Believe Me Natalie" by The Killers, "If You See Natalie" by The Eels, "Natalie" by David Crosby
LINER NOTES: R&B singer Natalie Cole first appeared on a record at age six, performing a duet with her father, Nat King Cole, on his Christmas album; her son Robbie regularly plays with her on tour.

Nikka, Nika

ENGLISH: Variation of Nike, goddess of victory
ROCK AND ROLL: Dazzling, lighthearted
RELATED ARTISTS/SONGS: Nikka Costa, "Nikka" by Amar Arshi, "Nika" by Vicious, "Nika" by The Library Fire
LINER NOTES: Nikka Costa has one daughter, Sugar McQueen Stanley; Nikka is she's also one of Frank Sinatra's goddaughters.

Nita

HINDI: Friendly
ROCK AND ROLL: Fresh, kindhearted, youthful
RELATED ARTISTS/SONGS: Nita Whitaker, "Nita Nitro" by The Wild-hearts, "Nita" by Billy Talent, "Nita" by John Coltrane, "Nita" by Paul Chambers
LINER NOTES: Soul singer Nita Whitaker was married to the voice-over artist Don LaFontaine; their three children are Christine, Skye, and Elyse.

Nona

LATIN: Ninth
ROCK AND ROLL: Soulful, from a strong family base, a great dancer
RELATED ARTISTS/SONGS: Nona Gaye, Nona Hendryx (LaBelle), "Nona" by Mötley Crüe, "Nona" by Erskine Hawkins, "Nona" by Paul Bascombe
LINER NOTES: Before LaBelle took off, Nona Hendryx was in a band with Cindy Birdsong (later of The Supremes) and Patricia Holt—better known as Patti LaBelle—called the Bluebelles.

Rhona, Ronna

SCOTTISH: Derived from Rhonwen, slender
ROCK AND ROLL: Modern, poetic, kind
RELATED ARTISTS/SONGS: Rhona Bennett, Rhona Mitra, Ronna Reeves, "Rhona" by Shakane, "Rhona" by The Killermeters
LINER NOTES: En Vogue member Rhona Bennett, known as "Miss R&B," was a member of the Mickey Mouse Club alongside Justin Timberlake, Christina Aguilera, and Britney Spears.

Rose

ENGLISH PLANT NAME
ROCK AND ROLL: Inventive, smart, shy
RELATED ARTISTS/SONGS: Rose Laurens, Rose Stone (Sly & the Family Stone), Rose Nabinger, "Rose" by A Perfect Circle, "Give My Love to Rose" by Johnny Cash, "Desert Rose" by Sting, "Sweet Rose" by Matt Cosat
LINER NOTES: Rose Stone, sister of Sly Stone, worked as a backup singer after the dissolution of The Family Stone, appearing on albums by Michael Jackson and Ringo Starr. She's currently part of Elton John's band.

Sade

NIGERIAN: Form of Folashade, honor confers a crown
ROCK AND ROLL: Sultry, mellow, earnest
RELATED ARTISTS/SONGS: Sade (Adu), "Sade" by Kenny G, "Sade" by Timco
LINER NOTES: Singer Sade Adu habitually performs barefoot; she has one daughter, named Ila.

Sharon

HEBREW: Forest

JONI MITCHELL:
"You sing for your friends and your family."

JOAN BAEZ:
"So precious to me."

XIU XIU:
"You try so hard to be as sweet as you can."

DAVID BROMBERG:
"She did a little dance that made me weak in the knees."

Sheila

GAELIC: Blind
ROCK AND ROLL: Blue-eyed, rosy-cheeked, sweet, adorable
RELATED ARTISTS/SONGS: Sheila E., Sheila Chandra, "To Sheila" by The Smashing Pumpkins, "Sheila Take a Bow" by The Smiths, "Sheila" by Morphine, "Sheila" by Tommy Roe, "Sheila Liked the Rodeo" by The Tear Garden
LINER NOTES: Prince protégée and muse Sheila E. is the goddaughter of Latin music legend Tito Puente; she is also the biological aunt of Nicole Richie.

Sunshine

ENGLISH NATURE NAME
ROCK AND ROLL: Optimistic, bright, welcoming
RELATED ARTISTS/SONGS: Sunshine Anderson, "Sunshine of Your Love" by Cream, "Ain't No Sunshine" by Bill Withers, "Good Day Sunshine" by The Beatles, "Pocketful of Sunshine" by Natasha Bedingfield, "Walking on Sunshine" by Katrina and the Waves
LINER NOTES: Sunshine Anderson has one daughter, Alexia Skyy.

Tamia

JAPANESE: Little gem
ROCK AND ROLL: Outspoken, kindhearted, sophisticated
RELATED ARTISTS/SONGS: Tamia Hill, "Tamia" by Tinku, "Tamia" by Nazca
LINER NOTES: R&B singer Tamia Hill has two children with the Phoenix Suns' Grant Hill: Myla Grace and Lael Rose.

Valerie, Valarie

LATIN: Valiant

THE ZUTONS:
"I miss your ginger hair."

STEVE WINWOOD:
"She was like jazz on a summer's day."

JERRY GARCIA:
"Valerie, won't you be good to me?"

THE MONKEES:
"I wouldn't live without her, even if I could."

Veda

SANSKRIT: Knowledge
ROCK AND ROLL: Spiritual, a deep thinker, enigmatic
RELATED ARTISTS/SONGS: Veda Brown, "Veda Very Shining" by Letters to Cleo, "Veda" by Buddy Collette, "Veda" by John Norum, "Veda" by The Veldt
LINER NOTES: Soul singer Veda Brown was born Mildred Whitehorn; Brown was her mother's name and "Veda" was picked at random in a contest held by Stax Records.

BOYS

Amos

HEBREW: Borne by God
ROCK AND ROLL: Classically trained, alternatively inclined
RELATED ARTISTS/SONGS: Amos Lee, Amos Milburn, "Amos" by Emil Richards
LINER NOTES: Amos Milburn was one of the key R&B musicians transitioning away from boogie-woogie to the louder "jump" blues that influenced The Rolling Stones.

August, Augustus

LATIN: Majestic
ROCK AND ROLL: Warm, starry-eyed
RELATED ARTISTS/SONGS: Augustus Pablo, "August" by Rilo Kiley, "August" by Umphrey's McGee, "August" by Love
LINER NOTES: Augustus Pablo pioneered the use of melodica in rock,

an instrument that had previously been used mostly as a school-children's toy.

Barry, Berry

CELTIC: Spear
ROCK AND ROLL: Dapper, loves show tunes, the man with the plan
RELATED ARTISTS/SONGS: Barry Gibb, Barry Manilow, Barry White, "Barry's Theme" by Love Unlimited Orchestra, "Barry" by GusGus
LINER NOTES: Barry White has had a beard since he was thirteen years old.

Booker

ENGLISH: Book lover
ROCK AND ROLL: Leader of the band, soul man
RELATED ARTISTS/SONGS: Booker Little, Booker T. Jones (Booker T. & the MG's), Booker T. Washington White (aka Bukka White), "Booker" by Harry Connick Jr., "Booker T." by The Velvet Underground
LINER NOTES: Booker T. Jones's first professional recording was as a saxophonist on the Stax hit "Cause I Love You" by Rufus and Carla Thomas. Booker was sixteen at the time.

Cody

ENGLISH: Considerate
ROCK AND ROLL: Faithful, friendly, old-fashioned
RELATED ARTISTS/SONGS: Cody Chesnutt, Cody Votolato (The Blood Brothers), Commander Cody, "Cody" by Mogwai, "Cody" by John Stewart, "Cody" by Bowling for Soup, "The Ballad of Iron Eyes Cody" by The Mummies, "Cody, Cody" by The Flying Burrito Brothers
LINER NOTES: The Roots' song "The Seed (2.0)" was a remake of Cody Chesnutt's soul classic "The Seed."

Craig

GAELIC: Rock
ROCK AND ROLL: Party animal, perfect for an entourage
RELATED ARTISTS/SONGS: Craig David, Craig Finn (The Hold Steady), Craig Mack, "Craig" by Stephen Lynch, "Craig" by Vile Richard
LINER NOTES: R&B singer Craig David has an honorary doctorate in music from Southampton Solent University.

Curtis

FRENCH: Polite
ROCK AND ROLL: Brash, great at guitar, funky
RELATED ARTISTS/SONGS: Curtis Blow, Curtis Mayfield, Curtis Fuller, "Curtis" by Medeski Martin, & Wood, "Curtis" by the Hang Ups, "The Ballad of Curtis Lowe" by Lynyrd Skynyrd

LINER NOTES: Curtis Mayfield had ten children with his wife, Altheida.

Desmond

IRISH: From Munster
ROCK AND ROLL: Happy, kind, the British champion
RELATED ARTISTS/SONGS: Desmond Child, Desmond Dekker, Desmond Williams, "Don't Worry, Desmond" by the Mighty Mighty Bosstones, "Desmond" by Smudge, "Desmond Blue" by Paul Desmond, "Desmond" by Chumbawamba

"Easily beats all his challengers."
—CHUMBAWAMBA

Dobie

ENGLISH: Variation of Robert, bright flame
ROCK AND ROLL: Talented, sharp
RELATED ARTISTS/SONGS: Dobie Gray, "Dobie" by Lance Martin, "Dobie" by Art Webb, "Dobie" by Lionel Newman
LINER NOTES: Northern soul musician Dobie Gray gained a huge following in South Africa for being the first performer to convince the apartheid authorities to let him play to an integrated audience.

Ernie

ENGLISH: Variation of Ernest, sincere
ROCK AND ROLL: Heroic, punctual, a reliable messenger
RELATED ARTISTS/SONGS: Ernie Isley (The Isley Brothers), Ernie Watts, Tennessee Ernie Ford, "Theme for Ernie" by John Coltrane, "E.R.N.I.E." by Madness, "Ernie (The Fastest Milkman in the West)" by Benny Hill, "Ernie's Tune" by Dexter Gordon, "Ernie" by Fat Freddy's Drop
LINER NOTES: Funk guitarist Ernie Isley appeared as a musician on R. Kelly's 1995 self-titled album.

Garnet

ENGLISH: Red semiprecious gem
ROCK AND ROLL: Lively, entrancing, folksy
RELATED ARTISTS/SONGS: Garnet Clark, Garnet Mimms, Garnett Silk, "Garnet" by D'espairsRay, "Garnet" by Khors
LINER NOTES: Reggae musician Garnett Silk began performing when he was twelve under the name "Little Bimbo."

Gerald

GERMAN: Rule of the spear
ROCK AND ROLL: Dreamy, boisterous, magnetic
RELATED ARTISTS/SONGS: Gerald Casale (Devo), Gerald Levert, Gerald Wilson, "Gerald" by The Lurkers, "Gerald Did What" by Evergreen Terrace
LINER NOTES: R&B singer Gerald Levert's father was Eddie Levert of the legendary soul group The O'Jays.

Gregory

GREEK: Vigilant, careful
ROCK AND ROLL: Mellow, nobly born, a lover and not a fighter
RELATED ARTISTS/SONGS: Gregory Hines, Gregory Isaacs, "Royal Gregory" by Holy Fuck, "St. Gregory" by The Twilight Singers, "Gregory" by The Dead Youth
LINER NOTES: Reggae singer Gregory Isaacs was nicknamed "Cool Ruler" for his smooth style.

Jackie, Jacky

ENGLISH: Variation of Jack, God's grace
ROCK AND ROLL: A school buddy, laid-back, polite
RELATED ARTISTS/SONGS: Jackie Gleason, Jackie McLean, Jackie Wilson, "Jackie" by Sinead O'Connor, "Jackie" by The New Pornographers, "Jackie" by Scott Walker, "Jackie" by Placebo, "The Return of Jackie and Judy" by Tom Waits
LINER NOTES: Soul singer Jackie Wilson's stage name was "Mr. Excitement" for his lively stage performances.

Kip

ENGLISH: Pointed hill
ROCK AND ROLL: Rambunctious, fun-loving
RELATED ARTISTS/SONGS: Kip Tyler, Kip Winger, Kip Anderson, "Kip" by Serge Chaloff, "Kip" by Mick Harris
LINER NOTES: Soul singer Kip Anderson wrote "A Knife and a Fork," a novelty hit warning an overeating girlfriend not to "let a knife and fork dig your grave."

Leon

GREEK: Lion
ROCK AND ROLL: A friend, ambitious, dreams big
RELATED ARTISTS/SONGS: Kings of Leon, Leon Russell, Leon Ware, "Leon" by Kinky, "Leon" by Roger Daltrey, "Leon" by Rush, "Leon" by Elaine Dempsey
LINER NOTES: Soul singer Leon Ware's songwriting partner was Arthur "T-Boy" Ross, brother of Diana Ross; Ware wrote songs for Michael Jackson, The Miracles, and Marvin Gaye.

Levi

HEBREW: Joined to

ROCK AND ROLL: Studly, smooth, the center of attention

RELATED ARTISTS/SONGS: Levi Celerio, Levi Seacer Jr., Levi Stubbs (The Four Tops), "Levi" by Dala, "Levi" by Barbara Harris, "Levi" by Greg Ross

LINER NOTES: The Four Tops' Levi Stubbs is the voice of the man-eating plant Audrey II in the movie of the musical *Little Shop of Horrors*; he had five children: Deborah, Beverley, Raymond, Kelly, and Levi Jr.

Lionel

LATIN: Young lion

ROCK AND ROLL: Nurturing, dreamy, urbane

RELATED ARTISTS/SONGS: Lionel Hampton, Lionel Richie, "Lionel" by DNA, "Lionel" by Allen Karl

LINER NOTES: Lionel Richie was mentioned on *Spongebob Squarepants* by the name "Lionel Fishy."

Luther

GERMAN: Soldier

ROCK AND ROLL: Confident, romantic, affable

RELATED ARTISTS/SONGS: Luther Allison, Luther Dickinson (North Mississippi Allstars), Luther Vandross, "Luther" by Boxcar Willie, "Luther" by Dale Watson

LINER NOTES: Luther Vandross appeared on the second ever episode of *Sesame Street*, in 1969.

Major

ENGLISH OCCUPATION NAME

ROCK AND ROLL: Important, confident, a leader

RELATED ARTISTS/SONGS: Major Harris, Major Lazer, "Major Tom," by David Bowie, "Me and the Major" by Belle & Sebastian, "We Major" by Kanye West, "Major Leagues" by Pavement

LINER NOTES: Soul singer Major Harris performed in a slew of soul groups, including The Charmers, The Teenagers, Nat Turner's Rebellion, and The Delfonics.

Marv

ENGLISH: Form of Marvin, sea hill

ROCK AND ROLL: Tough, rugged, has a good heart

RELATED ARTISTS/SONGS: Messy Marv, Marv Johnson, "Marv" by A Fourth World, "Marv" by Global Stage Orchestra

LINER NOTES: Early Motown singer Marv Johnson was signed to the label when Berry Gordy saw him perform on a carnival float.

Otis

GREEK: Wealthy
ROCK AND ROLL: Warm, gritty, romantic, lively
RELATED ARTISTS/SONGS: Otis Redding, Otis Rush, Otis Spann, "Otis" by The Durutti Column, "Otis" by Medeski Martin & Wood, "Otis" by Christian Vander
LINER NOTES: Otis Redding, the King of Soul, had three children with his wife Zelma: sons Dexter and Otis III, and daughter Karla.

Percy

FRENCH PLACE NAME: Derived from Perci-en-Auge
ROCK AND ROLL: Funky, confident, eccentric
RELATED ARTISTS/SONGS: Percy Faith, Percy Mayfield, Percy Sledge, "Percy's Song" by Bob Dylan, "Remnants of Percy Bass" by Rasputina, "Percy" by Vudu Hippies, "Pot Luck Percy" by The Toy Dolls
LINER NOTES: Soul singer Percy Sledge wrote "When a Man Loves a Woman" after his girlfriend left him for a modeling career; he has twelve children and fourteen grandchildren.

Philip, Phillip

GREEK: Lover of horses
ROCK AND ROLL: Clever, artistic, avant-garde
RELATED ARTISTS/SONGS: Philip Bailey (Earth, Wind & Fire), Philip Glass, Philip Rudd (AC/DC), "Philip" by The President, "Phillip" by The Hollow Men, "Phillip" by The River Detectives
LINER NOTES: Earth, Wind & Fire singer Philip Bailey appeared in both *Matlock* and *Full Metal Jacket* as Private Bobby Thomas.

Prince

ENGLISH ROYALTY
ROCK AND ROLL: A funky pixie, brash, stylish, prone to changing his name
RELATED ARTISTS/SONGS: Prince, Prince Buster, Prince Paul, "Prince" by Madness, "Prince" by Deftones, "Prince" by Vanessa Carlton
LINER NOTES: Prince's childhood nickname was Skipper. He also had the high school nickname "Gazoo," after the alien on *The Flintstones*.

Quincy

LATIN: Fifth
ROCK AND ROLL: Innovative, the brains of the operation
RELATED ARTISTS/SONGS: Quincy Jones, "Quincy" by Wally Pleasant, "Quincy Punk Episode" by Spoon, "Quincy the Pigboy" by Orange Goblin
LINER NOTES: Quincy Jones is the father of *Parks and Recreation* actress Rashida Jones. He has six other children: Jolie, Martina, Quincy III, Kidada, Rachel, and Kenya Julia Miambi Sarah.

Ray

ENGLISH: Variation of Raymond, protector
ROCK AND ROLL: Brainy, friendly, funky
RELATED ARTISTS/SONGS: Ray Charles, Ray Davies (The Kinks), Ray LaMontagne, "Gamma Ray" by Beck, "Worried About Ray" by The Hoosiers, "Sister Ray" by the Velvet Underground
LINER NOTES: Ray Charles was a chess fanatic, playing games in between sets and backstage at concerts.

Rocco

ITALIAN: Rest
ROCK AND ROLL: Protective, funky, energetic
RELATED ARTISTS/SONGS: Rocco DeLuca and the Burden, Rocco Prestia (Tower of Power), "Rocco" by Death in Vegas, "Rocco" by Don Caballero, "Rocco" by Umphrey's McGee
LINER NOTES: When funk bassist Rocco Prestia auditioned for Tower of Power, he could only play four chords; he attributes getting into the band to his "good hair."

Ronald

NORSE: King's counsel
ROCK AND ROLL: Fun-loving, cheerful, well rounded
RELATED ARTISTS/SONGS: Ronald Laws, Ronald Bell (Kool & the Gang), Ronald Frost, "Run Ronald" by Electro Hippies, "Ronald" by The New Jack Hippies, "Ronald Dean" by Box Elders
LINER NOTES: Kool & the Gang's Ronald Bell, who now goes by his Arabic name Khallis Bayyan, has one daughter, named Kahdijah Tavia.

Rufus

LATIN: Red
ROCK AND ROLL: Laid-back, part of a musical family, funky
RELATED ARTISTS/SONGS: Rufus Thomas, Rufus Wainwright, "Rufus" by Archie Shepp, "Rufus" by Ron Carter, "Rufus" by The Skillet Lickers
LINER NOTES: Soul singer Rufus Thomas began as a stand-up comedian in the 1930s with the band The Rabbit Foot Minstrels.

Sam

HEBREW: Variation of Samuel, name of God
ROCK AND ROLL: Has great potential, solid, a good friend but has a temper
RELATED ARTISTS/SONGS: Sam Cooke, Sam Phillips, Sam & Dave, "Sam's Town" by The Killers, "Sam Hall" by Johnny Cash, "Telegram Sam" by T-Rex, "Sam" by The Meat Puppets, "Sam" by Olivia Newton-John

Shuggie

ENGLISH: From Sugar, sweet
ROCK AND ROLL: Cool, friendly, mellow
RELATED ARTISTS/SONGS: Shuggie Otis, "Shuggie" by Los Pasteles Verdes, "Faberge Falls for Shuggie" by of Montreal, "I Know Shuggie Otie" by Raphael Saadiq
LINER NOTES: As a twelve-year-old, Shuggie Otis used to put on a fake mustache and dark glasses to sneak on stage and play with his father, R&B godfather Johnny Otis.

Sly

LATIN: Variation of Sylvester, from the forest
ROCK AND ROLL: A prodigy, sharp, wily
RELATED ARTISTS/SONGS: Sly Stone, Sly Dunbar (Sly & Robbie), "Sly" by Massive Attack, "Sly" by Herbie Hancock, "Sly" by The Cat Empire
LINER NOTES: Sly Stone married his girlfriend Kathy Silva during a concert at Madison Square Garden in an effort to boost ticket sales.

Smokey

AMERICAN INVENTED
ROCK AND ROLL: Casual, refined, and pleasant
RELATED ARTISTS/SONGS: Smokey Robinson, "Smokey" by Funkadelic, "Smokey" by Stan Kenton
LINER NOTES: Smokey Robinson—born William—got the childhood nickname "Smokey Joe" from his uncle. He kept it because it reminded him of a cowboy name.

Stevie

ENGLISH: Form of Steven, crowned
ROCK AND ROLL: Optimistic, precocious, talented
RELATED ARTISTS/SONGS: Stevie Wonder, Stevie Ray Vaughan, "Stevie" by Pat Travers, "Stevie" by Parsley Sound
LINER NOTES: Stevie Wonder, whose legal name is Stevland Hardaway Morris, has seven children; his daughter Aisha was the inspiration for his song "Isn't She Lovely."

Teddy

GREEK: Variation of Theodore, God's gift

ROCK AND ROLL: Loving, comforting, a nurturer

RELATED ARTISTS/SONGS: Teddy Geiger, Teddy Pendergrass, Teddy Thompson, "Teddy" by Connie Francis, "Teddy" by The Residents, "Teddy" by The Bobettes, "Teddy Picker" by The Arctic Monkeys

LINER NOTES: Teddy Pendergrass's 1984 album *Love Language* featured a duet with the then unknown singer Whitney Houston.

Terence, Terrence

LATIN: Form of Terentius, clan name

ROCK AND ROLL: Philosophical, introverted, artistic

RELATED ARTISTS/SONGS: Terence Trent D'Arby, Terence Wilson (UB40), Terence Blanchard, "Terrence" by Stellar, "Terence" by Last Straw

LINER NOTES: R&B singer Terence Trent D'Arby, born Sananda Maitreya, was a Golden Gloves champion boxer before he began his musical career.

Tyrese

ENGLISH: Form of Tyrone, from the land of Owen

ROCK AND ROLL: Outspoken, charming

RELATED SONGS/ARTSTS: Tyrese Gibson, "Tyrese" by Dirty Harry

LINER NOTES: Tyrese Gibson has one child, daughter Shayla Iylana.

Tyrone

IRISH: Land of Owen

ROCK AND ROLL: Groovy, a thrill-seeker, laid-back

RELATED ARTISTS/SONGS: Tyrone Davis, Tyrone Wells, "Tyrone" by Larry Young, "Tyrone" by Larry Coryell, "Tyrone" by Erykah Badu

LINER NOTES: Soul singer Tyrone Davis began his career working as a chauffeur for blues singer Freddie King.

Zapp

DANISH: Lively

ROCK AND ROLL: Wacky, inventive, unique

RELATED ARTISTS/SONGS: Zapp & Roger, "Zapp" by Kool Keith, "Zapp" by Lion of Judah, "Zapp" by 121 Crew

LINER NOTES: The original members of 1970s band Zapp & Roger are all brothers: Roger, Lester, Tony, and Terry "Zapp" Troutman; Roger Troutman was also childhood friends with funk impresario Bootsy Collins.

Match the Musicians to Their Middle Names

You might think that you already know everything about your favorite artists—pants size, pet names, favorite sandwich—but do you know his or her middle name? Some of them are real doozies—Sphere? Hercules?—and other are more traditional middle name territory. Take our quiz to see how well you know rock middle names.

1. Quincy Jones
2. Thelonious Monk
3. John Lennon
4. Frank Zappa
5. Kurt Cobain
6. Kim Gordon
7. Joan Baez
8. Elton John
9. Grace Slick
10. Billy Joel
11. Bruce Springsteen
12. Pete Townshend
13. Roy Orbison
14. Neil Young
15. Leonard Cohen

(a) Sphere
(b) Winston
(c) Althea
(d) Frederick Joseph
(e) Barnett
(f) Norman
(g) Dennis Blandford
(h) Donald
(i) Martin
(j) Percival
(k) Kelton
(l) Hercules
(m) Delightt
(n) Vincent
(o) Chandos

1 (m) 2 (a) 3 (b) 4 (n) 5 (h) 6 (o) 7 (c) 8 (l) 9 (e)
10 (i) 11 (d) 12 (g) 13 (k) 14 (j) 15 (f)

Girls' Names
That Mean "Song"

If you want something a little more literal, there are many mellifluous, lovely music words that could make interesting names.

ARIA, an operatic choice, is Italian for "melody."

BINALI in Hindi means "musical lady."

CAROL should remind you of a popular Christmas activity. No hints.

CHANTAL is French for "singer." Also might make a good stand-alone name for a budding diva.

GITA means "song" in Hindi.

LYRA, the Latin word for "song," makes a nice alternative to Laura or Leila.

MELE is the traditional Hawaiian word for "song," as in the ukulele holiday song "Mele Kalikimaka."

RONI makes a modern twist on Ronnie, and means "joyful song" in Hebrew. As long as it's not short for Macaroni.

SHIRA is a popular Israeli name; in Hebrew it means "my song."

TARANEH in Persian means "melody" or "song."

Funk Baby Names

Funk takes soul music to its most danceable extreme: It's fun, it's sassy, and it also happens to be a great source for unusual names from the era when James Brown was the undisputed king of the radio.

GIRLS	BOYS
Alfa	Ahmet
Betty	Archer
Cissy	Bohannon
Dawn	Bootsy
Elva	Brent
Ervella	Cedell
Fania	Chuck
Inez	Clinton
Lyn	Cordell
Mallia	DeLisle
Marva	Ernesto
Maxyann	Giancarlo
Mazie	James
Parlet	Jheryl
Rhetta	Jubu
Rose	Lucius
Starleana	Marlon
Syreeta	Onnie
Tati	Roger
Umpeylia	Stanton
	Sylver
	Timothius
	Tuck

2000s and Beyond

For those who are looking for up-to-the-minute inspiration, there's plenty coming from the radio right now. From the Justin takeover—Timberlake, then Bieber—to the vigorous reimagining Lady Gaga did of Judas, the new millennium promises to have a lot more rock names in store.

GIRLS

Adele

FRENCH: Variation of Adelaide, sweet
ROCK AND ROLL: Serious, soulful, earthy
RELATED ARTISTS/SONGS: Adele, "Adele" by Bangkok Blue, "Adele" by Jay Gruska
LINER NOTES: Adele was classmates with Leona Lewis and Jessie J at the BRIT School for Performing Arts & Technology in Croydon, England.

Adrienne, Adrianne

FRENCH: Dark one
ROCK AND ROLL: Angelic, often pined after
RELATED ARTISTS/SONGS: Adrienne Bailon (The Cheetah Girls), Adrienne Young, "Adrienne" by Tommy James & the Shondells, "Adrienne" by The Calling
LINER NOTES: Adrienne Bailon got her start when singer Ricky Martin heard her sing with her church choir group.

Amy, Amie

LATIN: Loved one
ROCK AND ROLL: Quirky, inspiring, religious
RELATED ARTISTS/SONGS: Amy Winehouse, Amy Ray (Indigo Girls), Aimee Mann, "Amy" by Ryan Adams, "Amy" by Elton John, "Amy" by Yann Tiersen, "Amie" by Damien Rice
LINER NOTES: A bar in St. Lucia, where Amy Winehouse spent many months, named itself "Rehab" after the singer's hit single.

Ashanti

AFRICAN PLACE NAME
ROCK AND ROLL: Chipper, chic, popular
RELATED ARTISTS/SONGS: Ashanti (Douglas), "Ashanti" by Bob James, "Ashanti" by Leslie Butler, "Ashanti" by The Buccaneers
LINER NOTES: Ashanti's mother named her after the Ashanti Empire of Ghana; her childhood nickname was Bon Bon.

Ashley, Ashleigh, Ashlee

ENGLISH: Meadow, clearing
ROCK AND ROLL: Dynamic, a daydreamer
RELATED ARTISTS/SONGS: Ashlee Simpson, Ashley Roberts (Pussycat Dolls), Ashley Tisdale, "Ashley" by The Dodos, "Ashley" by Yo La Tengo
LINER NOTES: Ashlee Simpson was the youngest person ever admitted to the School of American Ballet, entering at age eleven.

Ashton

ENGLISH: Forest
ROCK AND ROLL: Preppy, capable, confident
RELATED ARTISTS/SONGS: Ashton Shepherd, "Ashton" by The Papers, "Ashton" by Wicker Hollow, "Ashton" by Orion's Room
LINER NOTES: Ashton Shepherd grew up in rural Alabama "picking peas in the daytime and picking guitars at night"; her biggest influence is Patsy Cline.

Avril

FRENCH: April
ROCK AND ROLL: A skater girl, has a tough exterior but kind at heart
RELATED ARTISTS/SONGS: Avril Lavigne, "Avril" by Paris Combo, "Avril" by Lindsey Horner, "Avril" by Jon Smith, "Avril" by Yves Nadeau
LINER NOTES: Avril Lavigne has a pizza with olives named after her in her hometown of Napanee, Ontario; she owns more than one hundred pairs of Converse sneakers.

Catherine, Cathryn, Katherine, Katharine, Kathryn

GREEK: Wholesome
ROCK AND ROLL: Enviable, attractive, high-minded
RELATED ARTISTS/SONGS: Catherine Wheel, Kathryn Calder (The New Pornographers), "Catherine" by PJ Harvey, "Katharine" by The Durutti Column, "Katherine Kiss Me" by Franz Ferdinand, "Catherine" by Swells, "Cath . . ." by Death Cab for Cutie
LINER NOTES: Death Cab for Cutie's song "Cath . . ." was written about the character Catherine Earnshaw from Emily Brontë's novel *Wuthering Heights*.

Eliza

HEBREW: Variation of Elizabeth, God's promise
ROCK AND ROLL: Spunky, tough, loving
RELATED ARTISTS/SONGS: Eliza Carthy, Eliza Doolittle, "Eliza" by Phish, "Eliza" by Jackson Jackson, "Eliza Jane" by The Jon Spencer Blues Explosion, "Eliza" by The Motions
LINER NOTES: Singer-songwriter Eliza Doolittle, born Eliza Caird, comes from a musical family: Her mother is musical theater actress Frances Ruffelle and her father is stage director/writer John Caird.

Eve

HEBREW: Life
ROCK AND ROLL: Adventurous, original
RELATED ARTISTS/SONGS: Eve (Jeffers), Eve 6, "Eve" by The Carpenters, "Eve" by Backstreet Boys, "Eve of the End" by August Burns Red
LINER NOTES: Rapper Eve is sometimes listed in liner notes as "Eve of Destruction" or "pit bull in a skirt."

Fantasia

GREEK: Imagination
ROCK AND ROLL: A free spirit, passionate, revels in drama
RELATED ARTISTS/SONGS: Fantasia Barrino, "Candlelight Fantasia" by Symphony X, "Fantasia" by Argent, "Fantasia" by Dizzy Gillespie
LINER NOTES: Fantasia Barrino's cousins are the 1990s R&B singers K-Ci & JoJo; she has a daughter named Zion Quari.

Fergie

SCOTTISH: Short for Ferguson, son of Fergus
ROCK AND ROLL: Sassy, vivacious, has occasional trouble with wardrobe
RELATED ARTISTS/SONGS: Fergie (Stacy Ann Ferguson), Fergie (Robert Ferguson)
LINER NOTES: Before joining The Black Eyed Peas, Fergie did voice-over work as Sally Brown in two made-for-TV Charlie Brown films.

Fleur

FRENCH: Flower
ROCK AND ROLL: Delicate, pretty with a dark side
RELATED ARTISTS/SONGS: La Fleur Fatale, Flëur, "Ma Fleur" by The Cinematic Orchestra, "Fleur de Saison" be Emilie Simon, "Fleur" by Beautiful Disease, "Fleur" by Crowfoot
LINER NOTES: Singer Rihanna has a tattoo of the phrase "rebelle fleur" on her neck.

Gwen, Gwyn

CELTIC: White
ROCK AND ROLL: A party girl, stylish, a bombshell
RELATED ARTISTS/SONGS: Gwen Guthrie, Gwen McCrae, Gwen Stefani, "Blues for Gwen" by McCoy Tyner, "Gwen" by Clark Terry
LINER NOTES: Gwen Stefani and Gavin Rossdale have two sons, Zuma Nesta and Kingston James; older brother Kingston nicknamed his brother "Baby Zooms."

Haley, Hailey, Hayley

NORSE: Heroine
ROCK AND ROLL: Precious, sunny, and warm
RELATED ARTISTS/SONGS: Bill Haley, Hayley Aitkin, Hayley Williams (Paramore), "Hailey" by The Wooden Birds, "Haley" by Taylor Barton, "Hailey's Song" by Eminem
LINER NOTES: Hayley Williams formed Paramore at her high school in Franklin, Tennessee; the band was originally a funk cover band.

Janelle

AMERICAN: Variation of Jane, God's gracious gift
ROCK AND ROLL: Bright, idiosyncratic, courageous
RELATED ARTISTS/SONGS: Janelle Monáe, "A Letter from Janelle" by Chiodos, "Janelle" by Born Against, "Janelle" by Cold Chisel, "Janelle" by Cochese, "Janelle, Janelle" by The Queers
LINER NOTES: Janelle Monáe never appears publicly wearing anything but a tuxedo, noting in an interview that "I bathe in it, I swim in it, and I could be buried in it."

Katie, Katy, Catie, Caty

GREEK: Variation of Katherine, pure
ROCK AND ROLL: Courageous, cheerful, loyal, and golden-haired
RELATED ARTISTS/SONGS: Catie Curtis, Katy Perry, Katie White (The Ting Tings), "Katie" by Muddy Waters, "Katie" by The Mighty Mighty Bosstones, "Katy" by Count Basie, "Katie Bell Blue" by Townes van Zandt, "Catie" by Daniel Johnston
LINER NOTES: Katy Perry has a cat named Kitty Purry.

Kelly

IRISH: Church
ROCK AND ROLL: Ambitious, beautiful, a stargazer
RELATED ARTISTS/SONGS: Kelly Clarkson, Kelly Rowland (Destiny's Child), "Kelly Watch the Stars" by Air, "Kelly" by Del Shannon, "Kelly" by The Easybeats, "Kelly" by Smudge, "Song for Kelly Huckaby" by Death Cab for Cutie
LINER NOTES: Kelly Rowland's full name is Kelendria Trene Rowland; her group Destiny's Child took their name from a passage in the Bible's Book of Isaiah.

Kesha, Keyshia, Keisha

HEBREW: Variation of Keziah, cassia tree

ROCK AND ROLL: Center of attention, a party animal, loves glitter

RELATED ARTISTS/SONGS: Kesha Sebert (aka Ke$ha), Keyshia Cole, Keisha White, "Kesha" by Youngbucalinos, "Keisha's House" by Ghostface Killah

LINER NOTES: Ke$ha is a huge Prince fan; she once hiked onto Prince's property in order to try to give him her demo tape.

Lacey

ENGLISH: From Lassy

ROCK AND ROLL: A risk-taker, a temptress

RELATED ARTISTS/SONGS: Lacey Brown, Lacey Strum (Flyleaf), "Racy Lacey" by Girls Aloud, "Lacey" by John Chambers, "The Ballad of Lacey" by Jimmy Jacobs, "Cadmium Lacey" by Alex Mauer

LINER NOTES: Flyleaf vocalist Lacey Sturm has one child, a son named Joshua.

Leona

GREEK: Feminine variation of Leon, lioness

ROCK AND ROLL: Warm, sophisticated, gets emotional easily

RELATED ARTISTS/SONGS: Leona Lewis, Leona Naess, "Leona" by Conway Twitty, "Leona" by Stonewall Jackson, "Leona" by Wet Willie

LINER NOTES: Leona Lewis has said that she could sing before she could talk, crooning along to Michael Jackson songs in her car seat when she was tiny.

Madigan

IRISH: Little dog

ROCK AND ROLL: Bubbly, cute, outspoken

RELATED ARTISTS/SONGS: Madigan Shrive (Tattle Tale), "Madigan" by Tennis, "Elvira Madigan" by James Last

LINER NOTES: Riot grrrl Madigan Shive's parents were part of a nomadic hippie commune and changed her name every few years; she changed her name from Running Pony to Madigan when she was a teenager.

Meg

ENGLISH: Variation of Margaret, pearl

ROCK AND ROLL: Mysterious, cute, mischievous

RELATED ARTISTS/SONGS: Meg Christian, Meg White (The White Stripes), Meg Frampton (Meg & Dia), "Meg" by Dogbowl, "Meg" by Satellites Four

LINER NOTES: Former White Stripe Meg White is married to Jackson Smith, the son of Patti Smith and MC5 guitarist Fred "Sonic" Smith.

Miley

AMERICAN INVENTED
ROCK AND ROLL: Young, rambunctious, sugary sweet
RELATED ARTISTS/SONGS: Miley Cyrus, "Miley" by Matt Monsoor
LINER NOTES: Miley Cyrus's real name is Destiny Hope Cyrus. Her father gave her the childhood nickname Miley because she was so "smiley."

Natasha

RUSSIAN: Form of Natalie, born on Christmas Day
ROCK AND ROLL: Caring, witty, introverted
RELATED ARTISTS/SONGS: Natasha Bedingfield, Natasha Bradley, Natasha Hamilton, "Natasha" by Rufus Wainwright, "Natasha" by Pig Destroyer, "Natasha" by Phil Coulter
LINER NOTES: When she was a teenager, Natasha Bedingfield formed a dance group with her siblings, Daniel and Nikola, called The DNA Algorithm.

Nelly, Nellie

AMERICAN: Short for Ellen or Cornelia, practical
ROCK AND ROLL: Lighthearted, loves to party, multifaceted
RELATED ARTISTS/SONGS: Nelly Furtado, Nellie McKay, "Nelly" by Daniel Binelli, "Nelly" by Oliver Knight
LINER NOTES: Singer Nelly Furtado was named after the Soviet gymnast Nellie King.

Nicole

GREEK: Feminine variation of Nicholas, victory
ROCK AND ROLL: Starry-eyed, trusting, innocent
RELATED ARTISTS/SONGS: Nicole Wray, Nicole Scherzinger, "Nicole" by Mary Lou Williams, "Nicole" by Ween, "Nicole" by Half Japanese, "Nicole" by Ash
LINER NOTES: Nicole Wray was the first artist signed to Missy Elliott's nascent Goldmind label; she later joined The Black Keys' hip-hop group Blakroc.

Nora, Norah

LATIN: Honor
ROCK AND ROLL: Precocious, bubbly, a jokester
RELATED ARTISTS/SONGS: Dear Nora, Nora Bayes, Nora Dean, Norah Jones, "Nora" by Blessid Union of Souls, "Nora" by Xavier Cugat, "Nora" by The Long Winters
LINER NOTES: Singer-songwriter Norah Jones is the daughter of Indian sitar icon Ravi Shankar.

Paris

FRENCH PLACE NAME

ROCK AND ROLL: Stylish, rich, a party girl

RELATED ARTISTS/SONGS: Sarina Paris, Paris Hilton, "I'm Throwing My Arms Around Paris" by Morrissey, "Paris" by Groove Armada, "I Love Paris" by Ella Fitzgerald

LINER NOTES: Heiress Paris Hilton claims that Michael Jackson named his daughter, Paris Michael Katherine, after her.

Pink

ENGLISH COLOR NAME

ROCK AND ROLL: Fierce, witty, flashy

RELATED ARTISTS/SONGS: Pink Floyd, Pink, "Pink" by Aerosmith, "Pink Moon" by Nick Drake, "Pink Traingle" by Weezer, "Pink" by Bobby Sanabria

LINER NOTES: Pink got her nickname from the movie *Reservoir Dogs*, after several of her friends claimed that she looked like the character Mr. Pink.

Robin, Robyn

GERMAN: Variation of Robert, famous

ROCK AND ROLL: Summery, bright, cheerful

RELATED ARTISTS/SONGS: Robyn (Carlsson), Robin Lee, The Robins, "Rockin' Robin" by The Jackson Five, "Robyn" by Nancy Moran, "Robin" by Seals & Crofts

LINER NOTES: Pop singer Robyn did the voice-over for the character of Anne-Marie in the Swedish version of *All Dogs Go to Heaven*.

Skylar, Schuyler

DUTCH: Scholar

ROCK AND ROLL: Bright, effervescent, lovely

RELATED ARTISTS/SONGS: Schuyler Fisk, Skylar Grey, Skyler Stonestreet, "Skyler" by Doc Hopper, "Schuyler" by Tony Gillam, "Skyler" by Brad Yoder

LINER NOTES: Schuyler Fisk, whose duet with Joshua Radin, "Paperweight," appeared on the soundtracks for *Dear John* and *The Last Kiss*, is the daughter of actress Sissy Spacek.

Stephanie, Stefani

GREEK: Variation of Stephen, crown

ROCK AND ROLL: Curious, courageous, ambitious, has the nickname "Alaska"

RELATED ARTISTS/SONGS: Stefani Germanotta (aka Lady Gaga), Stephanie Mills, "Stephanie Says" by The Velvet Underground, "Stephanie Knows Who" by Love, "Stephanie" by Milow

LINER NOTES: According to celebrity genealogist Chris Child, Madonna and Lady Gaga are ninth cousins once removed.

Victoria

LATIN: Victory

THE KINKS:
"Land of hope and gloria, land of my Victoria."

JUKEBOX THE GHOST:
"You are certainly my poison of choice."

THE VERVE PIPE:
"Twirling blur of legs, legs and lace."

OLD 97'S:
"Victoria, you dance so fast that no one else can see."

Willow

ENGLISH PLANT NAME
ROCK AND ROLL: Bubbly, young, cute, introspective
RELATED ARTISTS/SONGS: Willow Smith, The Willowz, "Weeping Willow" by Scott Joplin, "Weeping Willow" by The Verve, "Underneath the Weeping Willow" by Grandaddy, "Willow's Song" by The Doves
LINER NOTES: Willow Smith launched her singing career when she was just ten, with the hit single "Whip My Hair."

BOYS

Aaron

HEBREW: Enlightened, revered
ROCK AND ROLL: Sweet, boyish, bouncy
RELATED ARTISTS/SONGS: Aaron Carter, "The Words of Aaron" by ELO
LINER NOTES: Aside from his famous older brother, Nick Carter of the Backstreet Boys, Aaron Carter also has a twin sister, Angel, who works as a model.

Akon

WEST AFRICAN: Born at night
ROCK AND ROLL: Suave, worldly
RELATED ARTISTS/SONGS: Akon, "Akon" by Chalie Boy
LINER NOTES: Rapper Akon is so private that he refuses to divulge his birth date or given name; he once claimed that his full name is "Aliune Damala Bouga Time Puru Nacka Lu Lu Lu Badara," but

researchers found that "Damala Bouga Time" is the title of Akon's song "I Want to Fuck You" in his native West African.

Benji, Benjy

HEBREW: Form of Benjamin, son of my right hand
ROCK AND ROLL: Rowdy, fun-loving, energetic
RELATED ARTISTS/SONGS: Benji Madden (Good Charlotte), Benji Boko, Benji Hughes, "Benji" by George Kahn, "Benji" by Serengeti
LINER NOTES: Good Charlotte's Benji Madden has a tattoo of Benjamin Franklin covering his entire back.

Brad

ENGLISH: Short for Bradley, Bradford, or Braden; broad clearing
ROCK AND ROLL: Talented but modest, the nice one in the band
RELATED ARTISTS/SONGS: Brad Hargreaves (Third Eye Blind), Brad Paisley, Brad Whitford (Aerosmith), "Brad" by The Hanson Brothers
LINER NOTES: Brad Paisley's dog's name is Hollar, after the part of Tennessee Paisley came from.

Brandon

ENGLISH: Gorse-covered hill
ROCK AND ROLL: Beloved son, creative
RELATED ARTISTS/SONGS: Brandon Boyd (Incubus), Brandon Jay (The 88), Brandon Flowers (The Killers), "Brandon" by Caribou, "Brandon" by Mötley Crüe
LINER NOTES: Incubus front man Brandon Boyd has written two books of drawings and poetry, *White Fluffy Clouds* and *From the Murks of the Sultry Abyss*.

Bruno

GERMAN: Brown
ROCK AND ROLL: Smooth-talking, romantic
RELATED ARTISTS/SONGS: Bruno Gos, Bruno Mars, "Bruno" by Curlew, "Bruno" by Flook
LINER NOTES: Actor Bruce Willis recorded an album, *The Return of Bruno*, under the pseudonym Bruno.

Caleb

HEBREW: Servant of God
ROCK AND ROLL: Older brother, has a dark side
RELATED ARTISTS/SONGS: Caleb Engstrom, Caleb Followill (Kings of Leon), Caleb Rowdon, "Caleb" by Sonata Arctica, "Caleb Meyer" by Joan Baez
LINER NOTES: Kings of Leon singer Caleb Followill was once a judge on *Iron Chef America*.

Carter

ENGLISH: Courier, poker player

ROCK AND ROLL: Established, part of a legacy, confident

RELATED ARTISTS/SONGS: Shawn Carter (aka Jay-Z), Carter Beauford (Dave Matthews Band), "Carter" by Fred Eaglesmith, "This Is the Carter" by Lil Wayne, "Get Carter" by The Human League, "Ron Carter" by Bill Frissell, "The Carter Family" by Carly Simon

LINER NOTES: Jay-Z refers to Russell Simmons as "the godfather"; his favorite books are *The Seat of the Soul*, *The Odyssey*, and *The Celestine Prophecy*.

Clem

LATIN: Informal

ROCK AND ROLL: The wild one

RELATED ARTISTS/SONGS: Clem Burke (Blondie), Clem Cattini (The Tornados), Clem Clempson (Humble Pie), Clem Snide, "Clem" by The Autumns

LINER NOTES: Clem Burke played under the name "Elvis Ramone" for a cancer benefit concert with the remaining Ramones in 2004.

Enrique

SPANISH: Variation of Henry, home ruler

ROCK AND ROLL: Romantic, charming, smooth-talking, earnest

RELATED ARTISTS/SONGS: Enrique Guzman, Enrique Iglesias, Enrique Martin Morales (aka Ricky Martin)

LINER NOTES: Enrique Iglesias's album *Quizas* is about his father, singer Julio Iglesias; Enrique originally was billed as Enrique Martinez to avoid the connection with him.

Fred

ENGLISH: Variation of Alfred or Frederick, wise

ROCK AND ROLL: The brains behind the operation, studious, mildly unhinged

RELATED ARTISTS/SONGS: Fred Astaire, Fred Durst (Limp Bizkit), Fred "Sonic" Smith (The MC5), "Fred Bear" by Ted Nugent, "Fred" by Kid Rock, "Fred Jones Part 2" by Ben Folds, "Fred" by Rodney Carrington

LINER NOTES: Fred Durst was a tattoo artist before forming Limp Bizkit.

Howie

ENGLISH: Variation of Howard, watchman

ROCK AND ROLL: Sweet, suave, one to take home to meet the parents

RELATED ARTISTS/SONGS: Howie Beck, Howie Day, Howie Dorough (Backstreet Boys), "Howie" by Kristen Hall, "Howie" by The Tonettes

LINER NOTES: Howie Dorough may by the oldest member of Backstreet Boys, but he's the youngest of his family, and became an uncle at the age of four.

Jaden, Jayden, Jadon

ENGLISH INVENTED
ROCK AND ROLL: An up-and-comer, a prodigy
RELATED ARTISTS/SONGS: Jadon Lavik, Jaden Smith, Jaden Spears, "Jaden's Interlude" by Will Smith, "Waiting for Jaden" by Animal Liberation Orchestra
LINER NOTES: Jaden Smith presented the Oscar for Best Animated Short when he was just ten years old.

Jared

HEBREW: Ruler
ROCK AND ROLL: Brainy, serious, committed
RELATED ARTISTS/SONGS: Jared Anderson (Morbid Angel), Jared Evan, Jared Leto (30 Seconds to Mars), "Jared" by Jeff Green, "Jared" by Umphrey's McGee, "Jared the Gray" by Mousy Brown
LINER NOTES: Actor and 30 Seconds to Mars front man Jared Leto occasionally directs music videos under the pseudonym Bartholomew Cubbins.

Justin

LATIN: Just
ROCK AND ROLL: A total heartthrob, multitalented, starts his career young
RELATED ARTISTS/SONGS: Justin Bieber, Justin Townes Earle, Justin Timberlake, "Justin" by Korn, "Justin" by Against Me!, "For Justin" by Dashboard Confessional
LINER NOTES: Both Justin Bieber and Justin Timberlake are avid sneaker collectors; Bieber owns more than three hundred pairs, while Timberlake designs his own line of kicks under the label William Rast.

Lance

ENGLISH: Weapon
ROCK AND ROLL: Trustworthy, blond, suave
RELATED ARTISTS/SONGS: Lance Bass, Major Lance, "Lance" by The Dancy Warhols, "Lance" by The Rhythm Devils
LINER NOTES: Lance Bass's 'N Sync nickname was Scoop, because he always knew the band's itinerary.

Marshall

FRENCH: He who minds the horses
ROCK AND ROLL: Orderly, disciplined, cheerful
RELATED ARTISTS/SONGS: Marshall Mathers (aka Eminem), The

Marshall Tucker Band, Marshall Thompson (The Chi-Lites), "Marshall" by Pearls Before Swine, "Marshall" by DNA

LINER NOTES: Marshall Mathers, better known as Eminem, has one biological child, Hallie Jade, and two adopted children: his niece Alaina and his ex-wife's child from another relationship, Whitney.

Mika

RUSSIAN: God's child

ROCK AND ROLL: Perky, happy, good with words

RELATED ARTISTS/SONGS: Mika, Mika Tauriainen (ShamRain), "Mika" by David Matthews

LINER NOTES: Singer-songwriter Mika has four siblings; his sister Yasmine designed several of his album covers under the name DaWack.

Phoenix

GREEK: Dark red

ROCK AND ROLL: Resilient, fiery, persistent

RELATED ARTISTS/SONGS: Phoenix, Phoenix Farrell (Linkin Park), "Phoenix" by Daft Punk, "Phoenix" by Coleman Hawkins, "Phoenix" by Aimee Mann, "Phoenix" by The Cult, "Phoenix" by Dan Fogelberg

LINER NOTES: The original name for Linkin Park was Hybrid Theory; they changed their name in honor of Lincoln Park in Santa Monica.

Quentin

LATIN: Fifth

ROCK AND ROLL: A fisherman, a good friend

RELATED ARTISTS/SONGS: Quentin Cook (aka Fatboy Slim), Quentin Jackson, Quentin Smith, "Quentin" by Christian Kleine, "San Quentin" by Johnny Cash, "Quick to Quit the Quentin" by The Toy Dolls, "Keith & Quentins" by The Jayhawks

LINER NOTES: Before becoming widely known as Fatboy Slim, Quentin Cook scored a number one single in England with his band The Housemartins.

Ralph

ENGLISH: Wolf counsel

ROCK AND ROLL: Humble, low-key, silky smooth, compulsively honest

RELATED ARTISTS/SONGS: Ralph Burns, Ralph McTell, Ralph Stanley, "Ralph" by King Johnson, "Ralph" by Ben Wendel, "Ralph Wiggum" by Bloodhound Gang

LINER NOTES: Bloodhound Gang's "Ralph Wiggum" is named for the lovable oddball *Simpsons* character.

Rhett

WELSH: Variation of Rhys, fiery
ROCK AND ROLL: Dashing, smooth, dedicated
RELATED ARTISTS/SONGS: Rhett Miller (Old 97's), Rhett Lee, Rhett Tyler, "Rhett Butler" by Forward All
LINER NOTES: Rhett Miller has two children, son Max and daughter Soleil.

Ruben

HEBREW: Beloved son
ROCK AND ROLL: Smooth, Southern, soulful
RELATED ARTISTS/SONGS: Ruben Stoddard, Reuben Wilson, "Ruben" by Johnny "Guitar" Watson, "Ruben" by Elizabeth Cotten
LINER NOTES: While on the second season of *American Idol*, Ruben Stoddard earned the nickname "the velvet teddy bear."

Saul

HEBREW: Prayed for
ROCK AND ROLL: Politically active, clever, wry
RELATED ARTISTS/SONGS: Saul Williams, "Saul Bellow" by Sufjan Stevens, "The Velocity of Saul at the Time of His Conversion" by Okkervil River, "Saul" by Natalia Lafourcade
LINER NOTES: Progressive hip-hop musician Saul Williams starred in the award-winning 1998 movie *Slam*, based on his own experiences on the slam poetry circuit.

Stan

ENGLISH: Form of Stanley, stony meadow
ROCK AND ROLL: Eloquent, dark, cerebral
RELATED ARTISTS/SONGS: Stan Getz, Stan Rogers, Stan Kenton, "Stan" by Eminem, "The Ascent of Stan" by Ben Folks, "Happiness Stan" by Small Faces, "Stan" by The Lounge Brigade
LINER NOTES: As a result of Eminem's song "Stan," an overly enthusiastic rap song is sometimes referred to as a "stan."

Sullivan, Sully

IRISH: Dark eyes
ROCK AND ROLL: Boisterous, amiable, witty
RELATED ARTISTS/SONGS: Sullivan, Sully Erna (Godsmack), "Sullivan Street" by Counting Crows, "Sullivan's Social Slub" by The Fiery Furnaces, "Sullivan" by Caroline's Spine, "Sullivan" by Seething Grey
LINER NOTES: Godsmack's Sully Erna is an avid poker player, winning second place in VH1's Celebrity Classic. (He lost out to Anthrax's Scott Ian).

Timothy

GREEK: Honoring God

ROCK AND ROLL: Energetic, creative, likes to stay outside the spotlight

RELATED ARTISTS/SONGS: Timothy B. Schmit (The Eagles), Timothy Mosley (aka Timbaland), Timothy Wilson, "Timothy" by Jet, "Timothy Where You Been" by Timbaland, "Timothy Leary" by Guster, "Timothy" by Gucci Mane

LINER NOTES: Producer and rapper Timbaland has three children, sons Demetrius and Frankie and daughter Reign.

Trace

FRENCH: From Thracia

ROCK AND ROLL: Rough and tumble, a risk-taker

RELATED ARTISTS/SONGS: Trace Adkins, "Trace" by Brian Eno, "Trace" by John Tilbury, "Trace" by Mango, "Trace" by The Tonights

LINER NOTES: Trace Adkins has a permanently crooked pinky finger, the result of a work accident in which it was cut off. Trace asked the doctors to reattach it in a way "that makes it useful."

Tyler

ENGLISH: Innkeeper

ROCK AND ROLL: Happy, energetic, high-spirited

RELATED ARTISTS/SONGS: Tyler the Creator, Tyler Stewart (Barenaked Ladies), Tyler Hilton, "Tyler" by The Toadies, "Tyler" by UB40, "Tyler" by The Hollisters

LINER NOTES: When he was little, Odd Future's Tyler the Creator used to take his parents' albums out of their sleeves and use the sleeves to create covers and tracklists for his imaginary musical projects.

Usher

ENGLISH: Doorkeeper

ROCK AND ROLL: Suave, spiritual, debonair

RELATED ARTISTS/SONGS: Usher (Raymond), "Usher" by Eric Rhame, "Usher" by Lunarin

LINER NOTES: Singer Usher is the third Usher in his family; his two sons are named Usher V and Naviyd.

Watkin

ENGLISH: Form of Walter, warrior

ROCK AND ROLL: Adaptable, literate, the class clown

RELATED ARTISTS/SONGS: Watkin Jones (Die Antwoord's Ninja), Mary Watkins, Julius Watkins, "Watkins" by Delilah, "Watkin's Ale" by Hortus Musicus

LINER NOTES: Watkin Jones has a child with Die Antwoord bandmate Yolandi Visser named Sixteen Jones.

Wyclef, Wycliffe

ENGLISH: Dweller at the white cliffs
ROCK AND ROLL: Confident, energetic, politically active
RELATED ARTISTS/SONGS: Wyclef Jean, "Wycliffe" by Nigel Hess, "Wyclef Jean" by Tony Touch
LINER NOTES: Wyclef Jean is a visiting fellow in the Department of Africana Studies at Brown University; he has one daughter, Angelina Claudinelle.

Zoli, Zoll

HUNGARIAN: Version of Solomon, peace
ROCK AND ROLL: Playful, lighthearted, approachable
RELATED ARTISTS/SONGS: Zoli Adak, Zoli Teglas (Pennywise), "Zoll" by Sataan, "Zoll" by Kaly Live Dub, "Zoli" by Kamajota
LINER NOTES: Pennywise founder Zoli Teglas is a dedicated animal conservationist, heading the Pacific Wildlife Project to rescue pelicans.

Just Names:
Classics

Solid, simple, and traditional: If that's more your speed, then check out the Bible-inspired names that rock stars past and present have worn with style:

GIRLS

Amadeus (*Lover of god*/Child of a classical music fan, ambitious)
Beth (*God's promise*/Bodacious and brainy, keeps to herself)
Esther (*Star*/Innocent, fearless, a brave soldier, self-conscious about her looks)
Gabrielle (*God's messenger*/Darling, dark-haired, fond of shiny things)
Hannah, Hanna (*God's grace*/Young, long-haired, regal, high class)
Lilith (*Ghost*/Willful, a temptress, independent-minded woman)
Ophelia (*Help*/Regal, tempestuous, a sweetheart)

BOYS

Abel (*Vital*/Responsible, resourceful, a trustworthy confidant)
Adam (*Original man*/Inquisitive to a fault, a good caretaker)
Ben (*Son of my right hand*/The good guy and loyal friend; not a ladies' man)
Chris, Kriss (*Bearer of Christ*/Charismatic, scruffy, smart)
David (*Beloved*/Uncomplicated, has serious star power)
Elijah, Eli (*The Lord is my God*/Patient, trustworthy, a good friend)
Ezra (*God helps*/Jaunty, insightful, cerebral, has a way with words)
Gabriel (*God's messenger*/Swift and agile, has high moral standards)
Isaac (*Laughing*/Peaceful, courageous, lucky)
Jack (*"God's grace"*/Happy, ambitious, a rambler and a great cardplayer)
Jacob (*Heel-grabber*/Wise, lives life to the fullest)
James (*He who holds the heel*/Blessed, a young cowboy, has a heart of gold)
Jeb, Jebediah (*Dear friend*/Hardworking, amiable, a cowboy)
Jeremiah (*God exalts*/Adventurous, seafaring, a good friend, his spirit animal is a bullfrog)
Jonah (*Dove*/Fiercely ambitious and music-obsessed, avoid whales)
Joseph (*The Lord increases*/Colorful, adventurous, patient)
Joshua, Josh (*Salvation*/Adorable, articulate, a diehard romantic)
Matthew, Matt (God's gift/Mother's pride and joy, hardy, faithful)
Moses (*Savior*/Magnanimous, gentle, clever)
Noah (*Wandering*/Adventurous, principled, eccentric)
Samson (*Man of the sun*/Has great hair, strong, unlucky in love)
Santo (*Saint*/Loves the beach, sophisticated, bright)

WORLD TOUR: Italy

O n the European leg of every tour, Italy is a must. Not only are there throngs of adoring rock fans—think about The Beatles and their attendant mob in the 1960s—but Italian's fashion sense, with its bold patterns and skintight jeans, influenced many a band's look. For a name with a hint of worldly sophistication, try one of these:

GIRLS

Ariana (*Most holy*/Classy, has a head for business)
Bianca (*White*/Crush-worthy, but demanding)
Caralee (*Beloved*/Sweet, smart)
Concetta (*Pure*/Joyful, magnetic, loves to dance)
Gemma (*Jewel*/Bright, lively)
Lucia (*Light*/Child of the dawn, golden-haired, beautiful)
Seraphina, Serafina (*Ardent*/Elegant, exotic, stylish)

BOYS

Alessandro (*Great*/Dark, accomplished)
Guccio (*Endearment*/Loves luxury, wealthy, flashy)
Marco (*Warlike*/Debonair, sly, helpful)
Salvatore (*Savior*/Creative, a hard worker, multilingual)
Santo (*Saint*/Loves the beach, dapper)
Trey (*Three*/Inventive, laid-back, magnetic)

Sonic Youth: Indie Rock

Indie rock has its roots in the do-it-yourself creed of punk, crossed with a healthy dose of 1980s and 1990s alternative rock. Since its humble origins in basements and college radio stations, indie rock has since spread to encompass a whole world of genres, from emo twang to garage rock to dreamy indie pop. The names are equally diverse, from new inventions like Avey and old names made cool again, like Tilly and Abel. Plus, they'll probably look great on a home-stenciled T-shirt.

GIRLS

Adeline

FRENCH: Variation of Adele, noble
ROCK AND ROLL: A ray of sunshine, bubbly, fun
RELATED ARTISTS/SONGS: "Sweet Adeline" by Elliott Smith, "Adeline, Out of Tune" by The New Amsterdams, "Ruby Adeline" by Minnie Driver, "Adeline" by Dr. Dog
LINER NOTES: Elliott Smith's adaptation of the folk classic "Sweet Adeline" was inspired by his grandmother, who used to sing with a glee club called The Sweet Adelines.

Annabelle

ENGLISH: Combination of Anna and Belle, graceful beauty
ROCK AND ROLL: Lovely, hardworking, charming
RELATED ARTISTS/SONGS: Anabel Lamb, "Annabelle" by Black Rebel Motorcycle Club, "Annabelle" by Gillian Welch, "Miss Annabelle Lee" by Django Reinhardy, "For Annabelle" by Band of Horses, "Annabelle" by Fraternity
LINER NOTES: Band of Horses vocalist Ben Brinwell wrote the song "For Annabelle" for his daughter while his wife was pregnant with her; he has another daughter, Ivy.

Avery

ENGLISH: Ruler of elves
ROCK AND ROLL: Brave, modest, a bookworm

RELATED ARTISTS/SONGS: Avery Storm, "Dear Avery" by The Decemberists, "Avery Island" by Neutral Milk Hotel, "Avery" by Spy Island, "Avery" by Mari Anderson

LINER NOTES: The Decemberists' "Avery Island" is a ballad Colin Meloy penned in honor of the parents of soldiers fighting in Iraq.

Belle, Bella

FRENCH: Beautiful

ROCK AND ROLL: Tempting, bright, Nowadays mostly associated with *Twilight*.

RELATED ARTISTS/SONGS: Belle & Sebastian, "Belle" by Jack Johnson, "Belle" by Al Green, "Belle of the Boulevard" by Dashboard Confessional, "Belle" by Johnny Hallyday, "Bella" by Santana

LINER NOTES: Belle & Sebastian are named after a French children's book of the same name, about a six-year-old and his dog.

Beulah

HEBREW: Married

ROCK AND ROLL: Sensitive, smart, fiesty

RELATED ARTISTS/SONGS: Beulah, Beulah Robertson (The Cookies), "Beulah" by Pat Boone, "Beulah" by Devo, "Beulah" by The Harper Brothers, "Beulah" by Jimmy McCracklin

LINER NOTES: Indie rock band Beulah began as a project to record one song every six weeks for sixteen months.

Britta

SCANDINAVIAN: Strength

ROCK AND ROLL: Sprightly, stylish

RELATED ARTISTS/SONGS: Britta Phillips (Dean & Britta), Britta Persson, "Britta" by Ollie Adolphson, "Britta" by Evert Taube, "Britta" by Spike Logan

LINER NOTES: Britta Phillips was the voice of the protagonist of 1980s cartoon series *Jem*; her father, Peter, was Paul Simon's music teacher.

Bryn, Brynn

WELSH: Hopeful

ROCK AND ROLL: Gentle, nature-lover, beloved

RELATED ARTISTS/SONGS: Brynn Andre, Bryn Christopher, Bryn Loosley, "Bryn" by Vampire Weekend, "Brynn Star" by Cinder Cone

LINER NOTES: Before forming Vampire Weekend and writing the song "Bryn," Ezra Koenig was in a joke rap duo called L'Homme Run.

Cara, Kara

ITALIAN: Beloved

ROCK AND ROLL: Alluring, youthful

RELATED ARTISTS/SONGS: Cara Dillon, Cara Luft (The Wailin' Jennys), Kara DioGuardi, "Cara" by Lucio Dalla, "Cara Mia" by Jay and the Americans, "Kara Jane" by The Vines, "Kara" by New World

LINER NOTES: The Vines' "Kara Jane" is about front man Craig Nicholls's girlfriend and The Follow's bassist, Kara Jayne "K.J." Dickson.

Carrie

FRENCH: Short for Caroline, little and strong

ROCK AND ROLL: Badass, falls for the wrong guy

RELATED ARTISTS/SONGS: Carrie Brownstein (Sleater-Kinney, Wild Flag), Carrie Underwood, "Carrie" by Europe, "Carrie" by Cliff Richards, "Carrie Anne" by The Hollies

LINER NOTES: Carrie Brownstein named Sleater-Kinney after a freeway off-ramp in Olympia, Washington.

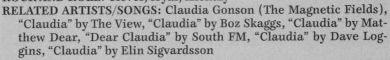

Claudia

LATIN: Feminine form of Claude, slow-moving

ROCK AND ROLL: Clever, loyal, friendly

RELATED ARTISTS/SONGS: Claudia Gonson (The Magnetic Fields), "Claudia" by The View, "Claudia" by Boz Skaggs, "Claudia" by Matthew Dear, "Dear Claudia" by South FM, "Claudia" by Dave Loggins, "Claudia" by Elin Sigvardsson

> *"Claudia, my friend . . .*
> *the guardian of all things."*
> **—ELIN SIGVARDSSON**

Devotchka

RUSSIAN: Girl

ROCK AND ROLL: Delicate, dramatic, has eclectic taste

RELATED ARTISTS/SONGS: DeVotchKa, Devotchkas, "Devotchka" by Plastic Assault, "Devotchka" by Cinder Cone

LINER NOTES: Long Island–based band Devotchkas got their name from *A Clockwork Orange*, which uses "devotchka" as a slang word for an attractive girl.

Emma

GERMAN: Whole

ROCK AND ROLL: Childhood sweetheart, angelic and beautiful, has a dark side

RELATED ARTISTS/SONGS: Emma Bunton (Spice Girls), Emma Paught (The Bobettes), "Emma" by Hot Chocolate, "For Emma" by Bon Iver, "Emma" by Alkaline Trio, "Emma Get Wild" by Sebadoh, "Emma, Get Me a Lemon" by The Walkmen

LINER NOTES: Bon Iver's song "For Emma" was written for an ex-girlfriend; he wrote the song while secluded in a log cabin for several months.

Frances

LATIN: From France
ROCK AND ROLL: Beloved friend, filled with righteous anger
RELATED ARTISTS/SONGS: Frances Faye, Frances McKee (The Vaselines), "Frances" by Jelly Roll Morton, "Frances" by The Impossibles, "Frances Farmer Will Have Her Revenge on Seattle" by Nirvana, "Frances the Mute" by The Mars Volta, "Frances" by Motorpsycho
LINER NOTES: Courtney Love and Kurt Cobain's daughter Frances Bean was named after Frances McKee, guitarist for the Scottish duo of The Vaselines. Her middle name "Bean" came from Cobain, who thought she looked like a kidney bean in her ultrasound.

Frannie, Franny

LATIN: Variation of Frances, from France
ROCK AND ROLL: Self-motivated, religious, independent
RELATED ARTISTS/SONGS: "Franny/You're Human" by Akron/Family, "Frannie's Blues" by Patrick Sweany Band, "Frannie" by The Exceptions, "Dancy Franny Dancy" by Floyd Dakil
LINER NOTES: Experimental folk artists Akron/Family self-released an album called *Franny & the Portal to the Fractal Universe of Positive Vibrations* in 2003.

Gracie

ENGLISH: Form of Grace, virtue name
ROCK AND ROLL: Youthful, gifted, elegant
RELATED ARTISTS/SONGS: Gracie Fields, "Gracie" by Ben Folds, "Little Gracie" by Buckethead, "Gracie" by Jimmy Smith, "Gracie" by Ryan Adams & the Cardinals
LINER NOTES: Ben Folds wrote the song "Gracie" for his daughter; he wrote "Still Fighting It" for her twin brother, Louie.

Helga

NORSE: Holy
ROCK AND ROLL: Outgoing, bubbly, throws a great party
RELATED ARTISTS/SONGS: Helga Hahnemann, "Madame Helga" by Stereophonics, "Helga" by The Kinks, "Helga" by The Subways
LINER NOTES: The Stereophonics song "Madame Helga" was inspired by Helga's Folly, where the band stayed in Sri Lanka.

Holly

ENGLISH PLANT NAME
ROCK AND ROLL: A beautiful vision, comforting, celestial

RELATED ARTISTS/SONGS: Holly Cole, Holly Golightly, Holly Sherwood, "Holly" by Smokey Robinson, "Holly" by The Lettermen, "Holly" by Andy Williams, "Holly Holy" by Neil Diamond, "Goodbye Holly" by The Left Banke

LINER NOTES: Holly Golightly was born Holly Golightly Smith, named after the protagonist in *Breakfast at Tiffany's*.

Hope

ENGLISH: Virtuous

ROCK AND ROLL: Divine, forgiving, sweet

RELATED ARTISTS/SONGS: Conspiracy of Hope, Hope Sandoval (Mazzy Star), "Hope" by R.E.M., "Hope" by Jack Johnson, "Hope" by Rush, "Hope" by Björk, "Hope" by Sublime

LINER NOTES: Mazzy Star's Hope Sandoval prefers to perform in near darkness, due to her difficulties with stage fright.

Imogen

ENGLISH: Image of

ROCK AND ROLL: Ethereal, spiritual, a dreamer

RELATED ARTISTS/SONGS: Imogen Bailer, Imogen Heap (Frou Frou), "Imogen" by Nick Barker, "Imogen Slaughter" by Porcupine Tree

LINER NOTES: Singer-songwriter Imogen Heap taught herself how to play guitar and drums mostly because she didn't like her boarding school music teacher.

Isabel, Isabelle, Isobel

GREEK: Variation of Elizabeth, God's promise

ROCK AND ROLL: Saucy, bright, hopeful, loves the nighttime

RELATED ARTISTS/SONGS: Isabelle Boulay, Isobel Campbell (Belle & Sebastian), "Isobel" by Björk, "Isabel" by John Denver, "Isabelle" by Jacques Brel, "Isabel" by Ray LaMontagne, "Dear Isabelle" by Lee DeWyze

"She's a mistress of the moonlight."
—JOHN DENVER

Juliana

LATIN: Youthful

ROCK AND ROLL: Poetic, smart, spunky

RELATED ARTISTS/SONGS: Juliana Hatfield (Blake Babies), The Juliana Theory, "Juliana" by Michael Nesmith, "Juliana" by Dark Latin Groove, "Juliana" by Pete Rodriguez

LINER NOTES: Juliana Hatfield wrote "President Garfield" about Henry Rollins; she was voted "Most Individual" in her high school yearbook.

Justine

LATIN: Just

LINDA RONDSTADT:
"The face of Aphrodite is a blank when it looks at you."

OCEAN COLOUR SCENE:
"You give them all of your affection."

BOB WELCH:
"She's made me dangerous."

THE CUSTOMS:
"Justine, climb down the balcony."

Karen

GREEK: Pure
ROCK AND ROLL: An outspoken, literary lady and a fashion pioneer
RELATED ARTISTS/SONGS: Karen O (The Yeah Yeah Yeahs), Karen Carpenter (The Carpenters), "Karen" by The Go-Betweens, "Karen" by The National, "Tunic (Song for Karen)" by Sonic Youth, "Karen Revisited" by Sonic Youth, "Karen" by The Surfaris

"Karen . . . this very special girl, and she works in a library."
—THE GO-BETWEENS

Kim

ENGLISH: Form of Kimberley, place name
ROCK AND ROLL: Fun-loving art school goddess
RELATED ARTISTS/SONGS: Kim Deal (The Pixies), Kim Gordon (Sonic Youth), Kim Schifino (Matt & Kim), "Kim" by Charlie Parker, "Kim" by Eminem, "Kim & Jessie" by M83, "Kim's Watermelon Gun" by The Flaming Lips, "Cool as Kim Deal" by The Dandy Warhols
LINER NOTES: When Kim Deal first joined The Pixies, she played under the stage name Mrs. John Murphy.

Lilah, Lila

ARABIC: Night
ROCK AND ROLL: Peaceful, loved, innocent
RELATED ARTISTS/SONGS: Lila McCann, "Lila" by Bright Eyes, "Lila" by Stillwater, "Lila" by Gary Peacock, "Lilah" by Don Henley, "Lila, The Divine Game" by Madina Lake
LINER NOTES: In Madina Lake's song, "Lila" refers to the Hindu concept, meaning the cosmic aspect of playfulness.

Liz

ENGLISH: Form of Elizabeth, God's promise
ROCK AND ROLL: Feminist sweetheart, wry, whip smart
RELATED ARTISTS/SONGS: Liz Carroll, Liz Phair, Liz Story, "Liz" by Rick Nelson, "She (For Liz)" by Parachute
LINER NOTES: Liz Phair has one son, Nicholas; she wrote "Little Digger" about her son meeting her new boyfriend.

Luna

LATIN: Moon
ROCK AND ROLL: Kindhearted, dreamy, poetic
RELATED ARTISTS/SONGS: Luna, "Luna" by The Smashing Pumpkins, "Bella Luna" by Jason Mraz, "Luna" by Chico Freeman, "Luna" by Fanfarlo
LINER NOTES: Dean Wareham formed Luna after the breakup of Galaxie 500; to avoid confusion with the new age act Luna, he originally had the band go by $Luna^2$.

Mae, May

ENGLISH: Fertile
ROCK AND ROLL: Breezy, bright, chipper
RELATED ARTISTS/SONGS: Mae, "May" by Ricky Peterson, "May" by Big Heavy Stuff, "May" by Rossy, "Maggie Mae" by The Beatles, "Maggie May" by Rod Stewart
LINER NOTES: Indie rock band Mae's name stands for "multi-sensory aesthetic experience," a phrase that drummer Jacob Marshall took from a college course.

Marnie

HEBREW: Form of Marnina, cause of joy
ROCK AND ROLL: Charming, loves wild animals, lovely
RELATED ARTISTS/SONGS: Marnie Stern, "Marnie" by Minotaur Shock, "Marnie" by Nat King Cole, "Marnie" by The Jazz Butcher
LINER NOTES: Guitarist Marnie Stern earned the nickname "the lady who shreds" for her fast-paced, Van Halen–esque guitar playing.

Megan, Meghan

WELSH: Form of Margaret, pearl

ROCK AND ROLL: Cheerful, loyal, creative

RELATED ARTISTS/SONGS: Megan McCauley, Megan Rochell, "Megan" by The Smoking Popes, "Megan Is My Friend to the Max" by Reggie and the Full Effect, "Megan" by Jamaram, "Meghan Again" by Tokyo Rose

LINER NOTES: James Dewees of Reggie and the Full Effect wrote the song "Megan Is My Friend to the Max" about his ex-wife Megan.

Mimi

ENGLISH: Form or Miriam, wished-for child

ROCK AND ROLL: Glamorous, a girly girl, lovable

RELATED ARTISTS/SONGS: Mimi Fox, Mimi Maura, Mimi Parker (Low), Mimi Perrin, "Mimi Merlot" by of Montreal, "Mimi" by Al Green, "Mimi's Song" by Donna Summer, "For Mimi" by The Durutti Column, "Mimi" by Dean Martin

 "Oh, Mimi, you got me sad and dreamy."
—DEAN MARTIN

Mirah

LATIN: Admirable

ROCK AND ROLL: Creative, spiritual, poetic

RELATED ARTISTS/SONGS: Mirah (born Mirah Yom Tov Zeitlyn), "Mirah" by Dingo

LINER NOTES: Indie singer Mirah's middle name, Yom Tov, means "good day" in Hebrew.

Neve, Neva

HEBREW: Oasis

ROCK AND ROLL: Elegant, pure, sophisticated

RELATED ARTISTS/SONGS: Neve, Neva Dinova, Neva Pilgrim, "Neve" by Mina, "Neva" by Picastro, "Neve" by Ennio Morricone

LINER NOTES: Indie band Neva Dinova was named after lead singer Jake Bellows's grandmother.

Polly

ENGLISH: Form of Mary, lady

ROCK AND ROLL: Lovely, has good instincts, impressionable

RELATED ARTISTS/SONGS: Polly Jean (P.J.) Harvey, Poly Styrene (X-Ray Spex), "Polly" by Nirvana, "Polly" by The Long Blondes, "Pretty Polly" by The Byrds, "Polly Bee" by Deerhoof, "Polly" by Animal Collective

LINER NOTES: According to producer Steve Albini, while she was recording *Rid of Me*, PJ Harvey ate nothing but potatoes.

Regina

LATIN: Queen

ROCK AND ROLL: Brassy, loves lobster, sunny

RELATED ARTISTS/SONGS: Regina Belle, Regina Carter, Regina Spektor, "Regina" by The Sugarcubes, "Regina" by Possum Dixon, "Regina" by Lester Flatt

LINER NOTES: Singer-songwriter Regina Spektor was born in Russia and immigrated to the United States with her family when she was nine. The first English words she learned were "garbage" and "sneaker."

Saskia

DANISH: Valley of light

ROCK AND ROLL: Starry-eyed, everyone's in love with her

RELATED ARTISTS/SONGS: Saskia Laroo, "Saskia Hamilton" by Ben Folds, "Saskia's Life" by Hey, "Ganru Isalnd/Saskia's Gone" by Buckethead, "Saskia" by Ash

LINER NOTES: The Ben Folds song "Saskia Hamilton" is for the poet of the same name; Ben Folds wrote it for her because "she has a fantastic name for her line of work."

Sloan, Sloane

IRISH: Rider

ROCK AND ROLL: Forward-looking, trustworthy

RELATED ARTISTS/SONGS: Sloan, "Sloan Shore" by Kaki King, "Sloan" by C. W. McCall, "Sloan" by Chris Lake

LINER NOTES: Canadian group Sloan got their name from a friend, Jason Larsen, whose boss called him "Slow One," but whose French accent made the name sound like "Sloan."

Sophie

GREEK: Wisdom

ROCK AND ROLL: Picky, a glamorous nightclub queen

RELATED ARTISTS/SONGS: Sophie Ellis-Bextor, Sophie Monk, Sophie Tucker, "Sophie" by Jeff Beck, "Sophie" by Philip Glass, "Sophie" by Charles Aznavour, "Sophie" by Willy Mason, "Sophie" by Eleanor McEvoy, "Song for Sophie" by Aura

 "She was always like a feather in the air."
—AURA

Stacy, Stacey

GREEK: Variation of Anastasia, of resurrection

ROCK AND ROLL: Warm-hearted, scrappy, the dark horse

RELATED ARTISTS/SONGS: Stacy Ferguson (The Black Eyed Peas), Stacy DuPree, "So Kind, Stacy" by The Spinton Band, "Stacy's Mom" by Fountains of Wayne, "Stacy's Song" by Dead Meadow, "Stacy" by Garnett Silk, "Stacey" by Chico Hamilton

LINER NOTES: The Fountains of Wayne song "Stacy's Mom" was a tribute to The Cars. In the music video for the song, a license plate reads "I <3 RIC" in honor of Ric Ocasek.

Tilly, Tillie

ENGLISH: Form of Matilda, warrior

ROCK AND ROLL: A dancing fool, a heartbreaker, charming

RELATED ARTISTS/SONGS: Tilly and the Wall, "Tilly" by The Jay Boys, "Tilly" by Allister Ivy, "Whoa, Tillie, Take Your Time" by Bessie Smith, "Ballad for Tillie" by Chick Corea, "Tornado Tillie" by Dick Curless

LINER NOTES: Indie rock band Tilly and the Wall's trademark is having a tap dancer keep time instead of a drummer.

Velouria

LATIN: Variation of Valens, strong

ROCK AND ROLL: Shining, ever youthful, adored

RELATED ARTISTS/SONGS: Velouria, "Velouria" by The Pixies, "Velouria" by The Bad Plus

LINER NOTES: The entire video for "Velouria" is one shot of the band running toward the camera, slowed down to last the length of the song.

Vivian

LATIN: Alive

ROCK AND ROLL: Heroic, stealthy, mysterious

RELATED ARTISTS/SONGS: Vivian Girls, Vivian Campbell, Vivian Green, "Vivian" by Eddie Quinteros, "Vivian" by Edison Woods, "Vivian" by Delta Spirit

LINER NOTES: Brooklyn lo-fi group Vivian Girls got their name from the work of outsider artist Henry Darger; in his book, "the Vivian Girls" are warrior princesses

Yoshimi

JAPANESE: To rejoice in beauty

ROCK AND ROLL: A sensitive warrior, bright

RELATED ARTISTS/SONGS: Yoshimi P-We (Boredoms), "Yoshimi Battle the Pink Robots, Pt. 1" by The Flaming Lips, "Yoshimi" by Vyvienne Long

LINER NOTES: The character Yoshimi in the Flaming Lips' album *Yoshimi Battles the Pink Robots* is based on Boredoms' Yoshimi P-We; P-We appears on the album as a drummer and backup singer.

BOYS

Abe, Abraham

HEBREW: Father of multitudes
ROCK AND ROLL: Merciful, noble, and patriotic
RELATED SONGS: "Abe" by Josh Hodges, "Bosom of Abraham" by Elvis Presley, "Abe" by Moving People
LINER NOTES: Two rock bands—Rainer Maria and Best Friends Forever—wrote songs that describe Abraham Lincoln's pants. ("My Head in Front of Your Head" and "The Contents of Lincoln's Pockets," respectively.)

Bishop

ENGLISH OCCUPATIONAL NAME
ROCK AND ROLL: Magnanimous, faithful
RELATED ARTISTS/SONGS: Bishop Allen, "Bishop's Robes" by Radiohead, "Amo Bishop Roden" by Boards of Canada, "Bishop" by Cedsing, "Bishop" by Uncut
LINER NOTES: The group Bishop Allen took their name from Bishop Allen Drive, a road in Cambridge, Massachusetts, where the band lived while attending Harvard.

Britt

ENGLISH: From Britain
ROCK AND ROLL: Inventive, passionate, easygoing
RELATED ARTISTS/SONGS: Britt Daniel (Spoon), King Britt, Britt Nicole
LINER NOTES: Spoon's Britt Daniel recorded solo material under the pseudonym Drake Tungsten; his first band was called The Zygotes.

Colin

IRISH: Young, victorious
ROCK AND ROLL: Spritely, talented but modest
RELATED ARTISTS/SONGS: Colin Burgess (AC/DC), Colin Greenwood (Radiohead), Colin Meloy (The Decemberists), "Colin" by Howard Shore, "Colin" by Allen Farnham, "Colin" by Malicorne
LINER NOTES: Colin Meloy's sister, Maile Meloy, is a celebrated fiction writer whose work has frequently appeared in the *New Yorker* and the *Paris Review*.

Conor, Connor

IRISH: Hound-lover
ROCK AND ROLL: A poet, a do-gooder
RELATED ARTISTS/SONGS: Conor Deasy (The Thrills), Conor Maynard, Conor Oberst (Bright Eyes), "Conor" by The Feeling, "Conor" by The Talons, "Connor" by Zee Zakima
LINER NOTES: Saddle Creek Records, the label founded by Conor

Oberst, originated in 1993 as a tape-only label called Lumberjack Records, funded by Oberst's brother Justin.

Damon

ENGLISH: Variation of Damian, subdued

ROCK AND ROLL: Mellow, introspective, hyper-literate

RELATED ARTISTS/SONGS: Damon Albarn (Blur), Damon Krukowski (Galaxie 500), "Damon" by Peter Kosh, "Damon" by Ganjaman

LINER NOTES: Damon Albarn, the front man of the animated group *Gorillaz*, has one daughter, Missy Violet.

Douglas

SCOTTISH: Black stream

ROCK AND ROLL: Intrepid, complicated, interesting

RELATED ARTISTS/SONGS: Douglas Colvin (aka Dee Dee Ramone), Douglas Hart (The Jesus and Mary Chain), Douglas Robb (Hoobastank), "Douglas" by The Rumble Strips, "A Song for Douglas After I'm Dead" by Current 93, "The Black Douglas" by The Corries

LINER NOTES: After he left The Jesus and Mary Chain, Douglas Hart directed videos for several bands, including Primal Scream and Babyshambles.

Dustin

NORSE: Warrior

ROCK AND ROLL: An optimist, a fun guy

RELATED ARTISTS/SONGS: Dustin Cavanos, Dustin Payseur (Beach Fossils), Dustin Kensrue (Thrice), "Dirty Dustin Hoffman Needs a Bath" by of Montreal, "All About Dustin" by Rebecca Runge

LINER NOTES: Kevin Barnes, who wrote a series of odes to Dustin Hoffman, named his band of Montreal after a failed romance with a woman "of Montreal."

Elliott, Elliot, Eliot

ENGLISH: Beloved of God

ROCK AND ROLL: Brilliant, brooding, a cult favorite

RELATED ARTISTS/SONGS: Elliot Brown, Elliot Easton (The Cars), Elliott Smith, "Turn Down Elliott" by Poison the Well, "The Rise and Fall of Eliot Brown" by Blackalicious, "Elliott" by Magnapop, "Elliott" by The Mumbles, "Eliot" by Sarah Slean

LINER NOTES: Elliott Smith was nominated for an Oscar for his song "Miss Misery," which appeared on the *Good Will Hunting* soundtrack.

Evan

WELSH: Young warrior

ROCK AND ROLL: Beloved, quirky, exuberant, humble

RELATED ARTISTS/SONGS: Evan Dando, Evan and Jaron, Evan Lurie (The Lounge Lizards), "Evan" by Juliana Hatfield, "(This Is) The Dream of Evan and Chan" by Dntel, "Evan Likes Driving" by Caribou, "Evan's Way" by Pants Yell!

LINER NOTES: Evan Dando of the Lemonheads has a small part in the 1994 cult film *Reality Bites*.

Fabrizio

ITALIAN: Craftsman

ROCK AND ROLL: Kooky, mysterious, worldly

RELATED ARTISTS/SONGS: Fabrizio Moretti (The Strokes), "Fabrizio" by Robotzen, "Fabrizio" by Silvio Pollozi

LINER NOTES: The Strokes' drummer Fabrizio Moretti is the cousin of The Moldy Peaches' Kimya Dawson.

Gabe

HEBREW: Short for Gabriel, God's messenger

ROCK AND ROLL: A soldier and a poet

RELATED ARTISTS/SONGS: The Gabe Dixon Band, Gabe Saporta (Cobra Starship), "Gabe" by Jerry Douglas, "Blues for Gabe" by Albert Collins, "Gabe" by Jason Collett, "Gabe's New Joint" by Antibalas Afrobeat Orchestra, "Gabe" by Vietnam

LINER NOTES: Cobra Starships' Gabe Saporta has a degree in philosophy from Rutgers University; his band wrote the theme song for the movie *Snakes on a Plane*.

Gideon

HEBREW: Destroyer

ROCK AND ROLL: A messenger, generally peaceful but has a serious temper

RELATED ARTISTS/SONGS: "Gideon" by My Morning Jacket, "Gideon" by Clinic, "Gideon's Bible" by John Cale, "Gideon Wrath, Part 1" by Anamanaguchi, "Gideon Tanner" by Kenny Rogers

LINER NOTES: Musical man Neil Patrick Harris named his twins Gideon and Harper in part because, he joked, "when we go to hotel rooms Gideon will feel at home."

Ira

HEBREW: Watchful one

ROCK AND ROLL: Heroic, quirky, misunderstood

RELATED ARTISTS/SONGS: Ira Gershwin, Ira Kaplan (Yo La Tengo), Ira Louvin, "Ira" by Charlie Louvin, "Ira" by Dariush, "The Ballad of Ira Hayes" by Johnny Cash, "Ira's Brief Life as a Spider" by of Montreal

LINER NOTES: Before forming Yo La Tengo, Ira Kaplan wrote music criticism for the *Village Voice*.

Jean

FRENCH: Variation of John, God is gracious
ROCK AND ROLL: Suave, high-class, well spoken
RELATED ARTISTS/SONGS: Jean-Benoit Dunckel (Air), "Jean the Birdman" by David Sylvian & Robert Fripp, "Jean Pierre" by Marcus Miller, "Jean" by Zoot Sims
LINER NOTES: Air's Jean-Benoit Dunckel released a solo album called *Darkel*, a play on his last name, which means "dark" in German.

Jed, Jedediah

HEBREW: Loved by God
ROCK AND ROLL: A Southern gentleman, rough around the edges, loves to dance
RELATED ARTISTS/SONGS: Jedediah Smith (My Teenage Stride), "Jedidiah" by Hot Hot Heat, "Jed" by Roland Hanna, "Jed" by The Dweebs, "Jed's Other Poem (Beautiful Grounds)" by Grandaddy, "Tennessee Jed" by The Grateful Dead
LINER NOTES: Grandaddy's "Jed's Other Poem (Beautiful Ground)" is written from the perspective of Jed the Humanoid, a robot with artificial intelligence who drinks too much.

Julian

LATIN: Youthful
ROCK AND ROLL: A star child, artistic, curious about the world
RELATED ARTISTS/SONGS: Julian Casablancas (The Strokes), Julian Lennon, Julian Marley, "Julian" by Boy George, "Pressure on Julian" by Blur, "But Julian, I'm a Little Older Than You" by Courtney Love, "Julian" by Circa Survive
LINER NOTES: Courtney Love's song "But Julian, I'm a Little Older Than You" is about her crush on Strokes' guitarist Julian Casablancas.

Ken

ENGLISH: Form of Kenneth, handsome
ROCK AND ROLL: A leader, strong and serious
RELATED ARTISTS/SONGS: Ken Coomer (Wilco), Ken Stringfellow (The Posies), Ken Vandermark, "Ken" by Beck, "Ken" by Saint Etienne, "Ken" by Kate Bush
LINER NOTES: The Posies' Ken Stringfellow, who has also worked with R.E.M. and Big Star, has one daughter, Aden.

Kevin

IRISH: Gentle birth
ROCK AND ROLL: Enigmatic, handsome, the strong and silent type
RELATED ARTISTS/SONGS: Kevin Jonas, Kevin Richardson (Backstreet Boys), Kevin Shields (My Bloody Valentine), "Kevin" by Elmo Hope, "Kevin" by Pansy Division, "Cousin Kevin" by The Who, "Full on Kevin's Mom" by Soundgarden

LINER NOTES: During his hiatus from My Bloody Valentine, guitarist Kevin Shields locked himself in his house with more than twenty pet chinchillas.

Murphy, Murph

IRISH: Hound of the sea
ROCK AND ROLL: The life of the party, sly
RELATED ARTISTS/SONGS: Murph Jefferson (Dinosaur Jr.), "Murphy" by Jackie DeShannon, "Murphy" by Pan, "Murphy" by Karl Williams, "Murphy" by Antoinette Costa, "Murph" by Sal Mosca
LINER NOTES: Dinosaur Jr. was originally just Dinosaur; they added the Jr. to differentiate themselves from the supergroup The Dinosaurs.

Orson

LATIN: Bearlike
ROCK AND ROLL: Theatrical, quirky, has a big personality
RELATED ARTISTS/SONGS: Orson, "Orson" by Nuspirit Helsinki, "Orson" by Duke Ellington, "Orson" by Herb Geller, "Orson" by Billy Strayhorn
LINER NOTES: Indie rock band Orson also plays under the names Halogen and Mr. Lady.

Pedro

PORTUGUESE: Variation of Peter, stone
ROCK AND ROLL: Spiritual, a philosopher
RELATED ARTISTS/SONGS: Pedro the Lion, Pedro Infante, "Pedro" by Richard Dyer-Bennett, "Pedro" by The Jolenes, "Pedro" by Raul Paz
LINER NOTES: Indie rock band Pedro the Lion got their name from the character of a children's book that lead singer David Bazan was planning to write.

Reggie

ENGLISH: Form of Reginald, advisor
ROCK AND ROLL: An old-fashioned heartbreaker, gets lonely
RELATED ARTISTS/SONGS: Reggie and the Full Effect, "Reggie Jax" by Public Enemy, "Reggie" by The Sounds, "Sad Reggie" by Mad Caddies
LINER NOTES: The Get Up Kids' James Dewees plays every instrument on Reggie and the Full Effect's recordings, recruiting various friends to take over the parts during his live shows.

Spencer

FRENCH: Keeper of provisions
ROCK AND ROLL: Confident, capable, tough
RELATED ARTISTS/SONGS: Spencer Krug (Wolf Parade), Spen-

cer Williams, Spencer Davis, "Spencer" by The Fall, "Spencer" by Gatmo, "Spencer" by Mayor West

LINER NOTES: Canadian guitarist Spencer Krug plays in three active indie bands: Swan Lake, Wolf Parade, and Sunset Rubdown.

Stephen, Steven

GREEK: Crowned in victory

ROCK AND ROLL: A heartthrob but a little bit of a wimp

RELATED ARTISTS/SONGS: Stephen Malkmus (Pavement), Steven Tyler, Steven Van Zandt (The E Street Band), "Hey Stephen" by Taylor Swift, "Steven" by Alice Cooper, "Stephen" by Ke$ha, "Saint Stephen" by The Grateful Dead; "Steve" by Rilo Kiley

"Stephen prospered in his time,
well he may and he may decline."
—THE GRATEFUL DEAD

Sufjan

ARMENIAN: Comes with a sword

ROCK AND ROLL: Sensitive, hip, poetic

RELATED ARTISTS/SONGS: Sufjan Stevens, "For Sufjan" by Jeremy Powell

LINER NOTES: Indie singer-songwriter Sufjan Stevens is working on a project to record an album about each of the fifty states; thus far he has completed Illinois and Michigan.

Thurston

NORSE: Variation of Torsten, Thor's hammer

ROCK AND ROLL: Youthful, artistic, effortlessly cool

RELATED ARTISTS/SONGS: Thurston Moore (Sonic Youth), Thurston Howe (Flayed Discipline), Thurston Harris, "Thurston" by Saint Sebastian's School for Wicked Girls

LINER NOTES: In the 1990s, Sonic Youth front man Thurston Moore had a side band with Richard Hell called The Dim Stars; Moore also directed the music video for Pavement's "Here."

Tunde

AFRICAN: He who returns

ROCK AND ROLL: Strong, cerebral

RELATED ARTISTS/SONGS: Tunde Adebimpe, Tunde Williams, Tunde Jegede, "Doctor Tunde Babs" by Yacht

LINER NOTES: TV on the Radio lead singer Tunde Adebimpe appeared in the film *Rachel Getting Married* as the groom.

Ty

ENGLISH: Form of Tyler or Tyrone, craftsman
ROCK AND ROLL: A good friend, jovial, warm-hearted
RELATED ARTISTS/SONGS: Ty England, Ty Segall, Ty Longley (Great White), "Ty Cobb" by Soundgarden
LINER NOTES: Ty Segall's first release was titled "Horn the Unicorn," his second was "Halfnonagon."

Xeno

GREEK: Foreigner
ROCK AND ROLL: Avant-garde, magnetic, soulful
RELATED ARTISTS/SONGS: Xeno and Oaklander, Xeno Volcano, "Xeno" by Panteon Rococo, "Xeno" by Pacou, "Xeno" by Pinx, "Zeno of Elea" by Kelley Polar
LINER NOTES: Synthpop band Xeno and Oaklander use only analogue instruments for their electronic music, drawing on the soundtracks from British murder mysteries like *Midsomer Murders* and *Inspector Morse* for inspiration.

Indie Rock Kids

For the latest in hipster cool, you couldn't do much better than check out what indie rock royalty are naming their kids.

BABY NAME	INDIE ROCK PARENT(S)
Agnes	Thom Yorke (Radiohead)
Cal	Julian Casablancas (The Strokes)
Coco	Thurston Moore & Kim Gordon (Sonic Youth)
Cosimo	Beck
Darla	Brian Eno
Erica	Robert Pollard (Guided By Voices)
Glory	Corin Tucker (Sleater-Kinney)
Henry Lee	Jack White (The White Stripes)
Irial	Brian Eno
Isadora	Björk
Lottie	Steven Malkmus (Pavement)
Malu Abeni Valentine	David Byrne
Marshall	Corin Tucker (Sleater-Kinney)
Panda	Kimya Dawson
Scarlett	Jack White (The White Stripes)
Sindri	Björk & Matthew Barney
Spencer	Jeff Tweedy (Wilco)
Sunday	Steven Malkmus (Pavement)
Tuesday	Beck

Record Label Names

Smokey Robinson and his wife Claudette named their daughter Tamla in honor of their record company, and it's not a bad idea. We wouldn't necessarily go with "Capitol" or "Rough Trade," but some independent names past and present make creative choices when it comes to names—or nicknames—for record-collecting parents.

GIRLS

Adeline	Joia		
Alta	Juana		
Anna	Kitty		
Bunny	London		
Cantora	Lyric		
Charnel	Mala		
Dallas	Marian		
Darla	Melodia		
Decca	Mimosa		
Dekema	Musea		
Duma	Nicola		
Echo	Nixa		
Elektra	Penny		
Europa	Rebelle		
Fania	Riva		
Geska	Roxy		
Giza	Savannah		
Harmonia	Suzy		
Harriet	Tamla		
Hosanna	Trix		
Indianola	Vena		
Isadora	Viva		
Jasmine	Wiija		
Jazz			

BOYS

Ajax	Kaifa
Almo	Kemado
Apollo	Lex
Ayler	Luke
Barclay	Malaco
Belvedere	Marlin
Body	Matty
Calabash	Mego
Clay	Mojo
Coronet	Nero
Cruz	Oliver
Dino	Pablo
Domo	Philles
Fogarty	Rajon
Fred	Rex
Gallo	Silas
Geffen	Stax
Gramm	Talo
Guy	Tino
Hall	Vee
Hep	Verve
Incus	Warner
Janus	Zarjazz
Jin	Zell
Johann	

Acknowledgments

I'd like to thank the many wonderful people who poured their hard work and music trivia prowess into this book. I am indebted to my editor, Cara Bedick, whose dedication, enthusiasm, and eye for a good YouTube video helped me through the writing process enormously. Thanks to Brandi Bowles, Caroline Stanley, and Judy Berman, who coaxed the idea from my head into a blog post and then a book. Thank you also to Rick Willet, Erica Ferguson, and the rest of the terrific team at Gotham. I'm also grateful to my friends and colleagues for their kindness, wisdom, and willingness to answer frantic late-night e-mails, especially Katie Porter, Elizabeth Wade, Aja Hazelhoff, Jessica Loudis, Anna Hartford, Nick Russell, Shay Howell, Susie Linfield, and Dennis Lim. Love and thanks to Eli Goldfarb, who helped me in ways both countless and immeasurable. And, of course, thank you to my wonderful family, and a particularly big shout-out to my brothers, Brendan and Conor, the most rock and roll people I know.

Index

Axl, 24
Ayler, 326
Azure, 247

Babette, 1
Baez, 134
Baker, 135
Banjo, 70
Barbara, 26, 47, 207, 230, 231
Barbra, 26
Barclay, 84, 326
Barnaby, 123
Barnett, 288
Barrett, 134
Barry, 135, 230, 280
Bartholomew (Bart), 240
Basie, 134
Basil, 247
Bay, 247
Bayan, 70
Baz, 176
Bea, 209
Beatrice, 111, 209
Beauregard (Beau), 96
Bebu, 135
Bechet, 134
Becky, 210
Belinda, 166
Bella (Belle), 309
Belvedere, 326
Ben, 306
Benjamin, 198
Benji (Benjy), 299
Benny, 95, 124
Berlin, 112
Bernadette, 270
Bernard (Bernie), 176
Berry, 280
Bert, 36
Bess, 50
Bessie, 50, 111
Bessy, 50
Beth, 158, 207, 306
Betsey, 98
Betsy, 98, 186
Bette, 27
Betty, 21, 51, 230, 290
Beulah, 309
Beverley (Beverly), 51
Beyoncé, 23, 95
Bianca, 307
Bijou, 116
Bill, 85, 93
Billie, 51, 113, 207

Billy, 11, 111, 133, 158, 207
Binali, 289
Bing, 36
Birch, 247
Bishop, 318
Bix, 60
Blaine, 219
Blake, 61
Blanche, 51
Blandford, 288
Blaze, 147, 158
Blue, 22, 48, 49, 111, 267
Bluebell, 49
Bo, 11
Bob, 47, 85, 162
Bobbi, 49, 210
Bobbie, 210
Bobby, 36, 95, 207, 210, 230
Body, 326
Bohannon, 290
Bolan, 134
Bon, 96
Bonham, 96, 158
Bonita, 47
Bonnie, 2, 48, 93, 113
Bonny, 2
Bono, 24, 133
Booker, 280
Bootsy, 290
Boris, 147
Bowie, 124, 134
Boyd, 11
Brad, 299
Brady, 113
Brandi, 27
Brando, 49
Brandon, 299
Brandy, 27, 73
Branford, 61
Brantley, 61
Bredda, 268
Bree, 98
Breeze, 267
Brenda, 2, 230
Brendan, 240
Brent, 290
Bret (Brett), 147
Brian, 85, 133, 269
Bridget, 75
Brie, 98
Brigit (Brigitte), 75
Britney, 27, 95
Britt, 318
Britta, 95, 309
Brittany, 27

Brix, 166
Bronx, 49, 112, 206
Brooke, 247
Brooklyn, 112
Bruce, 24, 113
Bruni, 135
Bruno, 299
Bryan, 85
Bryn (Brynn), 309
Bubba, 230
Buck, 220
Buckley, 134
Bucky, 220
Buddy (Bud), 12
Budgie, 95
Buffy, 98
Buju, 268
Bunny, 49, 326
Burke, 124
Buron, 12
Burt, 36
Byrne, 134

Cabell (Cab), 61
Caesar, 148
Caitlin (Caitlyn), 166
Cal, 325
Calabash, 326
Calcutta, 112
Cale, 134
Caleb, 230, 299
Caledonia, 2
Cali, 112
Calico, 206
Calilou, 231
Calliope, 70
Calloway, 134
Calum (Calumn), 176
Calvin, 240, 269
Camaron, 258
Camelia (Camellia), 116
Cameron, 230, 258, 269
Camilia, 116
Camille, 116
Cana, 231
Candace (Candy), 166
Cantora, 326
Cara, 309
Caralee, 307
Carey, 106
Carl, 12
Carla, 49, 271
Carlene, 210, 229
Carli, 27, 113
Carlos, 48, 85
Carlotta, 46

Damian (Damien), 241
Damita, 48
Damon, 319
Dan, 93, 221
Dana, 140
Dani, 234
Daniel, 106, 269
Daniella (Danielle), 190
Dannis, 230
Danny, 22, 177
Darby, 140
Darla, 4, 325, 326
Darlene, 191
Darrell, 148
Dave, 93, 113, 241
Davey, 86
David, 133, 207, 230, 306
Davis, 134
Davy, 86
Dawn, 247, 290
Dean, 37, 95
Deana, 29
DeAndre, 269
Deanie, 116
Deanna (Deanne), 29
Debbie, 167, 186, 230
Debby, 167
Deborah (Debra), 271
Decca, 326
Declan, 133
Dee Dee, 76, 177
Deirdre, 208
Dekema, 326
Delaney, 208
Delia, 73, 111, 231
Delightt, 288
Delilah, 140
DeLisle, 290
Della, 271
Delores, 29
Demeter, 46
Denim, 206
Denis, 86
Denise, 76
Dennis, 86, 113, 268, 288
Derek, 125
Deron, 149
Desdemona, 271
Desiree (Désirée), 96
Desmond, 93, 268, 281
Devendra, 107
Devotchka, 310
Dew, 247

DeWayne, 20
Dexter, 177
Deyjah, 267
Dez, 177
Diana, 29
Diane, 191
Dick, 13, 47
Diezel, 206
Dika, 168
Dillon, 107
Dina, 52
Dinah, 52, 113
Dino, 326
Dirk, 125
Diva, 206
Divine, 271
Dixie, 112
Dobie, 281
Dobro, 70
Dolly, 23, 47
Dolores, 29, 47
Dolorosa, 231
Domenic (Dominic), 107
Dominique, 96
Domino, 206
Domo, 326
Don, 37, 230
Donald, 288
Donavon, 107
Donita, 234
Donna, 116, 186
Donnie (Donny), 125
Donovan, 107, 134
Dora, 117
Doreen, 20, 117
Dori, 99
Dorine, 117
Doris, 30
Dorothy, 272
Dorraine, 231
Dorsey, 96
Dory, 99
Dot, 211, 230
Dottie (Dotty), 211
Doug, 221
Douglas, 319
Drake, 259
Drew, 149
Duane, 259
Dudley, 221
Duff, 208
Duffy, 272
Dulcian, 70
Dulcinea, 46
Duke, 24
Duma, 326

Duncan, 107, 111, 113
Dunn, 135
Durango, 111
Dusti, 267
Dustin, 319
Dwayne, 259
Dweezil, 206
Dwight, 222
Dylan, 107, 111

Earl, 259
Earnest, 222
Eartha, 272
Ebony, 272
Ecca (Ecco), 149
Echo, 326
Ed, 241
Eddie, 113, 149, 158
Eddy, 149
Eden, 46, 112
Edgar, 93, 126, 267
Edie, 77, 163
Edith, 30
Edna, 4, 46
Edward, 126
Egypt, 49
Eicca, 149
Eileen, 191
Eja, 229
Elaine, 117
Eleanor, 77, 93, 230
Elektra, 326
Elgin, 269
Eli, 306
Elias, 13
Elijah, 49, 306
Eliot, 319
Elisa, 96
Elisabeth, 117
Elise, 191
Eliza, 293
Elizabeth, 47, 95, 117
Ella, 52, 267
Elle, 52
Ellington, 134
Elliot (Elliott), 319
Elmer, 62
Elmore, 62
Eloise, 168
Elton, 24
Elva, 290
Elvira, 136
Elvis, 20, 24, 133
Emilio, 49
Emily, 47, 118
Emma, 49, 310
Enid, 234

About the Author

Margaret Eby's writing on music and pop culture has appeared in *Slate, Salon, The Los Angeles Times,* and other publications. Her obsession with music began when she was a DJ at WBAR, Barnard College's student radio station. Raised in Alabama, she now lives in Brooklyn.